Mahometism fully explained: containing many surprizing passages, not to be found in any other author. ... Written in Spanish and Arabick, in the year 1603, for the instruction of the Moriscoes in Spain

Muhammad Rabadan

Mahometism fully explained: containing many surprizing passages, not to be found in any other author. ... Written in Spanish and Arabick, in the year 1603, for the instruction of the Moriscoes in Spain. By Mahomet Rabadan, ... translated from the original manuscript, and illustrated with explanatory notes. By Mr. Morgan.

Rabadan, Muhammad
ESTCID: T172321
Reproduction from National Library of Scotland
London : printed for E. Curll, W. Mears, and T. Payne, 1723.
xxvi,[6],390p.,plates ; 8°

Eighteenth Century
Collections Online
Print Editions

Gale ECCO Print Editions

Relive history with *Eighteenth Century Collections Online*, now available in print for the independent historian and collector. This series includes the most significant English-language and foreign-language works printed in Great Britain during the eighteenth century, and is organized in seven different subject areas including literature and language; medicine, science, and technology; and religion and philosophy. The collection also includes thousands of important works from the Americas.

The eighteenth century has been called "The Age of Enlightenment." It was a period of rapid advance in print culture and publishing, in world exploration, and in the rapid growth of science and technology – all of which had a profound impact on the political and cultural landscape. At the end of the century the American Revolution, French Revolution and Industrial Revolution, perhaps three of the most significant events in modern history, set in motion developments that eventually dominated world political, economic, and social life.

In a groundbreaking effort, Gale initiated a revolution of its own: digitization of epic proportions to preserve these invaluable works in the largest online archive of its kind. Contributions from major world libraries constitute over 175,000 original printed works. Scanned images of the actual pages, rather than transcriptions, recreate the works *as they first appeared.*

Now for the first time, these high-quality digital scans of original works are available via print-on-demand, making them readily accessible to libraries, students, independent scholars, and readers of all ages.

For our initial release we have created seven robust collections to form one the world's most comprehensive catalogs of 18th century works.

Initial Gale ECCO Print Editions collections include:

History and Geography
Rich in titles on English life and social history, this collection spans the world as it was known to eighteenth-century historians and explorers. Titles include a wealth of travel accounts and diaries, histories of nations from throughout the world, and maps and charts of a world that was still being discovered. Students of the War of American Independence will find fascinating accounts from the British side of conflict.

Social Science

Delve into what it was like to live during the eighteenth century by reading the first-hand accounts of everyday people, including city dwellers and farmers, businessmen and bankers, artisans and merchants, artists and their patrons, politicians and their constituents. Original texts make the American, French, and Industrial revolutions vividly contemporary.

Medicine, Science and Technology

Medical theory and practice of the 1700s developed rapidly, as is evidenced by the extensive collection, which includes descriptions of diseases, their conditions, and treatments. Books on science and technology, agriculture, military technology, natural philosophy, even cookbooks, are all contained here.

Literature and Language

Western literary study flows out of eighteenth-century works by Alexander Pope, Daniel Defoe, Henry Fielding, Frances Burney, Denis Diderot, Johann Gottfried Herder, Johann Wolfgang von Goethe, and others. Experience the birth of the modern novel, or compare the development of language using dictionaries and grammar discourses.

Religion and Philosophy

The Age of Enlightenment profoundly enriched religious and philosophical understanding and continues to influence present-day thinking. Works collected here include masterpieces by David Hume, Immanuel Kant, and Jean-Jacques Rousseau, as well as religious sermons and moral debates on the issues of the day, such as the slave trade. The Age of Reason saw conflict between Protestantism and Catholicism transformed into one between faith and logic -- a debate that continues in the twenty-first century.

Law and Reference

This collection reveals the history of English common law and Empire law in a vastly changing world of British expansion. Dominating the legal field is the *Commentaries of the Law of England* by Sir William Blackstone, which first appeared in 1765. Reference works such as almanacs and catalogues continue to educate us by revealing the day-to-day workings of society.

Fine Arts

The eighteenth-century fascination with Greek and Roman antiquity followed the systematic excavation of the ruins at Pompeii and Herculaneum in southern Italy; and after 1750 a neoclassical style dominated all artistic fields. The titles here trace developments in mostly English-language works on painting, sculpture, architecture, music, theater, and other disciplines. Instructional works on musical instruments, catalogs of art objects, comic operas, and more are also included.

The BiblioLife Network

This project was made possible in part by the BiblioLife Network (BLN), a project aimed at addressing some of the huge challenges facing book preservationists around the world. The BLN includes libraries, library networks, archives, subject matter experts, online communities and library service providers. We believe every book ever published should be available as a high-quality print reproduction; printed on-demand anywhere in the world. This insures the ongoing accessibility of the content and helps generate sustainable revenue for the libraries and organizations that work to preserve these important materials.

The following book is in the "public domain" and represents an authentic reproduction of the text as printed by the original publisher. While we have attempted to accurately maintain the integrity of the original work, there are sometimes problems with the original work or the micro-film from which the books were digitized. This can result in minor errors in reproduction. Possible imperfections include missing and blurred pages, poor pictures, markings and other reproduction issues beyond our control. Because this work is culturally important, we have made it available as part of our commitment to protecting, preserving, and promoting the world's literature.

GUIDE TO FOLD-OUTS MAPS and OVERSIZED IMAGES

The book you are reading was digitized from microfilm captured over the past thirty to forty years. Years after the creation of the original microfilm, the book was converted to digital files and made available in an online database.

In an online database, page images do not need to conform to the size restrictions found in a printed book. When converting these images back into a printed bound book, the page sizes are standardized in ways that maintain the detail of the original. For large images, such as fold-out maps, the original page image is split into two or more pages

Guidelines used to determine how to split the page image follows:

• Some images are split vertically; large images require vertical and horizontal splits.
• For horizontal splits, the content is split left to right.
• For vertical splits, the content is split from top to bottom.
• For both vertical and horizontal splits, the image is processed from top left to bottom right.

$$\frac{e}{m}$$

2

The several Postures used by the Turks before, and at, their Devotions

MAHOMETISM
FULLY
EXPLAINED:

CONTAINING

Many Surprizing PASSAGES, not to be found in any other *Author*.

VIZ.

I. The previous *Difpofition* to, and the *Method* of, the CREATION: The *Fall* of ADAM and EVE; Their *Repentance* and *Sufferings*: Their *Pofterity* down to NOAH. With a particular Defcription of the DELUGE.

II. The *Wonderful Life* of ABRAHAM, and the *Diftinction* between the *Two Lines*, that of ISAAC, Father of the *Jews*, and of ISHMAEL, Father of the *Arabs*.

III. An *Hiftorical* and *Chronological Differtation* concerning the *Miraculous Prophetick* LIGHT, which fhone on the Forehead of MAHOMET, and all his *Progenitors*.

IV. The LIVES of *Hafhem, Abdolmutalib,* and *Abdallah,* the Three immediate Predeceffors of MAHOMET; With his own *Life, Pilgrimage to Heaven, Death,* &c The *Prayers, Ceremonies, Fafts, Feftivals,* and *other Rites* obferved by the *Mahometans* With a Remarkable Defcription of the *Day of Judgment.*

Written in *Spanifh* and *Arabick,* in the Year 1603, for the Inftruction of the *Morifcoes* in Spain.

By MAHOMET RABADAN, an *Arragonian* Moor

Tranflated from the Original Manufcript, and Illuftrated with Explanatory NOTES. By Mr. MORGAN.

LONDON·

Printed for E. CURLL, W. MEARS, and T. PAYNE.
M.DCC.XXIII. [Price 5 s]

TO THE
RIGHT HONOURABLE
EDWARD
Lord *HARLEY*.

My LORD,

PON my Arrival in
England, Three Years
since, from *Barbary*, a
Country wherein I have pass'd
Twenty Years of my Life, I had
no sooner determined to Translate
the Treatise of which I here intreat

Your

Your Lordship's Acceptance, than I designed to honour the Original with a Place in the *Harleyian Library.*

I shall not attempt to give Your Lordship any particular Account of this Work, the Author himself having done it so fully.

The Chief Motives of my undertaking the Translation, were, To give my Countrymen, more just Ideas of the Notions of the *Mahometans,* than they have hitherto received; and because I really thought many Things in the Author, were very Curious, and ought not to be buried in the little-known Languages (in this Part of the World) in which they are delivered.

How

[v]

How I came by the Manuscript, I have acquainted the Reverend and Learned Dean *Prideaux*, in a Letter hereunto annexed ; and shall only add, That, if the Original be thought worthy of Your Lordship's Acceptance ; and if either That, or the Translation, can give Your Lordship any Entertainment, it will answer all the Wishes of,

LONDON,
May 20. 1723.

My Lord,

Your Lordship's most Obedient

Humble Servant,

J. MORGAN.

To the REVEREND

HUMPHREY PRIDEAUX, D.D.

DEAN *of* NORWICH.

REVEREND SIR,

'RELYING on your Goodneſs, that
'you will Pardon my intruding on
'your better employ'd Thoughts, I
'make bold to proceed without fur-
'ther Apology, You being, un-
'doubtedly, the propereſt Perſon to
'be apply'd to in this Matter.

'In the Kingdom of *Tunis*, where (and in other
'Parts of *Barbary*) I reſided ſeveral Years, I pur-
'chaſed a *M.S. Anno* 1719. written *Anno Dom.* 1603.
'by one of thoſe ſeemingly converted *Moors*, called by
'the *Spaniards* CHRISTIANOS NUEVOS, whoſe profeſſed
'Chriſtianity being forced and unvoluntary, was,
'by Conſequence, never real. The Author's Aim in
'compiling this Work, was for the Inſtruction of the
'numerous and ignorant Multitude of his Nation and
'Perſuaſion inhabiting thoſe Kingdoms, concerning
'their erroneous Chronology, and the Rites and Cere-
'monies of that pernicious Sect. That being the Time
'when the *Inquiſition* was hotteſt againſt thoſe coun-

A 4 'terfeit

'terfeit Christians, and but few Years before their
'last General Expulsion, all who are not ignorant of
'the Bigotry and mistaken Zeal of the *Romish* Clergy,
'especially in *Spain*, may easily imagine the Confusion
'their Religious Affairs must be in after so rigorous a
'Prosecution, and of so long a Continuance; the bare
'Use of their Natural Language, being deemed a
'Crime worthy the Cognizance of that merciless and
'detestable Tribunal. But not to tire your Patience,
'or detain you upon a Subject you are so much better
'acquainted with than I can pretend to be, I proceed
'to give you some Account of the Book itself.

'He begins long before the *Creation*, with the
'previous Disposition in the Empyreal Heaven towards
'it, and brings it down to the Death of that Grand
'Impostor, whose Life you have so accurately tran-
'smitted to Posterity. Though his Orthography, or
'rather Cacography, is peculiar to himself, yet there
'is something Curious and Uncommon throughout the
'whole Work; Nor does it want a beautiful Extra-
'vagance, and an uncultivated Elegancy, not only
'in my Own, but in the Opinion of several
'Gentlemen of Learning and Sense. He has com-
'posed the whole in Metre, and for so doing, gives
'his Reason in a short Preface. The Language is
'*Spanish*, though not properly *Castillian*, but intermix'd
'with the *Arragonian* and *Valencian* Idioms (he being
'a Native of *Arragon*) with innumerable *Arabick*
'Words in *Spanish* Terminations: So that I may, with-
'out Vanity, affirm, there are very few in this Na-
'tion who can make any thing of it besides myself;
'Who by my long Continuance, and frequent Conver-
'sations with the Offspring of those *Exiles* in
'*Barbary*, am thoroughly vers'd in their Way of
'expressing their Sentiments. It may, without Scruple,
'be depended on as Genuine; for it can be scarce sup-
'posed, that, at such a Juncture, an *Alfaqui*, when
'his Flock were in such need of Spiritual Instruction,
'would give them any thing contrary to the firm

'Tenets

' Tenets of their Belief, at leaſt wilfully ; and, indeed,
' in ſeveral Places, he modeſtly pleads his own In-
' ſufficiency for ſuch an Undertaking, for want of
' Materials and Capacity.

' As he gives a more particular Account of ſe-
' veral of *Mahomet*'s Anceſtors, and of Himſelf,
' (and likewiſe moſt unaccountable Fables of many of
' the Patriarchs, but eſpecially of *Abraham*) than I meet
' with in other Writers, I was adviſed to publiſh it
' for its Curioſity, and I have, in Effect, tranſlated
' into *Engliſh*-Proſe, about a Sixth Part of it, with
' many Explanatory Notes, which ſeveral good Judges
' tell me, are in no wiſe Impertinent to the Matter,
' but rather very Uſeful and Inſtructive, *&c.*

' If you pleaſe, Sir, to give your Conſent, I am
' ready to ſend you the Sheets I have done, rough and
' unpoliſhed, juſt as they are, by any Conveniency
' you ſhall direct : The which if you will take the Pains
' to peruſe and ſend me your Sentiments, I ſhall reckon
' myſelf your Debtor, for whatſoever Service ſhall at any
' Time, or on any Occaſion, fall in my Way. And if
' you would be pleaſed to correct a few Pages, the
' Corrections of ſo eminent a Pen, I ſhould take as an
' Honour and Favour, and ſhall ſerve me as ſo many
' Rules in my future carrying on this Work.

' Now, having too long incroach'd on your Patience,
' I only beg you'll be pleas'd to grant me a ſpeedy
' Anſwer, and Leave to ſubſcribe myſelf,

Reverend SIR,

LONDON,
Auguſt 12.
1723.

Your moſt humble Servant
to Command,

JOS. MORGAN.

I take

I take this Opportunity, of returning my moſt hearty Thanks to Dean *Prideaux*, for his kind Compliance with my Requeſt, in a Reviſal of this Work, had he not been incapacitated, through his Ill State of Health, and very great Weakneſs, of which I received the following melancholy Account, from his *Amanuenſis*, the next Poſt after I wrote to him.

J. M.

The Anſwer *of Dean* PRIDEAUX.

SIR,

' I Write you this, by the Order of my Maſter
' the Dean of *Norwich*, who commands me
' to tell you, That he has received your Let-
' ter, and would be glad to ſerve you in the Matter
' you propoſe, were he in a Condition; But being now
' weakned by Age and Infirmity to ſuch a Degree,
' as he hath not Strength in his Hands to write his own
' Name, he deſires to be excuſed, and that you would
' not take it amiſs, that he cannot write to you him-
' ſelf.

NORWICH,
Auguſt *the* 18th,
1722.

I am

Your humble Servant,

THO. CHURCH.

To Mr. Joſ. Morgan, *&c.*

THE

THE

Mahometan Confession *of* FAITH;

OR,

A * TREATISE *concerning the* ARTICLES *which every good* Mussulman *is obliged to receive and believe, in order to be of the* Number *of the* FAITHFUL.

I.

Of GOD's *Existence.*

T HE Articles of our Faith, which every good Musulman is bound to believe, and to receive with an intire Assurance, are Thirteen in Number, whereof this is the first and principal.

---

* The Title of this in the Original is, *Tratado segundo de los Articulos, que tudo buen Muslim esta obligádo a créer y tener por Fé*; that is, *The second Treatise of the Articles which every good Musulman is obliged to believe and hold as Faith.* What is most remarkable in this M. S. is, that it is written in *Spanish*, with *Arabick* Characters. It is in the Publick Library at *Amsterdam*, and was lately translated into *French*, from a Latin Version taken from the Original. Mr. *Reland*, in his *De Relig. Moham.* frequently quotes it. Being short, and, in all Likelihood, Authentick and Genuine, I thought it not improper to be prefixed to this Work.

To

The Mahometan *Confeſſion*

To believe from the Heart, to confeſs with the Tongue, and, with a voluntary and ſtedfaſt Mind, to affirm, That there is but One Only God, Lord and Governor of the Univerſe, who produced All Things from Nothing; in whom there is neither Image nor Reſemblance, who never begot Any Perſon whatſoever, as He Himſelf was begotten by None ; who, as He never was a Son, ſo He never hath been a Father. It is this Lord and Sovereign Arbiter of all Things, whom we *Muſulmans* are bound to ſerve and adore. So that, none amougſt us may deviate from this Article, but every one muſt imprint it deeply in his Heart ; for it is unqueſtionable.

II.

Of the Prophet MOHAMED, *and his* ALCORAN.

The Second Article, *with its Principal* Reaſons.

WE muſt believe from our Hearts, and confeſs with our Mouths, That the Moſt High God, after having revealed Himſelf to Mankind by His Ancient Prophets, ſent us at length his *Elected*, the Bleſſed *Mohamed*, with the Sacred and Divine Law, which, thro' His Grace, He had (a) created, the which is contained in the venerable *Alcoran*, that hath been from Him remitted to us. By this Holy Law it is, that

---

(a) There are Controverſies among the *Mahometans* in Points of Religion, as well as among us. The Opinions of their Doctors were for ſeveral Ages divided concerning this famous Queſtion, *Whether the* Alcoran *was* Created *or* Uncreated? and it was at laſt thought the wiſeſt Way to leave it undecided. It ſeems this Author was for the Affirmative; whereas, on the Contrary, the Writer of the Abridgment of the *Mahometan* Religion, publiſhed by Mr. *Reland,* declares himſelf flatly on the Negative. Neither could I ever find in any Author that it is decided by the *Alcoran.*

God

God hath abolifhed all the preceding ones, and hath withdrawn from their Doubts and Errors all Nations and People, in order to guide them to a firm and lafting State of Happinefs. Wherefore, we are obliged exactly to follow the Precepts, Rites, and Ceremonies thereof, and to abandon every other Sect or Religion whatfoever, whether inftituted before or fince this Final Revelation. By this Article we are diftinguifhed, and feparated from all fort of Idolatry, lying Rhapfodies, and falfe Prophefies, and from all thofe Sects, Societies, or Religions different from ours, which are either erroneous, abrogated, or (a) exaggerated, void of Faith. and without Truth; as daily appears by the feveral Notions of the Infidels, who divorce and difannul their Statutes and Inftitutions, after having made them; every Moment changing their Principles, becaufe they are ignorant of God's Goodnefs; and who difhonour their own Rites and Ceremonies, by continual Innovations and Reformations.

III.

Of Providence *and* Predeftination.

The Third Article, *with its Principal* Reafons.

WE muft firmly believe, and hold as a Certainty, That, except God Himfelf, who always *was*, and always *fhall be*, every Thing fhall one Day be annihilated, and that the *Angel of Death*, fhall take to himfelf the Souls of Mortals deftined to a total and univerfal Extinction, by the Command of God our Powerful Lord and Mafter, who was able, and hath vouchfafed to produce out of Nothing, and, in fine, to fet in Form, this Univerfal World, with all Things there-

---

(a) In the *French* Verfion, which I follow, it is, *Ou erronées, ou abrogées, ou exaggerées, fans foi, & fans veri*.

in contained, both Good and Evil, Sweet and Bitter; and who hath been likewiſe capable, hath known how, and hath been pleaſed to appoint Two Angels, the One on the Right, and the Other on the Left, to regiſter the Actions of every one of us, as well the Good as the Bad, to the End that Juridical Cognizance may be taken thereof, and Sentence pronounced there-upon, at the great Day of Judgment. It is therefore neceſſary to believe Predeſtination; but it is not per-mitted to diſcourſe thereof, to any whomſoever, 'till after being perfectly well verſed in the Study of our Written Law, *viz.* the *Alcoran,* and of our *Sunna,* which is our Oral Law. As to the reſt, ſeeing all Things are to have an End, let us do Good Works, and deport Ourſelves ſo, that we may live for Ever; A Life, which is the real Life of Exiſtence, and which can never be obtained but through the Practice of Vertue: As hath been denounced by the Primitive Pro-phets, before the Sacred Volume of the *Alcoran* was ſent us from Heaven.

IV.

Of the Interrogation in the Grave.

The Fourth *Article, with its Principal* Reaſons.

WE muſt truly and firmly believe, and hold as certain and aſſured, the Interrogation of the Sepulchre, which will after Death be adminiſtred to every one of us by two Angels, upon theſe Four impor-tant Queſtions, Who was our Lord and our God? Who was our Prophet? Which was our Religion? And on what Side was our (*a*) *Kibla?* He who ſhall be in a Con-dition

---

(*a*) *K·b'a,* is the Point of the Compaſs towards which all *Mahome-tans* turn their Faces at their Devotions, and is, as near as they can gueſs, towards the *Caaba,* or Temple of *Mecca.* It is a miſtaken No-tion

dition to make Anſwer, That God was his only Lord, and *Mohamed* his Prophet, ſhall find a great Illumination in his Tomb, and ſhall himſelf reſt in Glory.   But he who ſhall not make a proper Anſwer to theſe Queſtions, ſhall be involved in Darkneſs until the Day of Judgment.   Let us then dread ſo terrible a Lot, where no Succour or Conſolation is to be expected from any Part ſoever; and let us look upon it as an Inſtance of the Divine Clemency, that Things are ſo diſpoſed for the Comfort of the Juſt, and for the Terror of the Ungodly.   For if we call ourſelves to an Examination in this Life, God will, after Death, vouchſafe us His Grace 'till the Day of Judgment.

V.

Of the Future Diſſolution.

The Fifth Article, *with its Principal* Reaſons.

WE muſt heartily believe, and hold as certain, that not only all Things ſhall One Day periſh, and be annihilated, *viz.* Angels, Men, Devils, *&c.* but likewiſe, that it ſhall come to paſs, at the End of the World, when the Angel *Iſrafil* ſhall blow the Trumpet, in ſuch ſort, that, except the Sovereign God, none of the Univerſal Creation ſhall remain alive, immediately after the dreadful Noiſe, which ſhall cauſe the Moun-

---

tion of thoſe who affirm, That they pray with their Faces always towards the *Eaſt,* ſome ſay the *South,* for it muſt only be underſtood of thoſe who reſide to the *North* and *Weſt* of that Temple, which is evermore their general Object, according to their reſpective Situations: And the *Hagges* or Pilgrims, when they arrive at *Mecca,* a they Yearly do in great Multitudes from all Parts, indifferently pray all round the ſaid Temple.

tains to tremble, the Earth to ſink, and the Sea to be changed to the Colour of Blood. In this total Extinction, the Laſt who ſhall die will be *Azarael* the Angel of Death: And the Power of the Moſt High God will be evidently manifeſted. Who would not apprehend ſo terrible a Noiſe, and ſo dreadful a Deſtruction? Who would not be touched at ſo diſmal a Solitude? Who would not labour to live well, and to abound in Good Works, in Hopes of an equitable and advantageous Compenſation? (*a*) Who would not (*b*) - - - - Of the Sun, and of the Moon? Who would not from this Moment begin to groan for his Sins, and to lament his laſt End, whether it happeneth by Night or by Day? Let us ſtop at theſe Thoughts, and let us walk armed with Hope and Good Works; for whatever is not of that Number, is only lent us in this tranſitory Life, and rendereth us obnoxious to Death and Puniſhment. Happy for us, if we give due Attention to theſe great Truths; all Things ſhall become beneficial and favourable to us; as well Poverty as Riches, Bitterneſs as Sweetneſs, Adverſity as Proſperity. Every thing ſhall elevate us, and give to our Souls that (*c*) Sublimity - - - - - - .

(*a*) See the 9th Article, wherein the Author explains this future Compenſation.

(*b*) This *Chaſm*, and all others which follow, are in the *French* Tranſlation, There is a Note, wherein the like are intimated to be in the *Latin M.S.* and perhaps may be the ſame in the Original.

(*c*) *Cette nobleſſe* - - - - - - The Gaps, as I have hinted above, are in the *French*. In this Place 'tis probable, the Author would have ſaid ſomething concerning the Activity and Agility required in the difficult Paſſage of the Sharp edged Bridge, which is treated of under the 11th Article.

VI.

Of the future Reſurrection.

The Sixth Article, *with its Principal* Reaſons:

WE are obliged cordially to believe, and to hold for certain, That the Firſt, before all others, whom God ſhall revive in Heaven, ſhall be the Angel of Death; and that He will at that Time recall all the Souls in general, and reunite them to the reſpective Bodies to which each belonged; ſome of which ſhall be deſtined to Glory, and others to Torment. But upon Earth, the Firſt whom God will raiſe, ſhall be our Bleſſed Prophet *Mohamed.* As for the Earth itſelf, it ſhall open on all ſides, and ſhall be changed in a Moment; and, by God's Command, Fire ſhall be kindled in every Part thereof, which ſhall be extended to its utmoſt Extremities, (*a*) - - - - - - God will then prepare a vaſt Plain, perfectly level, and of ſufficient Extent to contain all Creatures ſummoned to give an Account of their paſt Conduct. May this ſolemn, definitive, and irrevocable Judgment awaken us from our Security; for, to nothing that hath been created, ſhall Favour be ſhewed. Every Soul ſhall be judged there by the ſame Rule, and without Exception of Perſons.

(*a*) Here I can't gueſs what ſhould have followed.

[a]   VII. Of

VII.

Of the Day of Judgment.

The Seventh Article, *with its Principal* Reaſons.

WE muſt believe from our Hearts, and hold for certain, That there ſhall be a Day of Judgment, whereon God ſhall ordain all Nations to appear in a Place appointed for this great Tryal, of ſufficient Vaſtneſs, that His Majeſty may there be evident in Splendor. It is in this magnificent and ſpacious Station, that the univerſal Aſſembly of all Creatures ſhall be made, about the Middle of the Day, and in the Brightneſs of Noon : And then it is, That, accompanied by His Prophet, (*Mohamed*) and in the Preſence of all Mankind, God ſhall, with Juſtice and Equity, judge all the Nations of the Earth in general, and every Perſon in particular. To this Effect, every one of us ſhall have a Book, or Catalogue of our Actions delivered to us; that of the Good, in ſuch wiſe, that it ſhall be received and held in the Right-hand; and that of the Wicked, ſo, that it ſhall be received and held in the Left-hand. (*a*) - - - - As to the Duration of that Day, it ſhall be as long as the Continuance of the preſent Age. This ſhall be a Day of Sighs and Grief, a Day of Tribulation and Anguiſh, when the Cup of Sorrow and Miſery muſt be drank up, even the very Dregs thereof. But this is what ſhall be particularly experienced by the Ungodly and the Perverſe: Every thing ſhall preſent to them Ideas of Sorrow and Affliction. To them every thing ſhall become Aloes and Bitterneſs. They ſhall not obtain one Mo-

---

(*a*) In the *Mahometan* Catechiſm it is, *behind their Back*, becauſe they ſay, every one's Hands are ſo tied. Perhaps 'twas that which was omitted, and ſhould have filled the *Chaſm*.

ment

ment of Repofe. They fhall behold nothing that is agreeable, nor hear one Voice that fhall delight them: their Eyes fhall fee nothing but the Torments of Hell; their Ears fhall hear nothing but the Cries and Howlings of Devils; and their terrified Imaginations fhall reprefent unto them nothing but Spectres and Tortures.

VIII.

Of Mohamed's *Interceſſion.*

The Eighth Article, *with its Principal* Reaſons.

WE are bound to believe and hold as certain, That our venerable Prophet *Mohamed* fhall, with Succefs, intercede for his People at the great Day of Examination. This will be the firft Interceſſion; but at the fecond, God will be intirely relented, and all the faithful *Mufulmans* fhall be tranfported into a State of Glory, whilft not one Excufe or Supplication in the Behalf of other Nations, fhall be accepted. As to the Greatnefs of the Pain thofe among us are to undergo, who have been Offenders by tranfgreffing the Precepts of the *Alcoran*, it is known to God alone, as there is none but Him who exactly knoweth how long the fame is to continue; whether its Duration fhall be more or lefs than that of the Examination or Judgment. But to us it belongeth to fhorten its Continuation by our Good Works, by our Charity, and by all the Endeavours we are capable of; calling ourfelves to Judgment in this Life, with the intire Attention of all our Senfes and Faculties, before our Crimes and our Tranfgreffions cite us to God's Tribunal: fince He it is, who, through His Mercy, preferveth, and who granteth us this Time of Refpite, that we may, by a vertuous Conduct, put ourfelves in a Condition to approach Him.

IX.

Of the future Compensation at the Last Judgment.

The *Ninth* Article, *with its Principal* Reasons.

WE muſt ſincerely believe, and hold as a Certainty, That we muſt there every one of us give up our Accounts before God, concerning the Good and Evil we have tranſacted in this World. All who have been Followers of *Mohamed*, ſhall be, before all others, ſummoned to this Examination; becauſe they it will be, who ſhall bear Witneſs againſt all other ſtrange Nations. It ſhall come to paſs on that Day, that God will take away out of the Ballance of him who has ſlandered his Brother, ſome of the good Works, and put them into that of him who has been ſlandered; and if the Slanderer is found to have no good Works, He will then deduct from the Puniſhments of the Slandered, to include them in the Liſt of thoſe of the Slanderer; inſomuch that his great Juſtice will be fully manifeſt. At leaſt then, that we may not run the Hazard of this terrible Compenſation, let us not think of wronging others, nor of diminiſhing their Subſtance, their Honour, or their good Name; For, we may aſſure ourſelves, That if we injure our Brother, ſuch a Subſtraction ſhall be made from our good Works, or rather ſuch an Addition to our Debts, the which, nevertheleſs, at the Time of the laſt Affliction, muſt be paid; at the Time, when to quench our Thirſt, or only to refreſh our Tongues, we would willingly give, if poſſible, all the richeſt and moſt beautiful Objects our Eyes ever beheld here below.

X.

Of the Ballance, *and of* Purgatory.

The Tenth Article, *with its Principal* Reasons.

WE muft believe from the Heart, and confefs with the Mouth, That all our Actions, good and bad, fhall one Day be weighed in the Ballance, the one againft the other; infomuch that thofe whofe good Works fhall out-weigh their bad, fhall enter into Paradife; and that, on the contrary, they whofe bad Works fhall out-weigh their good, fhall be condemned to the Flames of Hell. And for thofe whofe Scales fhall be equally poifed, becaufe the Good they have done is equivalent to the Evil, they fhall be detained in a Station fituate in the Middle between Paradife and Hell, where Confideration will be made both of their Merits and of their Demerits; fince, befides their being confined in that Place, they fhall have no Punifhment inflicted on them, nor fhall they enjoy any Part of the Glory ordained for the Beatified Righteous. It is true, that all thofe among that Number who are *Mufulmans*, fhall be, at length, releafed from their Captivity, and fhall be introduced into Paradife, at the fecond Interceffion of our Bleffed Prophet *Mohamed*, whofe great Compaffion will be fignalized, by his engaging, in order to our Redemption, to fupplicate the Power and the Mercy of the Moft High, as well as his Juftice, already fully fatisfied by the long Captivity of the Criminals. Wherefore, let us from hence forwards weigh our Good Works, to the End that we may affiduoufly ftrive to increafe their Weight, and that they may have the Advantage over the Bad : except we rather defire that *thefe* fhould out-weigh *thofe* and, after our Examination, caufe us to be excluded from the Man-

fion

ſion of Glory. Let us not (*a*) - - - - - that which is the Centre of our Souls Felicity, leſt, at this Day of Darkneſs, we are obliged to weep and lament. Once more, Let us rather, from this Moment, adorn our Souls with the Charms of Vertue, whilſt we have Time to do it ; whilſt we have it in our Power to eſcape future Chaſtiſement, and that we have the requiſite Succour and Relief, as we may ſay, within our Reach. For it will be no longer Time, after this Life, to redeem ourſelves from Perdition ; there will be no farther Opportunity for Repentance ; nor ſhall we even find a Mediator or Security, 'till after having made Expiation for our Sins.

XI.

Of the Sharp-edged (b) Bridge, *and the unavoidable* Paſſage *thereof.*

The Eleventh Article, *with its Principal* Reaſons.

WE are obliged to believe from our Hearts, and to hold as aſſured, That all Mankind in the World, muſt paſs one Day over the *Sharp-edged Bridge*, whoſe

---

(*a*) The Chaſm here, it is preſum'd, may be ſupply'd with either *forget, omit, neglect,* or the like.

(*b*) This imaginary Bridge of theirs, I have heard them frequently deſcribe as it is here repreſented ; ſharper than a Razor, narrower than a Hair, and exceeding ſlippery. They ſay, The Sinners miſcarry through want of Reſolution, Strength, and Agility, being terrified with the Horrors of Hell, over which, it ſeems, it is extended ; whereas the Good, armed with Courage and Innocence, ſucceed happily. Monſieur *Chardin,* in his Voyage to *Perſia,* aſſures us, That the Apprehenſion of this Paſſage has a mighty Influence over their Morals ; that it is the Conſolation of the Injured, and the Terror of the Injurers ; and he reports, That ſeveral *Perſians* made him juſt Satisfaction, purely out of Fear of having a bad Paſſage at the Laſt Day. *Vide* Vol. ii.

Length shall be equal to that of this World, whose
Breadth shall not exceed that of one single Thread of a
Spider's Web, and whose Height shall be proportion-
able to its Extent. The Righteous shall pass over it
swifter than a Flash of Lightning; but the Impious
and the Ungodly shall not, in as much Time as the
present Age shall endure, be able to surmount the Difficulties thereof, and that through the want of Good
Works. For which Reason, they shall fall and precipitate themselves into Hell-Fire, in Company with the
Infidels and Blasphemers, with those of little Faith
and bad Conscience, who have done few Deeds of
Charity, because they were void of Vertue. There
shall be some among the Good, notwithstanding, whose
Passage shall be lighter and swifter than that of many
others, who shall therein, from Time to Time, meet
with Temptations and Obstructions, from every Precept which they shall have ill observed in this Life.
Good God! How dreadful to our Sight will this formidable Bridge appear? What Vertue, what secret
Grace from the Most High, shall we not need to be enabled to pass over it? What Desarts, what Monsters,
what Dragons, shall we not find in our Way? What
Hunger, what Drought, what Weariness, shall we not
be there exposed to? But what Anguish, what Grief,
what Affliction, shall there not be to devour all those
who have not meditated on this terrible Passage? Let
us pray to God, That, together with our Bodily Health,
he will also grant us His Grace not to remain his Debt-
ors in this Life; for the *Arabs*, and with Reason, are
wont to say, That *no Obstacle is so deeply concealed, as
that which cannot be removed by any Expedient or Artifice whatsoever.*

XII.
Of PARADISE.

The Twelfth Article, *with its Principal* Reaſons.

WE are ſincerely to believe, and to hold for a Certainty, That God did create a Paradiſe, which He prepared for the Bleſſed, from among the Number of the *Faithful*, by which are meant the Followers of the True Religion, and of our Holy Prophet *Mohamed*; where, with him, they ſhall be placed in perpetual Light, and in the Injoyment of Heavenly Delights; for ever beautiful, in the Vigour of their Age, and brighter than the Sun; and where they ſhall be found worthy to contemplate and adore the Face of the Moſt High God. As for thoſe who ſhall be detained in the Tortures of Hell, to wit, the Sinners and Tranſgreſſors, who have neverthelesſ believed in One Only God; they ſhall be releaſed at the Second Interceſſion of the Prophet, by whom they ſhall immediately be waſhed in the *Sacred Laver*; from whence being come forth whiter than Snow, and more refulgent than the Sun, they ſhall, with the reſt of the Bleſſed, behold themſelves ſeated in Paradiſe, there to enjoy all the Glory they can deſire. This is what ſhall befall the Body that was compoſed of Clay: And what then ſhall be the State of our Souls? To the which it ſhall be granted eternally to behold the Light and Brightneſs of the Divine Majeſty. Let us then continually have in our Hearts the Idea of - - - - - - and in maintaining our Faith, let us endeavour to do Works of ſuch a Character, that we may have no Cauſe to fear Hell-Fire; a Fire ſo intenſe and penetrating, that there is no Torment, either of Heat or Cold, to be compared therewith. Let us, I ſay, chiefly apply ourſelves to Good Works; let us not refuſe to exert our utmoſt Strength in the exact Obſervation thereof, and of the Faſt of our

venerable

venerable Month of *Ramadan*, and of the Prayers and Ceremonies which are ordained; and let us not defraud the Poor of the Tythe of all our Goods. We know what our Sacred Volume says upon this Subject; " Provide to thyself Happiness hereafter out of thy " Abundance; a good Name out of thy Riches; an in- " fallible Sustenance out of thy Poverty; out of thy " Infirmity, a perpetual Vigour; and out of thy Wis- " dom, the Health of thy Soul. "

XIII.

Of HELL.

The Thirteenth Article, *with its Principal* Reasons.

WE must sincerely believe, and hold for certain, That there is a Hell prepared for the Unrighteous, the Refractory Transgressors of the Divine Law, accursed of God for their evil Works; and for whom it would have been better that they had never been born, and to have never seen the Light of the Day. It is for such as those that a Place of Torment is appointed, or rather a Fire which burneth without touching them, a *Fire* of *Ice* and *North-Winds*, where there shall be nothing but Snakes and Serpents, with other venomous and ravenous Creatures, which shall bite them without destroying them, and shall cause them to feel grievous Pains. That Place shall be the Abode of the Impious, and of the Devils, where *These* shall, with all sorts of Cruelty and Rage, incessantly torture *Those*; and lest the Sense of their Pain should cause them to relent, a new Skin shall continually succeed in the Stead of that which has been burnt or mortified. It is for us good *Musulmans*, to conceive and entertain a just Horror of this detestable Place; such Reflections are the Duty of all God's Servants: As for those others who have declared

clared War againſt our Religion, they ſhall one Day ſee the Torments of Hell. Let us all dread this Puniſhment, and theſe frightful Terrors: Let us confirm our Faith by the Sentiments of our Hearts, and by the Confeſſion of our Tongues, and let us engrave it in the Bottom of our Souls.

THE

THE
Author's PREFACE.

Discreet *Mussulman* READER,

HE principal Motive which induced me to undertake the Compiling of this Treatise, was, among many others, My having been personally present at divers Assemblies, in Company with Persons of great Parts, Learning, and Genius of our own Nation and Belief, Natives of this Kingdom; at which Meetings I have heard Arguments of a most sublime and delicate Nature frequently handled and discussed; the Subject of which Conferences was generally concerning the great Excellencies of our glorious Chieftain, and most Beatified Prophet Mohamed, of ever-blessed Memory. Themes lofty and tender! At the Conclusion of these Discourses, the whole Congregation never failed to be seized with Astonishment, and inspired with ecstatick Raptures, glorifying the supreme Creator, who, in so particular a Manner, had vouchsafed to grant such distinguishing Mercies to those of that Family; strenuously affirming, and implicitely believing (a) those Di-

---

(a) Alluding to the Prophetick *Light*, shining on the Foreheads of all the *Elected* Males of that Family, so much treated of throughout this Work.

stin-

The Author's PREFACE.

stinctions to be the greatest and most convincing Proof of the Divine Favour, that His Almighty Goodness ever granted to any of His Creatures upon Earth, or even in Heaven itself; since thereby they had so peculiarly the Advantage of, and Preference to, all the rest of the Prophets and Patriarchs; not excepting even Isa *(or* Jesus) *himself; notwithstanding he was* The Breath of his Creator; *no Man having, in the least, been* Instrumental *towards his* Begetting.

Every one unanimously said, That it was a Misfortune, most deplorable, and never enough to be lamented, that there were no Writings now extant amongst us, which were able to give us a perfect and satisfactory Account of the true Genealogy of that most Illustrious Family. Some few, indeed, we had, which made slight, transient Mention of (b) Abdulmenaf *and his Son* Hashem; *but the true Descent of the Line was intirely obscure, and remained buried in Oblivion; and which, none can dispute, had been transmitted, in a direct Line, from Father to Son, without Mixture, or Interruption, from* Adam, *of venerable Memory, down to our Lord* Mohamed, *who was the* Last of all the Prophets.

This being so, and the Times so much corrupted and confused; the poor unhappy Mussulmans *so grievously oppressed, dispirited, and persecuted, that, for want of being better instructed, they confounded the Line of* Isaac *with that of the* Light, *making them both but one and the same Lineage, being wholly unacquainted with the Difference, and with what caused that Difference; but carried it from* Adam *unto*

(b) See the Life of Hashem, Pag. 269, &c. — Dean *Prideaux's* Life of *Mah.* Pag 3. and *D'Herbelot* under the Names *Haschem, Abdallah, Mohammed,* &c.

Abra-

Abraham, *and from thence unto* Mohamed *of* Blessed Memory. *To all which may be added, That they were chiefly led into this Error by the common Voice, and Opinion of the* Christians, *who so positively, and with so much Certainty, affirm the same, laying Blots and Imputations upon the Just* Ishmael, *and all his Male Posterity, and Lineage; unjustly and maliciously depriving him of the* (a) Honour *of the Sacrifice, giving it to* Isaac; *casting scandalous Objections upon the Good* Abraham, *and, by Consequence, upon our Beatified* Leader; *insinuating, that being descended from a spurious Line, he could not be a Prophet: And, notwithstanding our Religion and Belief was (by the Grace of the Most High God) firmly established amongst us in this Kingdom; yet, nevertheless, such Things as these are always want to cause, in the weak and vulgar Sort of People, a certain Lukewarmness; and those of superior Understandings are apt to be scandalized thereat; especially when they occur in a Nation so ill-instructed, (as ours has been of late) and so strictly confined within such narrow Bounds; surrounded with so many Incitations, Inducements, and Temptations; so threatned, and tormented by* Unbelievers, *who, in persecuting us, center their principal Glory and Satisfaction.*

Seeing then, all these Circumstances so notoriously conspicuous in the Light of the Sun; and, that our Leader and Protector (who was the Light of all God's Messengers, and himself one of them, for whose Sake all Things were created) is not only his Equal, but he and all the other Prophets were highly pleased;

(a) They deny that it was *Isaac* whom *Abraham* went to offer up as a Sacrifice. The Story is at large in the Life of *Abraham*, See Chap. VII. and VIII.

nay,

nay, they gloried in being the Annunciators and Pre-sagers of his sanctified Mission: With this Conside-ration I determined to stand forth in his Defence; like unto the Soldier, who, though rashly, resolutely throw-eth himself into the Battle, amidst his Enemies, to revenge some grievous Injury, or Affront, done to his General; though better furnished with the Ardency of his Zeal, than with a competent Strength or Ability, sufficient to accomplish his Undertakings. So I, with the Consent and Assistance, and at the Request of the above-mentioned Persons; but, above all, with the Help and Protection of the Divine Bounty of God, who assisteth and encourageth every good Intent; and withal recollecting, that His Sacred Majesty com-mandeth us, that his Holy Law shall be manifested to the whole Universe; and that the Name, the Doc-trine, and the Precepts of His Messenger shall be defended, by Dint of Sword, or otherwise, as best we can; and, that His true Religion shall be expanded and maintained:

For these Reasons, I say, I set my Hand to this Work, explaining the Original and Progress of the Light *of our most Blessed Prophet, with the proper Distinction between the Line of* Isaac, *and that of* Ishmael, *shewing the true Source of each, with ne-cessary Discourses thereupon: A Subject which we* Mussulmans *are under so mighty an Obligation to be acquainted with, and to retain in our Memories; which, as* El Hassan *says, is one Half of our Be-lief, and the Second Article of the* (a) *Unity.*

(*a*) The Confession of the *Mahometan* Faith, and, by Consequence of God's *Unity*, is contained in these Words; *La illah illallah, Mu-hammed Resoul Allah,* which is literally thus There is no God but God, *Mohamed* is God's Messenger. The latter Part of which, he here seems to mean by the *Second Article* of the *Unity.* See the Confessi-on at large hereunto prefixed.

I like-

The Author's PREFACE.

I likewise, with the same unquestionable Veracity, give evident Proofs of the Purity and Chastity of Abraham, intirely confuting all Doubts and Asperfions which have been, or may be made thereon; restoring unto Ishmael *his Right, and unto the Musfulmans a Subject of Joy, as for the most estimable Grace and Mercy wherewith God of His Divine Goodness ever blessed any Nation. This is all declared and layed open, without any Confusion, Prevarication or Fraud whatsoever, or any one Article that may cause Surprize to my Readers, or may be thought an Imposition upon them. In Compiling the which, God (who alone knoweth it) will be my Witness, what Pains and Troubles I have been at, in searching for, and procuring the Writings of the most authentick Authors in innumerable Parts of this Kingdom, which had long since, for Fear of the* Inquisition, *been either lost, or buried in Obscurity: To the better furthering whereof, His Sacred Majesty, of His Infinite Bounty, was, in many Respects, affisting to me, in such Manner, that, recalling to Mind what I had studied in my Youth (of all which at first I had but transitory Remains, and faint Ideas) yet, whatsoever I had Occasion for towards the completeing, and bringing to Perfection my present Purpose, came readily into my Memory, without Difficulty.*

I have composed the whole in plain and easy Verse, that Things so Sacred, and so worthy to be treated of, and kept in Remembrance, may, with the greater Pleasure and Delight, be learned by Heart, and retained in the Memory (a).

Now

(a) At the Town of *Teffitore*, in the Kingdom of *Tunis*, I heard some of the Inhabitants, of both Sexes, sing, in Concert, whole Chapters out of this Work, to the Sound of Lutes and Guitars. In

that

The Author's PREFACE.

Now, if in the following Treatise any improper or dissonant Word, any Expression misapplyed, or Sentence misplaced, shall be found, I intreat the Discreet Reader, he will be pleased to correct, and amend it with Prudence and Candour; piously considering the Fervency of my Zeal; and be assured, that in whatsoever I have errred, or done amiss, it hath not been through Design, but Ignorance, from which the wisest of Men are not always exempted; much less a Wretch of my poor Ability: And of all People, none are so desirous and ambitious of being in the Right, as those who undertake Matters of this Nature.

May it please His most Sacred Majesty, to give me Grace to perfect and finish it, to His Holy Praise, and to the intire Content and Benefit of the Mussulmans, *the unfeigned Believers and Followers of the Doctrine of* Mohamed, *of Everglorious Memory.* Amen.

---

that Kingdom. there are Ten or Twelve small Towns, built after the *Spanish* Model, which are, in a Manner, intirely inhabited by those *Spanish Moors*; They, among themselves, use that Language, and seldom marry their Daughters to *Arabs*, *Africans*, or even to *Turks*, except for Interest. They have all, besides their *Mahometan* Names, the Names and Surnames of their Ancestors, when in *Spain*. Of late Years, they begin to degenerate; and I was told for a Truth, that there now are but Two Men remaining alive, who can read the *Spanish* Tongue, of which one is, *Hamooda Bussisa*, the Person from whom I had this Manuscript. He is by Profession a Barber Surgeon. There is one miserable little Town, whose Inhabitants are *Catalonian Moors*, and who use that Dialect. The best of those Towns are *Suliman*, *Zaguan*, and *Tessatore*.

CHAP.

MAHOMETISM EXPLAIN'D.

❀❀❀❀❀❀❀❀❀❀!❀❀❀❀❀❀❀❀❀❀

INTRODUCTION.

The Mahometan *Author dedicates his Work to* GOD, *the Creator of all Things. His Address to the Prophet. To the* Mussulman *Reader. His Praise of Historians and Writers, particularly those who write in* Metre. *The deplorable Condition of the* Moors *in* Spain, &c.

Bismillahi el rahmani el rahimi, *i. e.*

In the Name of the Gracious and Merciful God.

O Thee, O Divine Monarch, King of the *Empyreal* Heavens, Lord of all Powers, and everlasting Director of all Things ! To Thee, who permittest, and graciously endurest the Frailties, Weaknesses, and Omissions of us thy Creatures, inhabiting this Earthly Globe, and bestowest on us large and bountiful Rewards, which we have in no wise merited : Thou, who art contented and satisfy'd with good Intents alone, and protectest and rewardest in the highest Degree those who are pure and

B   perfect

perfect: Thou, Lord, it is to whom I addreſs my ſelf, and to whom I dedicate this Work; ſince thou didſt never ſtop thy Ears from liſtening to thoſe, who in their Afflictions and Neceſſities made their Supplications unto Thee, and with a contrite Heart implored thy Divine Aſſiſtance. Succour therefore, O merciful King! this thy miſerable Servant; who caſting himſelf upon thy Bounty, and relying on thy Protection, launches out in the wretched tattered *Barque* of his weak Underſtanding, and ingulphs himſelf in a Tempeſtuous Sea, without *Oars*, or *Tackling*, his *Maſt*, and *Rudder* broken and ſhattered; with nothing but the diſconſolate *Prow* of his fervent Zeal, with which he hopes to make way thro' the mercileſs Waves; intirely confiding, that thou wilt graciouſly vouchſafe to grant him a favourable *Gale*, that the *ſcanty Sails* of his *diſtreſſed Veſſel* may conduct her ſafely to her deſired Port, to the Glory and Content of thy Holy Divinity: For, without thy Aſſiſtance, 'tis very poſſible, that in the midſt of her Voyage ſhe may be ſwallowed up; it being beyond the Power of Human Capacity to ſave her from Shipwreck. Thou, who cauſeſt Harmony and Sound to proceed from a Log of Wood, and melodious Muſick from a dumb and hoarſe Inſtrument; who cauſeſt the Stones and Rocks to reſound with reſponding Echoes, and giveſt a Voice to Veſſels of Iron and Copper, &c. Grant unto me, O Gracious Monarch! thy Love and Favour; give me Strength and Breath to enable my untuneable Voice and mean Capacity to accompliſh and bring to Perfection my wholeſome and well-deſigned Purpoſe, the which is offered and dedicated to thy Divine Bounty.

And thou, O *Meſſenger!* of whoſe Glory and Happineſs (tho' unworthy) I, languiſhing, covet to be Partaker; Thou in whoſe Tongue was ſtamped the only Way of Truth; I beſeech thee to intercee! for me, that I may obtain Favour; ſince my Deſign, is to thy Honour, and in thy Praiſe, to relate what my

Ruſticity

Rufticity and poor Underftanding will permit me, concerning thy *elected Lineage,* and *renowned Predeceffors ;* thofe who were poffeffed of that moft refplendent *Light,* which the All powerful Lord had (a) created fo long before the Formation or Fabrication of the Heavens, on purpofe to be inherited by Thee.

I will particularize the Original of all thofe moft eminent and fignalized *Heroes ;* and who, and how many they were, who were deemed worthy to carry that *Banner :* I will notify their Defcent from Father to Son, down from *That* our firft Father, without any Intermiffion, Interruption, or cutting the clear and apparent Thread, till I bring it to its appointed *Station,* which was thy *precious Forehead,* made and fuited to that Ufe, and with that Intent. I will give an impartial Relation of the notable Exploits and Atchievements of all thofe Juft *Meffengers,* Patriarchs, and Prophets, who carried this *Light ;* and I will fpecify their noble Deeds in the Defence thereof, together with the myfterious Miracles, and wonderful Protection with which the Almighty Lord favoured them ; the Mercies and Deliverances he fhewed them ; all tending to the Honour and Advantage of Thee, the true Lord and Owner, and Heir prefumptive to the fame, *viz.* the *Light.*

And Thou, *Muffulman* Reader, into whofe Poffeffion thefe my Verfes fhall happen to fall ; I befeech Thee, that thy great Candor and Benevolence will excufe and pardon all my Errors and Deficiencies, in Confideration of the Honour of *Him,* to whom I offer them : And I inform thee, Judicious and Prudent Reader, of what thou canft not be ignorant ; which is, That the Taftes of Mankind are various, and differing ; fome Palates relifh Profe ; others delight only in Metre : So God has been pleafed to ordain, in the

---

(a) See in the Beginning of the Chapter of the Creation, concerning their fabulous Ideas of this imaginary Light.

fame

ſame manner as he has the unaccountable Changes, Alterations, and Revolutions of Times.

Infinite are the Numbers of Authors, who by their Writings have tranſmitted to Poſterity the Heroic Trophies and Triumphant Actions of Great and Memorable Men; with indefatigable Labour, compoſing Voluminous and Exemplary Chronicles, whereby their Names and Memories ſhine, and will continue ſo to do in After-Ages, to the remoteſt Futurity; with no leſs bright a Luſtre, and their Laurels are as freſh, as thoſe of the very Worthies themſelves, concerning whoſe remarkable Tranſactions they have written. For it is inconteſtably certain, that had it not been for the laudable Pens of thoſe candid Hiſtoriographers, the notable Occurrences of Antiquity, and the Lives and Actions of our venerable Fore-fathers, would have been all obſcurely buried in perpetual Silence and Oblivion; neither would their Poſterity have edified from their Praiſe-worthy Examples; nor would the Palm of Honour have been given to thoſe, who were truly deſerving thereof.

For theſe Reaſons, it cannot be diſputed, but that an Author, who judiciouſly and impartially writes a Hiſtory, denoting and publickly bringing to light the Deeds and Sayings of Famous Men, *&c.* ought to be remembered, and mentioned with as much Reſpect, and Deference, as thoſe Heroes themſelves, who were the principal Actors therein, and on whoſe Account it was compiled

But He, who in Times ſo Modern as theſe, has had the Faculty of compoſing ſuch memorable Things, in a Method that they may be harmoniouſly ſung to the ſweet Sound of concording Muſical Inſtruments, in pleaſing and tuneable Accents; He, I ſay, deſerves more Praiſe than thoſe who write in Proſe; and the Pains He takes, are more meritorious than the others; it being to be ſuppos'd, that the Majority of Mankind are more taken with Verſe, and, by conſequence, the readier and more willing to give

Ear

Ear thereunto ; whereby thefe worthy Subjects, fo neceffary to be univerfally known, are, with the greater Succefs and Facility expanded and divulged. Seeing it is an undoubted Truth, that it is the Voice which teftifies, publifhes, and makes manifeft whatever the Soul and Body, in their fecret and unheard Imaginations, have cogitated, and in private agreed upon between themfelves Nor are there any other means of expreffing thofe Thoughts, but by the Voice ; it being She that ejaculates the fame, and makes them intelligible and familiar to others, whereby we partake of what would elfe be an Eternal Secret. Now it is Verfe, and not Profe, which occafions the Voice to refound with the fweeter and more agreeable Cadence and Melody, and fignalizes the Compofers thereof, to be Men compleat of Talent, and fublime in Genius: And how many Examples are there extant, of Perfons celebrated for their excelling in that Capacity, who have been advanced to the higheft Dignities ? For Inftance ; (a) *Belal*, the Son of *Hamama*, that Great and Famous *Cryer* ; who, for the tranfcendent Excellency of his Voice, was inthron'd in a Station the moft Honourable, and the only one upon Earth ; feeing the Verfes which he fung, for the Perfectnefs, and unparallel'd Goodnefs thereof, were worthy to be fung in thofe Glorious and Cœle-

---

(a) *Mohammed*'s Slave, afterwards manumitted, and became one of his greateft Friends and Confidants. He made him his *Muedin* ; that is, he who calls the People to Prayers, at the appointed Hours, from the Tops of the Turrets in the Mofques. *Vide D'Herbelot* in *Belal*. The *Mahometans* relate incredible Things of the Strength and Sweetnefs of his Voice. They fay, it was he who converted to *Iflamifm* that Nation of Blacks which are called *Soudan*, his Compatriots, of which every Year numerous Troops go in Pilgrimage to *Mecca*, under the Name of *Ruccib el Soudan*, as thofe of *Perfia* are termed *Ruccib el Ajam* ; thofe of *Damafcus* are *Ruccib Shaumi* ; from *Egypt*, *Ruccib Miffir* ; and the other Pilgrims from *Egypt* downwards, are comprehended under the general Name of *Ruccib el Migirbi*, i. e The Weftern Caravan of Pilgrims, which is the Signification of the Word *Ruccib*, from *Erkeb*, to ride or mount.

ftial

ftial Manfions of Everlafting Blifs. (*a*) *Omar*, that matchlefs Warrior, fallied out, finging in Verfe, when he went forth with the *Meffenger* to publifh his Holy Law. *David* finging, and playing upon his Divine Inftrument, expelled the Demons out of the Body of King *Saul*, notwithftanding their Perverfenefs: Nay, all the *Epigrams*, or *Pfalms*, he compofed in Acknowledgement of his known and publick Sins; All his facred Canticles, Hymns, Praifes, Thankfgivings; his lofty and echoing Invocations, are the fame Glorious Songs, which are, with fuch ravifhing and inchanting Voices, fung by the Angelic Choirs. It is Verfe, which, with its melodious and refounding Cadence, quickens, and enlivens our Intellectuals; inciting us, with the greater Alacrity, to renew our Memories: And it is moft requifite, that all rare and extraordinary Tranfactions in general, fhould be fung to the Sound of Mufick; becaufe the Remembrance, and Recollection of Things of that Nature, always exhort and ftir us up to imitate fuch laudable Examples. And although thefe *Metres* of mine, are far from being in any-wife worthy to be ranked amongft thofe I have above-mentioned, or to be compared with thofe Numbers of the more perfect Performances of fuch elegant Writers, who with their refined Pens have illuftrated and immortalized their Names; and that I am not ignorant of the Incapacity and Poornefs of my Talent: Yet of this I am certain, that the Subject I am about to treat of, will be an equivalent and fufficient Counterpoife, that all the

---

(*a*) *Omar Ben el Khattab.* was a very powerful and confiderable Man among the *Arabians*, and an early Profelyte to *Mohammed's* Impofture, by whofe Authority it was very much promoted and encouraged. He was the fecond Calyph after him, and was Inftalled in the Year of Grace 635. He reigned Ten Years and a half, and was then murder'd. See more of him in *Ockley's* Hiftory of the *Saracens*, and in *D'Herbelot.* *Hafsa*, one of *Mohammed's* Wives, was the Daughter of this *Omar*

Defects

Defects and Diffonancies which may be found in this Work, ought to be excufed, and obtain a favourable Reception, as Things to which my Weaknefs of Genius is incident, and that the Acceptance thereof, may be conformable to the Zeal of my Intent; I having nothing in View, but the being able to accomplifh the Manifeftation of thefe great Myfteries, towards the extending, divulging, and expanding of the which throughout the whole Univerfe, we are, by fuch mighty Obligations, bound ftrenuoufly to endeavour.

Although, as I have already faid, 'tis neceffary for us to call to Remembrance all the Prophets and Patriarchs, as they are all fpoken of in the reverend *Alcoran*, for the great Benefit and Advantage we may reap from the Example of their commendable Actions, conducive to the better Regulation of our tranfitory Bodies on Earth, and to the eternal Repofe of our immortal Souls in the Altitudes of Heaven: Yet, neverthelefs, the Precepts of none of them are to be compared with thofe we find in the Honoured *Alcoran*; By the facred Decrees of which, every good *Muffulman* is commanded to teach and publifh, to the utmoft of his Ability and Underftanding, all he knows concerning the Doctrine of our true Belief. O Sacred *Alcoran!* wherein the Words and Admonitions, and all the Fundamentals and Ways of our Holy Law, which is the (*a*) *El Iflam*, is contained! In it we are taught and enjoyned, that we fhould, with all our Might, diligently and indefatigably ftrive, either in Profe or Verfe, or in whatfoever Method we are beft capable of, or as may feem propereft or moft

---

(*a*) The *Mahometans* term their Religion *Din Iflam*, or the Law of Salvation, from the *Arabick* Word *Salám*, which implies Safety. In the Fourth Conjugation *Aflama*, to enter into the State of Salvation, hence *Iflam*, or *Eflam*, and *Muflimeen*, *i. e.* The Saved, or the Efcaped. They fay, all Mankind are born in *Iflamifm*, but are perverted by their Parents to other Religions.

con-

convenient, that our Religion and Belief may be exalted, propagated, and fpread abroad: This if we neglect to endeavour, God will deny us his Grace, and reward us with Torments and Punifhment.

Therefore, to acquit my felf of this incumbent Duty, and to enjoy an undifturbed Confcience, and that I might have no Neglect to anfwer for, in having concealed what my mean Talent and weak Judgment would furnifh me with, I determined to employ it on a Matter moft Sublime, as is this which I am about: A Subject highly worthy of my Conceptions, though as vaftly difproportionable to them, as is the little *Ant* to the great *Camel,* or the weak, infignificant *Worm,* when compared with the ftrong and mighty Body of the unwieldy *Elephant.*

Notwithftanding, 'tis to me a fufficient Confolation, when I reflect on many Inftances of thofe, who, armed with a pure and contrite Heart, and endowed with an implicite Faith, have overcome Difficulties, which had the Appearance of Impoffibilities; as *Noah* did the Deluge of Water; (*a*) *Abraham,* the Impetucfity of the Fire; *Daniel,* the Rage of Wild Beafts; and *Judith,* the invincible *Holophernes,* with many others whom I omit: And who, by only the Purity of their Faith, were delivered from thofe eminent Dangers, and have made their Names venerable in Heaven, and on Earth.

It is this fame Confidence which encourages me, and gives me hopes, that through the immenfe Power and Affiftance of God, I may be able to compleat what I have undertaken, and anfwer the Expectations of the Reader.

God having been pleafed to permit the *Moors,* in thefe Kingdoms, to be ftreightned and oppreffed with fo many Perfecutions, the Affairs of our Religion have been brought to fuch Extremities, that it is nei-

---

(*1*) *Abraham,* whom they call *Ibrahim.* See that Fable in his Life, Chap. IV.

ther

ther practiſed nor adminiſtred in Publick, nor in Private: The *Saláh* is layed aſide and forgotten, as of no Uſe; and if ſome few, very ſecretly perform their daily Prayers, 'tis very ſeldom; and then ill-performed, and without Reſpect. The Faſts (*a*) interrupted, either not kept at all, or if ever, far from the manner they ought to be. The accuſtomary Alms, &c. wholly aboliſhed, together with the uſual Annual Tythes, &c. The calling upon, and repeating (*b*) the Holy Names of God and of his *Meſſenger*, is what is now, in a manner, never heard of; that is to ſay, the calling them by their own *perfect Names* in our Language; (*c*) ſince they [the *Moors*] have been all forcibly baptized, and through Fear and

---

(*a*) As to the awful and profound Reverence, they uſe at their Devotions, the Strictneſs of their Faſts, with their Alms, Tythes, &c. ſee Sir *Paul Ricaut*'s Hiſtory of the *Ottoman* Empire, *Reland*'s *Mahom. Rel.* and others; and likewiſe in ſome Parts of this Book.

(*b*) See the 99 Attributes of God, at the End of this Work.

(*c*) The *Mahometans* hold it to be, in a manner, an Impiety to call God by the Names, thoſe they eſteem as Infidels, call him by. The *Andalouzes*, or *Spaniſh Moors*, very frequently uſe this Expreſſion, *Valga me Dios, ſi Dios es* Allah, *ſi no, valga me* Allah, that is, God help me, if God is *Alah*, if not, *Allah* help me; which the *Spaniards vice verſâ*, retort upon them, by ſaying, *Valga me* Allah, *ſi* Allah *es Dios, ſi no, valga me Dios.* Even the Learned and Religious among the *Turks*, ſeldom uſe the Word *Tangri* (which in their Language is the ſame as God) any otherwiſe than we ſay *Providence*, becauſe it is no where found, they ſay, in the Holy *Alcoran*: And in general all the Profeſſors of *Mahometiſm*, deem it as a Profanation of God's Divinity, to mention his ſacred Name by any other Appellation, than thoſe of his 99 Attributes, which ſee at the latter Part of this Work. The Word *Allah*, is abbreviated of *El Elah*, which anſwers to the Hebrew *Elohim* and *Adonai*, and is by all *Mahometars*, of what Language ſoever (as I have hinted) the General Appellation of God. *Mahomet* being interrogated by the Chriſtians, Jews, Magi and Idolaters, *What God it was he adored? and whoſe Precepts he preached?* anſwered thus, out of the *Alcoran*; *The God that is only One, who has his Being from Himſelf, from whom all Creatures have received theirs; who does not beget, and is not begotten; and in ſhort, him who has nothing Like him, among all Beings.* A farther Mention of this Head hereafter.

Terror,

Terror, are conftrained to profefs themfelves *Chriftians*; their Books are all loft, fcarce the Remembrance of them remaining. The *Alims*, [*i. e.*] Teachers are all difpatched or made away with; none to be found; being either dead, or in Cuftody: The *Inquifition* is difplayed againft us with the utmoft Fury and Oppreffion, committing Cruelties and Diforders in every Place, perfecuting us with unexpreffible Rigour, fo that few Parts of the Kingdom are free from Fire and Faggot: The new-baptized *Moors* are every-where feized, and daily punifhed with Gallies, Racks, and Fires. Thefe, and numberlefs other Adverfities, beft known to God, the Searcher of all Secrets, we have been now perfecuted with, during Seventy-fix Years, with greater Fury and Rigour than at the firft Beginning; for the Malice of our Enemies increafeth daily more and more towards us. Under thefe Afflictions and intolerable Torments, I fay, how is it poffible any Foundation or Light of our Religion fhould remain? And if in the Service of God we are difturbed and perplexed; and that whenever we perform any of our Rites, we are obliged to do it with all imaginable Secrecy and Dread; how can it be wondered at, if they are become ftrange and un-habitual to us? Withal confidering how many inveterate and inplacable Enemies we have to encounter, and to defend our felves againft. Adding to thefe, the World, and the Flefh, our moft pernicious Adverfaries, with their Incitations and Temptations, with their Snares and Delights, perpetually taking off our Thoughts from meditating on *That* our fupreme Welfare.

These, and fuch like Reflections and Confiderations, are what caufed me to take in Hand this Tafk, with fo fimple a Talent, and Capacity, with the Intent and Purpofe of declaring the Original Emanation, Growth and Progrefs of our Holy Law, and from what Stock it had its firft Beginning; that our diftreffed *Muffulmans* may receive the Content and Satisfaction of knowing and being acquainted with

the

the Bountiful Mercies which the Lord hath done for them, in blefling us in fo confpicuous a Manner, as to guide us in the Paths of a *Faith*, the Fundamentals of which were compofed in *Paradife*; and thither, as to its Native Source, it will return.

May the Difcreet *Believers*, to whom, and to no others, I offer this Hiftory, receive this Inftance of my Zeal with Candour, and favourably pardon my Faults, and Defects : And may the Divine Goodnefs of God Illuminate my Thoughts with the Sacred Light of his Grace, that I may be capable of properly fuiting my Expreffions, and of compleating the Whole, as I have propofed.

C H A P.

CHAP. I.

Of the previous Preparation in Heaven, in order to the Creation of Man. The Formation of all Things. Adam and Eve, our first Parents, created. Their Happy State. Their Disobedience and Fall. The dreadful Effects of their Prevarication.

THE sage *Malec*, in his incomparable Treatise, (*a*) intitled, *The Conferences*, &c. *of the Prophets*, communicates to us the memorable Secret of a most singular Transaction, which the King of the Heavens did in Favour of Mankind, long before the Formation of the Heavens, or of the Earth, or the Creation of our first Father *Adam* ; by which was manifested his tender and most compassionate Love to us. Which take as follows:

God designing to make known to his whole Choir of Angels, High and Low, (*b*) his Scheme concerning the

Crea-

(*a*) Many *Arabian* Authors of this Name are to be met with in D'*Herbelot* and others, who often quote them, but I can by no means gather which of them all is meant here.

(*b*) They affirm the Angels to be of several Degrees; Those which are of the first Rank, they call *Malaica el Mocareboun*, which is, The Angels which are nearest God's Throne of Glory. Those which are

employed

Creation, called the Arch-Angel *Gabriel* (c), and delivering to him a *Pen* and *Paper*, commanded him to draw out an *Instrument of Fealty and Homage*; in which, as God had dictated to his Secretary *Gabriel*, were specified the Pleasures and Delights he ordained to his Creatures in this World; the Term of Years he would allot them; and how, and in what Exercises their Time in this Life was to be employed. This being done, *Gabriel* said; *Lord, what more must I write? Thy* (d) *Pen resisteth; and refuseth to be guided forwards!* God then took the *Deed*, and before he folded it, signed it with his Sacred Hand, and affixed thereto his Royal Signet, as an Indication of his incontestable and irrevocable Promise and Covenant.

---

employed in bearing or carrying the Throne, are called *Hameloun el Arsch*. See *D' Herbelot*, in the Word *Arsch*. But of these more hereafter.

(c) The Angel *Gabriel*, or as they call him *Gibrael* or *Gebrael*, is by them introduced on all Occasions, and most frequently cited in the *Alcoran*: They hold him and *Mikeal*, i. e. *Michael*, to be the Two Principal Angels of the *Mocareboun*, those who approach nearest to God. He is often surnamed by them *Rouh*, or rather *Roh el Amin*, the Faithful Spirit. Some believe that by *Roh el Cods*, The Holy Spirit, mentioned in the *Alcoran*, is meant him. They believe, as we do, that this Angel brought the Tidings to our Blessed Lady, that she should conceive, and bring forth *Jesus Christ*. The *Alcoran* expresly says, *Wroever is an Enemy to* Gibrael, *shall be confounded.* They hold, that he is an implacable Enemy to the *Jews*, but a great Intercessor for the *Mussulmans*, because they reverence and respect the *Messias*, whom the *Jews* rejected. Many monstrous Fables are recorded of this Angel, some of which shall be inserted in their proper Places.

(d) The *Mahometans* believe and affirm, that before all other Things God created the *Table of his Decrees*, and after that *His Pen*: That this *Table* is of one intire Precious Stone, of an immense Magnitude; That the *Pen* is also of one Pearl, from the Slit whereof the *Light* distills which is the true and only *Ink* God (or rather the Angels by God's Command) makes use of to Register our Words and Actions. These are their Notions *Reland's Mah. Rel.* in the 6th Lesson, intitled, *Of the last Day.* Annot. 4.

Then

Then *Gabriel* was commanded to convey what he had written throughout the Hofts of Angels, with Orders that they all, without Exception, fhould fall down and worfhip the fame; and it was fo abundantly replenifhed with Glory, that the Angelical Potentates univerfally reverenced and paid Homage thereunto. *Gabriel* returning, faid; " O Lord! I have obeyed " thy Commands; what elfe am I to do? God repli-" ed, Clofe up the Writing in this *Cryftal*; for this " is the inviolable Covenant of the Fealty the Mor-" tals I will hereafter create fhall pay unto me, and " by the which they fhall acknowledge me ." *El Haffan* tells us, That no fooner had the blefled Angel clofed the faid *Cryftal*, but fo terrible and aftonifhing a Voice iffued out thereof, and it caft fo unufual and glorious a Light, that with the Surprize of fo great and unexpected a Myftery, the Angel remained fixed and immoveable; and although he had a moft ardent De-fire to be let into the fecret *Arcanas* of that wonderful Prodigy, yet all his innate Courage and Heavenly Magnanimity, were not fufficient to furnifh him with Affurance, or Power, to make any Inquiry. " From " whence, O Sons of *Adam!* we may eafily conje-" cture the Excellency and Perfection in which the " firft Scheme of our Creation was laid, abundantly " furpaffing even that of the Angels themfelves; fee-" ing that, as all our Teachers inform us, more than " Two Thoufand Years before *Adam* was created, the " All-powerful Monarch had vouchfafed to have the " Defign thereof drawn out, and endowed it with fo " refplendent a *Light*, preferving it for fo many Cen-" turies in that *Cæleftial Cryftal*, to the Intent that it " fhould be enjoyed by *Adam*, and by thofe of his " Male-Pofterity, whom his divine and incomprehen-" fible Wifdom fhould think worthy thereof, until it " was finally fixed on the Forehead of *Mohammed*, as " fhall be hereafter related ".

Now when the Omnipotent God was pleafed to or-dain, that the firft of all Men fhould be invefted with
Humanity,

Humanity, and become an Inhabitant of this our
World, he previoufly commanded the Chiefs of his
Angelic Subjects to prepare (*a*) a Throne; I mean, a
Place, a Fabrick, an Habitation, in fine, a World, for
the Reception and Accommodation of the *Beings* he
was about to create. In Obedience to the Command,
and exactly in the Manner as had been fpecified to
them, the Holy Angels formed a Mafs, an undigefted
Compofition, a *Chaos*, obfcure and dark, void of all
Manner of Light; which when they beheld, being
ignorant of the Secret Caufe, they were feized with
Wonder and Amazement, and turning towards their
Lord, faid unto him; " O King of Myfteries! what
" Fabrick, worthy of Admiration! is this which thou
" haft ordered us to erect? Have we, or any of us,
" been guilty of Difobedience to thy Divine Ordinan-
" ces? Is this frightful Place defigned for a Prifon
" for us? O Monarch! we comprehend not the
" Meaning of this fo hideous and difmal an Obfcu-
" rity! " To whom God faid; " I tax none of you
" with Difobedience; but I intend to form a per-
" verfe Generation of Creatures, of a fingular Com-
" pofition, who will tranfgrefs my Laws, and whofe
" Ways will be difpleafing and abominable in my
" Sight."
Then faid the Angels; " Accompany not us, Lord,
" with fuch difloyal Servants: Why wilt thou create
" them? What Ufe or Occafion haft thou for them?
" Are there not Millions of Legions of us, thy incef-
" fant Worfhippers? Befides, Lord! What Power,
" what Poffibility, can thefe thy intended Creatures
" have of ferving and adoring Thee, being involved
" in fuch aftonifhing Darknefs? " The Lord re-

(*a*) My Author has it after his *Spanifh* Pronunciation, *Una lare
entre todo los ala xes.* In *Arabick*, the Word *Al Arfch* or rather *El
Arfch*, fignifies a Throne: But more of that, when I come to mention the *Throne of God*, to which the Word is more properly applicable.

plied;

plied ; " This Maſs, which I commanded you to
" compoſe, ſhall have Light ſufficient to guide
" and direct the Inhabitants thereof, in all
" their Neceſſities. And it is my Will, That from
" henceforwards, you enjoy an Everlaſting and Eter-
" nal Reſt, nothing to interrupt your Repoſe, but
" your Time be intirely taken up in Contemplations
" on my Glory. As for thoſe I ſhall next give *Being*
" to, they ſhall undergo Afflictions and Joys, Trou-
" bles and Contents, Bitters and Sweets : They ſhall
" be liable to Heat and Cold ; Hunger, Thirſt and
" Wearineſs, with innumerable other Calamities du-
" ring their whole Life : Nevertheleſs, in all their
" Actions, if commendable and worthy of Reward,
" they ſhall enjoy free Liberty, nor ſhall any Thing
" diſturb or controul them in their Purpoſes : I will
" enjoyn them Precepts and Commandments, with
" other Duties, to be carefully kept, and ſtrenuouſly
" maintained by them, that they may acknowledge
" my Divinity, and revere my Power : They ſhall
" know in what Method I will be ſerved, and no-
" thing ſhall be required of them, but what is confor-
" mable to their Capacities and Abilities, and mild
" and eaſy to be performed.

" They ſhall be endowed with ſuch Knowledge of
" my ineffable Power, that they may be ſenſible it is
" conducive and requiſite to their future eternal Hap-
" pineſs, not to neglect or tranſgreſs theſe my Pre-
" cepts : Which if they inadvertently or rebelliouſly
" ſhould preſume to do, as an Atonement for their
" Crime, they may be trebly zealous in good and
" laudable Works, equivalent to the Omiſſions, in
" Hopes, and with the Proſpect of regaining my
" Grace and Pardon, and finding Mercy and Favour
" in my Sight. Thoſe among them, who with a firm
" and ardent Faith ſhall practiſe and obey theſe
" my Ordinances, none among the Nations of the
" Earth ſhall be equal to them in Dignity ; You,
" your-

" yourſelves ſhall be their Guardians (*a*) and Prote-
" ctors, that no Harm or Injury befall or happen to
" them : You ſhall be the Overſeers of all their Words,
" Thoughts and Actions, keeping a juſt Account of
" their Deſerts, which at the appointed Time ſhall be
" exactly weighed, compared, and computed in my
" unerring *Ballance*; of all which, you are to be im-
" partial Witneſſes, at the tremendous Tribunal of
" my Juſtice, on the Laſt Day, where you ſhall
" paſs a moſt ſtrict Examination before my Divi-
" nity. "

The Angels hearing ſuch wonderful Things, and ſo
amazing Myſteries, without farther Reply, or Inquiry, return'd to their uſual Occupation of chanting Divine Hymns, *&c.*

God then began his CREATION. He formed the
World in the Likeneſs of a Ball, perfectly round in all
its Parts : (*b*) He created the *Seven* Heavens. *Nature*

(*a*) The *Mahometans* hold, that every Man hath Two tutelar Angels conſtantly attending him, one at the Right Side, and the other
at the Left, who write down every individual Word and Action :
He on the Right, regiſters the Good, and the other the Evil.
For which Reaſon, at the Concluſion of each of their *Salaes*, or
daily Prayers, when they ſalute the ſaid Angels (which they do by
turning their Face, firſt to the Right, and then to the Left, pronouncing *Aſalamalic*, to each of them) they uſe more Deliberation
and Reſpect towards the Angel on the right Side, than to the Other.
This I have frequently ſeen and obſerved, and upon Inquiry, have
been told this, as a ſort of Secret ; for they are very reſerved in
thoſe Myſteries of their Belief, unleſs to their familiar Acquaintance. *Aſalamálic* is the uſual Salutation they give a ſingle Perſon, as *Aſalamalicum* is to a Company, or more than one ; though
this only to thoſe of their own Perſuaſion, for they refuſe it to all
others ; and think themſelves heinouſly affronted, if a *Chriſtian, Jew,*
&c. offered it them, they ſaying, the Angel *Gabriel* uſed that Form
of Salutation to *Mahomet*, at all their Interviews, and for that
Reaſon, they account all, who are not (as they call themſelves) *True
Believers,* unworthy thereof. The Word ſignifies, *Peace be with you,*
and the Anſwer to it is *Aliaſalám*, or *Alicum ſalim*, which is, *Peace
to you alſo.*

(*b*) They ſay there are Seven Heavens. See Dr. *Prideaux* L. *Mah.* p.
31, *&c.* and *Mahomet*'s Pilgrimage to Heaven in this Book, *Cap.* xxiii.

C   herſelf

herself had next her *Existence*, which was to be as a common Mother to all Things; but she was limited within convenient Bounds, that nothing superfluous or extravagant might be made, or have *Being*, but the Earth be replenished with what was requisite and necessary; upon which all Trees, Fruits, Plants, &c. were instantly produced. At the same Time, the Sun, Moon, Signs and Planets were created: God ordering his Angels that they might be so placed, that the regular Motions of the Heavens might be govern'd and directed thereby. He then created the Day and the Night, distinguishing them by such concording Divisions, that the transient and diminishing Hours, might, by that alternate Succession of Light and Darkness, be duly and regularly computed.

The East and the West (which were in the same Instant created to that Intent) were allotted to be the Limits, or, as we may say, the Walls thereof, by which the one is separated from the other. To the Moon was ordained her Conjunctions, her Increases and Decreases, by the which our Time is Yearly measured, and distributed into Twelve equal Parts, or Divisions, which we call Months (or rather Moons). The Firmament was beautifully adorn'd with brilliant Stars, by whose Direction the Navigators are guided and conducted to the remotest and most occult Corners of this capacious Globe. He created the Four Elements, of such different Species, and opposite Properties, that whensoever they meet, or are joyned one to another, they produce most contrary, and preposterous Effects. To the Fire he gave the Faculty of burning outrageously, and causing Liquids to boil, and of warming and cherishing, when kept within Compass and Moderation. The Earth was endowed with the Vertue of propagating and nourishing the Vegetables. The Air he ordained for the Habitation of winged Creatures, as Fowls, Birds, &c. The Water was allotted to be the Abode of the Fishes: The Rivers, Springs, and Fountains, though of so different

rent

rent Taſte and Nature from the ſalt Seas, are to be included in this Element ; by whoſe kindly Influence and ſeaſonable Aſſiſtance, the thirſty Earth is moiſt-ened (*a*) and made fruitful, to the unſpeakable Bene-fit of all Nations : Theſe were likewiſe created at that Time. The Froſty Winter, the Temperate Spring, the Delightful Summer, and the Ripening Autumn, he alſo created. He ſeparated the Heat from the Cold ; and commanded the Air to refreſh the Earth with ſalubrious Breezes ; and that the Fire ſhould be ſerviceable, not offenſive to us. He cauſed the Seas and the Rivers to diſcover, for our Uſe, the hidden Products of their Bowels ; forbidding them to conceal them from us, but that we ſhould be Partakers there-of. All theſe, and many Thouſands more of ſuch mi-raculous Myſteries, (the Recital of which is a Taſk too mighty for my weak Underſtanding) the Great and All-powerful Monarch accompliſhed in Six Days. This Stupendous Work being compleated, he reſted himſelf on his Throne of Glory.

The newly-created World, beautifully embelliſhed with all imaginable Delights, was ſolely dedicated to Man. He might take or leave, command or forbid whatever his Lordly and Arbitrary Will, or his Deſ-potick, Uncontrouled Fancy ſhould dictate. God, amongſt his other Wonders, had made a *Paradiſe* (*b*), a Place of Glory, inexpreſſibly delightful, appointed for the Reward of his truly dutiful Servants ; I mean,

---

(*a*) In the dryer and more Southern Parts of the World, much of the Land is in Summer overflowed with Water, by cutting Trenches, and making Channels to let it run through the Corn-Fields, Gardens, Orchards, &c. which would otherwiſe be barren, and produce nothing, except in very rainy Years ; a Thing not requiſite, and therefore, little practiſed in our Northern Climates. In *Spain* and *Portugal* they call them *Azequias,* corrupt'y from the *Arabick* Word *Sékia,* which implies the ſame Thing.

(*b*) By Paradiſe, is always meant a *Cœleſtial Paradiſe,* for they have no Notion of the Garden of *Eden,* or the Terreſtrial one. More of this ſhall be ſaid hereafter.

thoſe

thoſe who keep his Commandments, and obey his Holy Ordinances. This he was pleaſed to ſituate aloft near the Heavens. The dark and horrible Hell (*a*), being likewiſe created, was ordained for a perpetual *Priſon* for the Condemned ; who are thoſe that rebel againſt his Precepts, by denying, or oppoſing his Laws : This frightful Station, the Portion of Sinners, he placed below, in a diſmal Abyſs of Sorrow.

All being now compleated, and put in Order ; God ſaid to his Angels ; " Which of you will deſcend to " the Earth, and bring me up a Handful thereof ? " When immediately ſuch infinite Numbers of Cœleſtial Spirits departed, that the Univerſal Surface was covered with them ; where conſulting among themſelves, they all unanimouſly confirm'd their Loathing and Abhorrence to touch it, ſaying ; How dare we be ſo preſumptuous as to expoſe before the Throne of a Lord ſo Glorious and Sovereign as ours is, a Thing ſo filthy, and of a Form and Compoſition ſo vile and deſpicable ? And, in Effect, they all returned, fully determined not to meddle with it. After theſe, went others, and then more ; but not one of them, either firſt or laſt, dared to defile the Purity of their Hands with it. Upon which (*b*) *Azarael*, an Angel of an extraordinary Stature, flew down, and from the four Corners of the Earth brought up a Hand-

---

(*a*) The *Arabick* Word is *Gebennama*, which ſignifies *Hell.* D' *Herbelot* ſays, The *Arabian Mahometans* ſeem to have borrowed this Word from the *Jews* and *Chriſtians* The Original of the *Hebrew* Word comes from *Ghe Henmom*, that is, The Vale of *Henmom*, where the *Amorites* burnt their Children alive, ſacrificing them to the Idol *Moloch.* In Arabick *Gehennem* is properly a very deep Pit, and *Gehim* is one of a frightful deformed Countenance. *Ben Gehennem,* i. e. the Son of Hell, is the Name they commonly give to a very wicked Reprobate. See the *Mahometan* Ideas of Hell in D' *Herbelot,* at large, under the Word *Gebennem.*

(*b*) *Azrael*, the Angel of Death. According to all *Mahometan* Traditions, at the Day of Judgment, when *Aſrafil* or *Iſrafil* ſhall ſound the

Handful of what God had commanded: From the South and the North, from the West and from the East, took he it; of all which Four different Qualities Human Bodies are composed.

The Almighty perceiving in what manner *Azarael* had signalized himself in this Affair, beyond the rest of the Angels, and taking particular Notice of his goodly Form and Stature, said to him; " O *Azarael*, " it is my Pleasure to constitute thee to be *Death* it-

---

the Trumpet, all Creatures, Angels, Men and Devils shall dye; the last of all that shall dye is to be *Azarael Malec el Mavt.* Of the unaccountable Fables of the prodigious Statures of the Angels, Dr. *Prideaux* in his Life of *Mahom.* p. 31, &c. gives a particular Account. *Khondemir*, a celebrated Chronologist, quoted by many Writers, says; That when God had resolved to make *Adam*, he commanded the Angel *Gabriel* to take an Handful of Mould from every one of the Seven Depths of the Earth. The Angel went and acquainted the Earth with his Commission; to which she answered, That she fear'd, that Creature would rebel, and draw a Curse upon her, and prayed him to represent it to God. *Gabriel* did so; but God being resolv'd, sent *Michael* and *Israfil* on the same Errand, who both return'd as *Gabriel* had done. At last he sent *Azarael*, who took the Seven Handfuls by Force, without minding what the Earth said, and carry'd them to a Place in *Arabia*, between *Mecca* and *Thaif.* This harsh Method *Azarael* used towards the Earth, was the Cause that God gave him afterwards, the Charge of separating the Souls from the Bodies; and therefore, he is called *The Angel of Death.* When this Earth had been moulded by the Angels, God himself, form'd it, and was, when dry, a long Time exposed in Sight of the Angels, who often visited it. *Eblis*, or *Lucifer*, touching it, and finding it hollow, said; That Creature would often require *filling*, and be subject to many Temptations. He then asked his Companions, Whether, if God should require it of them, they would submit to that Creature? And they answering in the Affirmative, he seem'd to acquiesce also, but had other Designs. Some time after, God animated this Body, and cloathed it most gloriously, adorning the Soul with all Vertues and Sciences, and then commanded all the Angels to fall down, and pay Respect to the same. They all obey'd, only *Eblis* was refractory, who was therefore cursed, and drove out of Paradise, and his Place given to *Adam.* There *Eve* was taken out of his left Side, whilst he slept, and given to him for a Wife. *Vide D'Herbelot* in *Adam.*

" self;

" ſelf; thou ſhalt be him who ſeparateth the *(a)*
" Souls from the Bodies of thoſe Creatures I am
" about to make, Thou henceforth ſhalt be called
" *Azarael Malec el Mout,* or *Azarael* the Angel of
" Death.

Then God cauſed the *Earth* which *Azarael* had
brought, to be waſhed and purified in the *Fountains
of Heaven*; and *El Hoſan* tells us, That it became ſo
reſplendently clear, that it caſt a more ſhining and
beautiful *Light,* than the Sun in its utmoſt Glory.
Gabriel was then commanded to convey this lovely,
tho' as yet Inanimate *Lump of Clay,* throughout the Heavens, the Earth, the Centers, and the Seas, to the
Intent, and with a poſitive Injunction, that whatſoever had Life might behold it, and pay Honour and
Reverence thereunto.

When the Angels ſaw all theſe incomprehenſible
Myſteries, and *That* ſo beautiful an Image; they ſaid,
" Lord! if it will be pleaſing in thy Sight, we will,
" in thy moſt High and Mighty Name, proſtrate
" ourſelves before it:" To which voluntary Propoſal, God replied; " I am content you pay Ado-
" ration to *it,* and I command you ſo to do:" When
inſtantly they all bowed, inclining their ſhining Cœleſtial Countenances at his Feet; only *(b)* Lucifer
detained himſelf, obſtinately refuſing; proudly and

(a) Arokes. The Word in *Arabick* is *Roh,* in the Plural *Arrowah*;
it implies both Life and Soul, with ſcarce any Diſtinction.

(b) They call *Lucifer* ſometimes (as my Author does here, and
in many other Places) *Luzbel,* but more generally *Eblis,* which ſignifies *the Deſperate,* or one in Deſpair of recovering what he loſt.
They ſay his Name, before his Rebellion and Expulſion, was *Azazel,*
and during the Space of 8oooo Years, had been one of God's moſt
Obedient and Favourite Angels; 'till at laſt, for refuſing to render
Homage to *Adam,* he was caſt out of Heaven with all his Accomplices in his Diſobedience, among whom were the Angels *Arot* and
Marot, ſo often mentioned by ſeveral Authors. They give him ſeveral
other Names, of which in their proper Places. See *D'Herbelot* in
Eblis, &c.

arrogantly

arrogantly valuing himſelf upon his Heavenly Compoſition: To whom God ſternly ſaid; "Proſtrate "thy ſelf to *Adam*:" He made a Shew of ſo doing, but (*a*) remained only upon his Knees, and then roſe up, before he had performed what God had commanded him. When the Angels beheld his Inſolence and Diſobedience, they a Second Time proſtrated themſelves, to compleat what the haughty and preſumptuous Angel had left undone. From hence it is, that in all our Prayers, at each (*b*) Inclination of the Body, we make Two Proſtrations, (*c*) one immediately after the other. God being highly incenſed againſt the Rebellious *Lucifer*, ſaid unto him; "Why "didſt thou not reverence this Statue which I have "made, as the other Angels all have done?" To which *Lucifer* reply'd; "I will never leſſen or diſ-"parage my Grandeur ſo much, as to humble my-"ſelf to a *Piece of Clay*; I, who am an immortal "Seraphim, of ſo apparently a greater Excellency "than *that*: I, whom thou didſt create out of the "(*d*) Cœleſtial Fire, what an Indignity would it be to "my Splendor, to pay Homage to a Thing com-"poſed of ſo vile a Metal!" The irritated Monarch, with a Voice of Thunder, then pronounced againſt him this direful *Anathema* and Malediction; "Begone, "(*e*) Enemy; Depart, Rebel, from my Abode! Thou

 "no

(*a*) This ſhall be explained when their Prayers, *&c.* are treated of.

(*b*) The bowing of their Bodies with their Hands on their Knees, before they proſtrate themſelves at their Devotions.

(*c*) The Adoration they make when they pray proſtrating themſelves, and touching the Earth with their Foreheads, which is what the *Greeks* call προσκύνησις, when ſeven of our Members touch the Ground, *viz.* the Two *Feet*, the Two *Hands*, the Two *Knees*, and the *Head*. See a farther Explanation of this in *Reland*'s Abridgment of the *Mahom. Rel.*

(*d*) They hold, that the *Angels* and the *Genii*, were all made out of an exceeding hot Fire.

(*e*) A common Epithet they give the Devil, is, *Adou Allah*, God's Enemy. He is likewiſe called *El Ragim*, *i. e.* He that was ſtoned, or

' no longer ſhalt continue in my Cœleſtial Domi-
" nions. Go, thou accurſed flaming Thunderbolt of
" Fire! My Curſe purſue thee! My Condemnation
" overtake thee! My Torments afflict thee! And my
" Chaſtiſement accompany thee! " Thus fell this
Enemy of God and Mankind, both he, and all his
Followers and Abettors, who ſided or were Partakers
with him in his Pride, and preſumptuous Diſobedience : They were caſt, I ſay, by the avenging Arm
of God, into the loweſt Abyſſes of Everlaſting Torments, in which perpetual Dungeon of Endleſs Miſery, they ſhall remain to all Eternity.

The Conſequences of the Fall of this accurſed Generation, were not ſo inconſiderable, but that, according to the *Hebrew* (a) *El Taſfir*, and as (b) *Abou
el Khabar*, that Learned Doctor, informs us, the
Shock was ſo ſurprizingly great, when theſe pernicious Legions fell all at once, as they did, that the
whole Fabrick of Heaven, with the very Foundation
thereof, ſweated and trembled; Moſt terrible Earth-
quakes ſhook the vaſt Body of the lower Globe; The

---

or driven out of Paradiſe with Stones. This Name they give him
to incite every one to repulſe his Temptations with Violence and
Ardour. When they mention the Devil, whom they likewiſe call
Shietan and *Stiethar*, from the *Hebrew Shuthan*, they ever add a
Curſe, as *Allah enol hu, Allah Khuzze*, and very frequent v ſay,
Eouthou Billah min a Shietan Ragim, or, *God preſerve us from the vin-
quiſhed Satan.* This Expreſſion is before every Chapter in the *Al-
coran.*

(a) A Book ſo called. It ſhould be rather *Taſſir*, which ſignifies
an Expoſitor, and is the Title of many Books.

(b) The *Arabians* generally expreſs themſelves in a manner pecu
l ar to them alone ; for here *Abou el Khabar*, is the Title of a Book,
which literally ſignifies, *The Father of News*, and is alſo the Sirname
of ſeveral Men. Thoſe who are remarkable for any Perfection or
Imperfection of Body or Mind, or are addicted to any one Thing
in particular, they call him the Father of it. See *D'Herbelot* in
Abou, and Dr. *Prideaux* L. *Mahom* p. 82.

Rivers,

Rivers, Seas, and all running Waters were inftantly ftopped, and an unactive Sufpenfion of their *continual Worfhip* enfued, (*a*) fcarce advancing drop by drop in their Natural Courfes. In fine, an intire and univerfal Stupefaction followed ; all Things Animate and Inanimate, ceafed from their accuftomed *Adorations*, being wholly wrapped up in Amazement at the ftupendous and infcrutable Power of the Almighty Monarch, though it furpaffed their Imaginations, to dive into the Caufes of thefe fo wonderful Events. The Sun ftood ftill, faintly cafting an obfcure and difmal Light ; and the whole Surface was overwhelmed with Horror and Confufion : Nay, the moft pure and glorious Angels themfelves (thofe bleffed Cœleftial *Beings*) were fo difmayed with Aftonifhment, that they remained fixed and motionlefs in their (*b*) *Poftures.* Even the Natural Courfes of thofe Rivulets and Heavenly Springs which were among them, ceafed. And *Gabriel* himfelf (whofe Courage is fo incomparable, and whofe Magnanimity fo without equal) was, as much as is poffible for him to be, difmayed, lofing at once the Ufe of all his Faculties, being feized with a ftupid and unactive Lethargy ; yet ignorant of the real Caufe from whence proceeded the univerfal Aftonifhment, with which he felt himfelf oppreffed.

(*a*) The *Mahometans* affirm, that all Things Animate and Inanimate, the Mountains, Rocks, Seas, Rivers, Trees, Plants, Herbs, &c. perpetually ferve and worfhip God after their manner. *Prayer,* they fay, leads Half-way to Heaven ; *Fafting,* carries them to Heaven-Gate ; and *Alms,* gain Admittance. Notions worthy of a more believing People !

(*b*) According to the *Mahometan* Traditions, all the Angels in general have their particular Occupations affigned them by God, in which they are continually employed. Thofe who more immediately are Attendants on God's Perfon, they fay, ftand about him with their Hands folded over their Navels, and their Eyes inclining downwards, which they deem a Pofture of Humility and Refignation, and is the fame which the Pages, &c. ufe in the Prefence of their Emperors, Princes, and of all Men of chief Rank in general.

" Behold,

" Behold, O Sons of *Adam!* with what Rigour
" the damning Sins of Pride and Difobedience were
" punifhed; the Terrors they caufed, and with what
" direful Calamities they were accompanied; that
" they fhould affect, with their malignant Influence,
" the Heavens, the Earth, the Sun, the Moon, the
" Angels, the Courfes, the Seas, and every created
" Thing, caufing in every individual Part thereof,
" a Change; ftupifying, fhocking, infecting, ficken-
" ing, terrifying, and penetrating all exifting Bo-
" dies!

The accurfed Squadron, who before their Fall were
fo glorioufly beautiful, were transformed into fuch
hideoufly frightful and monftrous Appearances, and
fo much disfigured from what they once were, that
Imagination itfelf can comprehend nothing which
may be compared to have any Similitude, or bear
any manner of Refemblance to them: So ugly were
their Forms and Countenances, and fo unaccountable the Alteration, that nothing can be thought on,
which with any Likenefs may be juftly apply'd.
" Like unto a Delinquent, who has committed fome
" enormous Crime, and goes about feeking a Sanctu-
" ary, or fome Obfcurity, where to hide himfelf from
" the Eyes of Juftice, but finding none to protect
" him, he, trembling, expects his juft Chaftifement;
" uncertain when, yet fure 'twill come:" So this curfed rebellious Angel, both he and his Followers, feeing themfelves caft out of Glory, reflecting on their
prefent wretched Condition, and apprehenfive of
worfe (if poffible) went wandring about, feeking
Caves and difmal Solitudes, to avoid the farther
Wrath of the incenfed and offended God; but found
no comfortable Habitation, no Security, no Protection; wholly deprived of what might afford them
either Content or Reft. " O ye miferable Un-thron-
" ed! O Inheritances irrecoverably loft! Not the leaft
" Glimpfe or Profpect of being ever regained!

                                                This

This *Enemy* being thus routed, fubdued and van-quifhed; God now was pleafed to publifh and make manifeft his Defign of Animating *Man* out of that beautiful and refplendent *Cryftal,* and accordingly commanded *Gabriel* to breathe into the faid Veffel, that it might become Flefh and Blood: But at the Inftant, as the immaculate *Spirit* (a) was going to enter therein, *it* returned, and humbling itfelf before the Lord, faid; " O Merciful King! For what Rea-" fon is it, that thou intendeft to inclofe me in this
" loathfome Prifon? I, who am thy Servant, thou
" fhutteft up within mine Enemy, where my Purity
" will be defiled, and where, againft my Will, I fhall
" difobey thee, without being able to refift the Infti-
" gations and Power of this rebellious Flefh, whereby
" I fhall become liable to fuffer thy rigorous Punifh-
" ments, infupportable and unequal to my Strength,
" for having perpetrated the Enormities obnoxious to
" the Frailty of Human Flefh: Spare me, O Lord!
" fpare me! fuffer me not to tafte of this bitter
" Draught! To thee it belongs to command, and to
" me to fupplicate thee.

Thus fpoke the pure and unfpotted *Spirit;* when God, to give *it* fome Satisfaction to thefe Complaints, and that *it* might contentedly refign itfelf to obey his Commands, ordered *it* fhould be conducted near *his* Throne, where, in innumerable and infinite Parts thereof, it beheld certain Letters decyphered up and down, importing, MAHOMET *the Triumphant Leader!*

(a) *Aroh,* rather *Roh,* the Word is *Arabick,* and fignifies Spirit, Life and Soul promifcuoufly, as I have already hinted. *Cafchiri,* a noted Mahometan Writer, in his Book intitled *Fetouhat,* writes, That there are feveral Sorts of Creations: Some Things God cre-ated with only His *Fiat,* Be it done: others in which His Hands were employ'd only. And fome wherein He ufed, both his Word and his Hands. In the Beginning, He created Heaven and Earth with His fole Word, and then He created Man, and other Crea-tures with Matter, and the Concurrence of Second Caufes, which He had created before.

(a) And

(*a*) And over all the Seven Heavens, on their Gates, and in all the Books, he ſaw thoſe Words, ſtamped, exceedingly bright and reſplendent. This was the *Blazon* which all theAngels and other Cœleſtial Beings carried between their beautiful Eyes, and for their *Devices* on their Apparel.

The *Spirit* having ſeen all this, returned to the Throne of Glory, and being very deſirous to underſtand the Signification of thoſe Cyphers and (*b*) Characters, he asked, What Name that was which *ſhined* ſo in every Place? To which Queſtion, God anſwered; "Know, that from *Thee*, and from that *Fleſh* "ſhall proceed a Chieftain, a Leader who ſhall bear "*that* Name, and uſe *that* Language; by whom, and "for whoſe Sake, I thy Lord, the Heavens, the "Earths, and the Seas ſhall be honoured, as ſhall "likewiſe all who believe in *that* Name."

The *Spirit* hearing theſe Wonders, immediately conceived ſo mighty a Love to the Body (a Love

---

(*a*) The Four Sects which are among the *Mahometans* eſteemed as Orthodox, viz. The *Hanifeen*, the *Malikeen*, the *Shaffeen*, and the *Hambileen*, all unanimouſly agree, That the Name of the Impoſtor was, long before the Creation, Engraven all over the Heavens, and Recorded in the Sacred Regiſters thereof, in thoſe well known Words; *La illah illallah, Mohammed reſoul Allah*: But our Author has here, it ſeems, given us a different Expreſſion; I ſuppoſe, *Licentiâ Poeticâ*, (which he boldly and copiouſly aſſumes throughout his Work) not to lame his Metre.

(*b*) As throughout the whole *MS.* the Compiler has made no Scruple of *Spaniolizing*, al. *Spaniſhizing* moſt of his *Arabick* Words, I mean, giving them a *Spaniſh* Termination; I chuſe in this place to mention it once more for all He has it, *Alharſes*. In *Arabick*, the Letters or Characters of the Alphabet are *El harrof*, which is the Plural Number of *Haſf*, or rather *Horf*; but they uſually add *el* to all their Words, which is no other than the Article *The*, which the *Spaniards*, and all the *Europeans*, in Imitation of them, corrupt, by adding the Article to all thoſe Words beginning with *Al*, which are for the moſt part originally *Arabick*, as *el Alcarde*, The *Alcarde*, or Governor; *el Alquimia*, the Chymiſtry; *el Alcaſaba*, the Citadel; and ſo in innumerable others.

not to be expreffed, nor even imagined) that it long-
ed with Impatience to enter into it : Which it had no
fooner done, but it miraculoufly and artificially was
influenced and diftilled into every individual Part and
Member thereof, whereby the Body became Animated.

The Compofition of *Adam* was of divers and different Materials, anfwerable to the different Qualities and
Appetites which were to be incorporated in him.   His
Face and Head were formed from that illuftrious and
ever-famous Place, where *Abraham,* the Servant of
God, built the Holy *El Caaba* (a).   The Trunk of his
Body, from that where fince ftood the great and moft
fanctify'd Temple of (b) *Jerufalem.* His two Legs from
that where the Noble City of *Grand Cairo* (c) is fitu-
ated : His Feet, and Hands, from *Memphis :* His
Right-Hand from the Eaftward Part ; his Left from
the Weftward, oppofite thereunto, *&c.*   His *Nature,*
or his Private Parts, were compofed from *Aliftinche,*
(d) uninhabitable Mountains.   In fine, every Part and
Mem-

(a) The SquareChapel which is within the great and fumptuousTem-
ple at *Mecca,* held in mighty Veneration by all the *Mahometans* of what
Sect foever, towards the which they turn their Faces when they pray,
in what part of the World foever they be.   They hold, it was
begun by *Abraham,* and finifhed by *Ifhmael.* Edriffi an *Arabian* Geo-
grapher, in his Defcription of that Temple, fays, Its Length from
Eaft to Weft is Twenty-four Cubits, and Twenty-three from South
to North.   Its Gate ftands on the Eaft-fide, the Threfhold whereof
is Four Cubits from the Ground.   See more of this in *D'Herbelot,*
in the Words *Caaba* and *Meccah.* They affirm, That *Adam* built a
Temple where that at *Mecca* ftands, which they call *Sorah.*

(b) They call the Temple of *Solomon, Beit el Mocaddas,* the
Holy Houfe ; and that at *Mecca,* is generally called *Beit Allah,* the
Houfe of God.   My Author has it here *Al Magdiz,* meaning that at
Jerufalem.

(c) *Grand Cairo,* the Capital of *Egypt* ; the *Mahometans* all give it
the Name of *Miffir.* 'Tis here *Mucra.*

(d) *Su natvra de aliftinche de fierras inabitables.* This feems to be
obfcure, and fcarce intelligible ; yet this I am certain of, that the
wafhing

Member of him, necessary, convenient, or subservient to Human Life, were contained and included in the *Handful of Earth* which was conveyed by *Azarael*, the Angel of Death, and marvellously, and most artfully connected together, and so properly adapted and applied, to the Intent that Man might be in every Respect intirely perfect, exceeding all that Thought can conceive.

God furnished him with a Tongue harmoniously sweet and elegant, wherewith he might call upon, and glorify his Divine Name. He called him *Adam*, which is as much as to say, Father.

" Our Prophet has declared to us, the Reason
" why the First of Men was composed of so different
" Species, and from Places so distant and remote, one
" from the other ; for he tells us, That from hence it
" is, that Human Knowledge is distributed amongst
" all Mankind, and by which all People, in all Parts
" of the World, know one another. He who is born
" in the West, knows him who is born in the East,
" by only seeing him ; whereby it is evident, that
" seeing, upon a slender Acquaintance, and almost at
" the first Sight, Men of so distant Climates contract
" Friendships and Love, all Mankind are of the
" same Flesh and Blood."

The Supreme Monarch created *Adam* with his own Hands, suffering none but himself to touch him ; he formed him after the Image he thought fittest ; (*a*) Tall, Proper, Comely, and exceedingly Beautiful;

surpassing

---

washing of those Parts after Evacuation of either sort, is in *Arabick* called *Stina*, to which Word my Author seems to allude in *Alistinche* For the *Spaniards* use *ch* where we write the Consonant j, tho' not with so strong a Pronunciation The Consonant they always pronounce in the Throat, as they generally do the g, and the x.

(*a*) The *Mahometans* never say, That God created Man after his own Image, and hold it as the highest Impiety and Presumption in any who go about to give any Description of God's Form. Yet among the Vulgar, nothing is more common than to ask a Favour, or an

Alms,

ſurpaſſing the Riſing Sun. His Stature was of the moſt advantageous Size, (a); his Shape the beſt and moſt regular; And Rays of *Light* diffuſed ſo reſplendently from his Countenance, that none of the Angels were comparable to him.

God then aſſigned to him for his Habitation the *Cœleſtial Paradiſe*, with all its Territories, granting him free Liberty to go and come therein as he himſelf pleas'd; leaving it intirely to his Diſcretion to chuſe or to refuſe, to commit or to omit, to know or to leave unknown, whatſoever he would: But becauſe he ſhould not imagine himſelf to be abſolutely Lord, without a Superior; God enjoyned him (b) one only Precept to keep and obſerve, and that altogether eaſy and ſupportable, which was the firſt *Beginning* of our Miſery, and the *Middle* and *End* of all our Calamities!

Alins, *A la Widg Allah*, i. e. For God's Face; as we ſay, For God's Sake; but when any of the *A'lims* hear that Expreſſion, they rebuke them, ſaying, *Eſcoot Kafir! Allah m'andou Wdg*; i. e. Be dumb, you Infidel! God has no Face. *A'lim* ſignifies a Teacher, the Plural of which is *Oulemma* and *El Alm*.

(a) In the next Chapter he ſays, Thirty Spans.

(b) *Khondemir*, a famous Author frequently quoted by Monſieur *D'Herbelot*, and many others, has theſe Words, God forbad *Adam* the eating the Fruit of one Tree; but *Eblis*, aſſociating himſelf with the Peacock and the Serpent, prevail'd with *Adam* and *Eve* to eat of that *forbidden Fruit*. As ſoon as ever he had taſted the *Fatal Morſel*, their *Glorious Cloathing* dropt off, which made them ſenſible of their Sin, and aſham'd of their Nakedneſs, and run to a Fig-Tree to cover hemſelves with its Leaves; but it was not long before they heard the Voice of God, ſaying to them, *Go down, and depart this Place all of you, You ſhall, for the future, be Enemies to one another, and ſhall live and ſubſiſt upon the Earth for a Time.* ——— The general Tradition is, That *Adam* fell in the Iſland of *Serandib*, or *Ceilon*, *Eve* at *Guidda* or *Gidda*, a Port on the Red-ſea near *Mecca*: *Eblis*, or *Lucifer*, at *Miſſan* near Baſſora; the *Peacock* in *Indoſtan*; and the *Serpent* at *Naſibe*, or *Iſpahan*; that is, on the Places where thoſe Towns were afterwards built. *Adam* being miſerably diſtreſs'd, and inconſolable for the want of his Wife *Eve*, repented of his Sin, and lifted up his Eyes and Hands towards Heaven to implore Mercy. Then God ſent down a Tent by the Angels, and placed it where afterwards was the Temple of *Mecca*. *D'Herbelot* in *Adam*.

In

In this glorious Plain, so abundantly, and deliciously fruitful, replenished with Thousands of Charms and Allurements to content all his Appetites, one Tree there was reserved, and forbidden; Of which, God said to him; " Thou shalt keep especial Guard " over this Tree, the Fruit whereof thou shalt not " eat; neither shalt thou even touch it, on Pain of " my highest Indignation, Justice, Condemnation, " and Death : But take Notice; Thou wilt stand " in need of all thy *Light* to enable thee to " withstand the powerful Temptations of thy *known* " *Enemy.* In having given thee this Caution, I have " nothing more to say, or to advise thee; only, that " by thy Obeying this my One Command, I shall be " fully satisfy'd. It is a Thing reasonable, and of " no great Difficulty."

This Abode of inexpressible Delights, *Adam* enjoy'd alone, without a Companion; until he made his Supplications to God, that he would be pleased to vouchsafe him an Associate, with whom he might Communicate. When God immediately cast him into a deep Sleep, and before he awoke, took from his Left-Side a *Rib without Flesh*, of which he formed W O M A N, Beautiful, Fair, and superlatively Graceful; and named her (a) *Eve*, which signifies the same as Mother; from which Name so many innumerable Tribes and Lineages have proceeded.

Adam awaking, and beholding a Figure so exceeding lovely, and exquisitely desireable, was instantly for laying his Hands on her, without any more Respect, or farther Compliment; when he heard a Voice, saying, " Hold, *Adam*, detain thy self, and " pass no farther; fear the Lord who created Thee; " Thou must not approach her without my Leave." God then immediately called *Gabriel*, commanding him to go into *Paradise*, and there to treat of that

---

(a) The Name they call her by is *Hawah*.

first Marriage, and celebrate the Ceremony with
(a) a Festival and Lawful Dowry, and that the
Angels should supply the Want, and perform the
Office of (b) Parents, Relations, and Witnesses.

Thus those our First Parents were espoused, enjoying all that Happiness and Glory the Lord had been
bountifully pleased to allow them; their Wills and Desires being mutually conformable to each other's, never
in the least disagreeing; but continually praising and
glorifying their Maker, who had blessed them in giving them such spacious and ravishing Abodes.

'Twill be here reasonable I should declare what is
written concerning that pernicious Accident which
was the Source of so many Anxieties, so many Vexa-
tions, so many Calamities, so many Pains and Torments, such destructive Discords, Wars, and Desola-

---

(a) *Aras y Cidaque,* rather *Ars y Sidaak.* The Words are
Arabick. Ars is any Feast; but more-especially a Marriage Feast.
Sidaak is the Sum in Money or other Things the Husband is to give
for his Wife, according to Agreement.

(b) *Alguali,* as we pronounce, it is *Al Waali*; for the *Spanish gu.*
is equivalent to our *w.* The Word imports the Bride's nearest Relations, and particularly him or those who give her in Marriage.
More of this in another Place. I ought not to omit a Notion of
the *Mahometans* concerning the Creation, tho' a little improper here:
'Tis a Saying of no less a Person than *Giafar Sadik,* or *th Just.*
This Man was nearly related to *Aboubecre,* the immediate Successor
of *Mahomet* the false Prophet, and is of such Repute among them,
that it is held as an Authentick Tradition, that he was wont to say,
*Ask me Questions often, whilst I am among you, for none will come after
me, that can instruct you like me.* Of this *Giafar* it is recorded by a
noted Writer named *Rabi el Abiar,* that being ask'd, Whether there
was no *Adam* in this World before him that *Moses* speaks of? He answer'd, That there had been Three, and there would be Seventeen
more in as many great Revolutions of Years. And being ask'd, Whether God would create other Men after the End of this World? his
Answer was; *Would you have God's Kingdom remain empty, and his
Power idle? God is a Creator throughout his whole Eternity.* —— This
Giafar bore the Character of having never told a Lye in his Life,
and so his Sirname *Sadik* seems to imply, signifying, *One to be depended upon.* But this I leave to the Criticks to decide.

D

tions, Variances, Burnings, and Devaftations, Enmities, Affaults, and Afflictions; in fine, Deftruction and Death, and, what is infinitely worfe, Eternal Condemnation and Mifery.

I have already mentioned the Tree in that fragrant Garden, as likewife the ftrict Injunction that was laid upon that juft Couple, and the Regard and Reverence they were enjoyned to have towards the fame : Now, as the accurfed *Lucifer* was continually contriving with the utmoft Malice, Envy and Rage, how to bring about and execute his Revenge upon Man, againft whom he had conceived fo irreconcilable a Hatred, and for whofe Sake alone he faw himfelf caft out from fo much Glory, without any Hopes of ever recovering what he had loft, or being re-eftablifhed in his priftine Happy State; He envioufly, and impatiently beheld in what a diftinguifhing Manner God had enthroned M A N, and had given him the Poffeffion of the Station which was once his; where his Condition had been fo different from what he at prefent enjoy'd; and the better to accomplifh his evil Defigns, he imagined, that if by any Means, he could caufe him to defcend to the Earthly World, he fhould have him more ready at hand, and by his Falfehood and Treachery, advance himfelf, and by tempting and feducing Mankind to Sin, caufe their Condemnation to Hell.

Although this vile and curfed Angel ufed all poffible Endeavours to get Accefs to *Adam,* yet he found it impracticable, and altogether out of his Power to come at him; fo all his Projects and Snares had hitherto proved fruitlefs, and of no Effect.

This Inventor of all Evil and Wickednefs, full fraught with Mifchief, wandering about in this Manner, cogitating and revolving Thoufands of Fancies and Chimeras, by Chance happened to pafs by the refplendent Gate of Paradife, where, feeing the Guardian Angel, or, as we may fay, the Porter, he began thus to fpeak unto him; " I muft of neceffity, " upon a certain Bufinefs of great Importance, " fpeak with thofe Two Servants of thy Lord,
" whom

" whom thou haſt under thy Charge; 'tis to diſ-
" abuſe them, and to give them an Inſight into ſome
" Affairs which nearly concern them, and of which
" they are wholly ignorant.

According as we are informed by our Teachers, the Porter returned him a flat Denial : Wherefore, when this malignant Enemy perceived his little Succeſs in this Attempt, he intreated him to call the Serpent, which was then a Creature of a moſt beautiful Form and Shape. She came, and he deſired, that ſhe would oblige him ſo far, as to receive him within her : He artfully and ſubtly reiterated his Perſuaſions, and finally deceived her. The better to diſguiſe and give a more plauſible Gloſs to his Diſſimulation and Hypocriſy, he bid her conceal him in her moſt ſecret Part. With theſe Wiles, this Traytor fraudulently impoſed upon her Weakneſs ; ſhe hid him under her Palate, in the Roof of her Mouth, and in this manner conveyed him into Paradiſe ; and approaching near the forbidden Tree, the baſe Serpent would fain have diſengag'd herſelf from him, uſing many fruitleſs Endeavours to caſt him out of her Mouth ; But in vain ; he had got Poſſeſſion, and would not relinquiſh, but clove faſt to her Tongue ; and ſo involved in her, forced her to aſcend the *Reſerved Tree.*

The Reader muſt obſerve, That theſe Juſt, and 'till then Innocent, Perſons, were frequently accuſtomed to meet, and ſit under *that* Tree, to be the more careful and aſſiduous in guarding the ſame; and this Conſideration brought *Eve* thither, alone, at that time : When looking up towards the Tree, ſhe beheld the pernicious and treacherous Serpent, that Enemy of Mankind, who began to accoſt her in theſe Words ; " O moſt fair and beautiful
" *Eve !* Shouldſt thou but once taſte of this Fruit,
" the Glory which thou now enjoyeſt, thou wouldeſt
" poſſeſs to Eternity ! Thou ſhalt be equal to

God

" God himfelf in Wifdom and Knowledge! All
" Secrets and Myfteries, of which thou art now
" ignorant, will be manifefted unto thee!" In the
Interim, whilft thefe Words were fpeaking, came
Adam; to whom *Eve* imparted what was in Agitation: But he, with a ftern forbidding Afpect, reprov-
ed her, bidding Defiance to any fuch Temptati-
on, or Intent. She perfifted in importuning him.
The Blandifhments of *Eve* were fo many, and fo
perfuafive, that no longer had he the Power to refufe
complying with her; but at her Inftigations, renounced
the Fealty and Homage he had offered to God.

Con erning this Tree, there are many different
and incoherent Opinions, of what Sort of Tree it
was, and what was the Fruit it bore: But with
fufficiently convincing Reafons, the Majority agree,
That it was a Vine, and that the Fruit it produced,
was Grapes; they confidering the peculiar Effect
this Fruit has upon Men, which with its Juice,
caufes them to lofe their Senfes and Underftanding, depriving them of the Ufe of their natural
Faculties, and ingendering in them Difobedience, Brutality, and many other Enormities.

Eve ftretched out her Hand! " O unfortunate
" and dreadful Circumftance! How many Miferies
" didft thou caufe to the World, at that one In-
" ftant! O *Eve*! how many Millions of Souls didft
" thou, without Reafon, hereby condemn and deftroy!
" How many Lives haft thou fhortned and dimi-
" nifhed! How many Difobediences haft thou com-
" mitted for thy Pleafure, and to humour thy Ap-
" petite and Curiofity! And with only reaching out
" thy Hand, how many Throats haft thou parched
" and dryed up? Didft thou want in that Garden
" Thoufands of Thoufands of fructiferous and fhady
" Trees, loaden with fo many different Kinds and
" Species of delicious and *fugared* Fruits, befides this
" which thou now fo rapacioufly gathereft, where-
" with to fatisfy thy ravenous and infatiable Appe-
" tite?

" tite? Surely now with Anguish thou tastest the
" Bitterness of the Savour, which accompanies thy
" Lapsation! It might have been sufficient to
" content thee, to have considered, that a few Hours
" before, thou wast a *Vessel of Mud*, the vilest of all
" Metals, and that the Lord had exalted thee to the
" Cœlestial Choirs, surpassing in Excellency the
" whole Creation, the Creatures whereof, He had
" even caused to worship and adore (*a*) thee, and had
" placed thee in a Station above all Earthly Thrones, in
" such Freedom, Immunity, and Liberty, that thou
" mightest possess, enjoy, and uncontrouledly com-
" mand whatsoever thou could'st wish for! But in
" return for all these transcendent Mercies, thy pre-
" sumptuous Prevarication, and thy audacious Am-
" bition extended to equalize thy self in this man-
" ner to Him who gave thee thy very Being!"

In fine, as the Teachers affirm, she took of the
forbidden Fruit, Twelve Grains, or Berries, Eight
of which, she gave to her Husband, retaining Four
for herself, the which she swallowed without Delay.
From hence it remains for ever established, That in
all Cases of Inheritances, the Male claims as his
Right, a double Portion to what the Female can demand : As, likewise, that the Woman (in case she
has no Children) should inherit one fourth Part of
her Husband's Substance, on the Consideration of
those Four Grains, (or Berries) which she [*Eve*]
would keep to her self. In fine, *Eve*, as I have said,
swallowed them, and *Adam*, with the same Intent,
put those she had given him, into his Mouth; but
as he was about to proceed, as his Wife had set
him the Example, he heard a most terrible and
astonishing Voice; and being desirous of disgorg-
ing that which he repented his having touch'd, he
applied his Hand to his Throat, but by no means

(*a*) *Worship* and *adore*, here in the *Arabick* Sense, has no other
Signification than προσκυνεῖν in *Mat.* ii. ver. 2.

was able either to get it out, neither could he fwallow it ; fo much was he ftupified with that dreadful ecchoing Voice, that it would not pafs, but remained fixed in the Middle of his Throat, without going either backwards or forwards. The Voice faid, " O " Woe unto thee ! How foon haft thou forgot the only " Commandment thou hadft obliged thyfelf to ob- " ferve ! How haft thou violated the Purity of my " unfpotted Abode, with thy voracious Gluttony ! " My Habitation, wherein difobedient Vaffal never " fet his Foot unchaftifed !" *Adam,* difturbed, and wholly confufed, began to excufe himfelf, laying the Blame upon *Eve,* and fhe, in her Vindication, accufed the vile Serpent ; yet all was not fufficient to free them, or make them appear innocent.

" O how did they debafe and confound them- " felves ! and what a Load did they lay upon them- " felves, without being able to difcharge it ! How " blind is that Criminal, who forgets, and neglects " that which is of the greateft Importance to him ! " O guilty Sinners ! how near within your Reach " is your own Freedom and eternal Felicity ! It " intirely confifts in your own Power to be Happy: " With the fame Facility you may obtain the " *Much,* as the *Little,* a large Portion of Blifs, as " a fmall one ; nay, although you fhould defire an " Infinity of Glory, 'tis as eafily acquired, as the " fmalleft Atom.   Seek not Pretences and Evafi- " ons, nor accufe others with the Crimes you have " committed, as did thofe wretched Offenders, our " firft Parents. Return to your Creator, to whom " all your Sins are known ; to Him, from whom " no Secrets are hid ; fupplicate Him, that you " may be exempted from His Indignation and " Punifhment. Implore His Pardon, for thofe Of- " fences, which 'tis not in your Power to conceal " from him : Expofe to Him your Wounds ; mani- " feft your Sores, before they heal fuperficially ; " left the inward Corruption caufe a Mortification:
" Afk

" Afk of Him, for he is gracious and merciful, and
" never refufes to hearken to His Supplicants : He
" is all Goodnefs ; (*a*) All Pardon ; endeavour to
" learn no Language but this. " [To return from
this Digreffion]

The Voice of God thundered, commanding His Angels that they fhould immediately, without Delay,
drive them out of Paradife, and its Territories ; and
that they fhould defpoil them of the Robes, with
which their Nakednefs was covered, and deprive them
of the Crowns they had upon their Heads : They
with Tears and Lamentations, implored God's Compaffion, and that he would not banifh them from the
advantagious and delightful Seat he had been fo gracioufly pleafed to put into their Poffeffion :   But
without granting their Requeft, God faid, " Be gone ;
" Go out, ye difloyal Wretches ! Ye fhall no longer
" abide in this Place, fince you knew not how to de-
" ferve fo confummate a Happinefs. "   Then *Adam*,
laying faft hold of, and embracing the Boughs and
Branches of fome of thofe precious Trees, faid ; " Have
" Mercy, Lord ! on this thy miferable Servant ! fince
" thou, O King ! thy-felf, didft offer and promife me,
" That from my Loins, and from my Lineage, fhould
" proceed a *Son*, for whofe Sake, and through whofe
" Means, the whole World fhould be reftored and pre-
" ferved, and fhould have become as if it had been cre-
" ated a Second Time : For the Honour, (*b*) Vertue,
" and Excellency of whom, I implore thy Protection
" and Compaffion. "   God faid, *Caft him out !* But he
returning to his Intreaties and Supplications, faid ;
" Take Pity on me, Lord ! For thou it was who

(*a*) *Rahma* implies Mercy. The Word is *Arabick*, and in very
many Parts of the Original MS. is ufed in that Senfe.

(*b*) The Word in the Original is *Alfadila* ; rather *El Fadilah.* Its
Signification is Vertue or Excellency. See *D' Herbelot* in *Fadhael*,
which is the Plural of *Fadbilah*.

" gaveft

" gaveft me the (*a*) joyful Tydings, that from my
" Loins fhould be born a *Son*, who fhould be fo *upright*
" *a Walker*, that in the World he fhould be the Father
" of many Generations : Lord ! for the Love of *him*,
" and for the fake of the Honourable Tribes of *his*
" Pofterity, commiferate our Condition, and do not
" abandon us. " God replied ; *Let them be gone from
hence !* But *Adam* ftill perfifting in his Prayers and
Importunities, faid ; " Gracious Lord ! Thou didft
" offer me, and haft commanded, that from me
" fhould defcend a *Son* fo Important, that he fhould
" be admitted to converfe (*b*) *Hand to Hand* with thy
" *Divine Effence*. O Lord, of thy fo bountiful Mercy,
" take Pity on me ! " God, whofe Word had never
been oppofed, or contradicted, confirmed what He
before fpoke again ; faying ; *I command they go out,
and make me no more Reply :* But *Adam* inceffantly ap-
pealing, and mingling amongft the Angels, once
more faid ; " Thou didft promife me, Lord, a *Son* of
" my Genealogy ; thou wilt not now abandon me ! "
At laft, the Voice, more terrible and rigorous than
ever, replyed ; *Caft them out ! Caft them out !* The
Angels then preffed him to depart, without farther
Delay, and to be no longer difobedient to God, who
would admit of no Excufe.

(*a*) *Apiadadme, fenor que tu me albriciafte*, &c *Albricias* is a
Word the *Spaniards* have corruptly adapted to imply the Reward
for Good News, from *El Bifhara*, which in *Arabick* is Good News,
or Tydings. One of the Sirnames of *Adam* is *Aboul Bafhar*, that
is, *the Father of good News*, as if he brought the Earth Tydings
of its being inhabited.

(*b*) Their Expofitors all affirm, That when *Mahomet* made a
Vifit to God in Heaven (of which more hereafter) God took
him by the Hand, and laid his Hand on the Prophet's Shoulder,
which (at his Return, when he rehearfed that unfhapen Lye to his
Difciples) he faid was fo exceffive cold, that it pierced the very
Marrow in his Back. This is fpoken of by Dr. *Prideaux* in
Mahomet's Life, p. 76.

Adam,

Adam, before his going out, beholding the fragrant Fruits of thofe delicious, tender Trees, wept bitterly ; The Reflections he made on the glorious Bleffings he had fo indifcreetly deprived himfelf of, left him no Room for Confolation : Again he began his lamentable Complaints, in this Manner, " O compaffionate Monarch ! Thou, " who didft rejoice me with the good News of " my being the Father to a *Son*, juft and good, who " fhall highly excel all that fhall be born, or brought " forth, either among Humane Race, or any other " Creatures whatfoever ; upon whofe Account, thou " didft create that *Light* which thou haft recom- " mended to me ; I implore thee, for the Love of " *him*, and for the Sake of *his* fo refplendent *Light*, " that thou accomplifh to me thy faid Promife : " This is at leaft, what thou canft never fail to " perform.

O! how ferioufly ought Men to confider, and reflect upon thefe Things, and amidft the Misfortunes and Af- flictions incident to the Inconftancy of Worldly Affairs, be fervent, firm, and perfevering in their Prayers and Supplications to God. None fhould be diffident, nor defpair of Pardon, but center their whole Truft and Confidence in God's Mercy, and indefatigably intreat, beg, and implore Him, who is never weary of hearing Requefts of this Nature ; efpecially when fuch Means are pitched upon, as thofe which this juft Couple made ufe of in their Interceffion. For no fooner had *Adam* (the laft time) mentioned the Name of the Pro- phet, but the Almighty faid aloud ; " Unhand him ; " Let him alone ; Let him go out as he will himfelf, " and at his own Leifure ; for they have afked in the " Name of an *Interceffor*, for whofe Sake my Mercy " can deny them nothing. " So commanding the Angels to be kind and affifting unto them, and to take them under their Protection, they [the Angels]
obeyed,

obeyed, and carefully conveyed them down to this
World; but ſeparately, and to (a) far diſtant Places.

" Who can expreſs, or conceive the feeling Con-
" cern, the Anxiety, the Anguiſh of Mind, with
" which theſe unhappy Juſt Perſons were over-
" whelmed and oppreſſed, when they ſaw they muſt
" be parted one from the other? Their Eyes ſhed
" Tears of Blood, to find themſelves alone, in hor-
" ribly dark and diſmal Obſcurity; treading upon
" Thorns and Brambles, ſtumbling at every Step
" they made; with no kind of Covering to hide their
" Nakedneſs; ſubject to the Froſts and Colds of the
" tempeſtuous Weather; their amiable, comely and
" graceful Countenances, miſerably chopt and abuſed
" by the inclement Winds; weeping Tears of Blood

(a) It is the general Opinion and Tradition among all *Mahometans,*
that *Adam* was conveyed to the Mountain *Serandib,* in the Iſland of
Ceilon; which to this Day, is by the *Portugueſes* called, *Pico de
Adam,* or *Adam's* Mount. I find this Paſſage in D. *Manuel de Faria
y Souſa,* a Celebrated *Spaniſh* Writer, where he deſcribes the Iſland
of *Ceilon,* " In the County of *Denaraca,* which is in the Center of
" this Iſland, riſes that vaſt Mountain called *Pico de Adam,* becauſe
" ſome believed our Firſt Father lived there, and the Print of a
" Foot ſtill there to be ſeen upon a Stone on the Top of it, is his:
" The Natives call it, *Amala Sarapadi,* i. e. The Mountain of the
" Footſtep. Some Springs coming down it, at the bottom, form a
" Rivulet, where Pilgrims waſh, and believe it purifies them. The
" Stone on the Top is like a Tomb-ſtone; the Print of the
" Foot ſeems not Artificial, but as if it had been made in the ſame
" Nature, as when one treads in Clay, which makes it be looked
" upon as Miraculous." By the *Arabs* this Mountain is called *Ra-
boun.* The Place where *Eve* fell, they affirm to be at *Gidda,* a Port
of the Red-Sea, not far from *Mecca,* which Place, they ſay, was built
in remembrance of her, and from her called *Gidda,* which in *Arabick*
is Grandmother. They ſay, ſhe was buried there, and ſhew a Sepulchre of a large extent, which they affirm to be hers. *D' Herbelot*
recites many Fables of them, out of *Arabian* Traditions, under the
Names *Adam* and *Hauah,* and ſeveral others. The Cœleſtial Robes
of Purity, Piety, and Innocence, with which our Firſt Parents were
clad in Paradiſe, continued on them but half a Day, wherein the
Mahometans agree with the *Rabbies;* but the former ſay, That a Day of
Paradiſe, is equal to a Thouſand of our Years, ſo that it ſeems, they
were there about Five hundred Years.

" and

" and Anguifh ; trampling on, and wounding them-
" felves with Briars on every Side: Lonefome and
" Solitary, no Company but Serpents, and other
" fuch like Brute Creatures. O Mortals! Let us not
" bury this in Oblivion ! Let us continually remember
" this Draught of Bitternefs! Let us confider, that in
" the moft fhocking of our Afflictions, be our Con-
" dition ever fo defperate, or our Troubles ever fo
" numerous; yet it is impoffible they fhould arrive
" to the Hundredth part of that which our firft Pa-
" rents underwent, without the leaft Intermiffion,
" until God was pleafed, in fome meafure, to mitigate
" his Wrath. Banifhment, Solitude, Affront, and
" Nakednefs without compare; Fears, Tremblings,
" Terrors, Heats, Colds, Thirfts, Hunger, Sorrows,
" Pain and Wearinefs, innumerable and infupport-
" able bitter Miferies: A long and tedious Night,
" difmally dark and frightful, without the leaft Ap-
" pearance of Light. Let us ferioufly and judicioufly
" confider, how intolerable all thefe Calamities muft
" feem to thofe who were created in Paradife, and
" accuftomed to enjoy the inexpreffible Delights there-
" of! "

Now when God faw fit to put an End to *that* Night,
and that *Aurora* fhould fhew her beautiful Face; He
[*Adam*] perform'd thofe two Inclinations and Proftrations; which we, the *Muffulmans*, perform before
the Morning; the which we call (*a*) *the Trumpets of
the Dawn*: This he did very fecretly, and with a low
Voice, becaufe the Light was, as yet, but imperfect,
and his Fears exceeding great. But as the Day-light

(*a*) Hizo aquellos dos *Aracas*,que los *Muzlimes*,hazen antes de *azubbi*
y las Uaman annefilas de *Alfachri*, &c. *Ruccab* is the Proftration,
Subbah is the Morning, and *El Fejer*, is the Dawn of the Day , This
ferves to give a Tafte of the particular Care they take, to derive all
their Rites and Ceremonies from the remoteft Antiquity. Their
Muedins or Cryers, from the Turrets of the Mofques, before Break
of Day (befides the Words they fay at other times) repeat Twice,
Affalaat kheir mina noum, i. e. Prayers are better than Sleep.

began clearly to appear, the Sorrowful and Afflicted *Adam* was somewhat more determined, and began to take Courage, and to be of good Cheer: He then with an audible ecchoing Voice, pronounced *Allah* (a) *hu acbar!* that is, *God is great!* and performed the Two Morning Prayers with the proper Inclinations and Proftrations, whereby he manifeftly confirmed the Excellency of his Faith. From hence it is that our *Saláat el Sabbáh,* or our Morning Devotions, had their firft Original Appellation.

When *Adam* had recovered himfelf from his paft Confternation and Agony, and the bright refplendent *Phœbus* had now gilded the Earth, the Hills, and the Valleys, with his glittering Rays, the Light of the Sun afforded fome Comfort and Confolation to the almoft defpairing Patriarch. But as he beheld its fhort Continuance, he was again feized with melancholy Reflexions, and oppreffed with a Thoufand tormenting Thoughts; not without Caufe, apprehending that he had little Profpect of being ever delivered from thofe Perplexities and Afflictions.

In this comfortlefs Condition, and without tafting the leaft Suftenance, he continued Thirty Days; from whence our Annual Faft of the Honourable *Ramadam* had its Beginning.

At the Expiration of that time, the Faithful *Gabriel* defcended, and coming to the afflicted *Adam,* began to footh and carefs him, with his Seraphick Hands,

---

(a) It may be proper, and, perhaps, acceptable to many, to fet down here, the Words the *Muedins* ufe, when they call the People to Prayer. I therefore, genuinely give 'em *Verbatim,* with the exact literal Tranflation; *viz. Alah hu acbar,* Twice; *Efreddou inna la ilah ill'allah,* Twice; *Efheddou inna Mohammed Rafal Allah,* Twice; *Hai ala Salah,* Twice; *Hai alal Filha,* Twice; [Here, if in Morning before Day, as in the preceding Note] *Allah hu acbar,* Twice, *La ila ill'allah.* That is, *God is Great. Bear witnefs, that there is no God, but God; Bear witnefs, that Mahomet is God's Meffenger; To Prayer; To Succefs:* [meaning, that by ferving God they will fucceed and profper] *God is Great, There is no God, but God.*

ftroaking

ftroaking his Body, and with his Finger piercing thofe Parts, and making the (a) Hole from whence the filthy Dregs and Excrements of that *bitter Mouthful* of Gall and Aloes came out, the which, all this while for want of an Orifice, or proper Place of Evacuation, had not diftilled or paffed through him: But as the Glorious Angel had been always accuftomed to delicious Scents, and the fragrant Perfumes of Heaven, the naufeous and abominable Smell of thofe corrupted Dregs, almoft caufed him to fwoon. *Adam* aftonifhed, afked him, What he ailed? To which Demand the Angel anfwered; This Fainting and Alteration which thou beholdeft in me, proceeds from thy Difobedience; for the Savour of thy Excrement is moft offenfive and odious in my Noftrils. *Adam*, upon hearing this, conceived fo much Sorrow and Concern, that the Holy Angel was obliged to ufe many foothing Arguments and compaffionate Speeches, to appeafe and comfort him. The Difcourfe which at that time paffed between the Angel and him, was fo unconceiveably fublime, that it is beyond Human Underftanding to guefs, even in Dreams, at the Purport thereof.

At laft, by the perfuafive and irrefiftable Eloquence of the Charitable *Gabriel*, his Grief was in fome Mea-

---

(a) Whatever the Opinion of their Teachers is in this Point, I fhall not go about to decide; but of a certainty I know, that the Vulgar Notion is, that *Adam* was firft *broach'd* by the Devil, and (if I can without offending Decency exprefs it) the Reafon, by which I make this Affertion, is this: As few are ignorant, how much the horrid Sin of Sodomy is practifed, nay, even tolerated amongft them, though exprefly forbidden and exclaimed againft in the *Alcoran*, fo it is a very ufual Prank for them, when any one ftoops down, or ftands with his back towards them, to apply their middle Finger to his Pofteriors, which if the Party fo ferved, refents, their common Anfwer in Return is thus; *Khoya Is Shurr? Munkaddurfhe anna deer Sebbut fine el Shaitan hisfha, artaw?* which is, *Brother, is it any harm? May not I put my Finger where the Devil thruft his?* This is Word for Word from the *Arabick*. The *Turks* on the like Occafion, fay to the fame Effect, with little Difference; *Danilma Jinnum, Shaitanung birmoe ourodi girde, bennum ké ne-girm.fs ya? i. e. Be not angry, my Life, The Devil's Finger went in there, why may not mine enter too?* This I deliver not as an Article of their Faith.

fure affwaged, who in the next place taught him to
Till the Ground, and howby Art, Labour, and Induftry,
to obtain for himfelf a Suftenance, inftead of the State
of Glory and Happinefs he had loft for being Incon-
ftant.

To render him fit for the Service of his Creator, he
was commanded to purify himfelf from his Pollutions,
by wafhing all thofe Parts and Members of his Body,
which had been any-way Inftrumental or Acceffary
with him, in his Crime and Perpetration; Firft, His
Hands and Arms to the Elbows, as being the principal Actors; Next, His Head, Face, &c. as being
the Center wherein are contained and included all the
Corporal Senfes, which were Accomplices and Abettors with him in his Iniquity and Tranfgreffion.
Laftly, His Feet, which were the Suftainers and Up-
holders of thofe his Rebellious Members. From this
Wafhing took its Rife our (a) *Wadob*, now in ufe,
and daily practifed by us *Muffulmans*.

In this manner the good *Adam* remained in fome
meafure fatisfied and comforted, laborioufly delving
the hard and ftubborn Earth, fwallowing Sweat
mingled with Blood, continually undergoing and performing a moft fevere Penance, with incredible Au-
fterity, to try if by any Means he might poffibly re-
gain his Lord's Favour, that he might be reconciled
to him.

It is written, That for Forty Years together, without the leaft Refpite or Interruption, he underwent
the moft rigid and moft prevailing Penance imaginable, even beyond Expreffion; infomuch, that
through the extraordinary Greatnefs of his Penitence; and the Fervency of his Zeal and Contrition,

---

(a) My Author has it *El alguado*, which, I have already hinted to
be the *Spanifh* manner of writing and pronouncing fuch Words. The
Ceremonial Ablutions, the *Mahometans* ufe before they pray, they
call *Wadou* or *El wathou*. A more particular Defcription, fhall be inferted in the Chapter of their Rites, &c.

his

his Blood, which was before whiter than Milk, was changed to the contrary Extream, becoming excessively Black: When at last the terrible Voice said to him; *Why didst thou Sin?* Whereupon his whole Mass of Blood was altered, and reduced to the Likeness of what at this Day appears in his Progeny. This Corruption and Adulteration of his Blood, was the Source and Foundation of all Infirmities, from the Froth and Dregs of which, ever since have remained in our mortal Bodies those malignant Drops which incite us to Disobedience, Pride, Ambition and Avarice, and which rouze up in us Wrath, Hatred, Enmity and Malice, with all the other Vicious Inclinations which Original Sin brought with it. These Fatal Drops of polluted Blood, were taken from our Triumphant Prophet (*a*) by the most Holy Angels, when his Breast was opened by them for that Intent; for which Reason he never had the least Inclination to Sin.

Adam having now compleatly accomplished his penitential Purgation, and the Angel having denounced to him, that the Lord was appeased and satisfied with what he had performed and suffered, God now saw proper to rejoin him (*b*) with his Beloved Wife *Eve,* that they might cherish and comfort one another, as some Amends for their past Sorrows and

---

(*a*) This notorious Fable is at large in the 21st Chapter of this Book The *Arabick* Word for *Original Sin* is, *Hebat el Calb,* that is, the Grains of the Heart This the *Mahometans* allow to have been derived to us from our first Parents, and say, That it is the Ground of all Sin, and that their Impostor was Impeccable, because those corrupted Drops were taken out of his Heart, by the Angel *Gabriel.*

(*b*) The *Arabick* Name is *Hawah,* which they seem to have borrowed from the *Hebrews,* who call her *Khawah,* which, according to *D'Herbelot,* in the Name *Havah,* is the Name of a Root, and signifies *Life.* In *Arabick,* Life is *Haiat,* as *Hai* implies *Alive.* More concerning her hereafter.

Afflictions,

Afflictions, and that they might begin to People the Earth; fo they met together on the Top of the towring Mountain (*a*) *Arafat*, near *Mecca*, where weeping for Joy, they received each other with inexpreffible Love and Tenderneſs.

(*a*) This Word comes from *Araf* or *Arf*, which in *Arabick* is, *to know*. This Mountain, which is in *Arabia Petræa*, or the Stony, the *Mahometans* hold in the greateſt Veneration, and every Year, on the 9th Day of the Moon *D'ul Hagiat*, or *of the Pilgrimage*, incredible Numbers of Pilgrims meet there, to perform their Ceremonial Devotions, before they approach the Temple at *Mecca*, near which Place this Mountain is. They believe, that on the Top thereof, *Adam* and *Eve* firſt met, after a Baniſhment and Separation of 120, fome fay, 200 Years; all which Time, they underwent a moſt grievous Penance. According to all their Traditions, it is called *Arafat*, becauſe *Adam* there firſt *knew* his Wife *Eve*.

CHAP.

CHAP II.

Eve's wretched State in her Solitude, after she was banished out of Paradise. Adam's Comeliness, Stature, &c. His Resemblance to the Prophet Mahomet. They are pardon'd. The Hereditary Light (a) recommended by God to Adam, &c. Seth born. His Character, &c.

IT is the ordinary and usual Consequence, in all great Confusions, alarming Accidents, and mighty Revolutions, for us, on such Occasions, to neglect and forget that which is of the nearest Concern to us; giving a Loose to the Reins of the impetuously furious, and irresistable Destiny, by which Affairs are hurried on to the appointed Crisis: It has not happened otherwise, nor is that received Maxim and

---

(a) It may not be unnecessary or unacceptable in this Place, to give the curious Reader a Taste of what others say of *Eve.* The most ancient Eastern People, and almost the Generality of the *Mahometans,* hold, That the first Son she brought forth was called, *Abd al Hareth,* which literally signifies, the *Creature,* or Servant, of the *Tiller,* or *Labourer*; because *Adam* was the first that *Tilled* the Earth, according to the Words in *Genesis,* God put Man into Paradise to *till* it. Yet the *Arabs,* who abound in Fables, give another Account of the Reason of this Name, which is thus to be found related by *Hussain Vaez* an ancient Writer. He says, That *Eve* finding her-

E   self

and Obfervation, contradicted in this prefent Hiftory, as appears confpicuoufly obvious to our Sight, in that we have fo attentively employed our Thoughts on the Miferies and forlorn Condition of *Adam*, that we have been intirely forgetful of what was become of our forrowful Mother *Eve*, who was the firft Caufe, and principal Inventrefs of our Calamity, and the Source and Seed of the Perdition of all Human Kind.

If we ferioufly confider with mature Deliberation, we cannot reafonably fuppofe, or with any Probability conjecture, her Grief and Affliction to be lefs in any wife, than his ; as being a Woman, weak and helplefs by Nature, alone in an unknown Place, and in all refpects Comfortlefs ; and therefore, rather exceeding thofe of her Hufband. The Vehemency of her Anguifh was fo violently great, that I want Words to exprefs it. She had a Flux of Blood, of Red or Scarlet Hue, defcending from her moft fecret and occult Veffels, dying therewith the lovely Surface of her fo beautiful Limbs, accompanied by frequent

---

felf with Child, as fhe had begged of God, the Devil appeared to her in a Difguife, and asked her, Whether fhe knew what fort of a Creature fhe had in her Womb? And fhe acknowledging herfelf to be ignorant, he asked again, Whether fhe knew which Way it muft be brought forth, at her Mouth, Nofe, or Ears, or whether her Belly muft be cut open? *Eve*, in a Fright, went and told *Adam* what had happened to her, who was as much puzled, as fhe had been before. Whereupon the Devil appeared to him, and told him, That he was acquainted with the great Name of God, by Means whereof, he obtained whatever he demanded, and would make ufe of it to caufe *Eve* to bring forth with Eafe, and bear a Son like him, provided he would call his Name *Abd el Hareth*. The Devil's Aim in having this Name given him, was to engage the Son in his Service ; for this *Fallen Angel*, now call'd *Eblis* by the *Arabs*, had, they fay, in Heaven, *Hareth* for one of his Names ; fo that he would have *Adam*'s firft-born be called *Hareth*'s Servant, and not *Abd Adah*, God's Servant, as *Adam* had defign'd. The Devil fucceeded, they fay, in this Second Fraud, as well as he had done in the Firft, in Paradife.——The *Mahometans*, to this Day, honour a Cave on the Mountain *Geradim*, which they call *Gar Hawah*, *Eve*'s Cave, to which *Mahomet*, as they believe, often retired to pray.

Fits

Fits and dangerous Faintings : And what added
to her Affliction, and what she imagined made her
Condition the more deplorable, was, That as she was
created to be the Companion and Regale of Man, she
was now reduced to be subject to him, and obliged
to be at his Command, as a Punishment for her
persuading and inveigling him to eat of the Fruit
of that *Reserved Tree* : And *that* her Frailty and
wanton Curiosity she was possessed with, when she
incited him to Sin, she repayed with *that* her own
Blood, which the Malignancy of her Disobedience,
had ingendered within her; and her Deliberation,
I mean, her swallowing the Unhappy and Fatal
Mouthful, she payed with the grievous Tortures,
and the shocking Pains and Throws of Labour in Child-
bed. What was a further Grievance to her, was,
That she could by no means avoid, nor be exempted
from those pernicious and troublesome Purgations,
they coming unawares, and at disorderly Times,
discomposing and interrupting, and invalidating (*a*)
E 2 the

(*a*) Women at those Times, are among the *Mahometans* held as
unclean and polluted, and therefore, their Fasting is omitted, as
being of no Validity; but they, as well as the Men, are obliged to
fast at another Time, the same Number of Days they borrow, as
they call it, from *Ramadam*; nor are they allowed, even to borrow,
but on such Occasions, and dangerous Sickness, Child-bearing,
Travelling, or the like. Nothing can possibly be more strictly observed than this great Fast, which, notwithstanding the excessive
Rigour thereof, those poor deluded People, at least the Majority, keep
and observe with a most amazing Constancy, during the whole Thirty
Days of its Continuance; nay, very many of the more scrupulous
and superstitiously Religious, fast the Two preceding Moons, viz.
Rejep and *Shaaban*, but that is not obligatory, but voluntary.
Though most Writers say, they have Liberty to feast all Night
'till Sun-rising, I must crave their Pardons; for long before the
Break of Day, they wash their Mouths, and take nothing after 'till
Sun-set. They are not only to abstain from eating and drinking,
but from Tobacco in any kind, and from smelling to any Scents,
nay, even from putting any Thing into their Mouths, whether
eatable or not : To kiss a Woman would be a Breach of the Fast,
but

the Fafts fhe was ordained to obferve in Obedience to God's Commands. At length, the Lord was pleafed to permit, that they [our firft Parents] fhould be rejoyned together, being pardoned and abfolved from their former Tranfgreffion and Difobedience, the Lord having taken Compaffion on them, commiferating them by reafon of the great and heavy Penitence they had undergone; and now, as an Ornament to their Bodies, and a Covering for their Nakednefs, they had *Aprons*; which fome fay, were made of Deers Skins, others of Fig-leaves, or the Leaves of fome other Tree, contrived and fitted for them by the Angel, who was continually attending on them.

After all this, *Adam* remained exceeding comely and graceful, tho' not with that Cœleftial Refplendency he poffeffed before his Fall, but extremely well proportioned, and of a moft gallant Afpect; his Stature was Thirty Spans, his Countenance amiable and agreeable, and his Mien Noble and Majeftick. In fine, God had fo formed him, that there was a near Refemblance in him to *Mahomet* our Leader and Protector. The fame Mighty and Sovereign Lord,

---

but to meddle farther, an unpardonable Tranfgreffion. To drink Wine, or any other ftrong intoxicating Liquor, though by Night, would, in all the *Mahometan* Dominions, be punifhed with immediate Death, and that moft commonly, by pouring melted Lead down their Throats. *Mahomet* firft inftituted it in Imitation of our *Lent*, and, as is thought, to curry Favour with the *Chriftians*, whilft his Impofture was yet in its Infancy; and, as many affirm, to fpite the *Jews*, who, at that Time, had highly difobliged him, fo that he was ever after their implacable Enemy. Their *Paffua*, which they call *El Ayed ta'l Ramadham*, immediately follows it, as *Eafter* does *Lent*. The Etymology of the Word *Ramadham*, or rather *Romadham*, is *Arabick*, fignifying, according to *D'Herbelot*, a confuming Heat. It is the 9th Moon of the *Arabian* Year, which being Lunar, by confequence, this Faft happens at all Seafons, and by the Name, feems to have had its firft Inftitution in Summer, and by the Revolutions, once in about 33 Years returns: But this Suggeftion of mine, I leave to the Learned to folve. More of this Celebrated Faft fhall be inferted in other Places.

to give *Adam* and *Eve* some Confolation and Satisfaction for their paft Sufferings, influenced on *Adam* a *Branch of Light* in his Forehead, moft tranfcendently bright and glorious, which defcended from the Heavens, where it was fixed in that myfterious *Cryftal*, which before has been taken Notice of: This was the true and real Signal, which was fo confpicuous on that Beatified Countenance, whereby he was directed to the Way of Eternal Happinefs and Salvation; notwithftanding, this Sign was not altogether fo material or conducive thereto, fince there was a (*a*) greater Bleffing referved in Store for the Lord and Owner of *that Light*, peculiar to himfelf alone, the which he inherited from none of his Progenitors.

Lucifer, though he had been a glorious Angel, of thofe who are neareft to the Throne of the All-powerful Creator, found not fuch Mercy at the Hands of his incenfed Lord; for his Fall was to all Eternity, and his Chaftifement infinite, without Hope of Pardon or Remiffion; by which the High and Potent Monarch gives us to underftand, That in Grace and Excellency, we exceed the very Worfhippers before his (*b*) Supreme Throne (that is, when they rebel or are

---

(*a*) I conclude, he means in this Place, the Seal of the Impoftor's Miffion, the Impreffion whereof, they affirm, he had on his Back between his Shoulders.

(*b*) The *Mahometan* Writers fay, God has Two Thrones: The firft, called *Arfch*, is the Throne of God's Majefty and Glory. This is the *Cœlum Empyreum*. The fecond they call *Corfi*, which is properly his Judgment Seat. (The *Arabick* Word for a Chair, Stool, or fuch like, is *Curfi*.) The firft *Mahomet* fays, *God placed on the Waters, and that in its Production, he made Efforts*, or took Pains. This the Expofitors of the *Alcoran* cannot eafily digeft, or reconcile with God's Omnipotence. They fay, this Throne is fupported by 8000 Columns, of a Subftance whofe Nature and Value is unknown, and the Afcent to it contains 300000 Steps; that between each Step, there is a Diftance of 300000 Years Journey, and each Space full of Angels drawn up in Squadrons. Many Fables and Incoherences of this Kind, their Traditions abound with, by much too long to be inferted here. *D'Herbelot* in *Arfch*. See Dr. *Prideaux* in L. *Mahom.* p. 31, *&c.* *Reland*, and others.

difobediſobedient) and manifeſts to us, that he will ſhew his Bounty and Tenderneſs, and diſtribute his Bleſſing to every one of us, who with a perfect and contrite Heart unfeignedly implore his Mercy, as our firſt Father did, intreating for Pardon; implicitely confiding, that the Lord's Goodneſs and gracious Compaſſion, ſurpaſſed the Heinouſneſs and Atrocity of his Sin.

El Haſſan informs us, That notwithſtanding *Adam* had many Times the joyful Tidings admi-niſtred to him, moſt graciouſly denoting to him, that all his priſtine Offences were waſhed away by his unfeigned Penitence, yet his Breaſt was continu-ally unquiet and diſturbed, when he called to Remem-brance the Greatneſs of his Crime: And ſeeing with what great Benignity and Clemency the Lord had uſed him, was always relenting and melancholy, perpetu-ally ſighing and afflicting himſelf, impatiently endu-ring the endleſs Labour he was forced to undergo, to provide wherewithal to ſubſiſt.

His State being ſuch, and he, without Intermiſſion, continually contemplating on God, he on a ſudden, heard a Voice reſounding in his Ears, ſinging *Hymns* and Praiſes to the Almighty Creator, and with melo-dious Accents calling upon his moſt Sacred Name; At which being ſurprized, in a meek and humble Manner, he ſaid unto his Lord, " O Powerful Monarch! What " unuſual Voices are theſe, which eccho thus in my " Ears?" To which God replied; " Theſe are the " Hymns and Thankſgivings which are chaunted to " my Divinity by my *beloved* Servant, the great " and Warlike Leader *Mahomet*. He is now invok-" ing *that Light* which I have depoſited in thee, and " thy precious and elected Progeny: He it is, who is " the Principal Owner and Patron of the ſaid *Light*, " for whom, and upon whoſe Account alone, I have " created *it*. And take Notice, my well-beloved " *Adam*, obſerve theſe my ſtrict Commands: I charge " thee, and abſolutely enjoyn thee, that this *Light* " be held by thee in the higheſt Eſteem and Venera-

tion,

"tion, and that thou regard *it* with the utmoft Re-
"verence and Refpect; and that thou recommend
"*it* to thy Sons and Pofterity, in the fame Manner
"as I recommend *it* unto thee: Advertife them, that
"they deliver *it* up, into the pure and unfpotted
"Wombs of the moft chafte and vertuous Females,
"to the Intent, that from them it may defcend on
"the Males, who fhall for their Excellencies, be wor-
"thy to inherit the fame, until *it* be finally center'd
"on that *Honourable Man,* (viz. *Mahomet*) relin-
"quifhed by all thy Sons, and fixed in him. Go not
"in unto your Women, before you have (*a*) clean-
"fed and purified your Bodies; and let the fame
"Precaution be obferved by them alfo. I will re-
"veal to thee, when the appointed Hour and Time
"fhall be arrived, in which this *Light* is to depart
"from Thee, and be tranfmitted to Another, that you
"may prepare your felves by the requifite Purifica-
"tion. I command, that thou and thy Off-fpring
"carefully and vigilantly adore and worfhip me,
"and none but me alone, without prefuming to equa-
"lize any to me, or joyning with me any Second;
"for I will be ferved in (*b*) *Unity.* Let them, up-
"on no profane Matter, fwear by, or take in vain
"my Holy Name. Let them treat their Neighbours
"as they themfelves defire to be treated. I command,
"that they honour their Parents, if they themfelves
"would be honoured and refpected; and in fo doing

(*a*) *Tabarareis vueftros cuerpos, &c.* The Purifying and Cleanf-
ing with Water, is ufed on many Occafions, which they call *Tahar;*
its Signification is as I have rendered it. They call it alfo *Gas'l,*
which is the fame as *Wafhing.* Concerning thefe Immerfions or Corporal Ablutions, *Reland* in his *Abl. Mahom. Rel.* has given a particular Account. See Leffon VIII.

(*b*) They give themfelves the Epithet of *Mowahedoun, i e.*
Unitarians, in Contradiction and Oppofition to all other Religions
and Sects, which allow of Plurality of Divinities, whom they call
Mufhricoun, Affociators, *&c.*

E 4 "they

" they shall live comfortably many Days, and
" under my Protection. Let them not kill, for
" that is reserved to me; 'tis I who give Life, and
" I who shorten or lengthen the Thread thereof. Let
" them fly from the vile Sin of Adultery, for it is
" an abominable and odious Vice, most detestable
" in my Sight, and the Instrument and Foundation
" of all Wickedness. Let them be as careful and
" assiduous in preserving the Goods of another, as
" they would be of their own; Nor let them steal,
" nor take any Thing, but what they have justly
" acquired. Let them speak the Truth upon all Ac-
" counts, let them not lye upon any Occasion what-
" soever; nor affirm any Thing that is doubtful,
" or g've any false Testimony; nor covet that which
" belongs not to them; but be contented in their own
" Stations; for I have securely laid up in Store, the
" Portion of (*a*) Wealth, which is designed for, and
" belongs to every individual Mortal. In keeping
" and strictly observing these Precepts, in the same
" Manner as I have dictated and commanded thee,
" I offer and promise them, on my part, that they
" shall enjoy Everlasting Rest; but if they neglect
" so to do, and break or infringe upon these my Or-
" dinances; tell them, they shall be miserably tor-
" mented in *Gehennamma*, (*i. e.* Hell.)

From thence forwards, that is, from the Time *Adam*
had all these Injunctions laid on him, he was so extremely
punctual in obeying the same, and observing to a Tittle
every one of those Rites which the Lord had commanded him, that he was never after guilty of the
least Negligence or Disobedience, perpetually retaining in his Memory the past Warning.

(*a*) *Sus arizques figurados, &c.* The Word is *Rezk*, and *Rezkallah*
is the daily Subsistance Providence has appointed every particular
Man. *Vide D'Herbelot* in that Word.

It was God's Pleafure to permit our Mother *Eve* at her firft Bearing, to bring forth Two Sons. Which Sons gave a clear and evident Demonftration of what was for the future, to be expected in this forrowful and miferable World, and that by continual Wars and Ravages, the Number of *Adam*'s Pofterity was to be limitted, whilft the Earth was at all Times moiftened with Blood, no part thereof ever to be free from Tragical Events; For the elder of the Two, being blinded with Envy, (*a*) Hatred, and Jealoufy, (imitating the proud *Lucifer*) cruelly and inhumanly flew his Brother: From which deteftable Deed, Wars, Strifes, Divifions, and Parties, took their fatal Original. *El Haffan* fays, That *Eve* after thofe, had conftantly Two (*b*) at a Birth, a Son and a Daughter; but when God faw fit, that the *Elected* fhould come forth, and make his Appearance, he was ingendered and born alone: And no fooner had his Mother conceived him in her Womb, but the *Light* paffed away from *Adam* unto her, and was fixed on her Forehead; *Adam* remaining without the leaft Ray thereof: But when fhe was delivered of that glorified Infant, *it* departed from

---

(*a*) The *Mahometan* Traditions affirm (which is likewife the Opinion of the Eaftern Chriftians) that one of the principal Reafons why *Cain* (whom they call *Cabil*, as *Habil* is *Abel*) killed his Brother, was Jealoufy, becaufe *Adam* his Father refufed to let him marry his own Twin-Sifter *Aclimiah*, whom he defigned for *Abel*; as he did *Abel*'s Twin-Sifter *Leboudah*, for *Cain*; who liking his own Sifter beft, as being the more beautiful, conceived a mortal Hatred towards him, and finally flew him. They fay *Adam* mourned for *Abel* 120 Years, in all which Time, he went not in to his Wife. *D'Herbelot* in *Hedad*. They add, that after *Abel*'s Death, fhe was marry'd to *Seth*, though my Author gives *Seth*'s Wife a different Name, *viz.* *Hagualia*, according to our Pronunciation *Hawalia*. The Oriental Chriftians call her *Azrun* or *Azroun*, as they do *Abel*'s Sifter *Wain* or *Owain*. See *D'Herbelot* in the Names *Azrun, Cabil, Vain,* &c. *Reland* fays, They are called by the *Mahometans Azron*, and *Awin*, or *Auin*. In *D'Herbelot* under *Cabil*, this Story is at large, v.

(*b*) They fay Twenty, and every Time Twins, except *Seth*.

her,

her, and the beautiful Forehead of the new-born Child, darted forth Rays like thoſe of the Sun, aſcending to the higheſt Heaven.   This Child they named (*a*) *Seth*, and he was the Firſt-born of the *Light*.

In proceſs of Time, when he was grown up to Man's Eſtate, his Father *Adam* took him out with him one Day, into a green and fertile Field, from whence the Almighty was wont to accept all the Offerings and Sacrifices, and receive the Prayers and Petitions of thoſe his choſen and peculiar Servants; where they lifted up their Eyes to Heaven. *El Haſſan* ſays, That when *Seth* exalted his Head to look upwards with that his reſplendent and glorified Viſage, God at that Inſtant, commanded all the Cœleſtial Rivers, Springs, Currents, Fountains, &c. to ſtand ſtill, and ſtop their Courſes: The Air ceaſed from diſtributing its kind and delicious Breezes: The Trees ceaſed their Motion, and the Birds their ſweet Warblings: the Angels their Heavenly Hymns, and all the Creatures inhabiting the Seas, the Earths, and the Heavens, nay, the whole Hoſt of the Angelick Choirs, moſt earneſtly looked, advancing their Bodies out of the Windows, as if about to precipitate themſelves, and impatiently waiting to hear what thoſe charming Lips were about to utter and pronounce. "Moſt amazing Mercy! "Moſt wonderful Conſolation! That God ſhould "command all thoſe who were about him to lend

---

(*a*) My Author has it *Siz*, though corruptly, as are moſt of his Names.   All *Mahometans* call him *Sheith ben Adam*. From him thoſe the ſacred Scripture call *Bene Elobim*, the Children of God, are deſcended, who made continual War upon the *Caum Cabil*, *i. e.* the Poſterity, or People of *Cain*. This Righteous Generation was, as they ſay, thoſe endowed with the *Prophetick Light* ſo often mentioned.   He is held in great Eſteem, and is reckoned among the Eight principal Prophets, who, according to their Traditions, received Divine Scriptures from Heaven, *viz. Adam, Seth, Enoch, Abraham, Moſes, David, Jeſus,* and *Mahomet*, of which only Five brought New Laws and Inſtitutions into the World, *Adam, Abraham, Moſes, Jeſus,* and *Mahomet*.

"their

" their Ears with such Attention, only at the lifting
" up the Head of a Banished Man! Sure this Diftinc-
" tion feems to have fome Refemblance and Affinity
" with that firft State of Glory, when Man was but
" an Inanimate Stone, and yet all *Beings*, Cœleftial
" and Terreftrial, worfhipped and reverenced him!
" We might flatter ourfelves, that we were in hopes
" of recovering our priftine Excellency, feeing that
" in fo fhort a fpace, and upon fo fmall an Occafion,
" all Things were in fuch Diforder and Confufion.

What the juft *Adam* faid, at this his Holy Audience,
was this; " Divine and Moft High Lord ! Thou who
" haft recommended to me this *Light*, appointed for the
" Inheritance of thy peculiarly elected Servant *Maho-*
" *met*, with a ftrict Injunction, that I deliver it up
" to the worthieft of thy Creatures, diftilling it into
" the moft chafte and perfect Wombs, which already
" are, or hereafter fhall be created; I, to comply
" with, and to accomplifh what I am obliged to by
" this thy Precept, am come to know, if it be thy
" Pleafure, that this my Son, follow the Method or-
" dained by thee, for the propagating Mankind ;
" to the End, that this ever facred and venerable
" *Light*, may have its appointed Courfe, and proceed
" forwards ? If it is thy Will, that *it* fhall now be put
" in Agitation, I have pitched upon his Sifter *Hawaliá*,
" born at another Birth, that he may be married to
" her. She is a chafte and clean Veffel, and, I think,
" very proper for the expanding this *Light :* They
" both offer their Homage, and are obediently re-
" figned, and content to act as thou fhalt vouchfafe
" to command them : I only attend what thy Bounty
" is pleafed to ordain concerning the effecting this my
" Propofal. See, Lord, what is thy Will, I do in this Af-
" fair ?" God then immediately fent for *Gabriel* and
his Affociates, commanding them to defcend, in order
to celebrate the Marriage of that chofen Couple, Brother
and Sifter, their Father being *el Wáaly, i. e.* the Giver,
and thofe Angels I mentioned, were to be the Witneffes,

&c.

&c. The Lord alfo caufed Snow-white Garments from Paradife, to be carried to adorn the Bridegroom and the Bride, inftead of thofe their Parents loft, and were deprived of, for fwallowing the pernicious and fatal Morfel. In this manner *Seth* was married with great Content, Magnificence, and Solemnity.

At length, when the juft *Adam* perceived himfelf to be grown old and feeble, he took his Son *Seth* into a very private Place, and there difcovered to him a certain Cloth, of a moft rich and inimitable Compofure, of a Heavenly Contexture, which in paft Times, the Lord had beftowed upon him, on the which were ftamped and delineated all the (a) Prophets, who were to be fent, or intrufted with Miffions upon the Earth, together with all their Privileges and Immunities, their Decrees and Precepts, their Tribes, Nations, and Followers, and the Bleffings with which they were to be rewarded. *Seth*, with Wonder and Delight, beheld all this, and took particular Notice of One who was, in a very confpicuous Manner, diftinguifhed from all the reft, and who feemed to be far advanced in Pre-eminency and Degree beyond the other Tribes, and whofe Face was glorified with a *Light* of a more than ordinary Brightnefs, which reverberated from the Heavens, with exceeding beautiful and refplendent Rays: This he perceived to be *Abraham*, and that this moft honourable Stock, for fome Space, continued Single, and went on in a direct Path, without any Interruption

---

(a) As to any thing concerning this wonderful *Cloth*, I have little to fay ; but it is certain among the reft of their Fables, they have a Tradition, that God fhewed *Adam* all his Pofterity, which he caufed to affemble together, upon that Account in the Valley of *Nooman*, in the Forms of Ants, where he told them, He was their Lord ; to which they all anfwered in the Affirmative, and acknowledged him ; and therefore God faid, He had Witneffes againft them, at the Day of Judgment, if they fhould then plead Ignorance to his Covenant, by his Witneffes, meaning the Angels at that time attending on him. This, I affure you, is in a Book of no lefs Authority, than the *Alcoran* itfelf, the Expofitors whereof, fay, That *no Man can forget the Contract he then made with God.*

or Intermiffion; but at laft, another noble and illuftrious Tribe began to fpring forth, and have its Beginning; which, notwithftanding its appearing deprived
of that Myfterious *Light* the other Line was poffeffed
of, was neverthelefs of the higheft Nobility and Efteem.
Here was pointed out and demonftrated, Two principal and different (*a*) Religions, the refpective Tribes
each following their peculiar Leader, and their Holy
(*b*) Scriptures. *Adam* faid, " 'Tis proper that we take
" deliberate Notice of thefe which carry our *Light,*
" confidering, with particular Regard, the remarkable
" Bearers thereof, following it through all its Paths,
" directly from *Ifhmael,* the principal Founder and
" Patron of the elected Generation: He, who is the Firft-
" begotten Son of the chofen *Abraham,* and here ap-
" pears carrying the Standard of *Miffir,* [i e. *Grand*
" *Cairo*] erected aloft, which is the venerable Blazon
" and Device of our Illuftrious Lineage, with the
" which all the Tribes fhall be Triumphant and Glo-
" rious, until it be delivered up unto *Mahomet,* the
" proper Lord thereof, for whom it was at firft in-
" tended, and for whofe Sake and Benefit, it was
" from the Beginning appointed. And, mark me, be-
" loved Son, I charge you, that in all your Prayers,
" and in all your Offerings and Sacrifices, that this
" *elected Meffenger,* whofe Caufe we efpoufe, and
" whofe Dictates we follow, be by you compleatly
" (*c*) Saluted, and held in the greateft Veneration and
" Regard, with Honour and Deference. And I com-

(*a*) **Dos** *adines* fennalados que a dos caudillos feguian, *&c.* The
Word is *Dîn;* it implies Religion, *&c.* The Two Leaders were
Ifaac and *Ifhmael.*

(*b*) **Y** a fus *aliquitebes* fantos. El *Ketab* is a Book or Writing.

(*c*) Here he means, the fo much ufed Expreffion, at their Prayers,
and very frequently at other times, *viz. Affalaat wa falâm âle Sîdenah
wa Moulanab Mahommed;* which is, *Salutations and the Peace of God be
to our Lord and Owner* Mahomet. Sometimes they add the Word *Nabî-
nah, i. e.* Our Prophet. This is the Salutat on in particular adapted
to that Grand Impoftor.

" mand

" mand you, that you recommend this *Light,* which
" you now enjoy, and carry fixed on your Forehead,
" to the moſt exemplary and worthy Males, and to
" the chaſte Wombs of the beſt (*a*) guarded, and moſt
" vertuous Females, that *it* be not defiled, but remain
" pure and immaculate, for *this* is the Token and
" Banner which the Sovereign Creator gave us, to
" conduct us to the Way of Truth : And admoniſh
" your Sons, as I have done you, and lay the ſame
" Injunctions upon them. "

When *Adam* had finiſhed this Diſcourſe, he again
folded up that *Myſterious Cloth,* and delivering it to
his Son, enjoyned him to preſerve it as a moſt Sacred
Relick : At the ſame Inſtant, he alſo gave him his
Buskins and Shoes, which he had worn for ſo many
Centuries of Years, and were then as freſh and as whole
as if he had that moment put them on new. Theſe
are at this Day, in the Holy Temple at *Mecca,* in
which they are hung up, and dedicated as a Trophy,
(*b*) where, when a Prince is Inaugurated, it has ever
been the Cuſtom, that he Swear thereon.

(*a*) The *Arabick* Word, which is very proper and applicable here,
is *Mahajúbet* in the Femine Plural, and *Mahajúbeen* in the Maſculine;
the Singular is *Mahajúb,* which is, *covered, concealed,* &c. It is derived
from *Hájeb,* the Eye-brow. *Mahajúb* is the proper Name of many
Men, as *Mahajúba* is of Women. Recluſe Vertuous Women, are,
by way of Commendation and Excellency, called *Mahajúbet.*

(*b*) Y quando *melique* elijen los lleban a jurar, *&c. Melic* is in
Arabick a King or Prince, the Plural of which is *Melooo* : There is always a Prince, who governs the Cities of *Mecca* and *Medina,* of the
Race and Family of *Mahomet.* He is Independant; but makes ſome
Complimentary Acknowledgment to the *Grand Turk,* for the Preſents
he ſends him Yearly, along with the coſtly Covering for the *Caaba,*
or little Square Chapel before mentioned. All thoſe of that Sanctified Progeny, I mean *Mahomet's,* are *Shreefs,* [in *Arabick,* the Singular is *Shréef,* and the Plural *Shúrfa*] ſo his Title is, *Emir Shurfa;*
[*Emir is Prince*] and *Sultan Meccah wa Medinah,* and, according to
Dr. *Prideaux* in L. *Mah.* p. 3. *Emamo'l Hashem* Prince of the *Hashemites,* from which noble *Arabian* Tribe *Mahomet* had his Deſcent. Of
theſe *Hashemites,* ſee more in the Chapter of *Hashem.*

But

But to return to our Story : The good *Seth* had the joyful News denounced to him, by the Angel *Gabriel,* That he, and his Spouſe, ſhould prepare themſelves to receive the promiſed and deſired Fruit : So *Hawalia* conceived with Child ; and the uſual Time being accompliſhed, ſhe brought forth a Son, endowed with the *Hereditary Light :* This Child was extremely beautiful, well-proportioned, and graceful, and they called him by the Name of *(a) Enob.* He was under the Protection, and Guardian-ſhip of the Angel *Gabriel,* to defend him againſt the Wiles and Subtleties of *Lucifer,* who craftily and maliciouſly lay in wait to pollute and inſnare him.

By this Rule and Method, this clear *Light* continued paſſing on, in a gradual Deſcent of the moſt perfect and venerable Men, of the Lord's electing, (he always giving them timely Notice when, and on whom *it* ſhould be fixed) running from Father to Son, from one *Honourable* to another *Honourable,* without Inter-ruption, 'till *it* arrived to *its* proper Center. But be-cauſe thoſe memorable Perſons who, through the tranſ-cendent Excellency of their Merits, were exalted to the Supreme Dignity of carrying this *Banner,* and deemed worthy of this glorious *Light* ; thoſe ſancti-fied Men, I ſay, that they may not remain buried in Oblivion, and the *Muſſulmans* be debarred, from the Satisfaction they might reap, by knowing who they were, I will briefly recite their Names.

From *Enob* the *Light* paſſed to *(b) Cainam,* who was the Fourth Branch of the *Light :* This begot *Malaile,* from whom proceeded *(c) Jared,* who was the Father of

---

(*a*) He means *Enos.*

(*b*) This ſhould be *Cainaan,* whom all the Eaſtern Nations hold to have been one of the *Univerſal Monarchs* of the World.

(*c*) Becauſe my Author, is none of the exacteſt in his Genealogies, I preſume it may not be improper here, to let my Reader partake of the following Opinion of one of his own Belief, and with all probability (for the Reaſons he himſelf gives) more learned and better read.

of the moft holy *(a) Edris,* who for his extraordinary Piety, and vertuous Actions, was taken up into the Fourth Heaven, where he fhall live and remain, until the Trumpet of *Azarofiel,* fhall put an End to all that has been created. Concerning this Juft *Edris,* it is faid, That he made a folemn and inviolable Vow, of never defifting from doing *(b)* Deeds of Charity, whilft his Subftance lafted ; and that, one Day, being met in the Street by a neceffitous Perfon, who afked an Alms of him, and having nothing elfe about him to beftow, he gave him (both for Bleffing and Charity) his Garment, himfelf remaining in a manner naked, becaufe he would not refufe any Comfort he was capable of giving. Thoufands of other Occurrences of this Nature are recorded of that Bleffed Saint, the Truth of which is fufficiently proved, by God's taking him up, Soul and Body, into Heaven, where he lives in Glory and Blifs. He left behind him a Succeffor, his

---

read. I find it in *Reland,* taken, as that Author fays, word for word from the Arabick *Taart b,* or Chronicle. 1 *Adam,* 2 *Seth,* 3 *Enos,* 4 *Kainan,* 5 *Mahaliel,* 6 *Jered,* 7 *Idris,* 8 *Mathufhalah,* 9 *Lamech,* 10 *Nouh,* 11 *Sem,* 12 *Arphaxfhad,* 13 *Shaleg,* 14 *Phaleg,* 15 *Argon,* 16 *Seruch,* 17 *Nachor,* 18 *Azer,* 19 *Ibraham,* 20 *Ifaac,* 21 *Jacob,* 22 *Jehuda,* 23 *Kaz,* 24 *Amrou,* 25 *Daram,* 26 *Imram,* 27 *Abauan,* 28 *Salmon,* 29 *Zjabaz,* 30 *Oun,* 31 *Efche,* 32 *David,* 33 *Salomon,* 34 *Rehabeam,* 35 *Abis,* 36 *Afa,* 37 *Jehofca,* 38 *Philicos,* 39 *Mathan,* 40 *Imram,* 41 *Maria,* 42 *Jefus,* or *Ifa.*

(a) Enoch is by the *Arabs* and other *Ma'ometans,* called *Edris,* from the *Arabick* word *Ders,* which fignifies *Study* and *Meditation.* He is reckoned one of the Eight Prophets to whom God fent Divine Writings, of the which he had 30 Volumes, containing all the moft abftrufe Sciences ; which makes the Books of *Enoch,* be fo much talked of in the Eaft. They call him befides *Edris,* fometimes *Akhnokh* and *Ounoch,* from the Hebrew *Chanoch.* See more in *D'Herbelot* in the Name *Edris,* &c.

(b) De hazer *arahma* complida, &c. *Arráhaman* is one of God's Attributes, and fignifies *Merciful. Arráhma* in this Senfe implies *Çharity.*

Son,

Son, whoſe Name was *Matuſalem*, the Eighth Branch
of the *Light*, whoſe Son was *Lameq*; and he was the
Father of the great, and never-to-be-forgotten *Noah*,
who was the Second Father of all Humane-Race, in
whom the Firſt Age of the World had its End, and
from whom the Second derived its Original; on which
account, he merits our ſtricteſt Regard and Veneration, and whoſe memorable Tranſactions are related
in the following Canticle, or Chapter.

F   CHAP.

C H A P. III.

The Wickedneſs of Mankind. The World threatned with a General Deluge. Noah's *Piety and Up-rightneſs. The Ark built. Deſcrib'd. The People exhorted by* Noah *to Repentance. Their Obſtinacy. The Flood begins ; increaſes, and de-ſtroys the whole World. The Waters abate, and* Noah *and his Family come out of the Ark,* &c.

(a) OST of the Mortals of this Age, endeavoured to exalt their Memories to the higheſt pitch of Glory, and by ſo doing, thought to remain enrolled for ever in the Books of Fame ; vain-ly and ſtupidly imagining, that a long continued, and uninterrupted Series of Proſperity, was ſufficient to eternize their Names. Some puffed

---

(a) Monſieur *D'Herbelot,* in the Word *Eſlam,* quotes an *Arabick* Chronicle, called *Táarich Montekheb,* which ſays, there were but Eighty *Muſſulmans,* or *Believers,* in the World in *Noah's* Time, and that was the Number of thoſe which were ſaved in the Ark ; for moſt Men embraced Idolatry in the Days of *Jared* the Son of *Mahaleel,* the Father of *Edris* or *Enoh.* This I have likewiſe, often heard re-peated by ſome of their Learned Men, and it is indeed the general Notion of all *Mahometans.*

up with Pride, Pomp, and Ambition, fancied themfelves already in the Clouds, whilft others thought to
aggrandize their Names by Cruelty and Tyranny:
Some by inventing Herefies; and others by promoting Schifms and Idolatries; In a Word, giving a
Loofe to the Reins of all Sorts of moft deteftable and
abominable Sins and Outrages, as if in all Points
they had been Abfolute Lords of the Earth, and might
perpetually have continued thofe wicked and impious Courfes with Impunity.

But now, when their Iniquities and Abominations
were arrived to their Crifis, when they leaft expected,
or apprehended a contrary Change of Fortune, but,
fupinely, imagined themfelves in the greateft Security;
it was then, that the variable and unftable Wheel, at
one Turn, hurry'd them down to the loweft Abyfs of
Deftruction, where they received the Rewards of all
the prefumptuous Herefies and Enormities, in which
they had fo long triumphed.

If we look back to King (a) Baltbafar, or to his
F 2   Grand-

(a) He has thefe Names, *Baltafar, Bultanacar, Zamud, Namerud,
Faraon,* and *Abrabaca.* By *Zamud,* I cannot gather who he means,
and I know as little of *Abrabaca* as of the other; the reft are obvious. I can give no account by what Authority he mifcalls *Nebu-
chadnezzer,* whofe Name among the *Arabians* is, *Bakth'alnaffer,* which
is derived from *Bakbt,* or *Bokbt,* fignifying, *The Time,* or *Critical
Minute,* and *Náffer,* Fortune or Victory. This was given him, for
his great Exploits and Succefs in War, his own proper Name being
Rabam. By fome he is called *Gudarz,* as *Reland,* and *D'Herbelot*
obferve. Much is faid concerning *Nimrod,* in the Life of *Abraham.* But I can by no means deny my Readers the Satisfaction of
the following Fable. Though a little long, it is curious and remarkable; and Monfieur *D'Herbelot,* whofe Authority is, I may prefume,
undifputable, affirms to have found it in *Kondemir, Houfain Vaes,* and
other celebrated Writers: Neither am I wholly unacquainted with the
Story, having heard it under a different Name, as fhall be hinted at the
End of this Note. By the above-mentioned Name *Abrabaca,* I am con-
fident my Author means *Abrabab,* on which Word the aforefaid Learned *French* Gentleman, gives us the following Account of that Perfon,
—*Abrabab,* is he who is otherwife called *Abou-Macfoum,* with the Sirname

name of *Al-Aſtram*, ſignifying in Arabick, *Trat h. d a Gaſh on his Face*; as alſo, *Dhou Al-fil*, i. e. Maſter of the Elephant. He was a Prince or Governor of *Jeman* [pronounced *Yeman*] or *Arabia Fælix*, in the Reign of *Negtoſhi*, who was Emperor of the *Abiſſins*, in the Time of *Abdalmothleb*, *Mahomet's* Grandfather. The 105th Chapter of the *Alcoran*, intituled, *Sourat Al-fil*, that is, *The Chapter of the Elephant*, makes mention, of the Puniſhment of this Prince, who had many Elephants in his Army, when he came to beſiege the City *Mecca*. The whole Story is thus related, by the chief Interpreters of that Chapter. —— *Abrahab*, who governed in *Sanaa*, the Capital of the Province of *Yeman*, perceiving that a a certain time of the Year, moſt of the *Arabs*, travelled to the Province of *Hegtez*, which is on the Borders of *Arabia Deſerta*, to viſit the *Caaba*, or Square Houſe, which is the Temple of *Mecca*, thought fit to divert them from that Superſtitious Worſhip, by erecting another Place that might attract their Curioſity and Devotion; and therefore reſolved to build a Temple at *Sanaa*, exceeding that of *Mecca* in Structure and Ornaments. This was a moſt ſtately Church, the *Abiſſins* being Chriſtians. Yet *Abrahab's* Deſign could not ſucceed without Force, becauſe the *Arabs*, who were not Chriſtians, inclined to Idolatry, and found ſomething agreeable to their Superſtition in the very Stones about *Mecca*, and in its Temple. However, the *Coreiſhites*, who had the Charge of that Temple, perceiving the Concourſe of People, and conſequently their Gain, decline, cryed down, as much as they could, the Church of *Sanaa*, and at laſt made uſe of a notable Cheat, to deſtroy its Reputation among the *Arabs*. To this purpoſe, they ſent thither one of the Family of *Kenanah*, who getting in to be an Officer belonging to the Church, found his Opportunity, on a Feſtival, when it was to be richly adorned for the People to come in at Night, to profane it with Ordure. As ſoon as he had done it, he fled, and ſpread the News of this Profanation all the Way he went. *Abrahah* underſtanding what had happen'd, was ſo incenſed againſt the *Coreiſhites*, that in Revenge he reſolved to make War againſt them, to beſiege *Mecca*, and deſtroy the Temple. Accordingly he marched his Army, the greateſt Strength whereof conſiſted in the Elephants, towards the Province of *Hegiaz*, riding himſelf at the Head of it on one of thoſe Beaſts, called *Mahmondi:* This Elephant excelled the reſt in Bulk, and in Whiteneſs, for which reaſon he was eſteemed as the Chief and Maſter of all the reſt. When the *Coreiſhites* heard of this Prince's March, and that he had ſuch Beaſts, which had never, till then, been ſeen in *Arabia*, they deſpaired of defending their Town or Country with their own Forces, and therefore reſolved to abandon it, and fly, with their beſt Effects, to the neighbouring Mountain. *Abrahah*, meeting with no Oppoſition, plundered all he found in his March, and being come to the City, aſſigned his Troops their ſeveral Quarters; but when he thought, to advance in Perſon to view the Place, his Elephant, at the bare ſight of the City Walls, turn'd away his Head from them ſo violently, that all the reſt of the Elephants in the Army, who followed his as their Leader, did the

same,

fame, and routed the whole Army. The *Coreifbites*, who were intrenched on the Edge of the Mountain, feeing what had happened, knew not what to think of this fudden Counter-March of their Enemies; when immediately they efpied a vaft Flock of Birds coming like a Cloud from towards the Sea, and falling all together on *Abrabab's* Army. Thefe Birds had black Feathers, and green Beaks, and were followed by another Flock, that had green Feathers, and yellow Beaks. Each of thefe Birds had three Stones, one in their Beaks, and one in each Claw, and, they fay, each Stone had the Name of him it was to ftrike, writ upon it, and they all fell at once with fuch Force upon the *Abiffins*, that they were all flain, except *Abrabab*, who was deftin'd to carry the News of this dreadful Defeat into *Ethiopia*. In fine, when *Abrabab* had feen his Army perifh by this ftrange Accident, he repafs'd the Seas, and went to acquaint *Negiafhi* with his Difafter. But Divine Juftice, which had decreed to leave a notable Example of the Punifhment of thofe who had dared to undertake the deftroying a Temple built by *Abraham*, did not let this unhappy Prince efcape fo; for one of the Birds who had executed the Divine Vengeance, followed him all the way he went with the Stone in its Beak, fo that when he had told his fad Relation to the Emperor, that Prince asking what fort of Birds thofe were? *Abrabab* fhew'd that which flew over his Head, and at the fame Time, the Bird dropt the Stone, and killed him at the Emperor's Feet. Thus far Monfieur *D'Herbelot*. I was fome Years ago in the Tent of an *African* Prince, a very gallant Man, whofe Name is *Boazeefe*, Sheik or Chief of a noble Tribe of *Arabs*, called *El Hanaifha*, whofe Territories lie in the moft Eaftward Province of the Kingdom of *Algiers*. He was pitched with his Camp near the Ruins of an Ancient City, called now by thofe People *Tifefh*, which Place, by its miferable Remains, feems to have been a confiderable large and fortified Town. A certain *Talib* or Student, brought me about Twenty or more little Stones, of a very odd Make, their Shape was very irregular, fome inclining to be, as it were, long, others, as it were, round, but all in general Diamond-cut, and rather feeming to be Artificial than Natural. The largeft was about the bignefs of a Small Nut, and the leaft of a large Clove, or fuch like. In Colour they were for the moft part either Black, almoft like Jett, but fomewhat dull and rufty, or white and tranfparent; though four or five were blueifh and yellowifh, but not tranfparent. For a Trifle the Man let me keep 'em, and into the Bargain, told me the above Tale, with very little Difference; but inftead of *Abrabab*, he made the Leader of that imaginary Army to be *Nimrod*, and that old ruinated City, where fuch Stones are frequently found amongft the Rubbifh, to be built by 'him; but the Prince being a greater Student than himfelf, contradicted him, telling us, That the Name of that impious Unbeliever was *El Afhram Dhou el Fil*. The Stones, both the Prince, and the *Talib* affirmed, to be fome of the fame with which the Birds deftroyed that Sacrilegious Army; but to declare how they came, or why they are only to be found in thofe Ruins, and no where elfe, they were at

Grandfather *Nebuchadnezzar,* to *Zamud, Nimrod, Pharaoh* or *Abrahaca,* we fhall find them all, in the like impious manner, rebellioufly extending their Arms againft Heaven and their Creator; though, alas! how vain and fruitlefs were their audacious Efforts! and the Event how contrary to their Expectations! For inftead of obtaining the Victory, they wounded themfelves, precipitating their own ignominious Deaths, and, after that, everlafting Torment and Mifery.

Though I could recite infinite many other Examples of this kind, yet thofe I have already quoted, are fufficient for my prefent Purpofe; nor, indeed, are any others requifite towards the confirming and maintaining this Affertion, than the General Deluge, in which that Holy Patriarch (a) *Noah,* was fo principal a Tranfactor, whofe ever-famous and memorable Deede ought to infpire us with an awful Reverence and Veneration to his Memory.

The Remembrance of that never-to-be-forgotten Event, fure, might rouze up in us, and incline us to an implicite Obedience and Refignation, and incite us, to center our intire Confidence in God alone, and to reft affured, That in following and keeping the Precepts of God's Holy Law and Ordinances, we fhall acquire perpetual Fame and Renown in this World (fuch as it is) and eternal Blifs, a never-fading Paradife in the other. Not as thofe I mentioned above, neither thefe others I am going to treat of in the Univerfal Deftruction of that accurfed Generation of People, who, in one Moment, deprived themfelves of

---

a Non-plus. As for thofe I had purchafed, after I had kept 'em a long time, at laft a *French* Merchant begg'd 'em. This Story of *Abrahah,* is mention'd by Dr. *Prideaux,* under the Name *Abraham Al Afbram,* p 47.

(a) The Sirnames given by the *Arabians,* &c to *Noah,* befides, *Noah el Nabi,* or the Prophet, are, *El Nazi,* He that was faved, *Sheick el Morfelem, i.e.* The Ancienteft of thofe fent with efpecial Commiffions from God. See *D'Herbelot* in *Noah.*

Life,

Life, and damned their Souls, as I fhall make manifeftly apparent in the following Difcourfe.

After the Death of our Original Parents, *Adam* and *Eve*, their remaining Sons founded and carried on the Lineage. Of thefe Sons, one, with great Purity and Conftancy, ftrenuoufly followed the *Light*; but the reft were all in general Adulterers, Murderers, Sodomites, Idolaters, imperious, haughty Tranfgreffors, daring Blafphemers, and, in fine, a vile and infamous Race of Men. They were grown to fuch a pitch of Wickednefs, that the Contagion daily fpread, the Corruption increafing more and more, 'till at laft it became, in a manner, Univerfal, comprehending all Humane Kind.

" How ferioufly and deliberately ought Men, in
" this *borrowed*, tranfitory Life, to be cautious and
" circumfpect in their Choice of thofe with whom
" they affociate themfelves, or entertain Friendfhip,
" in order to pafs their Lives and Converfations,
" having fo notable an Inftance in this difmal
" Cataftrophe! "

The High and Powerful God beholding their notorious and incorrigible Difobedience, commanded his chofen Servant *Noah*, to erect and build an Ark; to which Effect the Angel *Gabriel* defcended with Inftructions concerning the Method, Order, and Plan thereof, with the Length, Breadth and Height it was to be of; and ftrictly enjoyning him, that whilft this Fabrick was going forwards, he fhould admonifh thofe employed thereon, together with all the reft of the People, to repent them of their abominable Sins, and be converted, in Pity to, and Confideration of, their Souls; which, if they did, they might expect Pardon and Remiffion; otherwife, he fhould let them know, that it was inevitably certain, that the Lord was fully determined to deftroy and annihilate them, by drowning and overflowing the intire Surface of the Earth with Water.

Noah

Noah was aged Five hundred Years when this memorable Injunction was laid on him by the Faithful *Gabriel* ; The *Prophetick Light* had already paſſed from him, and was tranſmitted unto his Beloved Son (a) *Sem* ; beſides whom, he had two others, whoſe Names were (b) *Ham* and *Japhet.* *Sem* was a Youth of excellent Qualifications, pure and without Blemiſh ; and by his laudable Actions merited the good Name the whole Univerſe beſtows on him : In a Word, He deviated nothing from his good Father, imitating Him who had walk'd uprightly before the Lord, in thoſe the worſt of Times, during the Space of Five hundred Years.

(a) The *Arabian* Chronology, intitled *Taarich Montekheb,* ſo often cited by the Learned Monſieur *D'Herbelot,* tells us, That the Patriarch *Shem* (whom they call *Sam el Nabi,* and *Sam ben Noah*) goes under the Denomination of *Abou'l Arab,* or the Father of the *Arabs* ; becauſe they hold, that they are deſcended from him : But they affirm, That all Prophets, whether *Arabs* or *Ajem* [*i. e.* Strangers, which Word imports the ſame as *Barbarians,* in the *Greek* or *Latin* Senſe] are, nevertheleſs, of his Race.

(b) It is in the *MS. Sem* (or, as he writes it every where, *Cem*) inſtead of *Ham,* which, I preſume, is a Miſtake though in no Place he mentions *Ham* at all, unleſs I may ſay he does it here. The *Mahometans* generally name but Three Sons of *Noah,* which they call *Sem, Ham* and *Jafed,* or, as they pronounce, *Yafedth.* They affirm, That *Noah* left Ten Books of Revelations and Orders he received from God, the which are all loſt, as well as thoſe of *Adam, Seth* and *Enoch.* In *Reland's Ab. Rel. Mahom.* in the 4th Leſſon, concerning theſe imaginary Sacred Books, they hold to have been compoſed and written in Heaven, he makes no mention of *Noah's* having any Share in them, but makes the whole Number to amount to 104, which were diſtributed in this manner ; To *Adam* 10. To *Seth* 50. To *Enoch* 20. To *Abraham* 10. To *Moſes* 1. To *Jeſus* 1. To *David* 1. To *Mahomet* 1. The Four laſt are what they call *El Taourat, El Zobour, El Engile,* and *El Coran,* and are the ſame with the *Pentateuch* or Five Books of *Moſes* ; The Pſalms of *David* ; The Holy Goſpel ; [*Engile* corruptly *quaſi* Evangelium] And laſtly, the *Alcoran* of *Mahomet* ; all but which, they ſay, are falſified and ſophiſticated. Of theſe more in proper Places.

When

When God's Command had, in this Manner, been fignified to *Noah*, he made no Delay to put it in Execution, with all poffible Diligence, providing all things requifite and neceffary, as Mafter-Builders, Carpenters, Architects, Joyners, with infinite Numbers of Labourers, fome to cut down the Timber, and others to conduct it to the Station where the (*a*) Ark was to be built.

In the mean time, he, without giving himfelf a Moment's Refpite, went about from Place to Place, exhorting the People to Repentance, fignifying and demonftrating to them their approaching Ruin and unavoidable Deftruction, with the moft terrible and tremendous Chaftifement with which God threatned them : He refted neither by Night nor by Day ; his very Throat was hoarfe with preaching and admonifhing them, in thefe, and fuch like Words ; " O wicked, vile, and mifguided People ! " return unto your Lord, and implore his Grace, " and your own Reftoration ; prevent and evade " thefe dreadful impending Evils ; give Ear unto " my Words ; Fear Him who created you ; Take " Notice, that his Juftice is fhut up and contain- " ed in this Ark, which he has commanded me " to build, with a bloody Rod, which menaces " your Lives, and the utter Condemnation of your

---

(*a*) That Library of Oriental Learning, Monfieur *D'Herbelot*, by whofe Authority I go in moft refpects, informs us, That a certain *Arabian* Author, *Ebn Abbas*, writes, That *Noah* being puzled about the Shape he was to give his Ark, God revealed to him in a Dream, that it muft be like the Belly of a Bird, and that he muft make it of the Wood of the Tree the *Arabs* call *Sag*, which is the *Indian* Plane Tree. *Noah* having received thefe Orders, he planted fuch a Tree, which in Twenty Years Time, grew fo big and fo tall, that it yielded Wood enough for his Work : And an ancient Tradition adds, That during thofe Twenty Years, no Woman was deliver'd of a Child, fo that all the Infants born at the planting of the Tree, were of Years to make their Advantage of *Noah*'s Preaching ; but they refufed, as well as thofe which were older. *Vide* in *Nouh al Nabi*.

" Souls :

" Souls: O ſhake off from your Necks, the inſup-
" portable Yoke and Bondage of Hell! whoſe
" Jaws are gaping ready to devour your Souls! "
Theſe were the Expreſſions he, indefatigably, repeated unto them : But to no purpoſe; for that ſinful,
hardned, and obſtinate Multitude, were both blind
and deaf to all the pious Exhortations of the juſt
Patriarch.

The Maſter-Workmen and Architects laboured,
with great Diligence and the utmoſt Aſſiduity, to
finiſh this mighty and vaſt Machine, which was full
One hundred Years before it was compleated, from
the time it was firſt put in Agitation; and all
that while, *Noah* continued his Admonitions to
that head-ſtrong Generation without ceaſing : But
the more he laboured towards their Converſi-
on, the leſs Effect it had upon them; and they
rather anſwered him, That he lyed in all he had told
them, ſince a hundred Years were already paſt, and
they ſaw no Sign of any ſuch Things, nor the
leaſt Appearance of a Flood or Deluge; and therefore, all that he had propheſied to them, ſeemed, they
ſaid, no other than Impoſtures, Lyes, and Impoſſi-
bilities.

The Fabrick of the Ark being intirely compleated,
with all the Diviſions and Appartments, neatly accommodated in the Inſide, and well caulked and
nailed without, that the Water might not penetrate;
the whole Edifice appeared to be of exquiſite Workmanſhip, and admirable Contrivance : It was formed after the Manner of a Ship; at the Prow was
figured a Pigeon's Head, and the Poop repreſented
the Tail of a Cock : It contained in Length Twelve
Hundred Cubits (a), from the Head to the Stern, and
Six Hundred in Breadth.

Noah

(a) In my Author it is *mil y dozientas varas*, &c. I have heard
it deſcribed and read in other *Arabick* Books, and the Word is
always

Noah then went up to the higheſt Part of his new-built Ark, and with a loud and audible Voice, began to call together the living Creatures of the Earth (which of all others were the moſt neceſſary for the Uſe of Mankind) that they might preſent themſelves, Male and Female, before him : They inſtantly came, being ſo commanded by the Lord, who ordained, that of every Kind Three Couple, with an odd Male, ſhould enter into the Ark, ſo that of each Sort they were Seven ; although the Honoured *Alcoran* tells us, they were not ſo many, and that there went in but one Male and one Female, and no more : It may be ſo, or as the *Alcoran* informs us, for that is not what is of the greateſt Importance to us. Whether the Number of thoſe which went in were ſo many, or not, I ſhall not diſpute; but thoſe which did go in, went very regularly, and in the exacteſt Order. A ſufficient quantity of Stores and Proviſions were pur-chaſed and depoſited in the Ark, to ſuſtain and nou-riſh them all for a whole Year, if in caſe it ſhould happen that their Confinement therein ſhould be of ſo long Continuance. In fine, *Noah* and his Wife, his Sons and their Wives, entered into the Ark, and ſhut up the Door and the Window, which was at the Top thereof ; this was covered with moſt clear and tranſ-parent (*a*) Glaſs, nor had they any other Hole left from whence they might behold the Water; and this, by God's eſpecial Command, was well daubed on the outſide with *Bitumen*, or ſome ſuch glutinous Matter, for the greater Security againſt the Impetuoſity of the Tempeſt.

---

always *Draa*, which in that Language is *the Arm*, from whence that Meaſure of theirs reaching from the Elbow to the Top of the middle Finger, takes its Denomination. The *Turkiſh* Meaſure is Two Foot, or very near; but the Spaniſh *Vara* is about a Yard, as I am in-formed.

(*a*) It ſeems there was Glaſs in thoſe Ages, if we may give Cre-dit to their Aſſertions.

The

The People, when they perceived that *Noah* was entered into the Ark, and had fhut up himfelf and his Family therein, they mocked, fcoffed, and derided him, and laughing, faid, " Now thou art well " accommodated ; Now thou art mewed up in that " Cage with brute Beafts and Animals, which, in " truth, are the fitteft Company for thee. Such are " the Rewards which all Lyars and Impoftors ought " to receive in Payment : Where is thy Prophecy ? " Where is even the leaft Appearance or Similitude, " nay, any Likelihood of it ?

O. Sovereign and Compaffionate Lord ! Who, that confides in thy Divine Goodnefs, fhould ever defpair of thy Mercy and moft Gracious Pardon? Seeing that fo many Years thou didft defer and prolong the Punifhment of thofe *condemned* and *predeftinated* Wretches, after thou hadft paffed Sentence upon them ; whilft their obdurate Hearts refufed to acknowledge thy Power, till the Scourge fell upon them when they leaft expected it !

After the Ark was fhut up, God ftill detained the Flood of Waters for Seven Days ; nor in all that Interval of Time, was there the leaft Sign or Profpect of Storm or Tempeft ; mercifully with-holding His avenging Arm in Expectation that poffibly He might difcover in that wicked Generation fome Merits, whereby His Juftice might withdraw from them that bloody Scourge ; But at laft, feeing their Stubbornnefs and inflexible Obftinacy hurried them on to their Deftiny, and that no Human Means were capable of foftning their Obduracy, or diverting their Sentence (I mean that dreadful Stroke, the Univerfal Deluge, with which he had threatned them) At length, I fay, weary with Expectation, He ftretched out His fharp and deftroying Sword.

Now

Now the Cataracts of the Heavens are opened, the Bofoms of the Clouds are rent afunder, and the Waters (a) gufh out of the Earth ; all the Rivers overflow, and the Seas exceed their Bounds, advancing with moft amazing Fury and Violence : And certain it is, it would have been much worfe, and the whole Univerfe would have been intirely fwallowed up, paft Recovery, had not *Gabriel*, by God's Command, put certain Limits thereto.

The People who were marked out for Deftruction, began now to be forrowful and afflicted, and to fear the great approaching Chaftifement : Now they groan, and are difmayed, their Courage fails them, and they give themfelves over for loft : Some run, in Hopes to efcape ; others cry out at Sight of the outrageous Tempeft : Nothing is heard but Sighs, Groans and Lamentations, and every Place is filled with Weeping, Anxiety, and bitter Complaints. The impetuous Waves furioufly enter into every Houfe, and carry away the tender Infants, whofe wretched, difconfolate Mothers miferably tear their Breafts and Faces, following their beloved Children ; and, holding them dead and breathlefs in their Arms, call and beckon to their wicked Fathers and Hufbands to come to their Affiftance ; but they are prevented, by the univerfal Calamity from affording them any Succour, and fo are in that lamentable Manner drowned, clofely embracing their unhappy, guiltlefs Babes.

(a) *Mahomet* in his *Alcoran* introduces God, faying, *When the Time we had appointed for the punifhing of Men, was come, and the Oven began to boil up, and run over.* This *Oven*, in *Arabick*, is called *Tannour*, and differs from the common Ovens, which they call *Fourn*, pl. *Froun*, for it has a narrow opening at the Top, and is generally made of Stone. This fort of Oven, the *Mahometans* fay, *Eve* made ufe of to bake her Bread, which came by Inheritance from Patriarch to Patriarch down to *Noah*, and from this Oven, they fay, the Waters of the Deluge began firft to flow, as it were, boiling over, which agrees with the Opinion of the *Rabbies*, who affirm the Waters of the Deluge were *hot and boiling*. See *D'Herbelot* in *Nouh*, &c.

How

How many bitter Deaths did thofe Wretches fuffer at once! The forrowful Mother beholding her deareft Daughter perifh before her Eyes; the Wife her Husband fink in her Sight; the Brothers their Sifters, and the afflicted Father the Son he doated on; the Son hangs upon his Father, and both go to the Bottom, and are drowned Face to Face. In every Place miferable Outcries of *I fink! I drown!* were to be heard, and of, vainly, imploring Succour. The Foundations of the Edifices are loofened, and the Houfes fall, overwhelming their Owners, and all their pompous and coftly Furniture; the Ark was already encompaffed with the Planks, *&c.* of thofe ruinated Buildings.

In the mean while, thofe who were the wifeft, or at leaft the moft defirous of Life, omitted nothing they imagined might be conducive to their Safety; fome get up on the Tops of Hills, others on the higheft Towers; fome afcend into the largeft Trees, that they might hold by the Boughs, where, thronging in Multitudes, and clinging one to the other, they all fall together, and perifh. Thofe who were in the lofty Towers, and on the higheft Mountains, by Degrees, retreat to the moft elevated Eminencies thereof, but to very little Purpofe; for now the Waters purfue and give chace to them on all Sides, till they were drove and reduced to the utmoft Pinacles and Tops to feek an imaginary Refuge, where the Stronger exerted their Force and Cruelty towards the Weaker, mounting up upon them, every one endeavouring what he poffibly could, to prolong his Life, and to be the laft that fhould die: But, alas! how vain and fruitlefs are all the Efforts of thofe miferable Homicides! They undergo a Thoufand Deaths in one, beholding their neareft Friends, their Parents, Brothers, Sifters, Wives and Children, ftruggling in the remorfelefs Waves, wherein they are devoured; and yet all this is not enough to induce them to be refigned willingly to part with the feeble Remains of their *fiery rebelli-*

ous

ous Breath : But notwithstanding all they could do to delay their certain and inevitable Perdition, the grim Conqueror confronts them, staring them, visibly, in the Face, and already makes their *Beards* (a) *tremble* : They have now no Sanctuary remaining to resort to, not one Step more to ascend, but are overtaken and reduced to their latest Gasps.

No mention is made now of the Beasts and Animals of the Earth, either Wild or Domestick, they having long since perished ; only the Inhabitants of the Air, the Birds and Fowls, for some time supported themselves on those Wings Nature had provided them with, but they could not long subsist, or sustain themselves under the Vehemency of that tempestuous Storm, which was so terrifying and violent, that what with Fear, and what with a long continued Motion, they were at length tired and spent, and how high soever they flew, the Tempest and Waves still overtook them.

The Waters were advanced Forty Cubits above the Tops of the highest Mountains, and all Creatures which had Life were annihilated (b) and *darkned*, except those which I above hinted to have been preserved in the Ark : Those indeed were *illuminated* with the *Light* of the Great *Mahomet*, *i. e.* with that Branch of it, which was then in the Possession of the Just *Sem*, exceeding the Moon in Brightness.

The Rain had continued to pour down without Intermission for the space of Forty Days and Forty Nights, and One Hundred and Fifteen Days the Earth remained intirely covered with Water ; This stupen-

---

(*a*) A very usual Expression in *Arabick*, to say, *Fear makes Mens Beards tremble* ; and not uncommon in *Spain*.

(*b*) Here seems to be meant that Notion of theirs, That the Graves of the Wicked are dark, whereas those of the Righteous are gloriously enlightned. Hence that frequent Benediction of the *Arabs*, for any Favour received ; *Allâb aitic Dhou fe Cabric*, God grant you Light in your Grave.

dous

ous Deluge began on the Seventeenth Day of the Moon (*a*) *Rejep*, which is the Seventeenth of *April*, according to the Account of the *Christians* (*b*).

The Ark continued in Motion, according to the exactest Computation, full Six Moons, and then it rested on the holy and memorable Day of *Ashora* (*c*), which is the Tenth of the Moon *Muharam*, upon that Mountain of *Armenia* (*d*), so much celebrated through-

---

(*a*) *Rejep*, or *Arjem* (as it is called by some) is the Third Month, or rather Moon, in the *Arabian* Year; reckoned Sacred by the Ancient Heathen Idolatrous *Arabs*, being one of the Four in which they were forbid making War; the other Three I shall mention in another Place. It is by the Modern *Mahometans* likewise held in some Deference. The Word imports *Respected* and *Honoured*, and is the proper Name of many Men.

(*b*) *Por la cuenta* nazara, &c. *Nassara* is the Plural Number of *Nassarani*, by which Name the *Mahometans* call the *Christians*; as much as to say, *Nazarites*, or *Nazareans*. The Eastern Writers gave this Name to the *Greeks*, &c. by way of Anticipation, long before our Saviour's Time. of which *D'Herbelot* gives several Instances, too long to be inserted, and not very material.

(*c*) *Moharam* is the first Moon of the *Arabian* Year, the 10th Day of which is called *Ashora* or *Ashoura*, which in both *Hebrew* and *Arabick* signifies, *Ten* or *Tenth*. On this Day the most scrupulous *Mahometans* generally Fast, which was a Custom among the Idolatrous *Arabs* before *Islamism* was known, which they say, was on the Account of the Ark's resting, and *Noah*'s entrance, and going out from thence, which happened all on that Day. How they can make this out, I shall not pretend to determine, but leave it to others; nor is scarce any one unacquainted, that their Year is Lunar. Besides the Regard the *Mahometans* have for this Day, the *Persians*, and all other Followers of *Alli* (*Mahomet*'s Son-in-Law, Husband to the Impostor's only Daughter *Fatimah*, and his Cousin Germain, being the Son of his Uncle *Abou Taleb*) have a particular Reason to observe it, because *Houssain*, the Second Son of *Alli*, was then killed at the Battle of *Kerbela*; they therefore yearly celebrate the Memory of his Death, with Fasts, pompous Funerals, Lamentations and dismal Songs. The History of that Prince, see in Mr. *Ockley*'s *Sar. Hist.* Vol. I.

(*d*) The Name the *Arabians* give this Mountain, is, *Gioudi*; It is in the Country of *Moussal* or *Diar Rabiah*, otherwise, by the *Turks* called

throughout the World. Forty Days after that, the high Hills began to diſcover their lofty Heads, as a Signal that the Waters were abated; and then a Token appeared in the Firmament of Three different Colours, Red, (*a*) Blueiſh and Green, which, by its Aſpect, ſignified and denoted Blood, Death, and Hope: Of thoſe Three Colours, the Green was the principal or moſt predominant, which ſhewed, that the Effects of the other Two had ceaſed. This is the Sign which at this Day is diſcovered to us in the Bow we behold in the Sky, when the thick Clouds are expelled after Rain. 'Twas Forty Days more before they in the Ark opened their Glaſs Window, and then ſent forth a Crow to ſee the Land, and in what Condition the World had remained. The Crow departed, and flew towards the high Mountains, to which moſt of the People had retired, where finding ſuch vaſt Numbers of Carcaſſes, he was deſirous of feeding upon ſuch plentiful Prey, ſo (*b*) that he returned no more with the

G   expected

---

called *Diarbikir* in *Meſopotamia*, at the Foot whereof, is a Hill called *Thamanin* and *Corda*. Theſe are the *Gordian* Mountains, which the Scripture calls *Ararat*. There is a Tradition among the *Turks*, That the Ark reſted on a Mountain in *Armenia*, which is by them named *Bermac Daghi*, or the Mountain of the Finger, from its Shape; where they affirm, the Remains of the Ark are ſtill to be ſeen. See *D'Herbelot* in *Gioud*.

(*a*) The Word is *Gualdada*, which is in *Spaniſh*, Sky colour Blue.

(*b*) I chuſe this Place, to hint a very odd Notion of theirs concerning the Crow, which I never yet found mentioned by any Author, and may therefore, perhaps, not be unacceptable to ſome of my Readers. They generally affirm, That thoſe Birds were White, and ſome ſay, they became Black for not returning to the Ark. But the more General Opinion, is this; The Prophet deſigning to propagate his Holy Religion, and encourage the Profeſſors thereof, as much as poſſible, called the Crow (who, it ſeems, then exceeded the Snow in Whiteneſs) and delivered to him the *Barala* (or Bleſſing) of *Riches*, under his Right Wing, and the *Evalli* (or Curſe) of *Lice*, under his Left, with a ſtrict Injunction to caſt the firſt on the *Believers*, and the other on the *Chriſtians* or *Unbelievers*;

but

expected Anſwer. When *Noah* ſaw he came not, the next Morning he let fly a Pigeon, the which came back in the Evening, and brought a green Olive-branch; and the next Week he ſent her again a Second Time, but then ſhe returned not; by which *Noah* was certified, that the Waters were confumed and dried up: And although he might have then gone forth, yet he would not; but waited for Leave from his Lord to go out, as he had done at his Entrance. At laſt, when God was pleaſed to permit it, he and his Company, that is, his Family, made their Departure out of the Ark on the ſame Day they entred therein, having fully and exactly compleated a Year. They joyfully, and with great Sincerity, rendered Praiſes and Thankſgivings to the Almighty, who had ſo graciouſly and bountifully vouchſafed to deliver them from ſuch eminent Perils.

Noah then offered as a Sacrifice, thoſe Birds and Beaſts which he had obſerved, in the Ark, to be uncoupled, or odd ones; and God laid his Bleſſing upon him and his Company, that they might anew increaſe and multiply Humane kind; and ordained, that all Creatures ſhould aſſemble together, and obey his Commands in whatſoever he ſhould require of them. He commanded the Herbs, Plants and Trees to bring forth their Fruits in the greateſt Abundance, and that the World ſhould be Peopled better than it was before.

---

but the Knaviſh Crow, maliciouſly, or otherwiſe, made an unlucky Blunder, beſtowing on the *Faithful*, the *Curſe*, inſtead of the *Bleſſing*. This they commonly tell Travellers, if they upbraid them with their *Louſineſs*, to which they are extremely ſubject. I ſpeak of the *Arabs* and *Africans*, who dwell abroad in Tents. Nothing is more common among all the *Arabians* in general, when they recommend any Thing to another's Care, than this Expreſſion, *Aman't el G'rab el Khahab*, that is, *The Truſt of the Black Crow*, as if they ſaid, *Remember how the Crow was ſerv'd for Breach of Truſt*.

The

The Flood being over, the Earth at Peace, and all Creatures recovered from the general Confternation; *Noah* called together his Sons, and faid unto them; " Beloved Sons, Remember thefe my Words, with " which I admonifh you for the Health of your Souls: " Retain always in your Memories the late paft " Juftice which your Lord has executed upon thofe " mifguided and deluded People; and that his Scourge " is ftill in his Hand, which is lifted up to chaftife " thofe who keep not his Precepts; Him alone it is " you are to worfhip and adore; Him who admits " of no Equal or Companion; He it is who gives " you Life, and prolongs it; 'tis He who fuftains and " nourifhes his Creatures; and He it is alone, who " commands and governs all Things. Love and " cherifh one another with a fervent Affection and " Conftancy; and in fo doing, your Deeds fhall fhine " before him, and your Fields and Flocks fhall pro- " duce you Riches and Subftance, with Bleffings " and Abundance: And fo the Lord's Benediction and " mine be upon you." To his Son *Sem* (which was he who had inherited the *Light* from him) he, in particular, addreffed himfelf; and in the fame Manner as *Adam*, heretofore, had done to his Son *Seth*, he recommended that efpecial *Gift* to his Care.

After many Years were paft, and the defart, folitary World began, in fome Meafure, to be re-peopled, the Inhabitants were difperfed in feveral remote and diftant Parts, whither the good *Noah* made frequent Peregrinations, encouraging and exhorting the People to till, fow, and cultivate the Earth. His venerable Prefence raifed in them fuch an Emulation, that they ardently ftrove to excel one the other in Buildings, and fuch like Occupations; as alfo in the Knowledge of the Motions and Courfes of the Planets. He gave the firft Original to the Invention of Weights and Meafures, and all the other Sciences requifite to the furthering the mutual Traffick and

Cor-

Correfpondence of Mankind, at leaft thofe which were of the greateft Neceffity and Importance.

It happened one Day, that among other Experiments he made, he gathered fome ripe Bunches of Grapes, which grew on a neighbouring Vine; and preffing out the Juice, he drank plentifully thereof, being defirous to know what Effect that, and all other Fruits and Plants, would produce: Having drank this, he, prefently after, was deprived of his Speech and Senfes, to fuch a Degree, that, with a violent Qualm and Loathing in his Stomach, he fell to the Ground. " This feems evidently to confirm the Opini- " on of thofe, who hold, that this was the Fruit which " *Eve* eat of." Upon this, a Grandfon (*a*) of his chanced to come to the Place where his good Grand-father lay, in fuch an indecent Pofture, that he beheld his Private Parts, which were bare, without any thing to conceal them; and, inftead of covering them, with immoderate Laughter, he haftily called his Father *Jafed*, who, together with him, greatly fcoffed at, and derided the Holy Patriarch; 'till at laft *Sem* came, and modeftly hiding his Face, he concealed the Na-

(*a*) Whatfoever Books our Author has confulted for this, he feems to be very much out in his Chronology, by the Relations I have heard my felf, and by what I find written by their own Doctors. By this Grandfon he may be fuppofed to mean, *Gaanan* or *Canaan*, the Son of *Ham*, whom the Author of the *Taarich Thabari*, fays, *Noah* curfed, together with his Father *Ham*, wherein he fwerves not much from Holy Writ. He adds, That by Virtue of this Curfe, *Ham* was not only made fubject to his Brothers, but that the Colour of his Flefh was changed and become Black; and that when *Noah* beheld this fudden and furprizing Alteration, he was moved to Compaffion, and prayed to God to grant, that his Brothers might have Pity and Affection to him; which Interceffion of his was heard; for though the Pofterity of *Ham* are Slaves in all Parts of the World, yet they are generally fought after, and ufed with Humanity and Tendernefs. This I remember to have heard read out of the aforefaid Author, and is likewife repeated in a manner *Verbatim* in *D'Herbelot*, under the Name *Ham ben Nouh*. They fay, (as do the *Jews*) That the Thicknefs and Largenefs of the Negroes Lips, proceed from *Ham's* thrufting out and extending his, when he mocked his Father.

kednefs

kedneſs of his venerable Parent with his Mantle: This he did with great Reſpect and Reverence, rebuking his Brothers for their ſhameleſs and undutiful Laughter and Deriſion.

When *Noah* came to himſelf, and was recovered from his paſt Fit of Drunkenneſs, and underſtood how he had been ſcoffed and laughed at, he was extremely incenſed againſt his Son *Jaſed*; inſomuch, that he curſed him, and laid a Mark upon him, diſinheriting and depriving him of the Poſſeſſion of any of his acquired Goods and Subſtance, or of his Grace and Benediction. From hence the ſacred *(a) Sunna* deprives and diſinherits the diſobedient Son, from the enjoying his Father's Riches and Protection, ſo that he who honours not his Parents, ſhall enjoy none of their Poſſeſſions.

The Curſe of *Noah* was ſo penetrating and extenſive, that it will endure in this World 'till its final Diſſolution, and whilſt there remain Creatures upon whom it may take Effect, on the Lineage and Poſterity of *Jaſed*; for they, among all other Nations, ſhall be diſtinguiſhed by their disfigured and diſcoloured Countenances. From him are deſcended the *Negroes* and the *Machuches*, *(b)* whoſe obſcure and diſmal

---

(a) *Sonnah* is the Name of a Book, among the *Mahometans* held in the higheſt Veneration. This *Arabick* Word, properly, ſignifies what the *Hebrews* call *Miſhnah*, the Second Law, or the Oral or Verbal Law, which was not writ by the Legiſlator, but only taken from what he ſaid or did, and preſerved by Tradition from Hand to Hand by Perſons in Authority. The plural Number of this Word is *Sonan* or *Sunen*, and ſeveral *Mahometan* Doctors have given this Title to their Works, wherein they gather all that is Obligatory or of Precept in the *Mahometan* Law, though it be not expreſly commanded in the *Alcoran*. See *D'Herbelot* in *Sonnah*.

(b) Deſte tomaron principio los Machuches a quien llaman los Negros, &c.

Com-

Complexions, they inherit from their (*a*) Original Anceſtor *Jaſed,* who had his Colour changed from White into Black, when he loſt that Grace and Perfection which he, at firſt, enjoyed. All that he loſt, revolved upon *Sem,* who by his laudable and vertuous Behaviour, obtained great Praiſe, and became the moſt perfect in all commendable Qualifications. This was he, whom the juſt *Iſa,* or *Jeſus,* at the Petition of the *Iſraelites,* raiſed from the Grave, from whence he came moſt ſtrangely disfigured ; his Beard and Head being half Black and half White; he imagining, that the Day of Judgment was come, and that he was called to render Account of his Actions.

Of this *Sem,* was born (*b*) *Arſaban,* from whoſe Name the *Hebrew* Language firſt had its Original: From him deſcended *Falaile,* and from thence the *Light* paſſed to *Sareg,* of whom was begotten *Argou,* and from him it was changed to *Tareh* or (*c*) *Terah.* This

---

(*a*) This is the greateſt Error I find my Author guilty of, throughout his whole Work ; for here he, unaccountably, confounds both the Poſterities, making thoſe of *Ham* and *Japhet* to be but one and the ſame , wherein he deviates from the general Opinion of all thoſe of his Perſuaſion, who all agree, that the Blacks are deſcended from *Ham.* Their univerſal Notion is, That all Good proceeded from *Shem,* and the contrary, I mean all pernicious deſtructive Generations, from *Japhet,* whom they hold to be *Noah*'s eldeſt Son. By theſe Evil Generations, they mean the *Scythians, Turks, Tartars, Goths, Vandals,* and, in fine, all the Northern Nations, which have ſince over-run all *Aſia* and *Europe.* His Word *Machuches,* certainly is intended for *Gog* and *Magog,* which in *Arabick* is *Yagiouge* and *Magiouge.* *D'Herbelot* treats largely of this, under the Names *Nouh, Jafeth ben Nouh, Jagiouge wa Magiouge,* &c.

(*b*) For this and the following Names, look back in the Genealogy, p. 64.

(*c*) Of this *Tareh,* whom they make to be *Abraham*'s Grandfather, take what I meet with in *D'Herbelot,* under the Name *Abraham.* He has it thus; *Abraham,* whom the *Arabs* call *Ebrahim,* the Perſians and *Turks* *Ibrahim,* according to *Taarikh Montekheb,* was the Son of *Azar,* and Grandſon of *Tareh* : It is generally concluded, that *Moſes*'s

This was the Father of *Ezar*, that famous Idolater, upon whom God was, myfterioufly, pleafed to fix the Sacred, Hereditary *Light* ; but for what Reafon He alone knows, for no Mortal can dive into His Secrets ; and although, as to what concerned the Rites of Religion, and the Ceremonies we ought to praċtife in this Humane Life, he was an Unbeliever, yet in his Aċtions he was, otherwife, a good Moralift. *Abraham* was the Son of this Man : Obferve the Difference! For though the Father was an impious Idolater, the Son was abundantly replenifhed with Grace. On this Account, the Holy *Alcoran* tells us, " That " God caufes the Dead to proceed from the Living, " and the Living from the Dead ;" from a juft Man comes an Infidel, who begets a Generation, as *Ezar* fprung from *Terah*, and from *Ezar*, fuch a Patriarch as *Abraham* ; whofe notable Deeds require fome Refpite and Refrefhment, to enable me to fing them ; for my Voice is now too much tired to begin fo great an Undertaking.

Mofes's *Tareh*, was the *Azar* of the *Arabs*, becaufe, according to the *Hebrew* Text of *Genefis*, that Patriarch was the Son of *Tareh* ; for in all *Mahometan* Hiftories, *Abraham* is called the Son of *Azar* : Yet it appears, that the *Arabs* do not mean the fame Perfon by thofe Two Names, fince *Tareh* is by them made *Abraham*'s Grandfather. Had our Chronologifts, who have taken fo much Pains to reconcile the *Epocha* of *Abraham*'s Tranfmigration, with the Years of his Age, and the Death of *Tareh*, been acquainted with this Genealogy of the *Arabians*, perhaps they would not have needed to fly to a Second Tranfmigration of the Patriarch, not mentioned in Scripture ; and they might eafily folve all their Difficulties, by admitting of Two *Tarehs*, one of which, called alfo *Azar*, was Father, and the other Grandfather, to *Abraham* ; which is not repugnant to Scripture.

C H A P.

CHAP. IV.

The HISTORY *of* ABRAHAM.

Nimrod's Prophetick Dream concerning Abraham. *His Idolatry and Cruelty.* Abraham's *Birth. He is caſt out by his Mother into a Cave. His miraculous Preſervation there. His early Know-ledge of God, by Divine Inſpiration. Is perſe-cuted by his idolatrous Parents, and by the impi-ous* Nimrod. *Deſtroys the Idols in* Babylon, *and is caſt into a prodigious Pile of Fire, out of an Engine made by the Devil. That monſtrous Fire deſcrib'd. The Angel* Gabriel *defends and preſerves him,* &c. Nimrod's *miſerable Death,* &c.

 **I** TREAT next of Him, whoſe Superna-tural Endowments were ſuch, that they would rather incline us to imagine him of Heavenly, than Earthly Extraction ; Thoſe from whom he received his Birth being not, in the leaſt, worthy the Name of Parents ; having caſt him out, and abandoned him to the Care of Providence, before he had well ſeen the Light. Who, in Fourteen Days after his Birth, was in-ſpired with ſo uncommon a Portion of Divine Grace,

that

that he attained, in that moſt tender Age, to the true and perfect Knowledge of the Omnipotent Creator and Suſtainer of the Heavens, and their Motions : He, who inſtead of thoſe Blandiſhments, and that tender Care practiſed throughout the whole World, in the nouriſhing and breeding up Children in their Infancy, had Stones thrown at him by his inhumane, wicked, and deteſtable Parents, who, by the Ties of Natural Affection, ought to have been more careful of his Preſervation : Yet they, not having the Fear of God before their Eyes, moſt cruelly perſecuted him, and, in the end, delivered him up into the Power of his mortal and implacable Enemy, the impious *Nimrod*, by whom he was committed to the Fire. This ever-famous Perſon was the moſt holy and juſt *Abraham*, whoſe Mother was no ſooner Delivered of him, but ſhe carried him to a frightful, obſcure Cave, in a deſart unhoſpitable Mountain, that he might eſcape the Sword of that Idolatrous and Blood-thirſty King *Nimrod*, of whom ſuch infernal and diabolical Tranſactions are recorded.

This Monſter was terribly frightened in a Dream by a Viſion of Hell, whereby his guilty Conſcience became ſo inſupportable to him, that he could take no manner of Reſt : In this horrible Viſion it was revealed to him, that the Hour approached in which a Male-child ſhould be born, who would overthrow all his Falſe Gods, and aboliſh his abominable Idolatries.

We muſt take Notice, That this ſame wicked King had, not long before, iſſued out a Proclamation, expreſly ordaining, commanding, and compelling all his Subjects, without Exception or Diſtinction, to reſort to his Palace, and to fall down and worſhip him ; and to pay the ſame Adorations to him, that are due to the Moſt High and Supreme Creator, and to none but Him alone ; whilſt he himſelf, impiouſly, and preſumptuouſly, worſhipped and fell down before Statues, Idols, and Images made of Wood, Stone,

and

and Metals; among the which, was one, in particular, that was moft richly cloathed in Gold, and pompoufly adorned with precious Jewels; This Idol's Name was *Teraq.*

(*a*) The aforefaid Dream or Vifion, had fo great an Influence upon this idolatrous and vicious King, that he immediately caufed all the Southfayers and Magicians throughout his whole Dominions, to be affembled

---

(*a*) Not to depend, intirely, upon the Credit of this my Author, and likewife to let the Readers fee, that he does not invent thefe Fables himfelf; I thought fit to tranfcribe this Story of *Abraham*, as I find it tranflated by Monfieur *D'Herbelot*, out of an *Arabick* Book, entitled *El Maalem*; and fince it contains many notable Circumftances, as alfo fome Variations from that of my *Spanifh Moor*, I hope it will not be unacceptable to the Curious. Thefe are the very Words.———— " *Nimrod*, the Son of *Chanaan*, thought
" to be the firft King after the Flood, refided in *Babylon*, which
" City he himfelf had built. This Prince, in a Dream, faw a Star
" rife above the Horizon, whofe Light darken'd that of the Sun;
" and having confulted his Magicians about it, they all unanimoufly
" agreed, that a Child would be born in *Babylon*, who, in a fhort
" Time, would become a great Prince; whom there was great
" Reafon to fear, though he was not yet begotten. *Nimrod*, in a
" Fright, immediately order'd, that the Men fhould be parted
" from their Wives, and appointed an Officer to every Ten Houfes,
" to hinder them from feeing one another. *Azar*, one of the Prin-
" cipal Men of *Nimrod*'s Court, and his Son-in-Law, deceived his
" Guards, and lay a Night with his Wife, whofe Name was *Adna.*
" The next Day the Southfayers, who, during this Time, made
" their Obfervations every Moment, came to *Nimrod*, and told
" him, That the Child, with which he was threaten'd, was begot
" that very Night; for which Reafon, he order'd all the Women
" with Child to be ftriftly obferv'd, and all the Male Children they
" brought forth, to be put to Death. *Adna*, fhewing no Tokens
" of being with Child, was not taken Notice of; fo that, when fhe
" was near her Time, fhe had the Opportunity of going out of
" Town, to be deliver'd; as fhe was, in a Cave, and having fhut
" it up carefully, fhe return'd to the City, where fhe told her
" Husband, fhe had been deliver'd of a Son, who died as foon as
" born. However, fhe went often to the Cave to vifit her Child,
" and to give it fuck; but fhe always found him fucking his Fingers-
" Ends, one of which gave him Milk, and the other Honey. She
" was much aftonifhed at this Miracle, and no lefs overjoy'd, per-
" ceiving,

aſſembled together at his Capital; and upon a ſolemn Conſultation, it was finally reſolved, That, without Delay or Exception, all the new-born Infants ſhould be put to the Sword. Which inhumane Edict was inſtantly put in Execution, and performed by his Miniſters of Iniquity, without the leaſt Remorſe; inſomuch that this deluded and Blood-thirſty Tyrant (for fear he ſhould miſs of the right one meant in the Viſion, and miraculouſly preſerved in the Deſart Mountain) thought to make ſure of him, by cauſing the Throats of Twelve thouſand Innocents to be cut.

But

" ceiving, that Providence took care to nouriſh her Child, and
" ſhe had no more Occaſion to make any Proviſion for him; Yet
" ſhe could not forbear ſeeing him ſometimes; and ſhe perceiv'd,
" that he grew as much in a Day, as other Children did in a Month.
" Scarce Fifteen Moons were paſt, when her Son appear'd to her
" like a Lad of Fifteen Years of Age, and he not been yet out of
" the Cave, when *Adna* told *Azar*, That the Son ſhe had been de-
" liver'd of, and had made him believe was dead, was now living,
" and of a very uncommon Beauty and Comelineſs. *Azar* repairing
" to the Cave, and having ſeen his Son, bad *Adna* bring him to
" Town, intending to preſent him to *Nimrod*, that he might be ad-
" vanc'd, and ſettled at Court. At Night *Adna* went for him, and
" led him through a Meadow, where Cows, Horſes, Camels, and
" Sheep were grazing: *Abraham*, who had never ſeen any living
" Creature, beſides his Father and Mother, ask'd the Names of all
" thoſe Things he beheld, and *Adna* told him the Names, Qualities,
" and Uſe of every Thing he inquired about. *Abraham* ask'd again,
" Who had made all thoſe ſeveral Kinds of Creatures? *Adna* ſaid,
" There is nothing in this World, but has its Creator and its Lord,
" upon whom it has its Dependance. *Abraham* reply'd, Who is it
" then, that brought me into the World? And on whom do I de-
" pend? It is I, anſwered the Mother. Who is your Lord, ſaid
" *Abraham*? *Azar* your Father, ſaid ſhe. *Abraham* ask'd her,
" Who was his Father's Lord? And being told, it was *Nimrod*, he
" was then deſirous to know, Who was *Nimrod*'s Lord? His Mother
" finding herſelf too far preſs'd, ſaid; You muſt not be ſo inqui-
" ſitive, my Child; it may be of a dangerous Conſequence to you.
" At that Time, there were ſeveral Sorts of Idolaters in *Chaldea*,
" where *Nimrod* reign'd: Some adored the Sun, others the Moon,
" and the Stars; ſome fell down before Statues, in which they ac-
" knowledged ſome Deity; and, in fine, many own'd no other God
" but

But to return to our folitary and diftreffed Innocent:
When Night approached, and he began to be pinched
with Hunger, having as yet, fince his Birth, tafted no
Suftenance, the Angel *Gabriel* defcended, and putting the
Child's Two Fingers into its Mouth, it received a full and

" but *Nimrod*. *Abraham*, going by Night from his Cave to the
" Town, faw, and took Notice of the Stars; and, among the reft,
" in particular, that of *Venus*, which was by many adored; and
" faid to himfelf; Perhaps, that is the God and Lord of the World!
" But fome Time after, upon Second Reflections, he faid; I per-
" ceive, that Star fets, and vanifhes, fo that it cannot be the Lord
" of the World; for He cannot be fubject to fuch a Change! He
" afterwards look'd upon the Full Moon, and concluded as he had
" done of *Venus*; but feeing her defcend to the Horizon, and dif-
" appear, he made the fame Conclufion, as of the faid Star. Hav-
" ing fpent all the reft of the Night in fuch like Thoughts, he was
" near *Babylon* by Sun-rifing; and there beheld abundance of Peo-
" ple fall down, and worfhip that Luminary, whereupon he con-
" jectur'd, as he had done before; 'till feeing him decline like the
" others, he faid, That could not be his Creator, his God, or his
" Lord, any more than the reft. When *Azar* prefented his Son
" *Abraham* to *Nimrod*, that Prince was fitting on a lofty Throne;
" about which, ftood in Order many beautiful Slaves, of both
" Sexes. *Abraham* ask'd his Father; Who that was above all the
" reft? Who anfwer'd, That he was Lord of all thofe he faw there,
" and that all thofe People acknowledged him for their God.
" *Abraham* then looking at *Nimrod*, who had a very hard-favour'd
" Countenance; demanded of his Father, How was it poffible, that
" he, whom he called his God, fhould make Creatures fo much more
" agreeable and handfome than himfelf; fince, of neceffity, the
" Creator muft, in all Refpects, be more *perfect* than his Creatures?
" This was the firft Opportunity *Abraham* laid hold of to undeceive
" his Father, concerning Idolatry; and to preach to him the *Unity*
" of God, the Creator of all Things, whofe Omnipotence had
" been revealed to him. This his Zeal caufed him then to incur
" his Father's Difpleafure, and was afterwards the Occafion of his
" having great Contefts and Controverfies with the Chief Men of
" *Nimrod*'s Court, who would not conform to, nor allow of the
" Truths he taught them. The Report of thefe Differences at
" length reaching *Nimrod*'s Ears, that cruel and haughty Prince
" caus'd him to be caft into a burning Furnace; from which he
" came out fafe and found, without fuffering the leaft Damage by
" the Fire. "
This Difpute of *Abraham*'s, is mentioned in the *Alcoran*, in the
Chapter intitled *Anaam*.

fufficient

sufficient Nourifhment; for, from one of the Fingers diftilled moft fweet and delicious Milk, and from the other, Honey of an admirable Flavour. In this Manner was he nourifhed for Fourteen Days, and then opening his Eyes, and lifting up his Head, he beheld the Morning Star, and faid; " This, doubtlefs, " is the God whom I am to adore!" But when he had for fome Time gazed thereon, and faw it defcend by Degrees, and at laft go down below the Horizon, quite out of his Sight, he cry'd out, faying, " I'll " never worfhip any God, that vanifhes fo foon!" Prefently after, he faw the Moon fhining exceedingly bright and refplendent; but perceiving her to fet alfo, he cry'd out in a great Concern, " I fhall be utterly " loft, if not remedy'd by fome more *ftable* and more " *fubftantial* Deity!" And fo he paffed the fmall Remainder of the Night, in the utmoft Anxiety of Thought and perplexing Imaginations; *For that Soul which God touches, is feldom or never unactive.* But when it was perfectly Light, and he, with Amazement, beheld the chearful Appearance of the glorious Sun, he made a loud and joyful Exclamation, and faid, " This, certainly, is my Lord and God; for he " is greater and more beautiful than the others!" But when that Planet had likewife run its Natural Courfe, and difappeared like the reft, he then faid; " I believe " not, neither will I confide in Gods fo unfixed, " and of fo little Stability; All thefe are, of Necef- " fity, guided by *one Sole and Superior Motion*, and " in Him, by whom they are governed, will I con- " fide and believe all my Life: Him it is I revere " and adore: And I affirm, that the Heavens and " the Earth were created by *One, and only One*; To " Him, and none but Him, will I proftrate my Face, " without acknowledging, that He has any Equal " or Competitor, or that any is worthy to ftand in " Competition with Him.

No

No sooner had he spoken these Words, but he fell down prostrate upon the Ground, adoring and worshipping his great Creator; as having attained the true Knowledge of Him, by the Observations he had made of the Motions of the Heavenly Planets.

At the same Instant, his unnatural Mother was inspir'd by the Lord with a Maternal Care, to know what was become of her Child; 'Tis true, he had never been out of her Thoughts, from the Time she had so inhumanely abandoned him to perish in that dismal Solitude; but now she was resolved to go and see if he was dead: And indeed, how could she expect the contrary? So she hasten'd towards the Mountain, and when she arrived at the Cave, she beheld the Youth almost at his full Growth, in so few Days after his first Appearance in the World, and endowed with such Knowledge and Qualifications, educated without the Assistance of a Tutor, that she had not the least Suspicion who he was; but seeing him, as I have said, with his Face prostrate on the Earth, she accosted him in this Manner; *Have you not seen, Young Man,* said she, *an Infant I left here in this Cave about Fifteen Days since, and of whom I have had no Tidings, nor know I what's become of him?* Abraham, upon this, discovered himself, giving his Mother to understand, that he was the Son she inquired after, and with great Humility, kneeling down, craved her Blessing: She, tho' scarcely believing what he said, raised him up, and, with unexpressible Joy, receiv'd him in her Arms, and after many tender and Motherly Kisses and Embraces, ask'd him; *To whom it was he was making those Adorations, when she found him in that Posture of Humility? For,* said she, *Those Postures of Worship, belong only to Him whom we adore, and in whom we believe; nor ought they to be bestow'd upon any other.* To which he answered; " Most honoured Mother, I have seen " and observed the Heavens and their Motions, the " Sun, the Moon, and the Stars; and by the Remarks " I have made thereon, I perceive, that they all, and
" every

" every one of them, take their Natural Courſe, and
" then abſcond and diſappear, and that none of them
" all are fix'd and ſtable, nor is it in their Power to
" be ſo ; ſo that it is my Opinion, and I affirm it to
" be true, That there is, of a certainty, One only
" Great and Powerful Lord, who rules over all theſe,
" and by whom their Motions are governed ; Him
" alone it is I firmly believe to be perfectly Good
" and Holy ; in only Him it is I confide, and Him
" I revere and adore: And I further aver, That all
" Worſhip or Adoration whatſoever, that is, or ſhall
" be made to any other Deity, is falſe, idolatrous,
" and erroneous, the which I poſitively renounce
" and deny.

His Mother, being highly incens'd at this, with
the utmoſt Concern and Indignation let go her Arms,
which held him ſtrictly embraced ; and puſhing him
from her, uſed all the Perſuaſions ſhe was capable of
uttering, to induce him to embrace that curſed and
idolatrous Worſhip introduced by the Devil, which,
infallibly, leads the deluded Obſervers thereof to the
Flames of Hell. But to all her Arguments, her vertuous Son only reply'd ; *Do you not bluſh for Shame,*
to entertain and vindicate ſuch vile Thoughts and Imagi-
nations ? Believe what I believe ; and affirm, for an
inconteſtable Truth, what I affirm to be ſo ; which
is the only certain Way to Eternal Happineſs and Sal-
vation.

This ſuperſtitious and idolatrous Mother, hearing
this her Son's reſolute and determined Anſwer, lifted
up her Hand, and ſtruck him a great Blow on the
Face, and after that, blind with Fury and Indignation, took up Stones and threw at him, ſtill aiming at
his beautiful and lovely Face ; and ſo, in the greateſt
Rage and Paſſion imaginable, left him, and ran home
with all poſſible Speed to call her Huſband ; all which
ſhe did with a moſt diabolical Intent.

When ſhe found him, ſhe accoſted him in theſe
Words ; " Hear, O *Ezar*, with Attention, what I
" have

" have to fay to you, for I am going to divulge a
" Secret of very great Importance: You muft know,
" that when I was delivered of my Child fome Days
" ago, out of a Motherly Compaffion and Tender-
" nefs, and not to fee it Maffacred before my Eyes,
" as fo many Thoufands were, even in their Parents
" Arms, notwithftanding my weak Condition, I
" carry'd it out into yonder Mountain ; and, that
" this Action of mine might be the better concealed,
" I left it hidden in a certain Cave that is in the
" faid Mountain ; and to Day, returning thither,
" expecting to have found it had been devoured by
" fome ravenous Beaft, or dead with Hunger and
" Thirft for want of looking after ; I, to my great
" Aftonifhment, found him alive and well, but pro-
" ftrate with his Face to the Earth, paying his De-
" votions and Adorations to fome ftrange God, dif-
" ferent from Him whom we Worfhip and Believe
" in ; and altho' I omitted nothing, but us'd all ima-
" ginable Endeavours to perfuade, and to bring him
" over to conform himfelf to our Worfhip, and to
" convince him of his Errors ; yet, notwithftanding
" all I could fay, he, moft perverfely, continued ob-
" ftinate, with aftonifhing Contumacy : And if he, who
" was born, as it were, *but Yefterday*, fhews us fo
" little Deference and Refpect, what will he do when
" grown up to Years of Maturity ? It appears to
" me plain and evident, and is my firm Opinion,
" That this muft needs be Him, concerning whom
" our Wife-men, South-fayers, and Magicians have
" prophefy'd ; Him it moft furely is, upon whofe
" Account the cruel and bloody King *Nimrod* caufed
" the innocent Children to be deftroy'd with fuch an
" unheard-of Barbarity, thinking thereby to take
" Vengeance for thofe terrifying *Dreams* and *Vifions*
" he had, and the which had difturbed his Repofe
" fo exceedingly."

Ezar, hearing thofe wonderful, and hardly credible Tidings, fell into fo exceffive a Paffion, that
he

he could fcarce contain himfelf; but, guided by his Fury, flew to the Cave where his virtuous Son had been left; where being arrived, and they had mutually made themfelves known to each other, this *Prodigy of Infants* began to give him the fame Admonitions, and to ufe the very fame Arguments, in order to convert him to the Truth, as he had before ufed with his *mis-believing* Mother, making him the fame Propofals. But this *blind* and *perverfe* Idolater, taking the felf-fame *vile* and *prepofterous* Method as his *faithlefs* Spoufe had already taken, and his Eyes glowing with Rage and Choler, he fell upon him, beating, bruifing, and wounding his beautiful Face with cruel and mercilefs Blows, throwing Stones at him in a moft brutifh and favage manner; and then, like a *Fire-brand of Hell*, or a fierce and rapacious Tyger, or an hungry Dragon, he haftened away to *Nimrod*, with loud Exclamations, and coming, in this furious Manner, before that Tyrant's Throne, he caft himfelf upon his Knees, and faid:

" Know, O moft Powerful, and moft Mighty Mo-
" narch! that, of a Certainty, it is my Son whom
" your Majefty fearches for; for, no Doubt is to be
" made, but that he it is of whom the Southfayers
" have fo often Prognofticated; I am juft this Mo-
" ment come from him, and have left him in a Cave
" not far from hence, where he is making his De-
" votions, and paying Adorations to another Deity
" befides your Majefty: His Name is *Abraham:* And
" it is a Matter of the utmoft Confequence, that you
" fhould immediately fend to have him feized, or
" killed; for I am certainly of the Opinion, that
" if he is fuffered to live, he will extinguifh, or, at
" leaft, eclipfe your Glory, and intirely difturb your
" Repofe.

When *Nimrod* heard this, he, without Hefitation, inftantly difpatched away a great Band of his Warriors, with exprefs Orders to bring him dead or alive.

H   The

The Mighty Lord of Hofts, upon this Occafion, fhewed a moft miraculous and wonderful Myftery; for between *Abraham* and thofe who were fent out to apprehend him, He erected Three high, ftrong, and unaffaultable *Walls*; the outermoft whereof was compos'd of *Fire*. The Angel *Gabriel* defcended at the fame Time, encouraging *Abraham*, with many Exhortations, that he fhould fear nothing from his Enemies; telling him, That *his prefent Companion was ftronger, and more powerful than they.* However, they began the Affault very furioufly; but the *Fire*, which iffued out from *that outermoft, or moft advanc'd Wall*, falling upon them, they were every one of all that Number burnt, and fo perifh'd miferably: While the *Bleffed Youth*, protected by God, and the Holy Angels, remained joyful and unconcerned in that *miraculous Fortrefs*, without receiving the leaft Hurt or Detriment from thofe *perilous Snakes* which were laid for him, and the imminent Dangers his Life was threatned with.

He underwent many other Dangers and Perfecutions, worthy to be recorded (as they are by feveral Writers) and all thro' the Means, and at the Inftigation of his *unbelieving* Father, who was always his greateft and moft inveterate Adverfary; till at laft, in Procefs of Time, it was God's Pleafure to permit him to be delivered into the Hands of King *Nimrod*, who took him Prifoner; This the Lord permitted, that the Infidel People might be the better convinced of the great Myfteries He had depofited in the Breaft of this moft righteous and venerable Patriarch.

The chief Motive that induced the Tyrant, at that Time, to perfecute him fo feverely, was that memorable Action of his, fo artfully contrived and tranfacted by this Renowned Servant of God, upon the Day of their Great *Pafcua*, or principal Feftival, at the Time when all the Inhabitants of the City were affembled

to-

together to worfhip *Nimrod* like a Deity. Upon
this Occafion, that Prince would needs caufe his Father *Azar* to go to him with his Command, that he
fhould come to the Palace and make his Adorations
to him, as the reft did. *Abraham*, for an Excufe, feigned himfelf to be indifpofed; but as foon as his Father had left him, he repaired to the great and ftately
Temple, where all the Idols were kept, which, it
feems, *Azar* had caufed to be made, and fet up there,
and among the reft was the Mighty Idol *Teraq*,
which was held by all as a God, and worfhipped as
fuch, and efteemed much fuperiour to all the
others : When he came thither, he, with a *Battle-
Ax* he had brought with him, began to lay about
him on all Sides, cutting, hacking, and mangling
thofe deformed and ugly Statues, fpoiling and disfi-
guring their Faces, and hewing off their Limbs, till
he had cut them, in a manner, all in pieces; At laft
he went to that which was feated in the midft of all
the others, being that fame *Teraq*, which that blind,
idolatrous, and mifguided King held in fuch
high Efteem, and adored as his God. This Image
was moft gorgeoufly fet off, and adorned with
exceeding rich and precious Ornaments of Gold
and Jewels; yet *Abraham* mangled all its Face, and
put out both its Eyes, and when he had done, took
the Weapon, fix'd it in the Idol's Hand, in fuch wife,
that it remain'd refting upon his Right Shoulder.
Soon after, when the *accurfed* and execrable *Nimrod*,
with a vaft Multitude of Followers (returning from
acting their abominable and deteftable Impiety, of
paying their Worfhip to that King, as I have faid
before) entered into the Temple, and beheld the
ftrange Deftruction of his Idols, all hewed to pieces,
and his great and adored *Teraq*, among the reft, fo
miferably treated and disfigured, he fet up a difmal
and horrible Outcry, and, greatly incenfed, faid;
Woe be to the Wretch who has committed this Indignity

to my Gods! Grievous fhall be the Torments I will inflict upon him!

After the firft Tranfports of Fury, they began to confider, and to make their Conjectures, who it could be that had done it; when, calling to mind the many Occafions *Abraham* had given, both in Publick and in Private, to fufpect him to be the Author of this prefumptuous Deed, they remembred how often he had fpoke revilingly and difrefpectfully of thofe Idols, faying; *I'll certainly, one time or other, fpoil the Countenances of thofe Wooden Gods; I'll break 'em in pieces, and trample 'em upon the Ground under my Feet!*

This wicked Generation of People then, without more ado, laid their Accufation againft him, and inftantly departed in great Numbers to feek him out, and having found him, they dragged him away to the King; who wrathfully demanded of him, *For what Reafon he had committed fo great a Wickednefs?* *Abraham*, no wife terrified, with a compofed, ferene, and unconcerned Countenance, made him this Anfwer; " Do you feek for a farther Difcovery,
" and clearer Demonftration, when you have the
" Criminal here before you? This is undoubtedly the
" Malefactor whom you behold with the Weapon
" upon his Shoulder: It muft furely be him who
" has wounded all the others, becaufe they refufed to
" obey his Commands; and thefe being many, have,
" trufting in their Numbers, been wanting in their
" Refpect towards him, and have blinded him in both
" his Eyes, and put him in the Condition you fee:
" However he is come off victorious. If you defire
" a more ample Information, ask him, and he will
" fatisfy your Curiofity; for tho' he has received fo
" many dangerous Wounds, yet, neverthelefs, his
" Heart is undaunted and magnanimous."

The King replied; " Wretch as thou art! Thefe
" can neither fpeak, nor move from their Seats; nor
" have they any Senfes, or Faculties to do either
" Good

" Good or Evil. Why then, faid *Abraham*, blind,
" and deluded Wretches as you are, do you Wor-
" fhip and put your Trufts in fuch inanimate Sta-
" tues, made of Wood and Clay? 'Tis You your
" felves are the Wretches, the miferable and mifgui-
" ded Servants and Companions of the Devil, void
" of Senfe or Reafon, and who will be condemned to
" the everlafting Flames of Hell! Worfhip Him
" who made you out of Nothing, and who nou-
" rifhes and protects you, without any Deferts of
" yours."

Upon this, they were all in general fo inraged
and inflamed with Indignation and Refentment, that,
with Infernal Fury, they cryed out in one Voice, *Let
the blafphemous Traytor Die! The common Enemy! The
Difturber of our Peace! The Contemner of our Holy Belief, and our Sacred Rites! Let him Die! Let him Die!*

His fevere Chaftifement was unanimoufly concluded upon ; but there were many different Opinions as
to the Manner of it : Moft were for making him
fuffer the cruelleft Tortures could be invented ; Some
were for Hanging him up as a Magician, to be a publick Spectacle ; and fome for having him Stoned to
Death ; others, more moderate, were for condemn-
ing him to perpetual Banifhment ; whilft others ftill
propofed fome different forts of Punifhment.

In the the midft of this Confufion of Voices and
Opinions, the Devil, who always delights in Mifchief and Wickednefs, as being the Author thereof,
prefented himfelf amongft the Congregation, and,
with Gladnefs in his Countenance, faid; " What is
" moft convenient and requifite to be done in Re-
" gard to this Offender, is, in my Opinion, that he
" fhould be deftroyed by Fire ; and that, when he
" is burnt, his Afhes be caft into the Air ; by which
" Means, the King, and his whole Kingdom may
" enjoy Peace and Tranquillity."

This was the Counfel that blood-thirfty Dragon
Satan gave them, and which was generally approved

on, and immediately concluded to be best of all: The King then gave Orders, that a Quantity of Wood should be brought; and the People were so eager and diligent in obeying this Command, that they amassed together such a prodigious Heap, that a Pile was raised no wise inferior to a Mountain; which, as we find in the *Hebrew* Text, was full Nine Months before it was completed; all which Time *Abraham* remained in a Dungeon loaded with Fetters.

When at last all was ready, and the Fire kindled, the Quantity of the Fuel was so prodigiously great, and the Fire so furious and intense, that the very Clouds were melted by the Flames thereof, which reached almost to the Skies; and the Heat was so excessive, that none dared to approach within a Mile of its vast Circumference.

They were now at a Loss how they should manage it to get *Abraham* conveyed into that extraordinary and unaccountable *Bonfire*; and as they were thus at a Stand, not knowing how to bring it about, *He, who for his Wickedness was cast down from Heaven*, appeared in the Likeness of an Holy Man, and shewed them a Machine he had prepared for that purpose, to cast him into it at that Distance; a Thing so subtly contrived, that it could never have reached the Capacity of any but that of this *Infernal Ingenier*, so diabolical was the Invention.

(a) Into this Hellish Engine *Abraham* is put, stark naked, with his Hands and Feet fast tied, and, like
an

(a) The Persian *Magi*, or Worshippers of Fire, affirm, That *Nimrod* was of the Religion of *Zoroastes*, and consequently of the same they still profess in *Hindostan*: Now the *Mahometans*, who borrow Fables from all Sects, and adapt them where they think proper, agree with them in this, and that *Andeschin*, who, they say, was Chief Priest of the Fire had, by that Idolatrous Prince's Command, a very warm Dispute with *Abraham* concerning God's Unity, and that thro' the Patriarch's persevering to affirm the Truth thereof, he councill'd *Nimrod* to cause him to be cast into a fiery Furnace,

an Arrow, fhot into the midft of that burning Pile. He was inftantly furrounded by thofe furious Flames ; But, calling upon God, and imploring Succour from Him who is the true and only *Succourer* in Time of Neceffity, the Angel *Gabriel*, with a hafty and precipitate Flight, defcended to his Affiftance, and battled with the Flames in his Defence, to preferve him on fo preffing an Occafion, till he was all on a Sweat.

This Heavenly Remedy being fo feafonably applied, the Flames received him with fo much Temperance, that not only they neither fcorched, nor offended him in the leaft, but he fat therein with the greateft Eafe and Pleafure imaginable ; and to Regale him, the Trees of the Cœleftial Paradife bent down their fructiferous Branches, loaden with fragrant and delicious Fruits, and afforded to the Holy *Abraham* a moft exquifite and nourifhing Repaft. And in this Manner that juft Perfon remained in the middle of the raging Furnace unhurt, accompanied with the Angel of God, the Bleffed *Gabriel*, with whom he paffed the Time in difcourfing of Heaven, and of its Joys and Glory.

On the Third Day after, at the Time when this *Artificial Hell* was raging and burning in its greateft Fury, and the King was making a mighty Feftival and Rejoycing, that he had, as he thought, obtained his Defire, and accomplifhed his Revenge, the Fancy

---

nace, to make Trial of the Divinity of the Fire : This, they all unanimoufly acknowledge, was put in Execution, and that *Abraham.* being protected by the Angel *Gabriel*, came glorioufly off from this fiery Trial. But the Original Source of this Fiction, is, what the Scripture fays concerning *Abraham's* coming from *Ur* of the *Chaldeans*, which many of the *Rabbins*, and all the *Mahometan* Expofitors, will have it, that *Ur*, in that Place, fignifies *Fire*, and is not the Name of a City, as our Tranflators expound it. —— Whatever the Word may be in the other Oriental Tongues, I fhall rot meddle with ; but *Fire* in *Arabick*, is *Nar*, or rather *Nabar*. Something to this Purport the Curious may find in *D'Herbelot*, under the Names *Andefchan, Zeraafcht*, &c.

H 4

took

took the Tyrant to go forth out of his Palace, as it were, to triumph over his Enemy, whom he imagined was long fince reduced to Afhes; but as he came nearer the Fire, he was unexpreffibly aftonifhed to behold *Abraham* fitting alive and unhurt, and very much at his Eafe, in the midft of the Flames with which he was furrounded, and not fhewing the leaft Token of Fear or Concern.

Great was his Amazement at this Sight; and being out of his Senfes, he vomited out, like a Dog, this blafphemous and impious Exclamation, That he was refolved to wage War with Heaven, and to conquer it, becaufe God had protected *Abraham* his Enemy. This he had the Prefumption to attempt, (*a*) but fucceeded fo well, that a little infignificant *Gnat*

(*a*) This *Nimrod*, whom the *Arabs* call *Nameroud*, and fometimes *Nemrodd*, they fay, derives his Name from *Mared*, which fignifies, A Rebel, a Name fuitable enough for his Rebellion againft God in building the Tower of *Babel*. The *Perfians* hold him to be the fame as their *Zhbak*, and that his Name came from the *Perfian* Word *Nemurd*, Immortal, becaufe of his long Reign; which Name was likewife given to *Caicous*, an ancient *Perfian* King of the firft Race, who reign'd One Hundred and Fifty Years, as all their Writers agree. *Mirkond* in his *Taarich* likewife mentions, that this *Caicous* was charg'd with attempting to climb up to Heaven, which fuits with the Defign of the Tower of *Babel*; tho' he feems to contradict it, by adding, That it is hardly probable, that fo wife a Prince as *Caicous*, fhould be guilty of fuch a Madnefs. The Author of the *Leb Taarich* fays, That *Nimrod* was the Son of *Canaan*, and Grandfon of *Ham*, the Son of *Noah*, and that he was Brother to *Cous*, furnamed *Fil Dendan*, that is, Elephant's Tooth. This *Cous* may perhaps be *Chus* the Son of *Canaan*, from whom the *Ethiopians* defcend. The fame Author, who relates the foregoing Story of *Abraham's* Birth, &c. fays, That when *Nimrod* had caft him into the fiery Furnace, and faw that he came to no Hurt, he built the Tower of *Babel* to go up to Heaven, that he might fee *Abraham's* God; This Tower being twice overthrown, he fays, *Nimrod* caus'd himfelf to be carried up by four monftrous Birds, mention'd in the Old Eaftern Romances, call'd *Kerkes*, (and by others *Roq*) and having been a long time flying about to no purpofe, he fell down on a Mountain with fuch a Shock, that he made it tremble. *Nimrod*, nothing difcouraged

Gnat caused him to die a miserable Death; and, such was his Distemper, and so exquisite the Tortures that little Creature gave him, that to afford him some sort of Asswagement and Respite to his intolerable Pain, he was forced to employ his Servants to be continually striking upon his Head with Mallets, without one Moment's Intermission. In this Manner this Servant of *Satan* expired in Torments, after he had lived on the Earth Six Hundred Years.

After *Abraham* had been so miraculously preserved from that Tyrant's Hands, he returned home to his Father, who still persisted in his Idolatry, and deporting himself very dutifully towards him, would often, with great Humility, represent to him his Errors, saying, " O my Father! Why are you so blind, and " unadvised, as to confide in, and worship Idols, " which neither hear nor see? They do you infinite " Harm, but can do you no manner of Good! O " Father! Why will you be a Servant to the *Accur-* " *sed* and *Rebellious* Satan? Think, that if you go on " in your Blindness, you are apparently in a State " of Perdition. Be not your own Enemy and De- " stroyer! O my dear Parent! I have received the

---

couraged by these Disappointments, would still cause his Subjects to worship him as a God, and persecuted all those who refus'd it; for which God depriv'd him of the greatest Part of them by the Confusion of Tongues, and punish'd his Adherents, destroying them with Gnats. The Author of the *Lebal* tells us, That one of those Gnats getting up *Nimrod*'s Nostrils, made way to the Membranes of his Brain, where, growing bigger and bigger, it cas'd him such terrible Pain, that he was forc'd to have his Head continually beaten with a Mallet to take some Rest, and that he underwent this Torture for Four Hundred Years, God, by the least of his Creatures, punishing him, who insolently and presumptuously endeavoured to be Lord of All. *Ebn Batrick* says, That *Nimrod* was of the Religion of the *Magi*, and the first who set up the Worshipping of Fire. Some Historians call the ancientest *Babylonian* Kings by the Name of *Nemared*, or the *Nimrodians*; for, in *Arabick*, *Nemared* is the Plural of *Nemroud*, and signifies, in that Language, Rebels and Tyrants.

" Gift

" Gift of the Knowledge of Truth from Heaven, a
" Bleſſing you have not yet been ſo happy as to
" enjoy, for your Comfort and Conſolation : But
" if you'll follow me, I'll guide you to the Path of
" Purity and Salvation. I will interceed with my
" Lord for a Remiſſion of your Sins and Errors :
" Conſider theſe Words in your Heart, dear Father ;
" or elſe, be aſſured, that the Torments of the Damned
" will be your Portion ! " But, notwithſtanding, *Azar*
continued in his Obſtinacy ; the Eyes of his Reaſon
were Blind, and both his Ears were *lock'd up with
Iron* ; ſo that he remained a perverſe Idolater all
his Life, and died without any Merit, or Knowledge
of God, and his Soul went to inherit eternal Torment for the Recompence of his Unbelief.

When *Azar* was dead, the vertuous *Abraham* began
to think of, and prepare for his Marriage with *Sarah*,
a Kinſwoman of his, a very beautiful, and moſt
deſerving Damſel, whoſe Parents were likewiſe Idolaters. When the Parents of this worthy Virgin perceived that their Daughter followed the Precepts of
Abraham (*a*) their Nephew, and that beſides ſhe bore
him a moſt ardent Affection, from which, by no Perſuaſions, they were able to break her, they ſtripp'd
her of all her rich Ornaments and Jewels, and with
only a very ordinary, coarſe Woollen Garment to
cover her Nakedneſs, they turned her out of Doors ;
and *Abraham* was likewiſe forced to flee in the ſame
wretched Condition ; ſo that thoſe two Lovers, deſtitute of all Help, were obliged to betake themſelves
to the Deſart ; Where, as they were alone, and in

(*a*) According to *Abn Batrick* (that is, The Son of the Patriarch,
who was an Orthodox Biſhop of *Alexandria*, and the Author of
ſeveral Books in the *Arabick* Tongue) *Sarah* was the Daughter of
Tareh and *Tehmiah*, who was his Second Wife, the Name of his
firſt being *Jounah*, who was *Abraham's* Mother. *Abraham's* Wife
Sarah was Daughter to *Aakhor*, and Grandchild to *Tuerah*, and
conſequently Niece to *Abraham*, and not his Couſin. *D'Herbelot* in
Batrick.

the

the Condition I have described, their Matrimonial Ceremonies could not poffibly be performed, there being neither (a) *Alwaali*, Witneffes, nor any of the Things requifite; nor had *Abraham* any thing to give the Bride for her *Azedaque*, or *Sidaak*.

But that this Marriage, which was to be of fuch Importance, and fo very beneficial to the whole World, might meet with no Hindrance, but might be happily effected, the Angel *Gabriel* defcended from Heaven, and brought with him Three of his Companions, who were *Mikael*, *Ifrafil*, and (b) *Reduan*, the Porter of Heaven Gate.

When thofe Bleffed Angels approached, *Gabriel* faid, " O *Abraham!* The Lord of Truth commanded " me to tell you, That it is His Pleafure, that by " Promife you affure unto your Spoufe her *Azedaque*, " and whatfoever is her Right, and properly belongs " to her; for the Performance of which He Himfelf " will be Security; And that nothing may obftruct " the Confummation of your Marriage, we are " fent to fupply the Places of *Alwaali*, and " Witneffes, and will fee every thing that is " neceffary performed, fo that nothing fhall be want- " ing." In this manner *Abraham* was Married, to

---

(a) *Alwaali* is the Bride's Father, or any other Relation or Friend, who officiates as fuch, by giving her in Marriage. A Woman, if her Matrimonial Agreement is not Sign'd by, at leaft, two Witneffes it is invalid; nor can fhe, upon parting from her Husband, demand her *Azedaque*, or rather *Sidaac*; i. e The Sum of Money, or whatever elfe had been agreed upon, and fpecify'd in the written Contract, and is, generally, to be paid half at their coming together, and the other half at parting. This is the Way of Marrying amongft the *Mahometans* throughout *Europe*, *Afia* and *Africa*.

(b) *Reduan*, *Redhouan*, *Reihuan*, or *Rezwan*, for they pronounce it all thofe ways, is a proper Name, and fignifies in *Arabick*, The Good-will God bears his Creatures.

his

his great Joy and Content, and leaving *Chaldea,*
(*a*) went to dwell in the Land of *Canaan.*

(*a*) *Chaldea* is by the *Mahometans* called *Erac,* and *Canaan* is
Kenaan. The Patriarch *Joſeph* is by the Eaſtern Authors called *Camar Kenaani,* or, The Moon of *Canaan,* for his great Beauty: But
of him in a properer Place.

C H A P.

CHAP. V.

Abraham *commanded to go into* Arabia, *to lay the Foundation of the Temple at* Mecca. *He departs with* Sarah *his Wife. They are carry'd before the King of* Ægypt. *Are in great Danger, but are miraculously delivered, and highly caress'd by that King.* Hagar. *the King's Daughter, refolving to accompany them, petitions her Father, who confents. They arrive in* Arabia. Abraham *marries* Hagar, *and* Ifhmael *is born. At* Sarah's *Requeft,* Hagar *and her Son are carried to the Defart. Their Mifery there. Relieved by the Angel* Gabriel. *The Temple built, &c.*

BRAHAM, the Servant of God, being now fettled in the Land of *Canaan*, led a pleafant and comfortable Life in that fruitful and delicious Province, in Company with his dearly beloved Wife *Sarah*, in the full Injoyment of all the Bleffings and Mercies, the Almighty had fo bountifully and gracioufly beftowed upon them; but, as yet, they had no Child.

One Night, the *Faithful* Angel of the Lord, *Gabriel*, came down and appeared to *Abraham*, and faid unto him; " *Abraham*, It is thy Lord's Pleafure, and by " me He commands thee, That thou leave this Coun- " try, and with none but *Sarah* thy Wife, thou, with- " out

" out Delay, depart from hence, bending thy Steps
" full South, **towards** *Arabia,* and there to repair to
" a certain Place, the which his Divine Majefty has
" chofe to fix therein the Throne and the Scepter
" He has, long fince, defign'd for His Elected *Ma-*
" *hommad,* and after him, to his great and noble
" Pofterity, and worthy Succeffors.   Thou there art
" to lay the Foundation for the building a moft glo-
" rious and magnificent Temple, the which for (*a*)
" Excellency, Sanctity, and the Vertues to be prac-
" tifed therein, fhall be abundantly fuperior to any
" Temple in the whole Univerfe.   In it, fhall be ce-
" lebrated, in After-Ages, the moft Holy Rites that
" are poffible to be performed by Mortals in this
" World, in Imitation of thofe who inhabit the other
" World of Everlafting Life.   The Name of this
" fanctified Place, is *Mecca,* and it is the Spot of
" Ground chofen by God himfelf, to be the Metro-
" polis, and Capital, for the Founding and Propa-
" gating His moft Holy and moft Divine Law.

When the Bleffed Angel had delivered this Meffage,
he fuddenly departed, without ftaying for any Reply : *Abraham* then, being exceedingly joyful at thefe
happy Tidings, awakened his Wife *Sarah,* and communicated to her, all the Angel had told him ; How
that the Lord had been fo gracioufly Merciful to him,
as to vouchfafe, that a Work fo Pious, and fo full of
Sanctity, fhould be begun by his Hands.

(*a*) The Word here is *Alfadila :* It fhould rather be *El Fadhilah,*
the Plural of which is *Fadhail,* and with the Article *The* prefix'd to
it, is *El Fadhail.* It fignifies Vertue and Excellency, as I have
hinted elfewhere   The *Muffulmans* affign Five principal Vertues,
in which the Spiritual Life confifts ; which are, 1. Confidence in the
Divine Providence : 2. Conformity to the Will of God   3. Self-
Denial : 4. Prayer : 5. Contemplation.   Thefe they call *El Fadhail.*
There is a Book called, *Fadhail, Miffir* or *Mefr,* the Excellencies of
Ægypt.

Sarah,

Sarah, at this good News, was no leſs rejoyced than her Huſband; and that very Day, with all imaginable Diligence and Expedition, they got all Things in a Readineſs for their Journey; and taking their Leaves of all their Family, they ſet out, travelling with the utmoſt Speed, and never making any Stay, but when it could not poſſibly be avoided.

As they were proceeding on their Journey, they were, of Neceſſity, obliged to paſs through the Territories of King *Agar*, who, at (*a*) that Time, reign'd in *Ægypt*; and as they were near a certain Mountain, they were attacked and ſeized by ſome *Spies*, who were out upon Duty, performing the Commands of that King, and were by them carried to his Palace.

Abraham, as they were going along, guarded and conducted by thoſe Soldiers, adviſed his Spouſe, that, in Caſe ſhe was examined, and had it put home to her to declare who he was, and what Relation ſhe was to him, that ſhe ſhould not own her-ſelf to be his Wife, but ſhould ſay, She was his Siſter: But *Sarah*, either not hearing what he ſaid, or not rightly underſtanding him, becauſe he was forced to deliver his Mind to her partly in Signs, and partly in Whiſpers, when ſhe was introduced into the Libidinous King's Preſence, who was wonderfully ſmitten with her exceeding Beauty (her Eyes ſeeming to obſcure the Light of the Sun) ſhe made a quite contrary Anſwer to what her Huſband had injoyned her to ſay.

The King thinking fit to examine them ſeparately, had, beforehand, ordered *Abraham* to be brought in firſt; The firſt Word *Agar* ſaid to him, was, *Whither art thou going with that Beautiful Damſel? Is ſhe your Wife, that you go ſo lovingly together? Let me know that, and likewiſe, whither you are bound?*

(*a*) The Author of the *Tarick Montheckheh*, who has this ſame Story, with ſome Variations, ſays, this King's Name was *Senan ben Ulvan.*

Abraham,

Abraham, being interrogated after such a Manner, reply'd; " The Woman, my Lord, you inquire about, " is my Sister; I am conducting her into *Arabia*, the " nearest Part of it from hence : The Occasion of our " Journey thither, is, some Affairs of Moment, which " concern us both very particularly : I intreat you, " my Lord, to suffer us to proceed on in our Way, " without detaining us any longer; for our Business " is of that Consequence, that it requires our utmost " Haste, and we have still many Days to travel.

After this, *Abraham* was ordered to withdraw; so he was taken away, and *Sarah* was brought in by the Command of *Agar*, who was desirous to know, if all that *Abraham* had told him was Truth, or whether he had been guilty of any Prevarication.

She, being ignorant of what had pass'd, when the same Questions were put to her, as had been before to her Husband, innocently answered, That she was *his dearly beloved Wife.*

The King, highly incensed at this Double-Dealing, and being, besides, desirous and impatient to gratify his lustful Inclinations (for the uncommon Charms of the amiable *Sarah*, had extremely raised his Appetite) he sent for *Abraham*, and, in a great Rage, asked him; How he had dared to have the Presumption, to tell him such Falsehoods to his Face? *Abraham* replied, " My Lord, I have told you no Falsehood, God forbid " I ever should be guilty of that Sin. If I said this " Woman is my Sister, it is Truth, for she is my " Cousin-Germain by Blood, which, in our (*a*) Law, is " allowable to be termed a Sister.

(*a*) The *Moors* and *Arabs* more frequently call those who are so nearly related to them as Cousin-Germain, *Khoyz* and *Hokhte*, that is, Brother and Sister, than they call them *Ben*, and *Ben't Amme*, which signifies Cousin of either Sex; yet, notwithstanding, they always chuse to intermarry in that Degree of Consanguinity, much rather than with Strangers, except some Inconveniency or Dislike put an Obstacle.

This

This reafonable Anfwer had no Manner of Influence upon the King; but he caus'd *Abraham*, for his malicious prevaricating Dealing (as he called it) to be hurry'd to Prifon, and ordered *Sarah* to be conducted into his rich and magnificent Bed-Chamber, in order to fatisfy his amorous Defires; for his luftful Heart was ftrangely captivated with her Beauty. So this charming, lovely Creature (whofe Face was brighter than the Day, and out-fhone the Moon) was carry'd away, and laid upon a fine Couch, in the private Appartment of that libidinous Prince.

In the mean while, 'tis worthy our Confideration, to guefs, what Tortures the good *Abraham* muft feel, to fee his dear Spoufe, who was dearer to him than his own felf, led away from him, to the Intent he might well imagine. The Pangs of Jealoufy he felt were fo violent, and caft him into fuch an Agony, that he had almoft render'd up his Soul with innumerable Sighs and convulfive Sobs. Under this Affliction, addreffing himfelf to his Creator in an humble Pofture, he utter'd thefe Words; " O King of the Heavens! " Look down upon the Sufferings of my tortur'd " Soul! This Tyrant's infernal Fury is more grie- " vous to me than the Bitternefs of the moft cruel " Death! It is Thou, O Lord, who removeft the Ago- " nies and Anxieties from thofe Hearts which are " overwhelmed with Sorrow!

Whilft *Abraham* underwent this fevere Tryal, the Lafcivious King haften'd to the Appartment where he had caufed *Sarah* to be convey'd, and where fhe had been all the while weeping and lamenting, and with her Soul full of Anguifh, imploring God's Affiftance to deliver her from the furious Tranfports of *Agar's* Luft. The Lord heard thefe her Petitions; for the King no fooner approach'd, and had laid hold of her to take her in his Arms, but his Limbs and whole Body were fuddenly feized with a ftrange Numb- nefs and Infenfibility, and he became intirely Cold, Unactive, and, in a Word, wholly Impotent.

I   Upon

Upon this he began to be fenfible of his Error, and fent immediately to fetch *Abraham* out of the Dungeon he had put him in, and where the Holy Patriarch had endur'd fuch Agonies: Being brought before him, he, with great Humility, Refignation and Contrition, intreated him to forgive the Injury he had offer'd him, and to implore his Lord to grant him his Life, and the Recovery of his Health. This the Good and Pious *Abraham* willingly complied with; and through his Means, and at his Interceffion, the King was perfectly reftored to his priftine State of Health and Strength, and the vertuous *Sarah* remain'd without Blemifh, free, pure, and unpolluted, and the King very thankful, and full of Acknowledgement for his great and miraculous Deliverance; offering, intreating, nay, commanding them, that they fhould ufe his Palace and his whole Dominions, as their own, into whatfoever Part of them they fhould pafs in their Journey; ftrictly enjoyning them, to make no manner of Difference between what he was poffeffed of, and what belong'd to themfelves. They kifs'd his Hands for the Favours he fo generoufly offer'd them, but begg'd he would give them Leave to proceed on their Journey without further Detention, feeing their Affairs required the greateft Expedition.

The few Days they continued with King *Agar*, they were ferv'd and entertain'd with all imaginable Magnificence, Gallantry and Deference, paffing their Time in Mirth and Rejoycing. This King had an only Daughter, whofe Name was (*a*) *Hechera* [rather *Hegira* or *Hegiar*] a moft beautiful, and accomplifh'd

---

(*a*) *Hagar.* Her Name amongft the *Arabs* is *Hagiar* or rather *Hegiar*, with the foft Afpiration *He*; whereas the *Ha* is the harfh One. 'Tis not this Author alone, but all *Mahometans* in general, pretend, That, far from being *Abraham*'s Concubine, or a Bond-Woman, fhe was his lawful Wife, and of Royal Defcent; and fo, by Confequence, her Son *Ifhmael*, both by his Elder-fhip, and by the Nobility of his Mother,

pliſh'd Young Lady, in the firſt Bloom of her Youth, and preſumptive Heireſs to his Crown, and all his Dominions. This Princeſs, enamour'd and charm'd with the endearing Converſation of *Sarah*, and being beſides touch'd with the great Zeal and Piety ſhe obſerv'd in *Abraham*, went to the King her Father, and falling down upon her Knees before him, with a moſt dutiful Humility and Reſignation, ſaid to him; " My Lord and Father! I intreat your Ma-
" jeſty, that one Favour your *Loving* and *Beloved*
" Daughter is come to petition you for, may be
" granted her, and not be denied: It is, That you
" will be pleaſed to give me your Permiſſion, that
" I may go into *Arabia the Happy*, in Company of
" the amiable *Sarah*, and the righteous *Abraham*:
" If I go in the Keeping and under the Protection of
" thoſe *Juſt* Perſons who follow the Path of God,
" it is impoſſible I ſhould err, or do amiſs. For it

Mother, was much ſuperior to his Brother *Iſaac*: For which Conſideration, he had the whole Peninſula of *Arabia* for his Inheritance, which is vaſtly Larger and Richer than *Paleſtine*, or the Land of *Canaan*, which was the Inheritance of the Younger Son of *Abraham*. *Hagar*, they ſay, died at *Mecca*, and was buried within the outward Incloſure of the *Caabah*, or Square Chapel, which Incloſure, or Wall, the *Arabs* call *Hathim*.——Though I ought to have mention'd the Place of her Birth, before that of her Burial, yet moſt of their Men of Letters affirm, That ſhe was born at the City of *Farma* in *Ægypt*, where the Kings of that Country kept their Court in *Abraham*'s Days, it being at that Time, the Capital: And *Abou Mawas*, in his Account of a Journey he took out of *Syria* into *Ægypt*, ſays, That he paſs'd through the Cities of *Gaza* of *Haſhem*, or the *Haſhemites*, which is *Gaza* in *Syria*, and *Farma* of *Hagiar*, or *Hagar*. Another *Arabian* Author, named *Ben Khalecan*, ſays the ſame, and adds, That this Mother of the *Arabs* is own'd by all the Tribes thereabouts, to have been born in that Capital, or in ſome Village near it. This City has, in Proceſs of Time, been ſo intirely deſtroy'd, that nothing now remains of it, but a ſmall Hill raiſed out of its Ruins, on the Left Hand, as the Caravans croſs over the Sands of *Cſſir*, in their Way from *Grand Cairo* into *Syria*. Their Hiſtories ſay, That this City *Farma*, was deſtroyed by *Baldwin*, the Brother of *Godfrey* of *Bouillon*, King of *Jeruſalem*. This *Baldwin* they call *Bardail*.

" is

" is my firm Refolution to defift from all Thoughts
" of inheriting the Empire ; From this Hour I renounce
" all Claim or Right to it, with all its Pomp and
" Majefty ; it being my Intent to feek the Heavenly
" Crown, the Throne whereof is Everlafting and
" Eternal: And as this my Requeft is equitable, juft
" and fincere, and my Petition is well grounded, I
" befeech you to be no Hindrance to me therein;
" but I rather confide in your Bounty, that you will
" be affifting to me in what I fo ingenuoufly defire,
" and earneftly requeft.

" O unheard-of Requeft! O pure and holy Incli-
" nation! O divinely infpir'd Breaft! Sincere and
" Praife-worthy Determination! Such a laudable Re-
" folution or Intent as this, has never yet been feen
" or heard of by any Mortal in this World, fo fin-
" ful and full of Vanity! how pioufly foever they
" might, otherwife, have been inclin'd. Thofe who
" have prevail'd upon themfelves to relinquifh and
" abandon their Worldly Pleafures, to betake them-
" felves to a folitary, recluse and retired Life, and
" to pafs the remaining Part of their Days in Aufte-
" rities and Devotion, have been look'd upon as
" Saints, and their fo doing, has been thought exceed-
" ing meritorious ; but that has feldom or never hap-
" pen'd, but to thofe whofe advanc'd Years began
" to call them on apace to leave the World and its
" Vanities, *for good and all*, and had left them unfit
" for the debauch'd and irregular Courfes, and the
" lewd Company they were wont to keep in their
" unbridled and *irreligious* Youth: Then indeed,
" call'd upon by the Stings of their Confciences for
" their paft Tranfgreffions, and difturb'd at their hav-
" ing led fuch diffolute Lives, they have determin'd
" to put a Stop to fuch Enormities, by retiring to
" fome folitary Hermitage. —— Thofe others, who, at
" the Expence of their Blood, and Hazard of their
" Lives, have magnanimoufly deliver'd their Coun-
" tries

" tries from Ruin and Deſtruction, have, in reality,
" been very worthy of Commendation; yet, I dare
" affirm, They had ſcarce ventur'd themſelves ſo far,
" had they not ſeen Death ſo near them, and already
" enter'd within their very Towns; ſo that they were
" forcibly compell'd, either to die, or gloriouſly to
" free themſelves: This it was that ſet them on, and
" inſpir'd them with Courage and Intrepidity; with
" the View, rather, of ſignalizing themſelves, and
" making their Names Famous to Futurity, than of
" obtaining Eternal Life. That ever great and memo-
" rable Matron *Judith,* when ſhe beheld her native
" City conquer'd, and deliver'd up into the Power
" of the *Aſſyrians,* and herſelf, as well as the reſt,
" liable to the Indignities and Outrages of an inſolent
" and imperious Conqueror, reſolutely went out
" into the Midſt of the Enemies Camp, and there
" depriv'd the Great Captain *Holophernes* of his
" Life, whereby ſhe gloriouſly obtained her own Li-
" berty, together with an unblemiſh'd Character,
" and by the ſame noble and heroick Action, freed
" her dear Country. But, notwithſtanding this moſt
" generous Deed of hers deſerves a never-dying Glory,
" and the higheſt Commendations, yet there was a for-
" cible Obligation of doing it. But the Heroine
" I now treat of, who was at the Fountain-Head of
" Happineſs, beautiful to Exceſs, in her tendereſt
" Bloom, and, more than all that, Heireſs to a mighty
" Empire, abounding in Wealth, and powerful in
" Vaſſals; Allurements, which are wont to attract the
" Minds even of the moſt Bigotted; For Her to be ſo
" marvellouſly inſpir'd with *Divine Love,* as to deter-
" mine, for the ſake thereof, to abandon her Father,
" and to relinquiſh her Country, Birth-right, Wealth
" and Inheritance, her Pomp, Ornaments and De-
" lights, to follow the pious Zeal of a Couple of
" poor Wanderers, is an Action without Example or
" Precedent. ————Well, O moſt illuſtrious and
" matchleſs Princeſs! Well doſt thou merit the *Name*

" (a) thou

" (*a*) thou art called by, ſince, O Zealous Princeſs!
" Thou haſt been thought worthy to be the elected
" Source and Fountain, through which the glorious
" and refulgent *Light* was to be conveyed.

Now when *Agar* had heard, and thoroughly conſidered, his Daughter's juſt and reaſonable Requeſt,
he thought ſo laudable a Propoſal and Reſolution
highly deſerved a favourable Anſwer; ſo that, without
Heſitation, he not only willingly gave his Conſent
to all ſhe aſk'd, but that very Day renounc'd his
Idolatry and Falſe Belief, and embrac'd *Iſlamiſm*, the
true Faith that leads to Salvation; and after having
beſtow'd many rich and noble Preſents upon them all
Three, he ſuffered them to depart in purſuit of their
intended Journey, which they did without Loſs of
Time: And, in a few Days, they arrived within Sight
of the Confines of *Arabia*, where they, with great
Devotion and Humility, returned infinite and joyful
Thankſgivings to God their Creator for that Mercy.
But when the Lord was pleaſed to conduct them to
that Holy Station, which was appointed for their
Journey's-End, they there ſet down their Baggage
to take ſome Repoſe, in Expectation of freſh Orders
from the Almighty concerning what was next to be
done, and in what Method they were to proceed in
the important Affair which was to be put in Execution.

Abraham with *Sarah* his Wife made their Abode
in *Arabia* many Years, having the Princeſs *Hagar* continually in their Company, where they led their Lives
very comfortably, and with an exemplary Sanctity
and Piety: But when *Sarah* beheld her-ſelf to advance
apace in Years, and ſeeing ſhe had bore her Huſband
no Children in all the Time they had been together,

(*a*) *Hagar* is by ſome called, *Omm el Arab*, or, The Mother of the
Arabs; but many hold their Original to be of an ancienter Date.

ſhe

ſhe began to deſpair of ever having any, and was very urgent in her Intreaties to *Abraham*, that he would take the Princeſs *Hagar* to Wife, (who had accompanyed them out of *Ægypt*) that the Lord might be pleaſed to vouchſafe him a lawful Succeſſor through her Means ; which Bleſſing there was little or no Probability he could ever expect to enjoy from herſelf.

This Propoſal of *Sarah*'s was received by her Huſband with a great deal of Lukewarmneſs and Indifference, and he remain'd, for ſome Time, irreſolute and undetermin'd what he ſhould do in this Caſe, or whether he ſhould embrace or reject the Counſel his Wife had given him : But while he was thus wavering in his Mind, the Angel *Gabriel* deſcended from Heaven, and brought him expreſs Commands, That he ſhould, without Delay, cónſummate what *Sarah* had propoſed to him ; That the Lord had decreed it ſhould be ſo ; That He had promiſed to pour down His Benediction upon them ; and that they ſhould partake of His Grace in Abundance.

Abraham obey'd God's Command, and that ſame Day the Marriage was celebrated, according to the Directions of the Angel ; and, in a little Time after, the Bride perceived herſelf to be with Child, and the *Hereditary Light,* which ſhined on *Abraham*'s Forehead (and, by God's Promiſe, to be center'd in *Mohammed*) paſſed away from him to the beautiful Princeſs ; ſo that her Countenance became as bright as the (*a*) Moon when at the Full, and in its greateſt Glory.

(*a*) This may ſound to ſome Ears, an odd Sort of a Compariſon ; but I can aſſure them, that no Compliment can be paſs'd upon a *Mahometan* Lady, that will be more pleaſing to her, than to call her, *Widg el Camar,* or *Moon's Face*; eſpecially if the Gallant who makes it her, adds, *When 'tis Fourteen Days old.*

At Nine Months End ſhe was deliver'd of a Son, as beautiful as the Morning-Star, and the Name they gave him was (a) *Iſhmael.* · He was born with that reſplendent and royal *Banner* of *Light* upon his Forehead, which he inherited from our firſt Father, and was ordain'd to deſcend gradually, 'till it finally fixed itſelf upon *Mohammed.*

(a) The *Mahometans* in general, tell the Story of this *Iſhmael* the Son of *Abraham* by *Hagar*, as our Scriptures do that of *Iſaac* the Son of *Sarah*; only add, That the Place where he was to have been ſacrificed, was the very ſame where *Abraham* and *Iſhmael* afterwards built the *Caabah*, the Square Chapel, which is within the Temple at *Mecca*, and which has ſince aſſumed the Holy Title of *Beit Alah*, God's Houſe, and the City itſelf is called *Mecca el Moadhemah*, i. e. Magnificent. My Author, as may be ſeen in ſome of the following Pages, ſays, the Sacrifice was performed upon the Top of a Mountain, whereas the City of *Mecca*, and, conſequently, the Temple, is ſituated in a Plain between Mountains : It has Two, at three Miles diſtance on the North, the Name of the one is *Abou Cau*, and the other *Gerabim*, in which is *Eve*'s Cave, where *Mahomet* uſed to retire, and paſs his Time in Contemplation, before he publickly ſet up for a Prophet : This Cave is held in high Veneration by all his Followers. Beſides thoſe Two Mountains on the North, there is another on the South called *Thout*, where the Impoſtor hid himſelf when he fled from *Mecca* to *Jathrib* or *Medina* ; of which more in other Places. ——This *Iſhmael* is looked on by the *Arabs*; to have been the firſt Father and Founder of their Nation and Language, though, in Reality, their firſt Original is from *Cathan*, or *Joctan* the Son of *Heber*. They ſay, he lived One hundred Thirty Seven Years, and that he and his younger Brother *Iſaac*, ſpread *Iſlamiſm*, or the True Religion, throughout *Arabia* and the Land of *Canaan* The Affinity or Reſemblance between the Words *Iſlamiſm* and *Iſmaeliſm* (though in their Language they have no Words with that Termination, which to them would ſound intirely barbarous) is ſuppoſed by many, to have been the Reaſon, that ſeveral of the *Mahometan* Doctors have confounded them, and maintain, That the Religion *Mahomet* taught his Followers, is the ſame which *Iſhmael* preach'd to the *Arabs*. —— The *Iſhmaelites* or Race of *Iſhmael*, whom ſome Authors will not allow to be pure *Arabs*, but mixt, had, at the Beginning, much Contention with the *Giorhamides*, ancienter Inhabitants of *Arabia* than themſelves, about the Temple at *Mecca* ; but at laſt, theſe two Races, uniting by Alliances, became for the future but one Nation.

Abraham

Abraham was tranfported with Joy at this fo fignal a Bleffing, infomuch that he pafs'd whole Days and Nights in Thankfgiving, and in praifing the Name of the Lord of Heaven. But, as Human Minds are fo corrupted, fo full of Envy and Malice ever fince that fatal Moment in which the Accurfed Angel fell from his glorious Station in Paradife, and this unhappy *Seed of Difcord* has fo univerfally fpread itfelf through all the World, that no Part thereof is free from that *pernicious Legacy*; it came to have fo great an Influence upon the Hearts of *Hagar* and *Sarah*, as to difturb and break off that Union and Amity, which had hitherto, for fo many Years, been cultivated between them ; For they now began to hate one another as much as they had lov'd before : There was now nothing but Quarrels, Difputes, Differences, and Difcontent between them ; fo great an Effect had the Contagion of Difcord to deftroy and diffipate that priftine Content and Unanimity they once enjoy'd. I am not able to determine whether or no it proceeded from *Sarah*'s being jealous at the exceeding great Joy and Satisfaction the Princefs had conceived at her being bleft with fo ineftimable a Jewel as fuch a Son as *Ifhmael* ; or whether that the Princefs herfelf was not fomewhat elevated with the Thoughts of her being the Mother of that Son, and fo endeavour'd at a Superiority over *Sarah* upon that Account ; as likewife feeing that *Abraham* had fo great a Value for her, and treated her with fuch extreme Fondnefs and Tendernefs. It probably feems to be from one or both of thefe Caufes, that the Hatred and Enmity between the Pofterity of the two Sons of *Abraham* had its Original Source, which they fuck'd in with their firft Milk, and which continues even to this Day, as is obvious to be feen : The like happen'd to *Rachel*, with her own Sifter *Leah* ; for the Malice of her Sons againft thofe of *Rachel*, proceeded from the Envy and Jealoufy between their Mothers.

The

The good Patriarch, obſerving all theſe Diſquiets, reſolved, to avoid thoſe Confuſions, and to make his Life eaſy, that they ſhould be ſeparated; and to that Purpoſe he took the Princeſs and her Son, and conveyed them out of the Way into an uninhabited Mountain; where, leaving with them what Proviſions he had brought with him, he took his Leave of them, and return'd to his Houſe; but very melancholy, and exceedingly troubled in Mind.

In the mean while, *Hagar* and her beloved Child, being left in that ſolitary Mountain, were brought to ſuch Extremity for want of Food, that they were forc'd to eat the wild Plants and Roots of the Earth, becauſe, for ſeveral Days, the Holy Patriarch, had neglected to carry them any Proviſion: *For it is a common Thing, too eaſily to forget thoſe who are in Neceſſity, even by the beſt and moſt vigilant Perſons !* They were, at laſt, ſo oppreſſed with Hunger and Thirſt, and brought to ſo low a Condition, that the poor Infant could no longer go nor ſtand, nor had his Mother ſcarce any Life left in her.

The diſconſolate Princeſs, overwhelm'd with Grief and Affliction, and no longer able to bear ſo ſhocking an Object, left the Child, in that miſerable and languiſhing Condition, behind a Rock, and went up to the Top of the Mountain, and there proſtrated herſelf before the Lord, glorifying his Holy Name, who had been pleaſed ſhe ſhould undergo all that Extremity of Sorrow.

When ſhe had continued there in earneſt Devotion, 'till ſhe thought ſhe might reaſonably conjecture that her dear and deſtitute Child had render'd up its Soul to the Creator, ſhe return'd to the Place where ſhe had left him, in order to be ſatisfied; Where, inſtead of finding him pined away and dead, as ſhe apprehended, ſhe beheld him ſitting, with a briſk and lively Countenance, at the

Brink

Brink of a delicious Spring, with great Abundance of refreshing and choice Viands placed all round about him.

This Mountain is the same which is called (*a*) *Zimzim* ; and that ever-famous Well, which is constantly visited, and held in such high Veneration by all the *Haggis*, or Pilgrims, is called by the Name of *Zimzim.*

Do

(*a*) This *Zimzim*, or *Zemzem*, is the Name of a famous Well near *Mecca*, mightily reforted to by the *Mahometan* Pilgrims, and by all of that Sect in general, held in great Efteem. *Khondemir* gives the following Account of it. The *Giorhamides*, an ancient Tribe of *Arabs*, inhabiting *Arabia Felix*, were the firft that met *Hagar* or *Hegiar* wandering in the Defart, and they, by the Flight of Birds, difcover'd where that wonderful Spring was, and therefore they pretended, that both the Well and the Country round about it, of Right, belonged to them : But *Abraham* coming to vifit *Ifhmael*, and having built the Chapel or Temple called *Caabah*, or the *Square Houfe*, he gave that and all the Territory about it, which was afterwards named *Of Mecca*, to his Son *Ifhmael*. The eldeft Son of *Ifhmael*, whofe Name was *Thabeth*, made good his Poffeffion of thofe Places ; but leaving his Children under Age, *Madhabd ben Amrou*, their Grandfather by the Mother's fide, took Charge of their Education, and at the fame Time, made himfelf Mafter of the *Caabah*, and of the holy Well *Zemzem*. *Thabeth's* Children being grown up, would not contend with their Grandfather *Madhabd* for the Poffeffion of thofe Places, fo that they remain'd to him and his Children after him, 'till the *Giorhamides* took them by Force ; but *Ifhmael's* Pofterity attacking them, they were overthrown, and obliged to quit the Temple and the City *Mecca*, which was built by Degrees by the Concourfe of People, and they caft the *Black Stone* (of which more in another Place) which is fo highly honoured in that Temple, with the two Goats of beaten Gold, prefented to the Temple by a King of *Arabia*, into the Well of *Zemzem*, which they quite ftopp'd up. The Well continued thus filled up, 'till the Days of *Abdelmothleb*, Grandfather to *Mahomet*, who one Day, heard a Voice, which faid to him ; *Dig the Well of* Zemzem. He asked the Voice, *What* Zemzem *was?* The fame Voice replyed ; *It was a Spring that rofe under the Feet of* Ifhmael, *of which he and his ufed to drink.* *Abdelmothleb* ftill ignorant were this Well was, the fame Voice continued, faying ; *The Well* Zemzem *is near the two Idols of the* Koraifhites, *which are called* Affaf *and* Nailah ; *and exactly where*

Do but confider within yourſelves, the inexpreſſible Joy and Satisfaction this Princeſs muſt conceive, to find her Son, whom ſhe thought had periſhed for Want, thus plentifully and providentially

---

where you ſhall ſee a Magpie *peck the Ground, and diſcover an* Ants Neſt, *there you muſt dig.* Abdelmothleb, not doubting but the Voice came from Heaven, went about to obey it; and notwithſtanding great Oppoſition from the *Koraiſhites,* who would keep up their Idols in that Place, he prevailed, and dug the Well. When the Work was done, the *Koraiſhites* demanded Part of the Treaſure he had found therein, which was refuſed them by *Abdelmothleb,* alledging, that it belong'd to the Holy Houſe, that is, the Temple called *Caabah,* built by *Abraham* and *Iſhmael.* To decide this Controverſy, they agreed to repair to a famous Soothſayer, call'd *Ebn Saed,* who lived on the Borders of *Syria,* and was by the *Arabs* accounted a great Prophet, ſo that they generally made Choice of him to decide all their difficult Queſtions. They ſet out towards *Syria,* and, by the Way, the Heat was ſo exceſſive, that *Abdelmothleb,* being extremely thirſty, was forced to aſk ſome Water of the *Koraiſhites,* who, fearing they might want themſelves, refuſed it him. *Abdelmothleb,* in this Extremity, had Thoughts of leaving them to ſeek for Water elſewhere, when a plentiful clear Spring guſh'd out from under one of his Camel's Feet, which not only abundantly furniſhed him and his, but ſerv'd alſo the *Koraiſhites,* who had before deny'd him a Draught. They, moved by this Miracle, would not proceed any farther to ſeek after the Soothſayer, but ſubmitted themſelves to *Abdelmothleb,* looking on him as a Perſon particularly favoured by God. In ſhort, he was a Man ſo intirely devoted to God's Service, that he had made a Vow to ſacrifice one of his Children, in caſe he had Ten, to imitate *Abraham,* from whom he was lineally deſcended by his Son *Iſhmael.* At length, *Zemzem* was dug and cleanſed, and *Abdelmothleb* gave to the Temple of *Caabah* the two Golden Goats, and all the Money he cou'd make of the Arms and other Accoutrements he had found in the Well; and the Vow he had made of Sacrificing one of his Children, was, by the Lord's Appointment, chang'd into a Number of Sheep, which were ſlaughterd at the new Dedication, as we may ſay, of the famous Temple of *Mecca.* The City of *Mecca* had, for a long Time, no other Water but that of the Well of *Zemzem,* 'till the great Reſort of Caravans thither obliged the Caliphs to build an Aquaduct, which now furniſhes Abundance of Water to all Comers. *Mahomet,* to make the City of *Mecca,* where he was born, more conſiderable, to heighten the Devotion of the People, and to
draw

ally supply'd with Cœlestial Nourishment! And this Joy and Amazement was increased, when, immediately after, she saw the *faithful* Angel *Gabriel* descend to them, inspiring them both with Courage, bidding them to fear nothing, and bringing the happy Tidings, that God would certainly bless, and provide for them.

After all these Things had happen'd, as I have declared, when in Process of Time *Ishmael* was grown up to be a fine Youth, and *Abraham*'s Affairs were all at Quiet, he leading a contented Life, the Angel *Gabriel* came down once more, and drew out the Plan, and Circumference for the Foundation of the Holy Temple, after the Model, and on the same Spot of Ground, where the Almighty had designed that the Sacred Fabrick should be erected.

The Ground was marked out in four Sides, the two (a) longest of which measured one hundred and forty Feet, but the Breadth was only forty: And to

---

draw more Pilgrims thither, made great Elogies upon the Water of this Well; for there is a Tradition deliver'd from him by the *Caliph Omar*, That the Water of the Well of *Zemzem* is a Sovereign Remedy, and restores to Health him who drinks thereof; and that he who drinks of it in Abundance, and quenches his Thirst therewith, obtains Pardon for all his Sins. —— This Water is preserv'd in Bottles by the Pilgrims, and brought very often some thousands of Miles to present to their Friends, as the most acceptable Present they can make them. They affirm, That they who drink of it with Devotion, and an implicite Faith, shall be blessed with a vast Strength of Memory; and a great Doctor among them formerly, whose Name was *El Hafedth*, and famous for his prodigious Memory in quoting Traditions, as the Name implies, obtain'd that Blessing through the Virtue of that Water. *D'Herbelot.*

(a) Sure my Author is here mistaken in his Measuring; for *Edrissi*, in his Geography, writes, That the *Caabah* or Square Chapel which is in the Temple at *Mecca*, is, on the Sides from East to West, twenty four Cubits long, and from North to

to the End that this Work might be compleated with-out Labour, the bleffed Angel taught *Abraham* fome Words (he fays *four Words*) to repeat, by the Virtue whereof the Holy Edifice was accomplifhed.

Ifhmael was prefent in Company with his Father at whatever was tranfacted upon that Occafion, as one who might juftly lay Claim and Pretenfion of being a principal Sharer in a Work of that Nature.

When all was finifhed, the Angel faid to *Abra-ham* ; " You are now to be informed and to take
" Notice, that this Fabrick is erected as the Mo-
" del, and in Imitation of Seven others which are
" in Heaven, and that this alone fhall furpafs in
" Excellency thofe Cœleftial ones all together ;
" fince this is defign'd for the Station, the Refidence
" of the *Seal of Pardon* and Remiffion of Sins, and
" is appointed to be the Seat and Manfion of the
" moft *elected Lineage* that ever has been, or ever
" fhall be created upon the Face of the Earth, who
" are to publifh, expand and propagate the *chofen*
" and *divine* Law of God. This venerable Manfion
" fhall be reforted to, and vifited by the Flower of
" thofe People who excel all other Nations in the

---

to South, it is 23 Cubits in Breadth, the Gate is at the Eaft-End, and the Threfhold of it is about 4 Cubits above the Ground ; fo that there being no Steps to go up to it, thofe that come to pray there lean their Foreheads againft it: At the Corner of it is the *Black Stone* which is held in fuch high Veneration by all *Muffulmans.* The *Caabah* is twenty feven Cubits high ; its firft Roof is not expofed to the Weather, there being another over it for the Rain to fall on. The ancient *Arabs* were wont to cover the Outfides of this Temple with the Works of their beft Poets, wrought upon Silk in Letters of Gold ; and now the *Mahometans* cover the firft Roof, and the Walls, with the richeft Silks and Cloth of Gold, formerly provided by the Caliphs and Sultans of *Ægypt,* and now by the *Ottoman* Emperor. —— The Cover-ing which is now fent every Year from *Conftantinople,* I have been often inform'd by credible Eye-Witneffes, is of Green Vel-vet richly embroider'd. —— This *Caab. b* they call *Beit Allah,* or God's Houfe : Some of their Writers fay, it was not built 'till after *Hagar's* Death.

" World

" World for Nobility ; and who, as they hold the
" firſt Rank upon Earth, are likewiſe the moſt
" regarded in Heaven."

When *Gabriel* had ſaid theſe Words, he departed ;
and *Abraham* began and went on with this pious
Undertaking, as to what concerned that meritorious Work, being continually accompanied with
Iſhmael his Son. He omitted nothing of what he
had been enjoyn'd by the Angel, ſo that the ſanctified Space of Ground which had been mark'd out,
having had the Foundation laid, was ſoon encom-
paſſed with ſtrong and beautiful Walls, and, in fine,
compleatly finiſhed : At which, *Abraham* (as
well he might) being well pleaſed, and full of
Joy, made this ſhort Prayer to the Lord his
God ; (*a*)

" Accept

(*a*) I find theſe Lines in *D' Herbelot*, under the Name *Abraham*, which, becauſe they mention ſomething of this Prayer of
Abraham, may, perhaps, be neither impertinent to the preſent
Purpoſe, nor unacceptable to the curious Reader. " One of the
" principal Fictions the *Mahometans* have concerning *Abraham*,
" is this that follows. — In that Chapter of the *Alcoran*, which
" bears the Title of *Abraham*, that Patriarch prays to God
" thus ; *Lord! make this Land free, and grant, that neither I, nor
" my Son, may ever worſhip Idols.*" The Country here meant, is
the Territory of *Mecca*, which ſtill enjoys perfect Freedom ;
for it is not lawful to put any Man to Death therein, nor to
hunt any Beaſt, or ſhoot Birds. Some of the Interpreters will
have it, that *Abraham's* Prayer was fully heard, becauſe that
neither *Iſhmael*, nor any of his Race, ever adored Idols ; but in
this Point, they diſagree, others holding them to be abſolute
Idolaters. In the Sequel of the ſame Chapter, *Abraham* ſays to
God, *Lord! Thou haſt placed one of my Sons in a barren Valley, near
thy Holy Houſe.* Upon thoſe Words, the Interpreters ſpeak
thus ; " *Sarah*, Wife to *Abraham*, not being able to endure
" *Hagar* or her Son *Iſhmael* in *Paleſtine*, uſed many Intreaties
" with *Abraham* to ſend them into a deſart Country where
" there was no Water. *Abraham* was mightily concern'd at this
" Propoſal, but *Gabriel* the Archangel bid him do as *Sarah*
" deſired ; and at the ſame Time he tranſported the Mother
" and the Son to the Country of *Mecca*, which was barren
" and without Water, where the Angel made a Spring to
guſh

" Accept, O merciful and gracious Lord ! this
" Work, which I have brought to Perfection in Obe-
" dience to thy Command, and to Thee alone, and
" to thy Glory and Honour, it is dedicated. O
" Lord ! of thy infinite Mercy and Goodnefs, give us
" the Grace to become *Muffulmans* and true Belie-
" vers, and that our Nations and Pofterity may
" follow thy Path. Teach and inftruct them in
" their Duty, that they may be capable of ferv-
" ing and walking before thee, in the manner
" that thou willeft that all Creatures fhould do, in
" order to appear before thy Judgment-Seat. In-
" fpire their Hearts with a true and perfect Peni-
" tence; for we are not ignorant, that thou art al-
" ways ready to accept, receive, and reward a fin-
" cere Contrition and Repentance of our Tranf-
" greffions. Send down to them (I mean, to us
" and our Pofterity and Tribe) *Prophets* and *Mef-*
" *fengers* from among themfelves, and out of their
" own Tribes, who may inftruct them in the My-
" fteries of thy moft Holy and Divine Law, and
" may teach and difclofe to them the *Arcana* of
" thy facred Scripture. Cleanfe and purify their
" Souls, that under thy Almighty Protection they
" may live and enjoy the Life Eternal and Ever-

" out under *Ifhmael's* Feet, which was the only Water in the
" Country about, and is a very famous Well among the *Ma-*
" *hometans,* called *Zemzem,* &c. The Temple of *Mecca* was
" not then built ; but there was in the fame Place, a great
" Structure, called *Sorah,* after the Manner of a Temple which
" had been there ever fince *Adam's* Days, if we will give
" Credit to the *Mahometan* Traditions. That Antiquity ren-
" der'd it venerable, and it was reforted to by all the People
" of the Country, who would ask any Mercy or Favour from
" God. *Abraham* pray'd to God, *That the Place might be Peo-*
" *pled, and produce abundantly the Fruits of the Earth.* His Prayer
" was heard, for the Tribe of *Giorham* came and fettled
" there; and there are now found at *Mecca,* Fruits belonging
" to the four Seafons of the Year, all at once, and in great
" Plenty.

" lafting;

" lafting ; for thou art Gracious and Bountiful in
" all thy Doings, and thy Knowledge is infinite.
" I implore, O Lord ! thy Bleffing and Protection
" for this City, that thou wouldeft vouchfafe to
" guard and defend it from the evil Wifhers and
" Enemies thereof. Grant thy Benediction to the
" Fruits and Seeds of the Earth, that they may mul-
" tiply and bring forth for the Ufe and Nourifh-
" ment of Mankind ; I mean, of thofe who know
" and acknowledge thee, by maintaining the Truth
" of thy Divinity : But thofe, O Lord ! who
" do not ferve nor believe in thee, let them be
" confounded, and caft into endlefs Torments. *Amen.*

This glorious Fabrick, when it was intirely compleated, the Walls and Roof thereof appeared as
fhining and as beautiful as the Sun. (a)

(a) As to the Defcription of the *Caabib,* fee the Note a little
before, where I have faid fomething to that Purpofe. Temples
are by the *Arabians,* fince *Mahomet's* Days, called *Juamma,*
i. e. Places of Congregation ; but more properly, *Mefged,* from
which Word, the *Spaniards* corruptly write *Mefquita,* and the
French from them *Mofquée,* and we *Mofque.* The two moft
venerable Temples among the *Muffulmans,* are, this at *Mecca,*
which is the chief and principal one, and by way of Excellency has (added to its other Titles) the Name of *Mefged el
Haram,* or the facred Temple, and that at *Medina,* which
Mahomet caufed to be built when he fled thither (See Dr.
Prideaux L. Mah. p. 41, &c) called *Mefged el Nabi,* or the Prophet's
Temple ; in this he preach'd, pray'd and was buried. This
is generally vifited by the *Mahometan* Pilgrims after they have
been at the firft. Thefe are both together peculiarly called *Ha-
ramain,* the Two Sacred Places.

I have met with no Author who gives fuch accurate and impartial Accounts of the Pilgrimage to thefe Places, and of the
Places themfelves, as *Albertus Bobovius,* whofe Treatife is annexed to
the *English* Verfion of *Reland's* Mah Rel p. 125. *& feq,* and
Pits in his Hiftory of *Algiers* (to which Books I farther refer
the curious Readers) fince they were Eye Witneffes of what
they relate, and, in every Refpect, agree with all the Defcrip-
tions I have heard f o n feveral *Hagg*'s, or Pilgrims.

The

The *Grand Signior*, after all his lofty Titles, ftiles himfelf, The Servant of thefe Two Holy Places. —— In the fecond Chapter of the *Alcoran*, call.d *El Bacrah*, there are thefe Words ; *We have eftablifhed a Houfe or Temple to be the Means for Men to gain much Merit*; and farther on in the Chapter *Amran* ; *The firft Temple that was built for Man, is that of Beccah, which ferves for a Bleffing and Direction for me, and in which there are fuch evident and remarkable Signs.* The Expofitors fay, That *Beccah* is the fame as *Mecca* ; that the Bleffing here mentioned, is both Spiritual and Temporal ; that the Sight only of that Temple, is as meritorious as all the Devotions a Man could perform for a whole Year, in any other. The remarkable Signs in this Temple are, the *Meccam Ibrahim*, or *Abraham's* Station, and the *Sanctuary*. As for the firft, they affirm, That there is the Print of *Abraham's* Feet on the folid Stone; that this Impreffion is fo deep, it reaches up to a Man's Ancles ; and that it has been preferved fo many Ages, againft all the Attempts of the Idolaters, who endeavour'd to deface it. The other Sign is, its being an *Azile* for all Criminals, who cannot be taken out upon any Account, provided they are in the Temple; and Sinners receive there the full Remiffion of all their Sins.

These are the Authentick Traditions of thofe People.

CHAP.

e *Mahometans* call *Abraham Kha'il Allah*, i. e. God's Friend,
utely *El Khalil*, that is, The intimate and familiar Friend;
efore the City *Hebron*, where he was buried, is often, in

THE TEMPLE OF MECCA.

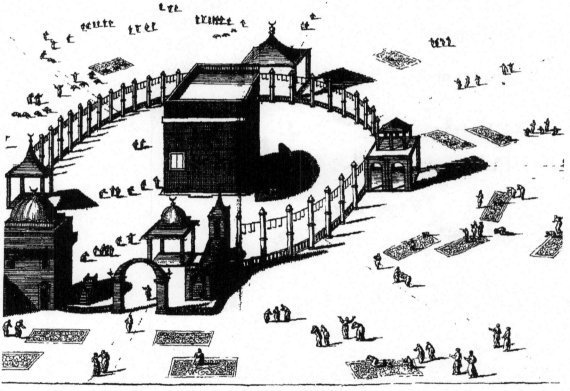

Hulett Sculp.

CHAP. VI.

The Angel Azarael, *surnamed* Malec el Maut, *or the Angel of Death, is sent to* Abraham, *with the News of his being elected for God's Friend. The Author's Reflections thereupon. That Angel describ'd. His Discourse with* Abraham, *and* Abraham's *Terror. His Humility and Resignation: With the Author's Encomiums upon that Subject.* Abraham's *Fear 'till the Angel was gone, and Joy at his Departure.*

S the Lord is so impartial, and His Justice so exact and great, that He never suffers any Crime to pass without Chastisement, nor any Deed of Piety or Goodness to be unrewarded; He, to recompence *Abraham* for his Uprightness and Integrity, and likewise, for his indefatigable Assiduity in serving Him, and observing His Holy Precepts, most graciously vouchsafed to elect him for his especial (*a*) *Friend*, which was the

K 2 most

(*a*) The *Mahometans* call *Abraham Khalil Allah, i. e.* God's Friend, and absolutely *El Khalil*, that is, The intimate and familiar Friend; and therefore the City *Hebron*, where he was buried, is often, in their

moſt eſtimable, and deſirable Grace and Favour
any Mortal, 'till that Time, ever had, or poſſibly
could enjoy ; and, for a Confirmation of this ineſtimable Election, the Almighty Lord of Lords commanded *El Malec el Maut,* or *The Angel of Death,* to
deſcend from Heaven with this joyful News, and to
deliver the Meſſage.

" O

---

their Books, called by that ſare Name. ——— Beſides the
Title *Abraham* has to this Name in Holy Writ, the *Muſſulmans* deduce another from theſe Words of the *A'coran,* in the
Chapter *Neſſa,* or of Women ; *God took* Abraham *for his Friend.*
Whereupon, the Expoſitors tell us how he came to obtain that
Favour of God, in the following Manner. ——— *Abraham,* as
appears by the Actions of his Life, being become the Refuge
and Father of all the Poor of the Country where he reſided,
and in a Time of Dearth, having emptied all his Granaries to
ſuſtain them, he was himſelf reduced to great Extremity of
Want, inſomuch, that for a Supply, he was obliged to ſend
his Servants, and Camels into *Ægypt,* to a Friend of his, who
was one of the principal Men in that Country, to procure him
Corn: But when that Friend underſtood what *Abraham's* Servants came about, he ſaid to them, *We are ourſelves in Fear
of a Famine in this Land ; and beſides, I am ſatisfied, that* Abraham *does not want Corn for his Family, but only for the Poor of
his Country ; and therefore, I do not think it reaſonable to ſend him
what ought to be kept for the Maintenance of our own Poor.* This
modeſt Refuſal was a great Concern to *Abraham's* People, who
were forc'd to return Empty ; and the more, when they were
near Home, fearing to be derided and laughed at by the Country People ; and therefore they filled their Sacks with very fine
white Sand they found in their Way. [In *Barbary* their fineſt
Flower or Meal very exactly reſembles that Sort of Sand.]
When they came to their Maſter, the chiefeſt of them whiſ-
per'd in his Ears how ill they had ſped, and *Abraham,* without
ſhewing the leaſt Concern, went into his Oratory to ſeek Comfort from God. *Sarah* his Wife was aſleep when the Camels
arrived, and knew nothing of what had happen'd ; ſo that ſeeing
the full Sacks when ſhe awaked, ſhe opened one of them, and
found therein very good Meal, with the which ſhe immediately
began to make Bread for the Poor. *Abraham* having perform'd
his Devotions, came out, and ſmelling the new Bread, ask'd
of *Sarah, What Meal ſhe had to make it of ?* Who reply'd, That
your Friend ſent you out of *Ægypt.* Nay, anſwered *Abraham,*
rather ſay, It was ſent me by the *True Friend,* which is God ;
for

" O unfathomable Mysteries! What Mortal is ca-
" pable of comprehending those mysterious and ob-
" scure Ænigma's which the Lord has shewed to
" Mankind in all Ages! To see that in all the Trou-
" bles, Persecutions, Afflictions, Calamities, Affronts,
" Indignities, Necessities, Imprisonments, and even
" Fire, which this Venerable Patriarch went through,
" his continual and inseparable Consolation, Fortress,
" and Defence, was the Holy Angel *Gabriel,* the
" Great *Comforter* in Affliction, and Time of Need;
" and that now, in order to rejoyce him with such
" glad and unprecedented Tydings, he should chuse
" the *Angel of Death,* to send the Message by; whose
" very Name is so terrible upon Earth, that the Ap-
" prehension of his Approach, deadens all our Content,
" and fills our Souls with Horror and Trembling, and
" makes a disagreeable Mixture of Bitter with all
" our Sweets; which, as they are only the Fruits
" and Product of this transitory World, no Autum-

---

for He never forsakes us in Time of Need. So that at this Time
Abraham called God his *Friend,* as God had taken him for *His.*

As much as the *Mahometans* extol this Prerogative of *Abraham's,*
they sometimes lessen it, out of a sort of Jealousy, saying, That
the Title of *Habib,* which they give their False Prophet, and signifies *Beloved Favourite,* is much greater than that of *Khalil,* which
is only a *Familiar Friend.* Thus they say, That *Abraham's* Friendship with God went no further than a Conformity to His Will in
any Condition; but *Mahomet's* Favour, was a State of perfect Charity, so that he had no Subsistance but in God. Yet, nevertheless,
they own, That the Stile of *God's Friend* is expresly given to *Abraham* in the Word of God, whereas, that of *God's Favourite,* given
to *Mahomet,* is only deducted by Inference, thus, *Mahomet* says in
the *Alcoran, Adhere to me, and God will cherish you.* Now, say they, *If
God cherishes those that Adhere to the Prophet, how much more will he cherish himself?* The *Mahometans* go yet further; for they say, That
Abraham only walked in the Lord's Ways, but *Mahomet* was rapt
and drawn away. These and more *Mahometan* impious Absurdities
are comprehended in one Distich by a *Persian* Poet, *Houssain Vaez,*
who says, That *Abraham* was but a great Officer in the Army of
God's Messenger, and the *Messiah* was the Master of the Ceremonies
in his Palace.

" nal

" nal Rays can poffibly have the Force or effica-
" cious Faculty of ripening and bringing them to Per-
" fection, or ever, intirely, to take away the abomi-
" nably naufeous and bitter Savour thereof: For it
" could never yet be found, that the Pleafures and
" Delights we enjoy in this World, were perfectly
" complete, but alloy'd with the Dregs of Aloes,
" Bitternefs and Difcontent; and all proceeding from
" the Terrors that Formidable Angel infpires our
" Souls withal.

This was *Abraham's* Cafe at that Juncture; for tho'
the Meffage he received, was the moft capable of filling a Soul with Joy, of *any* that had ever, 'till then,
been fent to Man; yet there was fomething fo great,
fo venerable, and indeed fo very fhocking and terrifying, in only the bare Name of the *Meffenger*, that
That alone was fufficient to damp his Joy, and to
make him quake with Fear.

But, that the Approach of this Dreadful *Meffenger*
might not have a fatal Effect on the Spirits of our Holy
Patriarch, God, of His incomprehenfible Bounty and
Clemency, was pleas'd to command *him* to affume a
moft glorious Form, and to appear before *Abraham*
with nothing able to ftrike Terror, but rather to in-
fufe a Thoufand Ecftatic Raptures.

In this Manner therefore the Strong and Mighty
Azaracl, departed from before the Throne of Glory:
The Form he had affum'd was fo exceedingly refplendent, that never any of the whole Cœleftial
Choir of Angels was before that Time known to appear under fo glorious a Figure, or fo fumptuoufly and
magnificently adorn'd. His Countenance was fo
fprightly, fo lovely, and fo ravifhingly glorious,
that he appear'd among the reft as furpaffingly beautiful as does a *Rofe* among other *Flowers*; and his Eyes,
in Brightnefs and Refulgency, refembled Two Suns:
His Garment was moft precioufly adorn'd with exceffive rich Embroidery and Flowers of Heavenly
Growth: His Tongue melodioufly fweet; and his
Speech

Speech engaging, perſuaſive, and eloquent, as if Honey
dropt from his Lips; and when he open'd thoſe graceful Lips to utter any Words, moſt exquiſite Perfumes,
and balmy, ſpicy Odours proceeded from his Mouth.
In a Word, he was ſo inexpreſſibly beautiful, and caſt
ſuch Splendor from him all around, that the whole Angelick Choir remain'd in Admiration.

Azarael, ſuch as I have deſcrib'd him, directed his
Steps towards *Abraham's* Habitation, and, without
any Ceremony, went in. However, he ſoon had
Notice of what ſort of a Gueſt he had got in his Appartment, by the uncommon Fragrancy of his Perfumes. He, who was the moſt jealous of all Men, beholding a Perſon of ſo extraordinary an Appearance
under his Roof, could not help being diſpleas'd, and
ſo, with great Concern and ſome Heat, ſaid to him;
" Tell me, I deſire you, Friend, what is your Buſi-
" neſs here? Or how came you into my Houſe with-
" out my Leave?" To which the *Angel of Death* reply'd; " The Owner of the Houſe ſent me hither, and
" likewiſe gave me Orders to come in, and ſo you are
" to blame to put your ſelf in a Paſſion, or to be
" concern'd at my being here. How! ſaid *Abraham,*
" Has my Houſe another Owner beſides my ſelf
" who live in it? Don't you know Him? ſaid *Azarael*
" ſternly; Are you ignorant, that He who created
" you, has the Diſpoſal of All whatever is or ever
" ſhall be created; and that it is He who commands
" Every-where, and that His Power is Univerſal? If
" then, anſwer'd *Abraham,* trembling, You are a
" Heavenly Meſſenger, as you ſeem to be, tell me,
" I beſeech you, who you are, and what is your
" Name? Keep me, I intreat you, no longer in Suſ-
" pence; for with only your Looks, you touch me to
" the Quick, but your Speech confounds my Facul-
" ties; you diſturb my Intellectuals, and cauſe the
" Blood in my Veins to run both hot and cold; my
" Body quakes, and my Joints tremble and ſeem diſ-
" located;

" located; my Heart violently throbs and pants,
" and will be no longer contained in its natural Sta-
" tion, the Compaſs whereof is now grown too nar-
" row for it, and it can find no reſting Place therein!

The Cœleſtial Meſſenger, who perceived the great
Conſternation *Abraham* was under, made him this Anſwer; " I am Him, at the Thoughts or Mention of
" whoſe Name, all Mortals tremble, even from the
" deepeſt and moſt profound Centers of the Earth,
" to the very Summits of the moſt lofty Edifices. I
" am Him who exempts none from the taſting of my
" bitter Cup; I make neither Difference nor Defe-
" rence; but to Me all are equally alike; the Little
" and the Great; the Rich and the Poor; from the
" meaneſt Peaſant to the moſt powerful Monarch;
" from the greateſt Emperor to the pooreſt Goat-herd.
" I am the only *Atalaya* [Watch-Tower] that over-
" looks All that has Breath; ſince no Creature that
" has Life, can, by any Means, abſcond or conceal
" itſelf from my Sight. I am Him who conſumes,
" deſtroys, and annihilates numerous Hoſts, and
" mighty and invincible Armies, and diſpoils the
" Bodies, depriving them of their *beloved Breaths.*
" I it is who People and Repleniſh the Burying Pla-
" ces with Inhabitants, and cauſe them to lie within
" the Narrow Confines of a Shallow Grave; when,
" at the ſame Time, and on the contrary, I depo-
" pulate the Manſions of the Living, and deprive
" them of their Owners: Cities, Towns, and Caſtles,
" I caſt down to the Ground; I turn into Ruins and
" Rubbiſh lofty Palaces and ſumptuous Fabricks,
" laying them level with their Foundations; ming-
" ling their Founders with the Duſt, and baffling all
" the Artifices they are capable of inventing by way
" of Prevention. The moſt magnificent and ſtately
" Temples I tumble down, and Heroes with their
" Pomp, Grandeur and Ambition, I make even with
" their Native Earth All this, and infinitely more,
" I do, without the leaſt Compaſſion or Remorſe for
" the

8

" the Sufferings of Mortals. It is I who change the
" moſt lovely and beautiful Countenances into hide-
" ous and diſcoloured Complections; and the pregnant
" projecting Heads of the moſt accompliſhed and
" learned Stateſmen, are by me converted into unſight-
" ly and frightful Sculls. The moſt delightful Com-
" panies, and the ſweeteſt and moſt endearing Con-
" verſations I diſturb and ſeparate, turning all their
" Mirth and Content into doleful Weepings and La-
" mentations. I am Him who ſowres all Pleaſures,
" and parts one Friend from another, without inquiring
" or conſidering whether he be Rich or Poor, Happy
" or otherwiſe. I am at Peace with none; I never
" give Ear to Reaſon or Arguments; I am a Friend
" to no Man, and I treat all exactly alike. The
" Title I am called by is, *Azarael the Angel of*
" *Death*; This is the Name of Him who never fears
" any, yet is feared by all the Generations of Man-
" kind. "

The *Preſence Abraham* was in, the *Harangue* which
had been made him, and, finally, the Mention of
the *Name* he had heard, amazed and terrified him
to ſuch a Degree, that, for the Space of an Hour, he
had neither Breath nor Motion. When he was ſomewhat recovered from his Lethargy and Aſtoniſhment,
he began to breathe, and making an Effort to ſpeak,
he faintly uttered theſe Words; *I humbly beſeech you
to let me know, What is your Pleaſure with me? But
I beg it may be in as few Words as poſſible!* Azarael,
in a mild, low and affable Accent encouraged him,
and with a pleaſant, ſmiling Countenance returned
this gracious Anſwer :

" Fear nothing, *Abraham*; The moſt High and
" Everlaſting Creator, who makes and unmakes, or-
" dains and diſpoſes of all Things according to His
" Divine Will, and can act in all reſpects what He
" pleaſes without Contradiction or Controll from
" any one, has vouchſafed to elect from among the
" Sons of Men, a *Friend*; One whom He condeſcends
" to

" to favour and honour with that fupreme Title, and
" deems him worthy thereof : And in order to re-
" joyce the Heart of that deferving Servant with
" thofe Bleffed Tydings, He commanded me to come
" down, and demand the *Albricias* [a Reward for
" good News] of that Perfon whom He has chofen
" for his *Friend.* .Now, tell me, *Abraham,* what you
" think ought to be required at the Hands of that
" *chofen* Servant ? and in what Manner he is obliged
" to retaliate fo mighty a Grace, and fo uncommon a
" Blefling ?

Abraham, who was very attentive in liftening to this
pleafing Difcourfe of the Angel 'till he had done fpeaking, with a Countenance full of Joy, faid ; " Direct me,
" my Lord, I intreat you, where I may obtain a Sight
" of this moft worthy and venerable Perfonage, that I
" may, in the Name of the Lord my God, adore the
" Duft of his Feet, and even the Ground he treads upon ;
" Conduct me where I may enjoy the Happinefs of
" communicating with him, and of beholding his
" Face and hearing him fpeak ; for he being fo
" faithful and beloved a Servant of God, I fhall
" greatly glory in being honoured with the Title of
" a faithful and obedient Servant to him ; and that
" the Water he drinks and the Bread he eats, I may
" be permitted to fetch all upon my Shoulders, and
" that he will vouchfafe to receive the fame at my
" Hands. If I may be thought worthy of this ho-
" nourable Employment, which I fhall efteem as my
" greateft Glory upon Earth, I'll go and caft my-
" felf proftrate at his Feet ; and, to the End of my
" Life, will honour, venerate, ferve and obey a Man
" of fuch tranfcendent Merit.

O rightly-plac'd Humility! O praife-worthy Ambition! O with what Grace art thou about to inveft
thy-felf! How defirable is the Glory thou coveteft!
How many, by fuch Humility as thine, have been advanced from the meaneft and loweft Conditions, to Stations far above the moft glorious Thrones, and has
                                                been

been the Means of obtaining for them a Throne of true Glory and Honour in the Cœleſtial Orb, which is to endure 'till *Iſrafil* ſhall blow his reſounding Trumpet, as happened to the Holy *Edris*, or *Enoch* (a). It was ſuch Humility and Reſignation as thine, that appeaſed the Vehemency of the General Deluge; it was *that* which put a Period to the Raging of thoſe Waters which no other *Veſſel* but *that*, could have contained. It was *that* which delivered *Lot* from thoſe

---

(*a*) The Patriarch *Enoch* the Son of *Jafed*, is by the *Arabians* call'd *Edris*, or *Idris*, and ſometimes *Akhoukh* and *Khangiouge.* The Word *Edris* has its Derivation from *Ders*, which ſignifies in *Arabick*, Study and Meditation, from whence a School or College is called *Meders* and *Medereſſa.* I have mention'd in another Place, that they hold *Edris*, or *Enoch*, to be one of the *Nabeyn Morſeleyn*, or Prophets expreſly ſent from God; that he had Thirty Volumes given him, containing all the Abſtruſe Sciences. Theſe Books of *Enoch* are much talk'd of in the Eaſt. The Author of the *Taarick Monteckheb* writes, That this Prophet was the firſt that made War upon the Race of *Cabil*, or *Cain*, which ſort of War is called in *Arabick*, *Gehed*, and *Gaza*, and he who makes it, *Mogiahed* and *Gazi*, which Surnames, the *Mahometan* Princes take upon them when they are at War with *Chriſtians.* The ſame *Edris*, they ſay, firſt made Slaves of thoſe Infidels he was at War with. They agree with our Scriptures, that *Enoch* liv'd 365 Years, and was taken up into Heaven; but they add, that he was ſent by God to convert the *Cainites*, who were grown wicked; and that they refuſing to hear his Doctrine, he wag'd War againſt them, taking their Wives and Children into Captivity. They ſay, That *Edris*, for his Portion, had *Wiſdom* and *Knowledge*, and that *Caroun* or *Korah*, had *Riches* for his Lot; that the firſt was taken up into Heaven, and the latter ſwallowed up by the Earth. They make him the Inventer of the Pen and of the Needle, of Arithmetick, and of Aſtronomy, and more eſpecially of Geomancy. He was, according to their Traditions, the innocent Cauſe of Idolatry; for an intimate Friend and Diſciple of his having loſt him when he was taken up, at the Devil's Inſtigation, made a Statue ſo very like him, that he ſpent his Time by it for whole Days together, and paid it ſuch ſingular Honours, that, by Degrees, the Regard he had to that Image of his departed Friend, degenerated into Superſtition and Idolatry.——The Eaſtern Chriſtians hold, that *Edris* or *Enoch*, was the *Hermes* of the *Egyptians*, ſurnamed *Triſmegiſtus*, that is, Thrice Great. Vide *Reland*, & *D'Herbelot* in *Edris.*

fiery

fiery Bolts, and from the Fury and Wrath of Heaven, at the Time when thofe finful Cities were deftroyed, and when nothing elfe could have preferved him. It was *that* which divided the Red-Sea into Twelve Paths, by which *Mofes* and his Tribes got fafe over, when the Waves rejoyning the haughty *Pharaoh* and his impious Followers were fwallowed up. The *fame* it was that fet (*a*) *Jofeph* at Liberty out of the Pit, freed him from Bondage and out of Prifon, ad-

---

(*a*) The Patriarch *Jofeph* is by them called *Toufowf ben Yacoub:* They give him the Surname of *Siddick*, or the true Witnefs, becaufe he made, as they fay, a Child in the Cradle fpeak, to declare the Truth of what had happen'd between his Mafter's Wife and himfelf. He was but Seventeen Years of Age when he told the Dream that made his Brothers fell him into *Ægypt*, where *Rian ben Walid* then reign'd. This Prince, who was alfo called *Pharaoun* the common Title of all the Kings of that Country, and in the *Ægyptian* Tongue fignifies an abfolute Monarch, was inftructed by *Jofeph* in the Knowledge of the True God; but had a wicked Succeffor, whofe Name was *Kabous ben Mefaab.—Ebn Batrick*, a Chriftian Writer, and Patriarch of *Alexandria* about the Year of our Lord Chrift 922, wrote a Book, wherein he fays, *Jofeph* was 30 Years old when he marry'd *Afimah*, the Daughter of the *Kahen* of *Ain Semfh*. The Word *Kahen*, taken from the Hebrew *Cohen*, fignifies Prieft, Sacerdote, Augur, or Diviner, and *Ain Semfh*, the Eye, or Fountain of the Sun, which is the Name of the City the Scripture calls *On*, and the Greeks *Heltopolis*. ——The fame Author, will have the Meafure for the Overflowing of the *Nile* at *Memphis* to be the Work of *Jofeph*, as alfo the *Canal* cut at *Grand Cairo*, for carrying off the Waters of the faid River, the which our Travellers call *Calu*. To thefe Works may be added, the Well and Publick Granaries, which to this Day bear that Patriarch's Name; and many will have it, that he had a Hand in raifing the Obelisks, and building the Pyramids. Much more is related to his Advantage, fo that his Memory is held in great Veneration: But what make him the moft famous among the *Mahometans*, are his Amours with *Zoleika*, Daughter to *Pharaoh*, and Wife to *Potiphar*. This Fable they have learnt from the *Alcoran*, and make Ufe of it to raife Mens Hearts above common and vulgar Loves, like the Book of *Canticles*; for they make *Jofeph* to reprefent the Creator, and *Zoleika* the Creature. They likewife affirm, That *Jofeph* had a fhining Speck on his Shoulder like a Star, which, they fay, was an indelible Mark of his Gift of Prophecy, and of his future Greatnefs. His extraordinary and incomparable Beauty, is highly extoll'd amongft them.

vancing

vancing his Name above that of Kings. *This* it was
that in like manner reftored *Solomon* to his Wealth,
(*a*) Empire and happy Condition, after he was become fo miferably poor and defpicable, that he was
fcorned and derided even by the Beggars and Mendicants. What but *this* was it that caufed the Lions to fawn upon *Daniel* when the *Affyrian* Tyrant
had caft him into the obfcure and difmal Den? *Ni-
nive* was through the *fame* Means delivered from the
impending Stroke, at the very Inftant when *it* feemed
to be juft upon the Point of falling, as we may fay,
upon its Shoulders; And, likewife, that great and
memorable Prophet *Jonas*, was by *this*, and nothing
elfe, preferved in that *monftrous Paunch*, and, to the
World's fo great Benefit, that *Leviathan* was forcibly compelled to difgorge him up again upon the
Shoar againft its Will. By *this* it was, that the Rebellious Angels were difcomfitted and overcome, when
the proud *Lucifer* waged that impious War upon
his Refufal to pay the required Homage to the new-
created Man : *This* it was that broke all their Meafures, and caft them down from Heaven into the
loweft Abyffes, where they fhall remain in perpetual
Torments to all Eternity. And, finally, all that
I have been faying is compleatly confirmed, as well
as innumerable other Miraculous and Triumphant
Myfteries and Trophies, in the never-to-be-forgotten
Hiftory of the venerable Perfonage I am treating a-
bout, who well deferves our greateft Regard and Reverence. By the Virtue and Efficacy of *this fame*, he

---

(*a*) See concerning *Solomon* and *Daniel* in the Ninth Chapter.

(*b*) They call the Prophet *Jonas, Younous ben Mathai.* In his Story
they differ not much from our Scriptures, only fay, He was Forty
Days in the Fifh's Belly : Tho', as may be feen in the next Chapter, my Author fays, but Three Days; and, in Truth, in abundance of the like Traditions, the *Spanifh Moors* in general agree
better with our Scriptures than the reft of the *Mahometans*, as the
Afiaticks and *Africans* make appear in all their Writings.

under-

underwent *Nimrod*'s fiery Pile ſafe and unhurt, and by *it* he is now ſeated and fixed in the firſt Rank, and in the moſt elevated Station among the Sons of *Adam*: Nor is it to be doubted, but that the Heavenly Meſſenger *Azarael* was ſo fully ſatisfied with the complete Reſignation and Humility of his Arguments and his Anſwer, which favoured ſo little of this World, that he required no other *Albricias* from him for his Meſſage, or the joyful News he brought him.

" Be joyful, O thou Man of Probity! ſaid the
" Angel to *Abraham*, for this Title belongs to thee,
" and to none but thee: The Almighty Lord who
" beſtows His Bounties and Mercies upon thoſe who
" have ſo true and perfect a Knowledge of His Divi-
" nity, has elected thee to be His *eſpecial Friend*,
" having vouchſafed, that, by thy Humility, thou
" ſhalt be exalted and inthroned in this ſo glorious a
" State of Dignity. Return therefore Praiſes and
" Thankſgivings to thy Creator, and glorify His
" Holy Name, who has been ſo wonderfully gracious
" as to beſtow upon thee Mercies of ſo ſublime a
" Nature, whereby thou art become the moſt Noble
" and moſt Honourable among Mortals!

Abraham having heard theſe Words, remained aſtoniſhed and quite confounded, not being able to gueſs how or through what Merits of all his former Services, Duties, or Devotions, he had deſerved ſo ſignal and ſo bountiful a Recompence: His Amazement was ſo great, that he knew not what he did, but fell down flat on his Face, giving Thanks and Praiſes to the Lord, who had been pleaſed to favour him with a Gift ſo ſuperlatively glorious.

In this proſtrate Poſture he continued Two long Hours, when riſing up, and looking for the Angelick Meſſenger, he found him not in the Place where he left him; but was gone, having returned the ſame Way he came.

When

When he had fought for him all about, and faw that he was not to be found, the good Patriarch rejoyced exceedingly ; for it is not to be difputed, but that (as he well knew *Azarael's* Employment was ever to feparate the Spirit from the Flefh, and that his Miffions never tended to the Content and Satisfaction of thofe Perfons to whom he was fent, but always proved fatal to them) he had been under terrible Apprehenfions ; never in the leaft imagining himfelf fafe from Danger after he had once feen him ; but was pofitively affured, that he was fent to take away his Life ; and thefe Thoughts and Reflections had infufed fo fhocking a Terror into his Imagination, that notwithstanding, as I have before declared, his Embaffy, his glorious Appearance, the Sweetnefs of his Voice, and his foothing and comfortable Words, his Shape, Gracefulnefs and fumptuous Apparel, were more than fufficient to infpire the Soul of any Mortal with Ecftafies and Joy ; nay, though that fo exquifitely beautiful Countenance caft forth a Thoufand refplendent Rays, thofe Eyes, thofe Lips, that Afpect and Cœleftial Form, and all thofe wonderful Perfections, tended to excite Raptures in the Beholders ; yet the bare knowing who he was, and the very mention of his Name, had fo far difquieted his Breaft, and difturbed and confounded him to fuch a Degree, that all thofe glorious Objects he had beheld, thofe ecftatic Tydings brought him, and that Bleffed Propofal, were not capable of reftoring his perturbated Heart to its wonted Repofe and Sedatenefs. But when he was intirely fatisfied that he was quite gone, and had left him to himfelf, he was exceedingly joyful, returning to the Lord infinite Praifes for his Deliverance.

C H A P.

CHAP. VII.

GOD *after having Three Nights sent his Voice to* Abraham, *on the Fourth commands him to offer up his Son* Ishmael *as a Sacrifice. His Grief upon that Account, and great Love to* Ishmael. *His Resignation to* GOD's *Will. He Dissembles with his Wife* Hagar, *whom he orders to make Preparation to Dress the Child to be present at the Offering he was going to make,* &c.

AFTER all these wonderful Mysteries had passed in the Manner as I have related above; after all the Extasies of Joy and Content, mixt with Terror and Apprehensions, that this *newly Elected Friend,* the Righteous *Abraham,* had conceiv'd at the Embassy of *The Angel of Death,* he esteemed his Obligation to the Munificent Donor, his Lord and God, to be of so extraordinary a Nature, and shew'd such Signs of Resignation, Humility, and assiduous Devotion, that he never employed a single Hour in any Occupation worthy Reproof; but his whole Time was taken up in the Service of the Lord his Creator : His Days he generally passed in Fasting, and the Nights in Watching ; and, in a Word, he indefatigably spent the greatest part of his Time

in

in Prayer, and other Works of Piety, fcarcely in-
dulging himfelf with a Moment's Repofe.

Having laid himfelf down upon his Bed one
Night, with his pious and vertuous Spoufe *Hagar*,
and his dearly beloved Son *Ifhmael*, in order to re-
frefh his wearied Limbs, and to recruit his Spirits
with a little Reft, being quite fpent and worn out
with the Fatigues of conftant Fafting, Prayer, and
fuch Holy Exercifes, he foon fell afleep: But he did
not long enjoy the Benefit of that Refrefhment, for
he was awakened out of his foundeft Sleep, by a
Voice, which, with a foft and pleafing Accent, uttered thefe Words ; `` *Abraham*, thou perfect Servant
`` of thy Lord! Liften to what I have to fay to thee.
`` Awake ; no longer indulge thy Senfes with foft
`` Slumbers, but rouze thy felf up, and fhake off
`` thy Drowfinefs. I require at thy Hands, that
`` thou pitch upon, and get ready a Sacrifice to
`` offer up in my Divine and Sanctified Name, the
`` which fhall, by me, be gracioufly and acceptably
`` received, (if thou choofeft right) as a Return and
`` Retaliation for what I have done for thee, in ex-
`` alting thy Name to fuch a Degree of Dignity,
`` that thou haft no Second or Partner in thy *Title* ;
`` and befides, at *the Day of Terror* thou fhalt be
`` further recompenfed ; and as now in this Age
`` thy Name is Bleffed, and has no Equal, fo in Af-
`` ter-Ages thy Memory fhall be held in Venerati-
`` on, and be called upon with the greateft Reve-
`` rence.''

Abraham awoke very much terrified and concerned ;
he paffed the Remainder of the Night revolving thefe
Words in his Thoughts, being dubious whether or no
this Revelation might not be fome Delufion of *Satan*
to infnare him, and caufe him to fin: However, as
foon as the Day appear'd, he got up, and in compliance, as he thought, with what he had been en-
joined, he kill'd a very large Camel; and when it
was cut in Pieces, he diftributed all the Flefh amongft

L

the

the Poor, and others in his Neighbourhood who might have the greatest Need thereof, and then, addressing himself to God, he said; "O my Lord! If this "my Sacrifice has been pleasing and acceptable to "thee, let me know it; but if the contrary, inform "me, by some Token, in what manner I shall ac- "complish thy most Sacred Command."

The very next Night, as he was in a most pro- found Sleep, he heard the same Voice again, which said thus; "Hear, O my beloved Servant! Ap- "proach towards me with the Sacrifice I required at "thy Hands, which I ordained thou shouldest offer up "in my sublime Name; and I will set it down to "thy Account, in a more singular and advantageous ", manner than ever was done to any mortal Crea- "ture; and the Reward thou shalt receive in Re- "compence shall be exceedingly singular and extra- "ordinary."

Abraham awoke when he heard the Voice, and in the Morning arose and sacrificed a Cow, distributing the Flesh to those who most wanted it, as he had done before, and then once more made his Address to the Lord in these Words; "O King of the Hea- "vens! If it has come to pass that this my Offering "has been accepted by thy Sacred Divinity, let it be "revealed to me this Night, that I may be satisfied "whether I have in all Points been able to fulfil thy "Holy Ordinance; so that in whatever I have been "defective, I may know how to rectify the Omissi- "ons or Misinterpretations to a Tittle, as by my "Obligation and Duty to all thy Commands I am "bound to do."

This was what he said the Second Time, and when the Third Night was come, he laid him down and fell into a sound Sleep as before, and soon after the same Voice began to call upon him in the same Terms as it had done the preceding Nights; upon which, being awakened, he instantly got up, and killed a fine large Fat Sheep, and, as he used to do,

gave

gave it all to the Poor. When he had done this, he said; "Moſt Sovereign Monarch! divulge and de-" clare to me, how I ſhall make a right Judgment, " that I may be able to accompliſh this myſtical Sa-" crifice!" But on the Fourth Night at the uſual Hour, the Voice once more ſaid to him; "*Abraham*, " make in my Name the Sacrifice I require, and " you ſhall enjoy Eternal Reſt!"

Abraham, who this Time was awake, and was re-volving in his Mind thoſe paſt Revelations, being under a deep Concern that he had not hitherto pitched on the Right Oblation which his Lord required of him, in any of thoſe he had already offered up, he made this An-ſwer; "Moſt powerful Lord! Thou knoweſt I have in " thy Name offer'd up Camels, Oxen and Sheep; and " my Comprehenſion extends not to the unravelling " this Myſtery: Expound, therefore, I implore thee, " O moſt Benign, moſt Wiſe, and moſt Omnipotent " Creator! the *Arcana* of this Ænigmatical Sacrifice: " Let thy ineffable Wiſdom put me in the right Way; " for my Capacity is too weak to dive into this Se-" cret, or to reach any further than the Knowledge " of thy wonderful Goodneſs, and thoſe bountiful " Mercies I have received from thee!"

The Voice of God now reſounded in his Ears like Thunder, ſaying; "*Abraham!* What I expect and " demand of thee for an Offering, is not Camels, and " ſuch like, as thou haſt ſacrified to me; but the Sa-" crifice I require at thy Hands, is, That thy beloved " and only-begotten Son: Him whom thou loveſt " dearer than thy own ſelf: Him who lies ſleeping by " thy Side: Him it is, I demand as an Offering, and " with *Him*, and nothing elſe, ſhall I be contented " and ſatisfy'd for all I have done for thee, and there-" with will all thy former Sevices be render'd accept-" able, and the Purity and Integrity of thy Heart " will become manifeſt."

O the Inſipidity of Earthly Content! O Pleaſures mixt with Gall and Bitterneſs! Almighty Lord of all

Secrets!

Secrets! O moſt High and Powerful Monarch! What humane Capacity is able to dive into thy hidden Decrees? Is it after this Manner that thou treateſt ſo ſignalized a Perſon, whom thou haſt elected for thy *eſpecial Friend* from amongſt all the Inhabitants of the Earth! The Angel, not long before, had rejoyc'd his Heart with the Tidings of ſo Supreme a Superiority over the reſt of Mankind; and thou hadſt bleſs'd him with an only Son in his declining Years, to be a Comfort and Support to him in his Old Age: Theſe were all certainly, and without diſpute, moſt eminent Tokens of a dear *Friendſhip*; yet now, when he is at the Summit of his Happineſs, when all his paſt Afflictions and Perſecutions are over, and his Life began to be eaſy and undiſturb'd, and he to be moſt ſenſible of, and thankful for thy uncommon Mercies and Favours to him; when his dear Son afforded him the greateſt Joy and Comfort, when he began to appear in his early flouriſhing Bloom, and gave him the greateſt Proſpect of Hope, and his Beauty and Qualifications attracted the Regards of all his Beholders; Now, I ſay, thou commandeſt his Throat to be cut by his own Father's Hands! O unheard of Sentence! What could Humane Judgments determine of this Matter! Not as of the Proceeding of a *Friend*, but rather as that of a profeſs'd *Enemy*; and that *Abraham*, under ſuch Circumſtances, and at ſuch a Juncture, would have chang'd all his wonted Piety, and indefatigable Application to God's Service, into Diſobedience and Neglect. How exquiſitely vile and groveling are Humane Conjectures! Such fatal and inconſiderate Thoughts as theſe can no wiſe conduce to the Welfare or Happineſs of thoſe who are ſo ſtupid as to harbour them in their Minds! How far do ſuch err from the Point! How far ſhort do they come of the Mark aim'd at by the Sovereign *Marks-Man?* Would Mortals but ſeriouſly conſider, how Gracious, how Munificent, and how ready the Lord is to protect us in our Adverſities; and, at the ſame Time, remember how impoſſible it is to

enjoy

enjoy perfect ·Content on this ſide of Heaven, that can be of any long Durance, without a Mixture of Sorrow and Diſquiet, they would then, without Doubt, commit fewer Errors than they do, nor would they make ſuch wrong Conjectures. But, O Omnipotent and Merciful Sovereign! if our low and earthly Imaginations ſhould Ignorantly or Inadvertently chance to fall into theſe Snares, be pleaſed, likewiſe, to conſider, that we are formed out of a Matter wherein are included our Four dangerous Adverſaries; and that it is not ſo much to be wonder'd at, if our Natural Frailty and Inconſtancy hinder us from reſiſting the Aſſaults of the Fleſh, eſpecially when ſuch myſterious *Ænigma's* as theſe I am treating about, happen to occur and fall in our Way.

But to return to our afflicted Patriarch: When he ſaw himſelf ſo evidently convinc'd how erroneous his Ideas of the Four preceding Revelations had been, it may eaſily be imagin'd, by a ſincere impartial Breaſt, what Agonies he muſt undergo, conſidering the tender Affection and fervent Love he bore his amiable Son, and the Abſoluteneſs of the Injunction. Not being able to take any Reſt all the Night, he paſs'd the Hours in ſtrange Agitations of Mind; and diſſolv'd, and, in a manner, drown'd in Showers of Heart-breaking Tears, he took his dear Child in his Arms, kiſſing him between the Eyes, on the Forehead, Cheeks, and Lips Ten thouſand times, bedewing his lovely Face all over with bitter Tears of Anguiſh, not ſuffering him to ſleep any more than himſelf, but held him all the while incircled in his cloſe Embraces, hugging him to his Boſom, and venting moſt lamentable Sighs. His great Love to him would have tranſported him much further, had he not ſtrove with all his Might, to ſuppreſs and ſtifle his Grief for fear of awaking *Hagar,* the vertuous Mother of *him,* he was beſtowing ſo many Kiſſes upon, and who was likewiſe lying by his ſide; he curbing his riſing Paſſion, and diſſembling what he felt as much as poſſible, being very unwilling to impart a

L 3

Thing

Thing to her which muſt needs be ſo·inſupportably ſhocking to her very Soul.

Yet all his Precautions were not ſufficient, nor could he vent his Paſſion ſo ſilently, but that ſhe heard his Sobs and Groans; and as by the great Love and Veneration ſhe had for her Husband, they gave her a ſenſible Diſquiet, ſhe was no longer able to refrain from ſpeaking and inquiring into the Occaſion of this unuſual Agitation: " From whence proceeds it, *Abraham,* ſaid ſhe, " that you have been ſo reſtleſs this whole Night, that " inſtead of ſleeping, you do nothing but ſigh and " lament? Nay, you likewiſe have quite tir'd my " dear Child *Iſhmael* to Death, by pulling him about, " and not letting him take a Wink of Sleep neither: " Pray, my Dear, let me know the Meaning of all " this!

" Nothing at all, reply'd *Abraham,* diſſembling the " true Cauſe, but the mighty Affection and Love " I bear the Child, which increaſes every Day more " and more, inſomuch, that I han't the Command of " my ſelf to conceal or diſſemble it any longer: But I " muſt deſire you, as ſoon as 'tis Day, not to neglect " what I am going tell you; You muſt dreſs him in " his beſt and neweſt Apparel; let every Thing about " him be perfectly clean, and well perfum'd; what " you have of valuable and coſtly be ſure to put " it him on, and anoint his Head with the moſt pre- " cious ſweet-ſcented Oyls, for 'tis my Deſign to take " him with me to be preſent at the Sacrifice I intend " to make.

The good *Abraham* concluded his Words with a moſt profound Sigh fetch'd from the Bottom of his very Soul; for as the unexpreſſible Grief he was under made him endure an Agony and Sentiment of the ſame Nature, and nothing inferior to the Anguiſh a Mother feels who has the Child of her Youth torn from her Arms never to behold it more, to contain the Inflammation of whoſe Breaſt the whole Univerſe is by much too narrow: So in the very ſame manner

was

was the Breaft of this holy Man inflam'd and in an Uproar: His Bed, tho' defign'd for a Place of Comfort and Repofe, could not contain him, but up he rifes, and throws himfelf proftrate upon the Ground, and, invoking the Name of the Lord, with Anguifh and Bitternefs of Soul, he made this fhort Supplication;

" O Lord! Who with thy All-powerful Hand haft
" created this Heart of mine of the fame Matter and
" Subftance as thou haft the reft of this my frail
" Flefh which is fo prone to be repugnant to thy
" Sacred Will and Ordinances; Grant, I befeech thee,
" out of thy unbounded Goodnefs, that both *that* and
" all my Faculties, and my five Senfes, may become
" all Obedience, and be intirely devoted to thy Plea-
" fure, unanimoufly to fulfil thy Commands in every
" individual Point: Permit, O Creator! that *they*
" may all bear the fame Countenance, and bend *their*
" Steps wholly towards thee: And as thy Effence is all
" Holy and Divine, let the Infinity of thy Mercy
" bear with my Weaknefs and Reluctancy upon this
" Occafion! "

Whilft *Abraham* was thus expoftulating with God, the Royal Princefs *Hagar* went about to put in Execution what her Husband had recommended to her Care. With many Kiffes and Embraces fhe awaken'd the tender and beautiful Youth, and wafh'd his Head (as fhe had been defir'd) with perfum'd Waters of moft exquifite Odours, in which had been diffolv'd Camphire, and other precious Gums, fuitable to fuch an Occafion, and which in thofe Days were made ufe of in Sacred Solemnities, and held in great Efteem.

When the good Child beheld all this unufual Preparation, he faid; " For what Reafon, my dear Mother,
" have you thus wafh'd my Head with thefe perfum'd
" and fanctify'd Waters, which are only us'd upon
" Holy Occafions?" To which Queftion, this great Princefs reply'd, " My Son, it is by your Father's Order,
" and fince he has been pleas'd to command it to be
" done, 'tis our Duties to obey him." Now when

Ifhmael

Ishmael was dress'd in all the Ornaments his Father had before given Orders he should put on, his glorify'd Countenance cast forth so great a Splendor, that it obscur'd the Light of the Sun; and his Father having privately taken a sharp keen Dagger which he always kept in good Order lock'd up in a Chest, he conceal'd it in his Girdle, on the left side under his Garment. As he was going, *Hagar* said to him; " Pray take " with you a little of something to eat and to drink, " that if the Child has a Mind, he may refresh him- " self with a Mouthful; and if he should complain of " any Ailing, bind his Head, and cover it with this " costly Sash; and so the Blessing of the Lord guide " and protect you both. "

CHAP.

CHAP. VIII.

Abraham *fets out with his Son* Ifhmael *to perform the Sacrifice. His difconfolate Condition upon that Occafion. His wonderful Profpect of the World's Situation. Is tempted by the Devil, but repulfes him. The Devil makes three feveral Attempts upon* Ifhmael *to feduce him to Difobedience, who, tho' he likewife repulfes his Temptations, yet feems to ftagger, and is terrified; but at laft refigns with admirable Piety and Refolution: He very pathetically encourages his Father, exhorting him to proceed in what he had undertaken. Abraham's Preparation and Prayer before the Sacrifice. He makes Tryal thrice to kill* Ifhmael, *but is prevented by Angels. Their Interceffion with God for* Ifhmael. Ifhmael's *Prayer. Abraham tries a fourth Time, but his Arm is withheld by the Angel* Gabriel, *who brings him a Ram from Heaven, which* Abraham *joyfully offers up inftead of his Son,* &c.

WHEN every Thing that was thought requifite and material for this Occafion had been prepared and got in Readinefs, (as I have hinted above) our holy Patriarch, having firft recommended himfelf to the Protection of Almighty God, and taken his Leave of the Princefs *Hagar* his moft pious and vertuous Spoufe, he fet forwards, with his lovely Son *Ifhmael* (whom he led by the Hand) in order to fulfil
the

the Lord's Command concerning the Sacrifice he had been enjoyned to offer up to His Holy Name.

The venerable, but difconfolate Old Man, overwhelmed with Grief and Affliction, and ruminating in his Mind the Unaccountablenefs of his prefent wretched Circumftances, went on his Way with an aking and heavy Heart. He beheld with Tendernefs, Love and Compaffion his dear Child at every Step he made; He look'd upon thofe his tender and delicate Limbs, as yet not arrived to Maturity: He gaz'd on that his moft beautiful Countenance, whereon the glorious *Hereditary Light*, created for the Ornamental *Blazon* of the *Lord's Elected*, appeared fo confpicuoufly refplendant. He examin'd, with the greateft Attention, this Miracle of Children, from Head to Foot; and then, Oh the racking Thought! he call'd to Mind, that this very Child, he fo doated upon; this only Child God had been pleas'd to blefs him withal, was now going to be fo inhumanely butcher'd by the Hands of his own doating and tender Parent. Such fhocking Reflections, fuch melancholy Heart-breaking Confiderations as thefe, are certainly much eafier to be conceiv'd in our Imaginations than to be exprefs'd by Words; and they took fo deep a Rooting in the Heart of the afflicted and forrowful Patriarch, that, at every Moment, he fetch'd fuch bitter Sighs from the very Bottom of his Soul, that each feem'd as if it was to be his laft.

But left a long uninterrupted Continuance of fo fevere a Tryal, might occafion this bitter Pill of Gall and Aloes to have too great an Influence over his almoft wafted Spirits, the Lord, to prevent it, and, in fome meafure, to divert his Thoughts, was pleas'd to fhew him a moft ftupendous and amazing Myftery: For, as he was proceeding on his Way, exceeding penfive, and little dreaming of fuch a Prodigy, behold! the Seven Earths were all opened to his View, infomuch, that nothing within the profoundeft Centers, occult Recefles and Abyffes thereof were concealed

from

from him, but all their Myftical *Arcane* expofed apparently to his Sight.

Tho' his Aftonifhment was great, as we may eafily imagine, yet neverthelefs, arm'd with a Heavenly Fortitude, he extended his Sight as far as his Eyes would reach, and beheld, O wonderful Profpect! this Earthly Globe the World refting upon the Point of a Bull's Horn, the Bull ftanding upon a great Fifh, which Fifh lay extended upon a vaft Lake of Water.

Thefe are, indeed, Myfteries and Prodigies which ftupify the Senfes, fhock the Underftanding, and are by far too fublime for Humane Comprehenfion! Yet from hence *Abraham* began to confider and reflect upon the Omnipotency and Supreme Divinity of God, and that his Works are wholly incomprehenfible, and that all and every one of His Creatures in general, are bound, tacitely, to conform to the leaft of his Ordinances with an implicite Obedience ; fo that, ftrengthen'd by thefe Reflections, he remain'd eafy, fatisfied, contented, and with a perfect Refignation ; purfuing his Way with a firm, determined, and conftant Refolution to perform the Sacrifice he had undertaken.

As he was going forwards, that accurfed Enemy of Mankind (a) the Devil (who has from the Beginning, openly

---

(a) *A propos* ; Now we are fpeaking of the Devil, I fhall give my Readers a notable Story the *Mahometans* tell of *Abraham* and that Seducer of Mankind ; There goes a Tradition, That the Devil looking one Day upon the Dead Carcafe of a Man the Sea had thrown up on the Shore, whereof the wild Beafts, the Birds of Prey, and the Fifhes had each devour'd fome Part, he thought this an excellent Subject for him to work upon, in order to infnare Mankind concerning the Point of the Future Refurrection. " For, faid he, how can they " conceive that the Parts of this Body, devour'd by fo many feveral " Creatures, can ever joyn again at the General Refurrection ? " God knowing the malicious and pernicious Defign of this common Enemy, order'd *Abraham* to go walk upon the Sea-Shore; The Patriarch did fo, and the Devil prefently appeared to him like a Man, feeming to be much afton'fh'd, and in the greateft Confufion, and propos'd to him
his

openly declared himfelf as fuch, and whofe Thoughts and Deeds are perpetually tending towards the difturbing and difannulling whatever may be pleafing in the Sight of God) to try, if, by laying any of his dangerous and pernicious Snares, he could bring to nought, or at leaft interrupt this Pious Undertaking, he, with this View, came and prefented himfelf before *Abraham,* under the Likenefs of a Grave Ancient Hermit, and fpake to him in thefe Words; " Stay, " *Abraham!* Whither is it you are dragging your " poor innocent Child? You are certainly going to " cut his Throat! Take Heed; this is, doubtlefs, " fome Artifice of *Satan's* which he makes Ufe of to " infnare you; It is not God's Will you fhould com- " mit this Wickednefs; neither did thofe Dreams and " Vifions you have had proceed from Him.

Abra-

---

his Doubt touching the Refurrection. When *Abraham* had heard all he had to fay, he anfwer'd; " What reafonable Ground can you " have to doubt, fince He who could deduce and draw together " all the feveral Parts and Particles of this Body out of the Abyfs " of *Nothing,* will eafily know how to find them again in the feveral " Parts of Nature, wherefoever they fhall be difpers'd, to put 'em " together again. The Potter when he pleafes, breaks in pieces an " Earthen Veffel, and makes it up again of the fame Clay. " However, God to pleafe *Abraham* (according to the *Alcoran)* faid to him, *Take four Birds, cut them in Pieces, and carry thofe Pieces and difperfe them in four diftant Mountains, and then call them, and you fhall fee all thofe four Birds will immediately come to you.* This Story, which *Mahomet* has introduc'd into his *Alcoran,* is taken, we prefume, from the Sacrifice of the Birds mentioned in *Genefis;* but the *Arabs* know many more Particulars of Holy Writ than *Mofes* ever left us, fo fruitful are they in their Inventions. Thefe four Birds were, they fay, a Pigeon, a Cock, a Crow and a Peacock; and that, when *Abraham* had cut them in pieces, he made a perfect Anatomy of them, and minc'd 'em all together. Some add, that he pounded them in a Mortar, and reduc'd them all to one Mafs, which he divided into four Parts, and carry'd to the Tops of four feveral Mountains: Then holding up their Heads, which he retain'd in his Hands, he call'd them feverally by their Names, and each of them inftantly came for its Head, and flew away. In the Second Chapter of the *Alcoran,* intitled *El Bacrah,* or, The Cow, we read, that *Abraham* made

Abraham, who immediately knew the *Rebel*, not-withftanding his plaufible Difguife, and perceiving his malicious Drift, made him this Anfwer; " Depart, " *Satan*; Begone from before me, thou Enemy to God " and Man! Thou Wretch! who waft driven out of " the Almighty's Prefence with (*a*) Stones! Thy " Malice and Deceit fhall work no Effect upon me, " nor fhall it be in thy Power either to obftruct or " delay this my holy Defign. "

The Traytor, when he found himfelf difcovered, and that the Holy Man fcoffed at him and derided him in fuch opprobrious Language, was quite confounded with Shame, and left him; but returned and appeared to *Ifhmael*, unfeen by his Father, faying to him; " How comes it about, O deceived Young Man! " that you fuffer your felf to be abus'd and impos'd

---

made this Supplication to God; *Lord! Shew me how you raife the Dead*, The Lord anfwer'd; *Have you not Faith? Yes, Lord*, reply'd he, *But I only beg this to fatisfy my Heart.*— The Fable of the Birds is thus allegoriz'd by the Author of the Book call'd *Anuar*: " All thofe, " fays he, who defire that their Souls fhould live a Spiritual Life, " muft flay and facrifice all their Paffions with the Sword of Mortifi- " cation, and make them to be fo confounded together, that they may " find themfelves in a Difpofition to be led away by the Ordinances " of God; for then, the Lord calling them, makes them run in the Way " of his Law, till they fly away to the Place of Eternal Blifs. " The Poet *Senai* makes another Allegory of the Fiction of thefe four Birds, faying, They are the Four Humours we are compofed of, and that having facrific'd them for the Service of God, if we make ufe of Faith, the Love of God, Reafon and Experience, we fhall, like *Abraham*, make them live again to Immortality. Some *Mahometan* Doctors pretend, that the divided Parts of thofe Birds came toge-ther again to denote to *Abraham*, that his Pofterity the *Jews* fhould again be re-united, after having been difperfed over the Face of the Earth; which Notion they have, perhaps, borrow'd from the *Jews*, as well as many others The Chapter *Amram* in the *Alcoran*, takes Notice of feveral of *Abraham's* Prerogatives in Relation to the Genealogy of our Saviour *J. fus Chrift*, which fhall be mentioned in a convenient Place.

(*a*) This I have explained in the firft Chapter, *p*. 23. Note (*e*)

" upon

" upon, by your unnatural Father, after this in-
" humane Manner? Don't you know, that he is
" going to cut your Throat, and to offer you up for
" a Sacrifice?" *Ifhmael* return'd him this Anfwer;
" No Father was ever heard of, that cut his Child's
" Throat without fome juft and equitable Caufe for
" fo doing: Your Words are incongruous, and incon-
" fiftent with Reafon!" To which the Devil reply'd;
" I'll tell you, unfortunate Youth! Your ungodly
" Father alledges for an Excufe, that, for four fuc-
" ceeding Nights, he has been admonifh'd in a Vifion,
" that he fhould cut your Throat, and offer you up
" for a Sacrifice: But, unhappy Young Man! I had
" no fooner feen you, than my Bowels yerned with
" Compaffion for you." The Pious Youth anfwer'd
him in thefe Words; " Since the Lord has ordained it,
" and it is His Holy Will it fhould be fo, moft juft it
" is that my Father fhould execute a Command fo
" reafonable and fo worthy of him: Far be it from
" him he fhould ever difobey his Lord·and Creator:
" And feeing God is pleas'd, that I fhould fall a
" Victim, and vouchfafes to be appeafed and con-
" tented with me for an Offering of Atonement, I am
" intirely refigned, and confirm and approve of my
" Father's Intention."

Satan feeing himfelf baffled, and finding all his falfe,
bafe and treacherous Artifices to be vain and of no Effect,
departed, and went away: And *Ifhmael*, being in a great
Concern at what the falfe, pretended, hypocritical
Old Hermit had faid to him, could not refrain from
fhedding abundance of Tears; the which when his
good Father perceiv'd, mov'd with a more than ordinary Paternal Tendernefs, he afk'd him, " What
" ailed him, and wherefore he wept? Conceal nothing
" from me, faid he, my Dear! my Darling! Thou
" Joy of my Life, and Comfort of my Soul!"
To which kind Expreffions, the innocent *Ifhmael*
reply'd; " My Dear and ever-honoured Parent!
" The Caufe of my Weeping and Concern proceeds
" from

" from the Words that the Old Man, who was with
" you awhile ago, faid to me; He told me that you
" was carrying me on purpofe to kill me; and this it
" is that makes me cry. Dry up thy Tears, faid the
" Righteous Patriarch: Weep not, my Deareft, but
" wipe thine Eyes; the treacherous old Thief is a
" malicious, lying, infamous Villain; I'll take Care,
" my Life! to protect thee that no Harm befal
" thee."

With thefe Words the Child took a little Courage
and was appeafed: But the Devil, not fatisfied with
what he had already done, nor difcouraged with the
Repulfes he had met withal, refolved to make another
Tryal; and, to that Intent, transformed himfelf into
a Bird, and fate before them in the Way they were
to pafs, with his Feathers all briftled up in a very
melancholy Pofture, and fhewing great Signs of Sorrow, faid to the Child; " O unhappy, wretched
" Youth! How miferable and unfortunate *is* thy
" Fate, that thou art now led to the Slaughter in thy
" tender Years, to be Butchered by thy cruel Father."
" Alas, O Bird! faid the Child, Have you ever feen
" any Father murder his Son without his having de-
" ferved fo violent a Chaftifement? Alas! reply'd
" that infernal Bird, Thy Father wickedly affirms,
" That he is obliged to do it by God's exprefs Com-
" mand. If that is true, anfwered *Ifhmael,* I am ex-
" tremely well fatisfied, and I receive the Stroke as
" a particular Grace and Mercy." Then turning towards his dear afflicted Parent, he faid to him; " Father,
" I fuppofe, what the Old Man faid juft now, is ftill
" frefh in your Memory, and now that Bird, you fee
" yonder, has told me the very fame Thing! My
" Life! replied *Abraham,* (*a*) the Language of Birds
is

(*a*) In the *Mahometan* Writers, abundance is to be found concerning the Language of Birds and Beafts, and many notable Fables
I have heard of Men who in all Ages underftood their Language:
Nay, I have met with Two Pretenders to that Knowledge; but,
however,

" is always myftical and intricate, ever concealing
" fome double Meaning, and fome fecret and unin-
" telligible *Ænigma*; nor are there fewer Falfities in
" what they tell us, than in the Words of Men:
" This, my Dear, as well as every Thing elfe, is by
" the Lord's Permiffion.

But the Enemy of God, the rebellious *Satan*, whofe
Subtlety and Malice had been baffled and brought to
nought, and his infernal Hatred to all Goodnefs having proved effectlefs in the cunning and artful Snares
he had hitherto laid againft this Holy Man, was now
once more refolved to make a Fourth Effort, to try
if he could hit the Mark he had already aimed at
Three Times, but had always miffed it; fo now, fan-
cying himfelf fure of his Aim, he flew away fwiftly
before them to the Top of the Mountain (which was
the Place where the Sacrifice was to be made) and
there concealing himfelf under the Rock 'till they
came, which was foon after, he then, like an Eccho,
faid thus; " Alas! alas! How I commiferate thy de-
" plorable Deftiny, thou unhappy, and never-enough-
" to-be-lamented Youth! In thy tendereft Years to
" be brought to fuch a difaftrous and untimely End!
" To Day, in this very Place, thou wilt have thy
" Throat moft barbaroufly cut; Here in this lonefome
" folitary Mountain, whither thou haft been bafely
" and treacheroufly inticed to thy Grave; Here, I fay,
" will thy innocent Blood be fpilt: And when thou
" haft fallen a Victim to the blind and fuperftitious
" Obftinacy of thy unnatural Father, thou wilt here
" be buried in a Hole, and never more fet thine Eyes
" upon thy Dear and Sorrowful Mother, 'till the Day
" of Judgment.

---

however, the *Mahometans* all unanimoufly agree, That none was
ever perfect in that fort of Learning, except King *Solomon*, of whom
much is fa'd in the next Chapter. Which fee.

This

This laft Circumftance, which ferved as a Confirmation of all the foregoing ones, wrought a great Effect
upon *Ifhmael*; infomuch, that the Child was, in a
manner, fcandalized to find himfelf fo often forewarn-
ed of what his Father defigned againft him; which
though he had denied, yet he could not forbear believing; and therefore, with his Eyes flowing with
Tears, he turned towards him, and fpoke thefe Words;
" My Righteous and Honoured Father; If, parad-
" venture, all that the Old Man told me was falfe,
" the Words of the Bird cannot be a Fiction likewife;
" but if the Bird is alfo a Lyar, how is it poffible, or
" even probable, that the Mountains themfelves, that
" are fixed and immoveable, and know no Change,
" how can they tell me of a Thing that is not true?
" Explain to me, I befeech you, this Riddle!

They were now, as has been faid before, arrived
at their Journey's End, which was the very Summit
of the Mountain, and when the good Patriarch faw
himfelf there, and upon fo forrowful an Occafion, he
was juft ready to render up his Soul, and expire with
innumerable Sobs and bitter Groans: Nor was he a
little touched with his Son's laft Words, to the which,
accompanied with a Flood of Tears, he returned him
this Anfwer;

" My deareft Child! To conceal the Truth no longer
" from thee, know, That for Four Nights fucceffively
" I had it revealed to me in a Voice from Heaven,
" That it is the Pleafure, Will and abfolute Com-
" mand of the moft High and moft Powerful Creator,
" that I fhould here, in this Place, fpill thy Blood,
" and offer it up as a Sacrifice to his Holy Name; nor
" is it His Divine Pleafure to accept of any other Of-
" fering. This, if I perform, His fupreme Majefty
" has promifed to enhance, at the laft Day, the
" Merit of my Obedience and Conformity to His Holy
" Will and Ordinance, above that of any Mortal who
" now lives, or has hitherto lived upon the Earth.
" Confider now, my dear Son! think well upon it,

what

" what thou wouldft have me do in fuch a Cafe, or
" what can be thought on to prevent my being difo-
" bedient, in not complying with what the Lord my
" God requires; nay, fo pofitively demands at my
" Hands!

The lovely Youth, when he was now clearly convinced and evidently confirmed upon what a Tragical Account he had been brought to that fatal Place,
was feized with Fear and Terror, trembling at the
Thoughts and Apprehenfions of approaching Death;
nor was he able to ftand the Shock without Horror,
notwithftanding all the poffible Efforts he made to
overcome his Pufilanimity and want of Refolution:
But what could be expected from one of his tender
Age? For, in Truth, he was but, as we may fay, an
Infant.

Under this Apprehenfion and Concern, he caft a
mournful Look towards his Aged, Sorrowful Father,
and faid; " Why, my Beloved Father! why did you
" not give me Notice of this before we came from
" Home? I might then have had an Opportunity of
" taking Leave of my Dear and Pious Mother, and
" might have received from her Mouth the laft Bleffing
" I fhall ever have from her in this World: I might
" then have had the Happinefs to have proftrated my-
" felf before her with a Filial Humility, and to have
" laid my Head under her Feet, and have im-
" plored her Pardon and Forgivenefs for what-
" ever I had offended her in, and fhould have
" had her Farewel *Salem*, before I had departed from
" before her Eyes, never to behold them more;
" before my Immortal Spirit had relinquifhed this
" Earthly Clay: This would have been to me an ex-
" ceeding great Comfort and Satisfaction.

To this Expoftulation *Abraham* made Reply; " I was
" cautious, my Beloved! nor dared I mention any
" thing of this important Affair to thee, fearing thou
" fhouldft have difcovered it to thy Mother, who,
" doubtlefs, would never have given her Confent; but
" would

" would have prevented my Proceeding in it, and not
" have fuffered thee to have come; whereby, I fhould
" have incurred the Lord's high Difpleafure, through
" my Difobedience in complying with what He had
" fo ftrictly enjoyned me.

" Far be it from me, faid *Ifhmael*, that I fhould
" be, in any-wife, inftrumental to your Difobedience:
" Accomplifh, my dear Father, the Holy Injunction
" of the Almighty; Obey, I befeech you, this His
" Divine Precept without the leaft Delay or Hefita-
" tion upon my Account; for, affure your-felf, that
" fince his Sacred Majefty vouchfafes to accept of fo
" infignificant and worthlefs a Victim as I am, for
" an Oblation, I obey the Holy Decree with a per-
" fect Refignation, and am intirely fatisfied it be in-
" ftantly put in Execution. Approach, my dear
" Father, I beg you, that I may kifs you *between*
" *the Eyes*, and give you my Farewel *Salem*; the
" which when I fhall have done, and taken my Leave
" of *them* for Ever, let then *thofe* Eyes be impartial
" Witnefles how patiently, and with what Humility
" and Refignation, I will, like an innocent Lamb,
" fubmit my Throat to your Knife to be offered up
" to the Lord as a Victim, fince it is for His Holy
" Service: And I intreat you, my Beloved Parent,
" as in this prefent Juncture there is no Remedy nor
" Medium, to mufter up all your innate Courage
" and Greatnefs of Soul: Let your Heart, that feems
" now to be fo tenderly touch'd with Compaffion and
" Reluctancy, become infenfible to Pity, and hard
" as a Rock; let it be, for a while, divefted of all
" Softnefs, or, as it were, of all Humanity: Forget
" that I am your Son; for, upon an Occafion where-
" in it is inconfiftent and inconvenient to harbour the
" leaft Spark of Compaffion, as in this Cafe it is al-
" together fo, then a Compaffionate Perfon is rather
" an Enemy than otherwife. No, the firft Thing
" you do, the firft Step you take, tye my Hands with
" a Cord very faft, that they may not be at Liberty

" to

" to make any Refiftance when you apply the Knife
" to my Flefh: And take Heed, my Honoured Fa-
" ther, that your Garments are not fpotted and de-
" filed with any Drops of my Blood; for fhould it
" fo happen that they be dyed therewith, that Sight
" would hourly bring the Remembrance of this Tra-
" gical Circumftance frefh into your Thoughts: And
" befides, take Notice, I befeech you, that if my
" Mother fhould chance to fee it, fhe will, every
" Minute, endure a moft cruel and bitter Martyrdom.
" Be pleafed, my Father, with humble Submiffion I
" beg it of you, to comfort her under her Affliction
" for my fake, and give her my laft Salutation; and,
" I intreat you, return her my Thanks for having
" conceived in her Womb a Son, whom the Almighty
" has been pleafed to deem worthy to be chofen for
" a Victim to be facrificed to his Holy Name and for
" His Service. I fear, O my good Father, when the
" fharp-edg'd Steel fhall pafs over my Throat, with
" my dying Groans, or my ftruggling Limbs, I may
" difcompofe you; for, in Effect, I am but Flefh
" and Blood, and fubject to all the Frailties incident
" to that bafe and earthly Compofition. By this, I
" am apprehenfive, left the Merit of my fpontaneous
" Refignation fhould be fullied and diminifhed. But,
" alas! my Parent! I too plainly perceive your Sor-
" row and Concern: I beg you not to give way to
" it; but do the Duty that is required of you, with-
" out any further Reluctancy: Take the Weapon in
" your Hand, and delay no longer to comply with your
" Obligation: Shake off the relenting Pity you have
" for me; but if you have not otherwife the Power,
" cover my Eyes and Face with the Veil you brought;
" and, when I am once Dead and Cold, then bury my
" Body out of your Sight: But I defire you'll be
" pleafed to interr me in the fame Cloaths I have on;
" but this *Al juba* [an Upper-Garment] my Mother
" put upon me this Morning when we left her, I
" beg you to return it to her again, that by often
" looking

" looking upon it, fhe may recall her Son fome-
" times into her Memory, and it may, perhaps, be
" fome little Confolation to her for the Abfence of
" her only Child fhe was fo fond of.

Abraham, when he beheld fuch wonderful Conftancy and Refolution, with fo fincere and unufual a
Piety and Fortitude in one fo young as was *Ifhmael*
his Son ; and, when he called to Mind the Arguments he had us'd to encourage him, and with what
an Heroick Intrepidity he was ready and fully prepared to embrace a painful Martyrdom ; When he recol-
lected all this, I fay, his Thoughts were varioufly and
differently employ'd : On one Hand he look'd upon
the fharp Weapon wherewith he was about to cut the
Veins and fpill the Blood of that innocent Child,
the very Sight whereof pierc'd him to the Bottom of
his Soul : On the other Hand, he was very much
heartned and comforted at the Fortitude he beheld
in his Son, and how foon he had fhaken off the Terrors and Apprehenfions of Death, to which he now
fo chearfully offer'd himfelf without the leaft Reluctancy or Hefitation. So that without any further
Delay, the zealous Patriarch began to make ready
to accomplifh the intended Sacrifice.

In order to this, he fet down what Luggage he
had about him, which confifted only of a Sort of a
Felted or Shag Upper Garment caft over his Shoulders, and a Wallet made of a Deer's Skin, tann'd with
the Hair, hanging by his Side, wherein he conftantly
put his Provifion whenever he went abroad to take
his Rounds about his Lands, as he frequently did :
He then, with great Reverence and Humility, began
his *Salah* or Devotion 'till the Sun was mounted up
about half Way towards the Meridian, that the Refulgent Rays of that glorious Planet, when in its
brighteft Splendor, might be Witneffes of the meritorious Proceedings, Oblation and perfect Refignation
of him and of his pious Son. When he had pro-

ftrated

ſtrated himſelf before the Lord, he made Him this
memorable Oration or Prayer.

Abraham's *PRAYER* before the Sacrifice.

Moſt High and Omnipotent Sovereign!

M*AY all the Cœleſtial Potentates of thy Bleſſed Seraphick Choirs give Praiſes to thy Holy Name, with
their melodious and ecboing Hymns, for Ever and Ever!
For, of all thy wonderful and inimitable Works, none was
ever done in Vain, or without the utmoſt Perfection!
No Creature ever felt the Effects of thy dreadful Wrath
and Indignation without having juſtly deſerved the ſame!
Thy Promiſes are as inviolable, and thy Covenants as
ſtable and immoveable, as thy fixed Throne! Thou never
didſt refuſe to ſend thy Succour and Aſſiſtance to them
who implored it : We have hourly Tokens of thy great
and boundleſs Love towards us ; and the Influence of
thy Divine Grace is continually diſtributed amongſt thy
Creatures, with the Intent, that they make the right
Uſe thereof for their Eternal Welfare.   In the Holy
Decrees of thy ſecret Judgments, there is neither a
Why, How, nor Wherefore : All is firm, ſure, and
inevitable ! They are all fix'd, irrevocable and infinite !
I am now, Lord ! upon the Point of Accompliſhing what
thou haſt commanded me to perform ; Grant, therefore,
I beſeech thee of thy unmeaſureable Bounty, that I may
be illuminated with thy Grace, ſo that I may be able,
perfectly to compleat what I have taken in Hand to thy
Honour and G'ory ; and that no Obſtacle may occur to
prevent this my Offering's being acceptable in thy Sight,
and to thy intire Satisfaction.   I ask not this Grace preſumptuouſly, or through the Merit of any of my paſt
Actions, or of my preſent proſtrate Poſture of Humili-
ation ; but I beg it out of the infinite Love and Compaſſion*

paſſion thou haſt always manifeſted to Mankind, and to me in particular, though unworthy of the leaſt of thy Favours. I implore it by the great Mercies thou didſt cauſe to deſcend down upon Adam : *By the unparalell'd Deference thou didſt ſhew to* Noah, *in electing him to be the Director and the principal Tranſactor in that ſo important and never-to-be-forgotten an Action : By all thy ſacred Precepts, which we are in Duty bound to obſerve ; and by all thy mighty Bleſſings, I beſeech thee, moſt Gracious Monarch ! to receive this my Oblation, which is, with an implicite Faith, Confidence and Reſignation, offered, directed and dedicated to thy Divinity, and in Conformity to thy Holy Will and Command. Thy glorious Planets, the refulgent Sun and the beautiful Moon, with all the bleſſed Seraphims that are Attendants about thy Throne of Glory, ſhall be all Witneſſes of my Obedience. And be thou alſo, O Faithful Seraphim ! moſt beauteous* Gabriel ! *I beg and ſupplicate thee, be Thou an Interceſſor for me, that this my Offering may find a gracious and favourable Reception ; as thou canſt teſtify, that I do it purely in Obedience to the Injunction laid on me by the Almighty Lord of Lords.*

Abraham, as ſoon as he had ended this Prayer or Addreſs to the King of Heaven, immediately laid hold of his beloved Child, and having firſt bound his Hands, he caſt him upon the Ground, and then, between Reſolution and Deſpair, he approach'd the Keen-edg'd Knife to the tender Throat of this Innocent, ſaying, at the ſame time, theſe Words, (a)
Biſmil-

(a) Theſe Words are conſtantly uſed by all *Mahometans* in general when they kill any Creature that is to be eaten, for which Reaſon, they don't care to eat of the Meat that is kill'd by *Chriſtians,* who never practiſe that Ceremony : But they are not altogether ſo very ſcrupulous in this Caſe as are the *Jews,* who have, beſides this, other Reaſons for not eating with any Sort of People, but thoſe of their own Religion, eſpecially Meat. —— The laſt Word is here ſuperfluouſly

Bifmillabi! *Allab bu Ackbar wa Adimu!* That is, In the Name of God! God is Great and Powerful!

At this Inftant the Earth, with the very Centres and the profoundeft Abyffes thereof, began to tremble; nay, the Heavens themfelves fhook, and were agitated: The Seas, the Rivers and the Springs were as unfettled as in the greateft Tempeft, or Hurrican; The Dolphins and the reft of the Inhabitants of that Element, funk down, in an unufual Aftonifhment, to the loweft Centres of the Deep, to hide themfelves for Fear. The Cœleftial Choirs of Angels were all, in general, almoft drowned in Tears, being extremely affected with Compaffion, Pity, and Concern at the Sight of fo moving an Object. The Fowls and Birds of the Air flew here and there in a promifcuous Confufion, chirping and lamenting in their Language; and the wild Beafts of the Earth fent forth moft frightful Howlings and Yellings. The Devils in Legions, fled away to fhelter themfelves, being as much terrify'd at the mighty Confufion they beheld, as full of Shame and Refentment to fee that all their Snares, their Subtlety, and their Malice, wherewith they had expected, nay, even made fure of interrupting or quite preventing this fanctified and pious Work, had proved Ineffectual.

" But, amidft all thefe Prodigies, we forget the
" Sufferings of the righteous, and much-to-be-pitied
" Father: What muft his Sentiments be under fo
" fharp a Tryal! To behold his dear and only Child
" bound and ftretch'd out at his Feet, his own Hand
" arm'd with a fharp and fatal Steel ready to táke
" away that innocent Life he would have preferved

---

fluoufly added by the Author, I fuppofe, as he often does, to make out his Verfe; for what the *Mahometans* fay, when they cut the Throat of any Creature whatfoever that is to be eaten (and as they affirm in Imitation of *Abraham* upon this Occafion) is only *Bifmillabi*, *Allab bu Ackbar*: Nor do they hardly do any thing at all without ufing the Expreffion of *Bifmillabi*, or In the Name of God.

a thou-

" a thoufand times rather than his own ; and yet,
" in Obedience to the Abfolutenefs of the Injunction,
" he was rather feduloufly diligent in that cruel Af-
" fair, than negligently lukewarm.

We are informed by facred Writ, That he felt at
once, *Four* different penetrating Afflictions, which
fearch'd and pierc'd into his fuffering Heart to fuch
a Degree, that it became, as it were, like melted
Wax; either of the which was abundantly fufficient
to reduce any Mortal, however courageous and refo-
lute, to his laft Gafp; as it undoubtedly had him,
if the Protecting Hand of his All-powerful Creator had
not been extended over him. The *Firft* was to fee
himfelf obliged to become the Butcher of his only
Child, and who was intirely fpotlefs, faultlefs, and
innocent, far from having, in the leaft, merited fo
deplorable a Deftiny. The *Second* was the fhocking
Thoughts, when he look'd upon the fharp Edge of his
Weapon, of what a cruel and intolerable Smart the
poor harmlefs Child muft endure when he received
the fatal Wound in his tender Flefh. The *Third* was,
when he reflected upon the exceffive heart-breaking
Sentiments of his Mother, when fhe fhould come to
hear of the miferable and untimely Death of the
Child fhe fo tenderly doated upon, and in whom
fhe had center'd her Delight, Joy and Expectations.
The *Fourth* was, that it was altogether out of his
Power, by any humane Means, to deliver his Child
from undergoing the bitter Cup, fince it was the exprefs and pofitive Command of the Eternal Monarch
it fhould be fo, with the which he was abfolutely
and inevitably obliged to comply.

" What a Tryal was here! How hardly muft this
" faithful Servant of the Lord, this Holy *Wreftler,*
" be put to it, to contend with Four fuch potent
" and contrary Adverfaries! Yet, neverthelefs, by
" his Conftancy, his Perféverance and Refolution, he
" prevail'd and got the Victory over them all ."

He

He now, animated with a pious Zeal, with Vigour
and Reſolution, graſp'd the mercileſs Steel in his
Hand, and, with his utmoſt Strength, drew the keen
Edge acroſs the delicate, tender, unreſiſting Throat
of the immaculate Victim : But without Effect ; for
the Angels of God had interpoſed ſome Obſtacle between the Knife and *Iſhmael's* Skin, and at the ſame
Moment cry'd out to their Sovereign in one Voice;
" Behold, O moſt Gracious Lord! thoſe thy Ser-
" vants and *Friends*, whom thou haſt elected from
" among all the Nations of Mankind ; ſee their Suf-
" ferings with thine own All-ſeeing Eyes ; Have
" Compaſſion upon them, ſince thou knoweſt their
" Integrity and Obedience : Pity the tender Nonage
" of the innocent Child, we beſeech thee of thy in-
" finite Mercy."

God anſwered the Bleſſed and Compaſſionate Angels
in theſe Words ; " I ſee it all ; I am an Eye-witneſs of
" what has been tranſacted : If they implore my
" Succour in this their Sorrowful Conflict, in this
" their terrible and bitter Tribulation, I, who am
" the moſt Merciful amongſt the Merciful, will aſ-
" ſuredly and infallibly aſſiſt and deliver them.

The zealous Patriarch again took hold of his Knife,
and, lifting up his Arm, he paſſed it with all his
Might, over his Son's Neck ; but the Endeavour
proved likewiſe fruitleſs and abortive. Then ſaid
Iſhmael to him ; " Alas, my Father! What means
" this! What's become of your wonted Strength, your
" priſtine Vigour and undaunted Reſolution? How
" comes it about, you are ſo ſtrangely altered from
" what you have always been? In the Lord's Name,
" ſhake off this Puſilanimity and inglorious Cowar-
" dice ; and if the Knife's Edge will not cut, thruſt
" it in Point-ways, then it muſt ſurely penetrate!
" Advance your fearful, trembling Arm with Vi-
" gour and Reſolution, that it may pierce my
" yield-

" yielding Flesh, without your giving Way to your
" unseasonable Reluctancy for me. Hasten, without
" farther Delay, to fulfil the Sacred Decree, in Spight
" and Opposition of your mortal and implacable
" Enemy the Devil, who is using all his possible
" Endeavours to obstruct and deter your Proceeding
" in the Accomplishing an Injunction so Sacred as
" is this you are about.

Abraham now tried that Way also, but notwithstanding he thrust forwards with all his Force, to make the sharp Point penetrate into the Child's Throat, imagining that by so doing, he might be able to make an End of him, and so put him out of his Pain at once; yet he could not possibly either wound or draw Blood of him; which when *Ishmael* saw, he got up, and throwing himself upon his Knees, he made his Address to the Almighty in this short Prayer.

Ishmael's PRAYER.

MY Bounteous Lord, who livest and reignest, for Ever and Ever, to all Eternity! Thou who art Absolute Monarch over all the Heavens, the Earths, and the Waters, there being none that dares contradict the least of thy Decrees! Vouchsafe, I implore thee, to cast an Eye of Compassion upon my tender Years, and commiserate the Gray Hairs of my afflicted, aged Parent. Grant, O thou just and impartial Judge! that this our Oblation may have a speedy Catastrophe, and that it may be accomplished to the Honour and Glory of thy Blessed Name. Thou perfectly knowest our Intentions, as we likewise are satisfied and convinced that with only thy Will it shall be so, it may be brought to a happy Conclusion, and I shall be out of my Pain and at Rest. As thou
knowest

*knoweſt what I am, ſo, in like Manner, I am not at all
ignorant, that what I ſhall be, or what is to become of
me, is wholly in thy Power and at thy Diſpoſal. And,
as thou art the only Victorious Conqueror, who never
was, nor never can be conquered, do not, I intreat thee,
diſpiſe this my voluntary Offering, leſt the Accurſed
Enemy the Devil ſhould remain with the Victory, and
I, notwithſtanding my pious Intent, be vanquiſhed and
confounded.*

As ſoon as the pious Youth had thus ended his
Prayer, he, with a ſurprizing Magnanimity and Reſolution, returned again, and laid down his Neck at
his Father's Feet, ſaying; " Come, my dear Father,
" diſpatch and make an End of me." *Abraham*
then made a Fourth Tryal to wound his Son's Throat,
but his Arm was now this Time withheld by the
Faithful Angel *Gabriel*, who, by the Command of the
moſt High and Sovereign Monarch, had deſcended,
and brought with him a fine, fat, and beautiful Ram,
which had been bred in the richeſt Paſtures of the Cœleſtial Paradiſe.

The Bleſſed Angel then, detaining and holding
back his Arm, ſaid to him; " Deſiſt, thou Upright
" *Friend* of the Almighty; Forbear, and ſet thy
" *illuſtrious* Child at Liberty; for he is not the Victim
" the Lord requires. Yet his Oblation is nevertheleſs
" compleatly accompliſhed: Let him go; and for his
" Ranſom, take and ſacrifice this choſen Ram, which
" thy Lord hath, with his own Hand, picked out of
" his Cœleſtial Flocks, on purpoſe to redeem the pi-
" ous *Iſhmael:* This is the Offering His Divine Ma-
" jeſty is pleaſed to accept of inſtead of thy Son, be-
" ing intirely ſatisfied with the Integrity of you
" both."

The good Patriarch upon this, with exceſſive Joy
and Content, unbound his Son, and inſtantly offered
up the Ram which the Faithful *Gabriel* had brought
from Paradiſe; the Fleſh whereof he got ready, and
they

they made a joyful and delicious Meal of it: And from hence is derived the venerable Ceremony of the (*a*) *Adaheas*, which the *True Believers* always perform at the Feaft of *El Corban*, that is, *Of the Sacrifice* which is left us as an uneccceptionable Precept by our Honoured Prophet *Mahommed*, and afterwards recommended to us by his excellent and venerable (*b*) *Sahaabah*, or Companions.

After

(*a*) *Adaheas.* Though I am tolerably well acquainted with this Word my felf, yet I rather chufe to infert (as I often do, that my Readers may fee, I give them the Authority of fo Authentick an Author) what Monfieur *D'Herbelot* fays under the Word *Adhha*, which is the true Pronunciation. He fays; It is a Feftival of the *Mahometans*, kept upon the Twelfth Day of the Moon *Debou'lbagiat*, which is the Twelfth and laft of their [Lunar] Year. This Name fignifies, *The Month of the Pilgrimage*, becaufe particularly obferved for the Ceremonies of the Pilgrims at *Mecca.* —— On that Day they folemnly facrifice a Sheep at *Mecca*, and at no other Place [He means the Ceremony there is folemnized after a peculiar Manner; for on that Day, which is the firft Day of their great *Beyram*, every one that is able, folemnly facrifices one or more Sheep, throughout the whole *Mahometan* Dominions] which bears the Name of the Feftival by the *Turks* commonly called the *Great Beyram* [and by the *Arabs Aayd el Kebir*, or *Aayd el Corban, i. e.* The great *Pafqua*, or the Feftival of the Sacrifice] to diftinguifh it from the Leffer one, which immediately fucceeds their Great Faft of *Ramadam.* The Eaftern *Chriftians* call it the *Mahometans* Eafter. This Feftival is likewife called *Jaum el Corban* or the Day of Sacrifice, becaufe on that Day every Pilgrim may facrifice as many Sheep as he pleafes. Thefe Victims are called [in the Plural] *Dhabiat.* They go out of *Mecca* to celebrate this Solemnity in a Valley called *Mina*, or *Muna*, and there they fometimes offer a Camel.——This is the only Sacrifice the *Mahometans* ufe; and this they obferve in the Commemoration of *Abraham.* It is pofitively afferted by their Authors, That the Horns of this very Ram, which was facrificed inftead of *Ifhmael*, were, by the *Arabs*, affixed to the Golden Gutter which received the Rain Water from the Roof of the *Caabah*, and continued there 'till *Mahomet's* Days, who caufed them to be taken away, to deprive thofe People of any Motive to Idolatry.

(*b*) *Sahaabah* or *Sahabah*, is the Plural Number of *Saheb* and *Afhab*, a Friend or Companion, and, in fome Senfes, a Mafter and Owner of any Thing But the Word, as it does here, always fignifies

After all this was over, they gladly began to defcend from the Mountain, and with joyful Countenances haftened their Steps towards the City; where
being arrived, they met the Child's Mother, who
having been in a great Care and Concern at their long
Stay, was coming out to look after them; and when
fhe beheld them coming, fhe ran and took her Son in
her Arms, and tenderly embraced him, kiffing his
lovely Eyes and Cheeks a Thoufand Times They
gave her a particular Account of all that had paffed:
At the Recital whereof, fhe was exceedingly terrified
and amazed; and although, from that Day forwards,
fhe was more than ordinary careful of her Son, and
would never venture him a Moment out of her Sight,
yet fhe could never be eafy; but was always under a
Jealoufy and a fufpicious Apprehenfion, left the like
Accident might befal him again: Nor did fhe ever
think him fecure, 'till one Day the *Faithful* Angel
Gabriel appeared to her, and affured her, That from
the Loins of *Ifhmael* her Son fhould proceed Men of
pure and exemplary Lives; and that he fhould be
the Father of infinite Generations, and the Founder of
innumerable Tribes of gallant and undaunted Warriors, from whom fhould defcend the noble and moft
illuftrious Chieftain, the great and famous Leader
Mahommed of ever Bleffed Memory, the laft, or as
we may fay, the *Seal* of all the Prophets; for the
Love of whom, and for whofe Sake alone, God created the Heavens with all their Illuminations, Planets
and Signs, the Earths, Plants, Seas, Rivers, *&c.*

The Great and Royal Princefs remained fatisfied,
joyful and content at this Affurance, returning Prai-

---

fies *Mahomet's* Companions, being Ten in Number, fome whereof were his immediate Succeffors, as *Abubeker, Omar, Otham, Ali,*
&c. They were all very famous for their Learning, Piety, Valour,
Employments or Dignities, and their Memories are held in great
Authority and Veneration among the *Mahometans,* They are fpoken
of by Dr. *Prideaux* in his L. of *Mahom.* Which fee.

fes

fes and Thankfgivings to the Lord of Heaven, who had-been pleafed to grant her fo mighty a Blessing: And the good *Abraham* fanctified the Hour of that great and memorable Transaction that had happened in the Mountain, with Two Proftrations and Humiliations, which are, to this Day, obferved by many pious *Muffulmans :* By which is meant, That Time of the Morning when the Sun is fo high advanced in his Afcent, that his Rays are upon the intire Surface of this Side of the Earthly Globe : This Point of Time is what we call *Adoha,* and is the fame wherein *Abraham* began firft to make ready to offer up his Son, when they arrived at the Mountain-Top : And for the Four different and contrary Afflictions he had to contend with all at once, as has been related, before he began to apply the Knife to his Son's Throat, the righteous Patriarch inftituted Four Proftrations, *&c.* as a Token of his grateful Acknowledgment to his Lord and Creator, for delivering him from Four fuch terrible Adverfaries ; which Devotions he performed as the Sun was juft mounted to the Zenith, or rather Meridian ; for the whole Time of the Sacrifice continued from the Sun's being, as I have faid before, in his *Adoha,* 'till full Noon, from whence our High *Salah* of the *Dohar,* or Noon-Tide, had its firft Original : The which, with all the reft of the Holy Precepts, are enjoyned us by the Sacred Law of our Bleffed Prophet *Mahommed* of ever Holy Memory, to the unexpreffible Benefit of all *True Believers.*

C H A P. IX.

The LINE *of* ISAAC.

The Angel Gabriel *brings* Sarah *Tydings of her bearing a Son in her Old Age. Her Diffidence. The Angel's Prophecy concerning the Posterity of* Isaac. Abraham's *Indifference.* Isaac's *Birth. His Character. That of* Jacob. *Of* Joseph. *Of* Moses. *Of* Joshua. *Of* David. *Of* Solomon, *with his strange Adventures. Of* Daniel. *Of* Jonas. *Of* St. John *the Baptist. Of* Jesus Christ; *and the Antichristian Sentiments of the* Mahometans *concerning him.* (a)

AFTER this great and memorable Sacrifice, which had, in every Particular, been transacted as I have before related; *Abraham,* who had taken up his Abode within the Confines of *Arabia,* where he had passed the greatest Part of his Life, was now growing towards his latter End, being full an Hundred Years old, and his Wife *Sarah* Ninety. She

---

(a) The Argument my Author gives this his 9th Chapter runs thus; *Cuentas en este Canto, la Linea de Yzhaq Patron de los Judios y Cristianos, y el asiento del Pueblo de Israel, y los grandes Hechos de los*

She was now paſt all Expectation or Probability of ever having any Children, as having been hitherto barren all her whole Life, and now arrived at an Age of, almoſt, Decrepidneſs; ſo that ſhe might, by the Courſe of Nature, very rationally be in Deſpair of ever becoming the Mother of a Son.

" But as the hidden Cauſes of all thoſe myſterious
" Secrets of Nature are known and manifeſted
" to the All-knowing Creator, and to none but Him;
" and as it is His Divine Pleaſure it ſhall be ſo, He
" never vouchſafing to permit any but Himſelf alone
" to be endowed with a conſummate and perfect Know-
" ledge, it becomes not us Mortals to be over-curious,
" but, in all Things, to ſubmit to His ſuperior
" Wiſdom.

For the Lord, notwithſtanding the apparent Im-poſibility, was pleaſed at that Time to diſpatch away the Seraphic *Gabriel*, with Orders to deſcend to the Earth, and there to deliver a Meſſage to the deſpairing Matron. He came to her and ſpoke thus; " *Sarah!* It is ordained by the Lord of Heaven, that " you conceive and bring forth a Son." To which ſhe, with a loud Laughter, made him this Reply; " My Lord! You are ſurely come to mock me: Your " Words and the Subject of your Meſſage are ſuch, " that I can't refrain from Laughter. What Pro- " ſpect or Probability can I have of bringing forth " Children, when I am come to my Journey's End? " How can it be expected or imagined, that I ſhould

---

los *Anauies* qui de a jui procedieron baſta yce aleb çalam, y las vertajas que de cada uno dellos eredamos: que fue el principal *Motibo de bazer eſte Libro*, por que auia muchos ygnorantes delles. That is; " In this " Canucle, or Chapter, an Account is given of the Line of *Iſaac* " Patron of t e *Jews* and *Chriſtians*, and the Foundation of the Peo- " ple of *Iſrael*, with the great Deeds of thoſe Prophets who pro- " ceeded from that Stock: Which was the principal Motive for " compoſing this Book, becauſe many were ignorant of thoſe " Things."

" ever

" ever hold a Son, to fuckle him at thefe Breafts of
" mine, which are, through Age, become fo wrink-
" led, lank and languid?

The Angel then anfwered her to this Purpofe;
" Mark well what I fay, thou worthy, though incre-
" dulous Woman! Liften attentively to my Words:
" The Son that fhall be born unto thee, fhall bear
" this very Name: He fhall be called *Laughter*: But
" he fhall be the Father of very numerous Genera-
" tions, and the Founder of an Illuftrious Genealogy,
" wherein fhall be many holy, pious and fanctified
" Prophets and Patriarchs; from whom fhall likewife
" proceed a wicked, perverfe and moft degenerate
" Race of People: For in the fame Manner as thou
" haft, fo inconfiderately, derided and made flight of
" the facred Word of God, fo fhall thy future Pofte-
" rity become the Scoff and Derifion of the Accurfed
" *Lucifer.*

When *Gabriel* had fpoke thus, he departed, leaving
Sarah not a little furprized and overjoyed; who immediately went forth out of her Houfe to feek for her
Hufband, to impart to him the glad Tydings the Angel had brought her; and that God had promifed them
a Son, who fhould prove the Ornament and Comfort
of his Houfe and Pofterity. She found *Abraham* in
Company with his Son *Ifhmael*, whom he fo dearly
loved, and whom he held in his Arms tenderly embracing. When fhe had told him the whole Caufe of
her Joy and Aftonifhment, he, with a kind of a cold
Indifference, only faid; " If the Lord pleafes but to
" preferve this I have already, I fhall be intirely fa-
" tisfied: Meaning, That his Son *Ifhmael* alone, was
what he had the greateft Love and Efteem for in this
World, and that he feemed to be doubtful and to
make Difficulties, and likewife to be indifferent, as to
his ever being the Father of another Child.

However, at the End of Nine Months, his Wife
Sarah was delivered of a fair Son, and they called
him by the Name of *Ifaac*, which Word fignifies
Laughter:

Laughter : This was done in Conformity to the Fore-warning the blessed Angel *Gabriel* had given to *Sarah* his Mother.

This *Isaac* was the Father, Founder, or Patron of the Tribes of *Beni Yfrael*, who are the *Jews* or Sons of *Jacob*, otherwise called *Israel*; a People in former Ages, exceedingly beloved, favoured and honoured by the Almighty. This just Patriarch *Isaac* took to Wife a chaft, fair and beautiful Virgin, of *Hebrew* Defcent, whofe Name was *Rebecca* : She was of noble and honourable Parentage, and had been brought up by *Batuel*, who was a very upright and devout Perfon, and took great Care of her Education. The Fruits of her Marriage with *Isaac* were two Twin-Brothers, *Jacob* and (a) *Esau*, who ftrove and contended mightily in

N 2   their

(a) *Esau* the Son of *Isaac* and *Rebecca*, and Twin-Brother to the Patriarch *Jacob*, is by all *Mahometan* Hiftorians, called *Aü Ben Ishac*. They tell all that Story with very little Variation from *Mofes*'s Account of it in *Genefis*; only add, That the Bleffing *Isaac* defigned for *Esau*, but gave to *Jacob*, by the Contrivance of his Wife *Rebecca*, particularly regarded *Jacob*'s Pofterity, out of which were to proceed the Prophets and Meffengers of God : And this Bleffing being, by God's Appointment, given away from *Esau*, he begged, that his Line might, inftead of Prophets, produce Kings, Emperors, and mighty Men ; and accordingly moft of the *Mahometan* Hiftoriographers affirm, That *Esau* had a Son called *Roum*, from whom all the *Greek* and *Roman* Emperors are defcended. *Esau*, they fay, married feveral Wives, and had by them a numerous Iffue. The firft was *Nahalat*, the Daughter of his Uncle *Ifhmael*. The fecond *Adah*, Daughter to *Elon Hefteen*, a *Canaanean*. After thefe he married *Greeks*, whofe Offspring remain'd in their Mother's Country. *Abou'l Farage* fays, That *Esau* made War upon his Brother *Jacob*, who at laft flew him with an Arrow. *Esau* is likewife furnamed *Edom*, being fo called becaufe he was Red-haired. This the *Arabs* have borrowed from the *Hebrew*, and call the Pofterity of *Esau*, *Edmioun* and *Edomijn*, the *Edomites* or *Idumeans*. They alfo give them the Name of *Banou* or *Bani el Asfar*, the Children of the Yellow, Fair, or Red-hair'd Man, which *Edom* fignifies in the *Hebrew* Tongue. But by this Name they do not only mean the *Idumeans* or *Edomites*, but apply it likewife to the *Greeks* and *Romans*, whom they believe to defcend from *Esau*. The *Talmudi*'s and mo-

                dern

their Mother's Womb, about who fhould be firft born: However *Efau* got the better there, and came out fore-moft, whom his Brother *Jacob* immediately followed at his Heels: So that *Efau,* by his Robuftnefs and an arrogant Refolution, got the Advantage of his meeker Brother, as to the Precedency of Birth-right; but (a) *Jacob,* in Retaliation, defrauded him of the Bleffing of his dying Father, and was endowed with a larger Por-tion of God's Grace.

Jacob was a moft Righteous Man: He went into *Mefopotamia,* where he married two Sifters, the Daugh-ters of his Uncle *Laban*; and afterwards he efpoufed two young Damfels who had been his Handmaids, infomuch, that the whole Number of lawfully wedded Wives he had, was Four: He had by thofe four Wives, Twelve Sons, Prophets and Patriarchs of high Efteem and Degree, from whom proceeded Twelve Tribes or Lineages. Of thefe Twelve Houfes or Stocks, all the whole People of *Ifrael,* that is to fay, the Nations of the *Jews,* had their Original Defcent; amongft which

---

dern *Jews,* have infufed this ill-grounded, foolifh Notion into the Heads of the *Mahometans,* with the malicious Defign of bringing down the Curfes the Prophets laid on the *Idumeans* o   upon the *Chriftians* in general, and even upon our   himfelf; but in this Refpect, they muft never harbou   of the *Mahometans* agreeing with them.

(a) They fay, *Jacob* is called *Ifrael* in *Syriac,* and that he was the Father of Twelve Sons, whom they generally call *Asbath,* that is, the Tribes, becaufe they were the Parents and Founders of the Twelve Tribes of the *Jews*; and, that of this Patriarch's Race came all the Prophets, except Three, who are *Aoub* or *Job,* *Shioab* or *Jethro,* Father-in-Law to *Mofes,* and *Mahomet*; which Three, they fay, defcended from *Ifhmael,* and were *Arabs* by Nation; though fome Writers leave out *Job,* and mention only the two others. The *Tzarich Montbekieh* adds, That not only the Gift of Prophecy continued among the Sons of *Jacob,* but alfo the Regal Power, which remained amongft them, 'till the Time of *Ija* and *Jahia,* that is, *Jefus Chrift* and St. *John* the Baptift; after whom the *Romans* and *Perfians* deftroy'd their Country. The fame Author fays, That *Jacob* dyed in in *Ægypt, &c.* all exactly as in the Bible.

People,

People, there have been a venerable Number of very vertuous and pious Men, Servants of the moft High God, whofe Fear was continually before their Eyes, and upon whom the Lord was pleafed to pour down very great and exemplary Mercies, and to beftow upon them uncommon Portions of his Divine Grace: Yet, notwithftanding, as I have before hinted, from this Favoured and Illuftrious Family, by their mixing with Strange and Idolatrous Nations, they, in fucceeding Ages, became fo degenerately adulterated, that the latter Generations of that once fo noble a Nation, have rendered themfelves infamous, defpifed, hated and contemptible throughout the whole World: They have had many and terrible Inftances of the Wrath and Indignation of their incenfed God, whofe avenging Arm hath not yet ceafed from purfuing that obftinate, wicked and perverfe People.

The moft worthy of all the Sons of *Jacob*, was that juft and ever-memorable Patriarch *Jofeph*. From this fame Stock defcended the Righteous Legiflator *Mofes*, that for-ever-famous Perfon, who was deemed worthy to converfe with God Himfelf, and to receive from His Divine Hands thofe Sacred Laws, which were written with God's Finger upon the Tables. *Aaron* the High Prieft was Brother to this Holy Man, and was a great Affifter to him, in the Publication of thofe Laws of the Moft High. From the fame Lineage likewife defcended that Renowned and Warlike Leader *Jofhua*, who won that miraculous Battle. As was alfo the Royal *David*, the famous and fanctified Author of (a) *El Zabour*, or the *Pfalms*, a Book re-

N 3 vifed

(a) *El Zabour*, or, as fome pronounce it, *El Zebour*, is the Plural Number of *Zebr*, which in *Arabick* fignifies a Book. The Word *Zabour* hath two Significations. In the Firft Place, it is the Name of the Book of the Divine Decrees, which the *Mahometans* otherwife call *Lough el Mahfouth*, The fecret Tables. In the next Place, as it is generally taken, it implies the *Pfalter*, or Book of *Pfalms*, wherewith they believe that God infpired *David*. They add, That this

vifed by God Himſelf, and ſigned with His own Hand: The Son of this Royal Prophet was the Magnificent and moſt Wiſe *Solomon*; he, who thro' the Tranſcendancy and efficacious Virtue of his Ring, obtained Univerſal Command, nothing daring to diſpute his Will. Of this People was likewiſe the holy *Daniel*, who was caſt to the Lions to be devoured. And *Jonas*, who was ſwallowed by the Whale, proceeded from the ſame Original. *Zacharias* the Sacerdote, that devout Man, who was eſpouſed to the vertuous *Anna* or *Hannah*, who was the Mother of the unſpotted (a) *Miriam*, or *Mary*, that chaſte and undefiled Virgin, whoſe Memory is of ſuch high Veneration in the World; and is the

ſame

---

this Royal Prophet ſung them himſelf, and cauſed the *Levites* and his Muficians to ſing them to the Sound of Inſtruments before the Holy Ark. However, the Book the *Mahometans* call *Zabour*, does not contain the ſame *Pſalms* we have in the *Pſalter*, but only a confuſed Extract of ſeveral Things, which have not the leaſt Relation to *David* or his *Pſalms*. They likewiſe ſay, That the *Engile* or *Holy Goſpel* was ſent by God to *Jeſus Chriſt* 1200 Years after *David* received from Heaven his Canticles or Songs called *Zabour*; and the *Sabis* or *Sabians*, who pretend they have *Adam*'s Book, do alſo boaſt, that they have the true *Zabour*: But this Book of the *Sabians* is ſtill more remote from *David*'s Pſalms than that of the *Mahometans*, and is rather the ſame with that they call *Deſſour*, which comprehends their Law, or Superſtitious Religion; and it is likely they rather call it *Zabour* from the general Signification of this Word, which is Book, than from that peculiar one the *Mahometans* give it. *D'Herbelot* in *Zebour*. Of theſe *Sabians*, ſee the ſame Author under the Words *Saba* and *Sabi*, where is a large Account of them.

(a) The *Arabick* Name *Mariam*, that is *Mary*, is taken from the *Hebrew* and *Syriack*. By this Name they always call the bleſſed Virgin Mother of our Lord. ever adding *Lella*, or Lady. It is the proper Name of many Women. The *Alcoran*, in ſeveral Places, makes very honourable Mention of our bleſſed Lady, and there is a whole Chapter that bears her Name; and ſome others ſpeak not only of her Birth, but of her Mother, *S. Ann*, being big of her, and likewiſe of her Education in the Houſe of *Zachariah*, and in the Temple; as alſo of her divine and miraculous Delivery;

to

ſame from whoſe Body was born the moſt Juſt and Holy *Iſa,* or *Jeſus,* whom the deluded *Chriſtians* blindly, erroneouſly and idolatrouſly worſhip, and
N 4   have

---

to all which the Expoſitors add ſeveral Traditions of the Eaſtern Chriſtians, which, but for them, 'tis probable, had been loſt, One of them is, That God (according to the *Alcoran*) pre-ſerved her and her Son from the Devil. *Houſſain Vaes,* a noted Hiſtorian, expounds this Preſervation in theſe Words; " No Child, " ſays he, is born into the World, that the Devil does not touch " and handle 'till he makes it cry, and except *Miriam* and her " Son, none were ever preſerved, and exempted from this Hard- " ling. " —— This Tradition ſeems to have ſome Alluſion to Original Sin, called by the *Arabs* (as I have ſaid ſomewhere elſe) *Hebat el Calb,* that is, The Grains of the Heart. —— As for S. *Ann,* the Bleſſed Virgin's Mother, ſhe is known by the *Mahometans* by her proper Name *Hannah,* of whom they ſay, That when ſhe was with Child of our Lady, ſhe vowed to dedicate to God what ſhe bore in her Womb, and accordingly performed her Promiſe as ſoon as ſhe was delivered, by offering up her Daughter in the Temple. *Mahomet* makes God ſay upon the Birth of the Bleſſed Virgin, " I have named her *Miriam*; " Which Name, ſay the Ex-poſitors, is the ſame as *Amat Allah,* God's Handmaid; an Expoſition taken from our Lady's Words to the Angel; *Behold the Handmaid of the Lord.* The Impoſtor *Mahomet,* who always inlarges upon the Truths of our Scriptures, ſays, That God gave *Mary* in keeping to *Zachary,* who ſhut her up in a Chamber of the Temple, the Door whereof was ſo high, that there was no coming to it but by a Ladder, the Key whereof he always carry'd about him. He very frequently went to ſee her, and always found by her great Store of the choiceſt Fruits the Land of *Paleſtine* produced, and ever in the wrong Seaſon, when they were no where elſe to be found, which at laſt, made him aſk her, " How ſhe came by that fine Fruit? " To which ſhe anſwer'd; " All you ſee comes from God, who furniſh- " eth whom he pleaſes with all things in Abundance. " —— They extol the Purity of the bleſſed Virgin in the higheſt Degree, and not many Years ago a *Turk* at *Conſtantinople* ſuffered the moſt cruel of all Deaths, being impaled alive, for uttering an unſeemly Ex-preſſion concerning her. —— There is an odd fabulous Tradi-tion goes among them, about a certain Princeſs, in former Ages, whoſe Name was *Alankara,* which *Khondemir* compares to the mi-raculous Conception of the Virgin *Mary.* The Story runs thus; She was the Daughter of *Gioubine* the Son of *Buldu* King of the *Moguls,* of the Race of *Kiat,* the Second that reign'd over them in the Northern *Aſia,* after the Re-eſtabliſhing of that Nation. This Princeſs

have equalized with God, by whom both He and all other Creatures were made. *Jahia,* or *John,* whoſe Life was ſo exemplary, and ſo exceeding pious, with

---

ceſs married *Doujoun* her Couſin Germain, then King of the *Moguls,* by whom ſhe had Two Sons, called *Belghedi* and *Bikghedi.* After the Death of her Husband, *Alankara* governed his Dominions, and brought up her Children with great Prudence. She being awake one Night in her Chamber, a very bright ſhining Light entered in at her Mouth, and paſſing through her Body, came out at her Private Parts, which ſurprized her very much; but far greater was her Amazement, when ſhe perceived herſelf afterwards to be with Child, without a Husband, or having had to do with any Man. She called an Aſſembly of the chief of her Subjects, and acquainted them with the whole Matter, and finding they would not be perſuaded to believe what ſhe ſaid, ſhe cauſed ſeveral of them to ſtay all Night in her Appartment, where they were all Eye Witneſſes of the ſame thing, which happened to her conſtantly every Night, whereby her Reputation was cleared When the Time was expired, ſhe was delivered of three Sons, The Firſt called *Boukoun Cabaki,* from whom deſcended the *Tartars* called *Cabakin* and *Kapgiak;* The Second *Boukin Selgue* from whom deſcended the *Selgiucides.* The Third *Bouzangir,* who was one of the Fore fathers of *Genghizkhar* and *Temur Langh,* or, as we call him, *TamerJane.* This ſtrange Fable was probably invented on purpoſe to aggrandize the Original of the great *Turkiſh* and *Tartarian* Families: And perhaps the *Moguls* being once *Chriſtians,* may have applied that miraculous Conception to this Princeſs, ſince their Fall, for their greater Reputation. —— The *Mahometan* Infidels charge the *Chriſtians* with making the Virgin *Mary,* the Third Perſon of the Bleſſed Trinity; yet ſome of their Authors clear us from that Imputation. *Abou'l Farage* writes, That it was a Tradition among the Eaſtern *Chriſtians,* That the bleſſed Virgin was but 13 Years of Age when ſhe conceived by the Holy Ghoſt, and that ſhe lived but 51 Years. They, I mean the *Aſiatick* Chriſtians, have a Faſt they keep before the great Feaſt of our Lady, which is on the 15th of *Aguſt,* by us called the Aſſumption. This Faſt begins on the 1ſt Day of the ſame Month, and the Feaſt of the Aſſumption is by them generally called *Futh Miriam,* The breaking up of *Mary's* Faſt, or the Feaſt of our Lady The Plant we call *Cyclamen Odoriferum,* and our *Lady's* Glove, is by the *Aſiaticks* called *Bokhour Miriam,* or *Mary's* Perfume; and they affirm, That by the bleſſed Virgin having laid her Hand upon that Plant, it received the Form of her four Fingers and Thumb, and drew from thence its odoriferous Scent.

very

very many others, too numerous to be all repeated here, were all derived from that noble and illuftrious Original.

But let us return to the Beginning, from whence we have made this Digreffion, to fee how the Genealogy was carry'd on. Something fhall be faid, though with all poffible Brevity, concerning the never-dying Actions of thofe venerable Perfons, whofe Names I have mentioned; And, likewife, we ought not to omit recalling to our Memories fome of the Precepts left us by them, whereof the Inftitutions in our Books of *El Sunna* are chiefly compos'd; fince the Doctrines and edifying Examples which we have inherited from thefe holy Prophets have been mainly conducive towards the Redemption and Eternal Salvation of our Immortal Souls.

(a) *Ifaac* the fecond Son of the Holy Patriarch *Abraham*, by his firft Wife *Sarah*, was, as I have already faid, the firft Founder and Patron of the People of *Ifrael*. He was an upright Servant of the Lord, and walked conftantly in his Paths. He never omitted vifiting his Father's (b) Sepulchre thrice every Day, paying great Honour,

Reve-

(a) In moft things, except the Sacrifice, the *Mahometans* agree with our Scriptures in what concerns *Ifaac*, whom they call *Ifbac ben Ibrahim*. They only add, That the Spirit of Prophefy, which before was intire in the Patriarchs, was, after the Death of *Abraham*, divided between *Ifhmael* and his younger Brother *Ifaac*; and that all the Prophets in general defcended from *Ifaac*, except *Shoaib* and *Mahomet*, who were of the Pofterity of *Ifhmael*. This *Shoaib* is *Jethro*, Father in-Law to *Mofes*, of whom I intend to make mention in another Place, and likewife of *Job*, whom a little before I have hinted to be, by many Authors, reckoned with the other Two.

(b) That *Abraham* was buried in the City of *Hebron*, from him likewife called *Khalil*, is the unanimous Opinion of all the Eaftern Nations. *Ben Schonah*, in the Year of the *Hegira* 513, which anfwers to the Year of our Lord 1119, under the Caliphfhip of *Mofterbaffbed*, 19th Caliph of the Houfe of the *Abbaffides*, tells us, That *Abraham*'s Tomb, wherein were alfo *Ifaac* and *Jacob*, was opened, and in it were

Reverence, Devotion and filial Duty to that venerable Monument. The Increase of his Flocks, and all his Cattle, he set apart for the Poor, and liberally bestowed it all upon them; taking particular Care to distribute his Charity so, that those who were most in Necessity might have the largest Share of his Bounty. He ever cultivated an amicable Correspondence, and maintained an inviolable Friendship with his Brother *Ishmael,* to whom he always shewed great Respect, and a Deference due to him as his Elder.

Jacob, the worthy Son of this so venerable a Parent, was no-wise inferior to his Father in Merit, and Piety, Charity, or Holiness of Life. He enjoyned himself to observe Four notable Vows, which he had made a solemn Promise to God never to violate, and the which for their Rarity, and their meritorious Sanctity and Charity, are highly esteemed of, and extolled by *Caebu el Khabar,* a learned Writer. The first was, He obliged himself never to taste the Meats that were set before him, but deemed them to be *Haram,* or Unlawful, 'till he had first performed two Prostrations before God, by way of craving a Blessing upon what he was about to eat, and to shew his thankful Acknowledgments for what his Lord had bountifully been pleased to send him for his Sustenance. The Second was; That he had bound himself under the like Obligation to eat of nothing that had been prepared for him, 'till he had given of it to such poor,

were found the Bodies of those Patriarchs very whole and intire, with several Lamps of Gold and Silver, of all which vast Numbers of People were Eye Witnesses. This Tomb is so much honoured by the *Mahometans,* that they make their fourth Pilgrimage to it, the three first being that of *Mecca,* that of *Medina,* and that of *Jerusalem.* There are several Books that treat of these Pilgrimages, and *Calami* has wrote a particular one concerning the Visitation of *Abraham's* Sepulchre, and intitled it, *Uns el Khalil,* that is, The Society or Familiarity that is contracted with *Abraham.*

weak,

weak, or fick People that were near his Habitation.
The Third was, That he had always as many Par-
cels of Provifions of all Sorts, laid up in Store for the
Relief of thofe who were in Want, as there are Days
in the Year, with a folemn Oath never to diminifh
them, upon his own Account, to whatfoever Neceffity he fhould happen to be reduced. The Fourth
was ; An inviolable Promife he had made, that the
Water of his Wells, Cifterns, and the like, fhould,
unexceptionably, be never refufed to Mân ôr Beaft
that were thirfty.

"O juft and venerable Patriarch! 'Twas not for
"nothing that all thy Undertakings were attended
"with fuch profperous Periods! Nor was it undefer-
"vedly that thy Fields and Paftures were continu-
"ally covered with exuberant Verdure, and thy
"Flocks fo fair and fo fruitful! Whoever can but ob-
"tain the Grace to follow thy Foot-fteps, will, un-
"doubtedly, gain the Palm of Honour in this World,
"and of everlafting Glory in that to come! It was
"thy tranfcendent Conftancy in doing Good Works,
"thy fcarcely imitable Perfeverance in thy bountiful
"Diftribution of Alms to the Diftreffed, that gave
"thee Strength and Refolution to exert thy felf, as
"thou couragioufly didft, when thou contendedft
"fo long with fo unequal a Match as the Angel
"fent from Heaven to try thy Force!

This great Prophet wreftled a whole Night, from
Sun-fet to Break of Day, with the bleffed Angel of
God, *Gabriel*, who came down to him in humane
Form to make Tryal of his Fortitude and Valour :
and after they had ftrove, as I have faid, all the
Night, and notwithftanding the Superiority of the
Antagonift *Jacob* had to contend withal, he remained
upon his Feet, unfoiled and invincible, having, by
that fo heroic and magnanimous an Action, gained
to himfelf an immortal Name.

"By

" By this, and such like Examples, we meet with
" in Holy Writ, we may plainly comprehend, and
" not scruple to conclude, That those of the Poste-
" rity of *Eve*, when inspired with divine Grace, and
" armed with a generous Emulation of exerting their
" Forces for the Glory and Honour of their Mighty
" Creator; Then, I say, they can never possibly be
" vanquished, nor is any thing in this earthly World,
" too difficult for them to undertake, and, by perse-
" vering, to bring to a happy Conclusion.

This was He, who, as he lay asleep, beheld a wonderful Ladder, the Bottom whereof was at his Feet,
and the Top reached up to Heaven, upon the which,
innumerable Legions of Seraphims were ascending and
descending without Intermission. And, in a Word,
it was this same Patriarch concerning whom our Expositors all agree in telling us, that since the Time of
Noah, none of all the ancient Patriarchs ever saw
such Mysterious Visions, or had so many Revelations
as the ever-venerable *Jacob*.

(*a*) *Joseph* his Son, of whom such honourable Mention is made in the Sacred *Alcoran*, had a Vision in
his Sleep, wherein he beheld the Sun, and the Moon,
with Eleven of the brightest Stars in the Firmament,
fall down and worship and do Homage to him. This
is He who was cast into the Pit or Well, and sold for
a Sum of Money to People of a Strange Nation, like
a Beast in a publick Market; and was afterwards
thrown into a dismal, lonesome, and filthy Dungeon,
where he continued Seventeen Years in inexpressible
Misery and Distress; which Misfortune befel him
only because when he was tempted and persecuted,
through the Means of his matchless Beauty, to violate his Chastity, he refused to consent. We read of
him, That whilst he continued in that loathsome and

(*a*) Of *Joseph* I have already said something, See. P. 140.

solitary

folitary Confinement, he was frequently wont to weep, becaufe the filthy Stench, and the fqualid Naftinefs of the Place, was an Hindrance to him from performing his daily *Salaat,* or Devotions ; and alfo, becaufe he was deftitute of Water wherewithal to wafh and purify himfelf with the neceffary Immerfions and Ablutions we *Muffulmans* are enjoyned to ufe, to prepare us for our daily Prayers : To fupply which Defect, or, at leaft, to atone in fome Meafure for the fame ; the Angel *Gabriel* appeared to him, and faid ; " *Jofeph!* When thou haft no Water, thou " mayft, in fuch a Cafe, make Ufe of Duft, or the " like, by rubbing thyfelf therewith inftead of Wa-" ter. " From hence our Holy *Sunna,* or Book of the Oral Law, has deduced the Original, the Form, and Method of our Purification called (*a*) *Tayahmam,* a Liberty and Privilege fo very requifite and commodious in many Circumftances, and upon feveral Occafions. " By this Incident we may gather, that the " worft of Misfortunes that can happen to us, may, " by fome Means or other, be turned to our Ad-" vantage, and made applicable to fome good Pur-" pofe. "

This Memorable Patriarch affiduoufly followed, and ftrenuoufly promoted the Precepts of his venerable Anceftor *Abraham,* which, to his immortal Praife, we inherit from him. He exhorted the ftrange Nations to ufe Circumcifion, and to diftribute Alms, (*b*) as well of

---

(*a*) Concerning this Ceremony fee *Reland's* Mah. Rel. p. 37. where, in the Notes, it is largely explained.

(*b*) The *Arabick* Word for Alms-giving, I mean thofe Alms which are enjoyned them by Precept, is *Zacah* or *Zacouah,* and is derived from *Zaca,* which fignifies to purify, becaufe it, as it were, purifies the remaining Part of what we poffefs, when that Obligatory Duty is performed. This Word, and that of *El Aafhor,* or the Tenth, fhould never be confounded with *Sadacah,* which is only a voluntary Alms. Our *European* Tranflators generally call it the *Tythe,*

of thoſe Things which, by Inſtitution, give a Fourth
Part, as of thoſe that give a Tenth, and ſo of all the
reſt. He reſtored the *Iſraelites* in his Time, from
theirSuperſtition, and prevailed with them to deſiſt
from their Obſervations of ſeveral Pagan Ceremonies, that were crept in amongſt them by their Com-
merce with ſtrange Nations. For this his Probity,
and for his tranſcendent Merit, the Lord advanced
him, ſetting him over the People of *Ægypt* to be their
Ruler and Director, inſomuch, that he at laſt came
to have ſo abſolute an Authority throughout that
large Kingdom, and had the whole Nation ſo intirely
at his Devotion, that he had their Subſtances, and
even their Perſons, as much in his Diſpoſal as if they
had been all his Slaves, purchaſed with his Money
in the Market.

(*a*) *Moſes* was a very eſpecial elected Servant of
the Lord, ſince He it was, who only could ever boaſt

Tithe, which is, certainly, very improper, both in Regard this
Portion is neither given to the *Imaums* or Rectors, nor to their
Moſques; but to whom the Donor pleaſes; as alſo becauſe it is not
a Tenth (except of ſome certain Things) but commonly riſes to a
Fifth Part of what a *Muſſulman* is poſſeſs'd of. Nay, charitably-
inclined *Mahometans* often part with a Fourth of what they are
worth to the Poor, and ſometimes a Third; nay, even in
Life with Half their Poſſeſſions to ſatisfy this Duty, and
their good Diſpoſitions. Nay, there have been Inſtances of
many who have beſtowed their All upon the Poor, as did *Haſſan* the Son of *Alli*, Couſin Germain, Son-in-Law, and Fourth Succeſſor to *Mahomet*. The 1ſt and 2d Tythes of the *Jews* have ſome
Affinity with this *Zacah* of the *Mahometans*. Vide *D'Herbelot* in
Zacah.

(*a*) The *Mahometans* call *Moſes Mouſſa* or *Mouſa ben Amran*,
ben Cabath, ben Laour, ben Jaccub, that is, *Moſes* the Son of *Amran*,
the Son of *Caath*, the Son of *Levi*, the Son of *Jacob*. His Titles are
Kelim Allah, becauſe he talked familiarly with God; and *Sahib el
Aſſa*, or the Owner or Maſter of the Rod, or Wand. According to
the *Taarich Montbekhib*, he was born 506 Years after the Flood, and
loſt his Father a Month after he was born: That *Pharaoh* who then
reigned in *Ægypt*, and was called *Walid*, had marryed *Amran*'s
Niece,

of that eminent Prerogative of speaking Face to Face
with the Mighty Creator of all Things : But he
through

Niece, whose Name was *Assiah* (and, of Consequence, was *Moses's*
Cousin Germain) by which Means *Amran* became a great Man in
Pharaoh's Court. Yet this Favour *Amran* was in, did not secure
Nagiah, Mother to *Moses*, from her Apprehensions lest *Pharaoh*,
out of his Inveteracy to the *Jewish* Nation, should cause him to be
put to Death, which made her, as the Scripture says, expose
him on the River, from whence he was taken up, and bred in that
King's Palace. There he continued 'till the Age of 41, when, for
his having killed an *Ægyptian* for abusing a *Jew*, he was forced to
flee into *Arabia*, where he was kindly received by *Shoaib* or *Jethro*
the High Priest of the *Midianites*. He soon after gave him his
Daughter to Wife, and would fain have had him continue with
him; but *Moses*, with an impatient Desire of seeing his Mother *Nagiah*, and his Elder Brother *Haroun* or *Aaron*, set out for *Ægypt*, by
the Way of Mount *Thôour* or *Tor*, which is *Sinai* ; at the Foot
whereof, he received the Gift of Prophecy, and God's Commands
to go up to *Pharaoh*, to require him to dismiss the *Israelites*. The
same Author agrees with the Scripture, in Relation of all the
wonderful Miracles wrought by *Moses*, and his carrying the Children of *Israel* through the Red-Sea into *Arabia*. The *Mahometans*
(as I have hinted somewhere else) reduce the *Jews* 40 Years wandering in the Desart to 40 Days, and say, That the Difficulties they
met with had not been to be surmounted, had not *Khedbir*, or the
Prophet *Elias* (of whom more in the next Chapter) assisted them
therein, whom God had sent to be their Guide. Thus they confound the Age of *Elias* with that of *Moses*, whose Times were so
very remote one from the other. Though the Story of *Moses*
is at length in the Chapter of the *Alcoran* called *Aa'raf*, yet the
Commentators add many fabulous Tales to it, taken from the
Books of the *Jews*, or some ancient Traditions. They say, That
Moses returning into *Ægypt* from the Country of *Midian*, on the
Banks of a River called *Atmen*, found a Prophet's Garment and a
Wand. As soon as he had put on the Garment, and taken up the
Wand, his Hand was covered with a bright Whiteness, and God
appearing to him, gave him his Commands to *Pharaoh*. — To
pass by many fabulous Circumstances which they add to the Scripture-
Truth, they write, That the Tables of the Law *Moses* brought down
from the Mount were Seven, and according to others Ten, and
each of them Ten or Twelve Cubits long. Some of their Authors
say, they were made of a certain Sort of Wood the *Arabs* call
Sedr, or *Sedrat*, something like the Lote-Tree, and grows, as they
affirm, in Paradise. Others will have them to be made of Rubies,
but the greatest Number hold them to be Emeralds, and the Characters

through the Merits of his righteous and pious Life, and more especially for his great Humility, was thought worthy of receiving the Laws written on the Tables, out of God's own sacred Hands, whereas all the other Prophets, Messengers, and Law-givers had His Divine Commands and Messages sent them by an Angel: But this Holy Man had a peculiar Deference shewed him.

This ever-venerable Prophet it was, who perform'd such famous and mighty Deeds, that he might accomplish the Redemption of his People out of the insupportable Bondage under which they had so long laboured: He never desisted, 'till he had brought them all safely out of the Land of *Ægypt*, in spite of, and Opposition to *Pharaoh*, that impious, infamous and idolatrous Tyrant, which he happily effected by his unparalell'd Constancy and Perseverance. For as that wicked, hardened and unbelieving King had pursued the flying *Israelites* to the very Brink of the Red-Sea, this chosen Leader of that persecuted Nation, with an implicit Confidence in his omnipotent Lord, forced a safe Passage for himself and all his numerous Followers through the Waves: Inspired with a divine Assurance, he lifted up his Arm, and struck the Waters with his Rod Twelve times, which were of such an Efficacy, that each Stroke penetrated the Waves to the very deepest Centres, and left them so many different Paths, dry, straight, and sufficiently wide and capacious for them all to pass

---

racters so engraven on them, that they could be read on all Sides. When *Moses* had broke those Tables, the Pieces were carried back to Heaven by Angels, excepting one Piece a Cubit long, left on the Ground, which was by *Noah* afterwards preserved in the Ark. This Table they call *Hodu u Rahmat*, The Table of Direction and Mercy: But enough of these incoherent Fables. —— Their Historians make *Moses* and *Aaron* Contemporaries with *Manougher* 7th King of *Persia* of the first Race, and reckon from his Death to the first Year of the *Hegira* 2347 Years, which most exactly agrees with our Chronology.

convени-

conveniently over, without incommoding one another, each Tribe taking a different Path, as he intended they should, by his making that Number ; when at the same Instant that they were out of Danger, the obstinate Tyrant, endeavouring to follow them, was, with all his mighty Army, devoured by the Waters returning upon them. When the good *Moses* and his Tribes had thus miraculously escaped, he led them through a barren Desart, in which unfertile Place, these infinite Multitudes were all the while very plentifully nourished with Sustenance of a (*a*) Heavenly Growth, that descended down from Paradise on Purpose to feed that then Favourite Nation.

O

Ma

(*a*) In the Chapter of the *Alcoran* entitled *El Bacrah*, the Impostor introduces God speaking to the *Jews* in these Words ; *Wa inzilna ailaicum el Mann wa'l Salua* ; That is, And I also sent you down *Manna* and *Salua*. That celebrated Author *Houssain Vaez*, expounding this Text, says; That the *Arabick* Word *Salua* answers to the Hebrew *Selav*, which most Expositors translate Quails, tho' he says, it likewise signifies Honey. Several other Expositors agree in the same Interpretation ; and it is certain, that the Bird they call a Quail is peculiar to *Arabia Felix*, and is something less than a Pigeon : It has neither Bones, Sinews nor Veins, and sings with a very sweet Voice. The same Author adds, That God caused so violent a Wind to blow, that it broke the Wings of all those Birds, insomuch that they fell, like a Cloud, upon the Camp of the *Israelites*, who easily took and eat them with *Manna*. Vide *D'Herbelot* in the Word *Salua*. Nor ought I to omit what they say of the Ark of the Covenant of the *Jews*, which they call *Tabout Moussa*, The Chest or Cabinet of *Moses* ; but they also give it a more lofty Title, *Cobbat el Zaman*, The Ark, or rather Cupulo of Time, for so they interpret the Hebrew Words *Aron Haedas*, The Ark of Covenant ; because *Edab* signifies both Time and Covenant. They say, this Ark was delivered by God, ready made, to *Adam*, and was transmitted from Hand to Hand, from Patriarch to Patriarch, down to *Moses* ; and they add, That in it were kept the Portraitures of all the Prophets that were to appear, in Process of Time, to the After-ages. I shall say something more of this Ark when I treat of the Prophet *Samuel* at the End of this Chapter, whom my Author has forgot to mention. —— The *Mahometans* make *Carun*, that is, *Korah*, to be Cousin Germain to the Patriarch *Moses*, whom they represent as a great Chymist, and that by that Art he had amassed so great a Quantity of Gold, that he loaded Forty Camels with nothing but

that

Many more were the memorable Deeds of this worthy and never enough to be honoured Prophet; all his great and remarkable Undertakings ever tending to the intire Good and unexpreffible Advantage of the

that Metal. ——He is looked upon, among them, as the Emblem of a very rich, avaritious, and uncharitable Mifer, even to a Proverb, and they fay, That when *Mofes* commanded the *Ifraelites* to pay Tythes, he utterly refufed; wherefore *Mofes* laid his Curfe upon him, and he was fwallowed up by the Earth. ——The Brevity my Author has ufed, is the Caufe of his omitting many Material Points in his Account of *Mofes*, as, likewife in feveral other Places, which I fhall endeavour to fupply, for the Satisfaction of the Curious, out of what is to be found in other *Mahometan* Traditions. ——That King of *Ægypt* who the *Hebrews* call *Pero*, and we *Pharaoh*, the *Mahometans* call *Feraoun*, which they hold to be a Title the firft Kings of that Country took, as the Succeffors of *Efcander* or *Alexander. the Great* did that of *Ptolomy*. That *Pharaoh* who reign'd when *Jacob* and his Family came thither, was furnamed *Rian*, according to the *Arabick* Chronicles, and his Succeffor's Name was *Maaffab*; but that Tyrant who perfecuted *Mofes* and the *Ifraelites*, was called *Cabous*, and *Walid*. The two firft, they fay, treated the *Ifraelites* with great Kindnefs and Humanity, but the third would be worfhipped as a God, and oppreffed the *Jews* becaufe they refufed to pay him that Honour; alledging, That *Jofeph* was his Predeceffor's Slave, bought for Money, and confequently they were all his: And accordingly he kept them in Servitude 'till they were delivered by *Mofes*. So fay the Expofitors of the *Alcoran*. The *Taarikh Montekeb* will have the *Pharaohs*, in the *Arabick* Plural *Faraenah*, to be of the Race of *Ad Pere*, of the Tribe of the *Adites*, and that *Wald* or *Weld*, who was drowned in the Red-Sea, lived in the Days of *Manugeher* King of *Perfia*, of the firft Race. The Scripture Truths concerning *Mofes* and the *Ifraelites* have been mixed by the *Mahometan* Writers with feveral Fabulous Circumftances of their own Invention. ——Among the reft, they write, That the Angel *Gabriel*, mounted upon a ftately Courfer, brought up the Rear of the Tribes of *Ifrael* when they fled out of *Ægypt*, and that when *Pharaoh*, following them, faw the Sea divided, he would not have ventured in after them, but that his Horfe, being drawn by the Scent of *Gabriel*'s Steed, carried him in by Force, and that all his Troops following him, they found themfelves in the midft of the Sea before they knew where they were; when the Waters joyning again, they were all fwallowed up and deftroyed. The *Ifraelites* not knowing what had happened to *Pharaoh*, were ftill afraid he would pafs the Sea in Ships, and purfue them; but God caufed *Pharaoh*'s Body, which was all clad in bright Armour, to fwim upon the Surface of

the People of *Iſrael*, whoſe Paſtor he was ; but they were never ſatisfied, always murmuring, unthankful and rebellious, never contented, nor ever acknowledging God's peculiar Mercies, and the uncommon Deference with which He ever diſtinguiſhed them; but have, from the Beginning, ever ſhewed themſelves a faithleſs, diffident and unbelieving Generation : And from this hardened and contradicting Spirit of theirs, ſprung the Source of that Idolatrous Schiſm they introduced when they ſet up the Calf for their Deity and the Object of their Adoration.

'Tis recorded of this great Prophet, That when he was in *Ægypt*, he was forced one Evening to flee out of the City, to avoid the Wrath of the tyrannick *Pharaoh*, who, upon ſome Account, was highly incenſed againſt him, and ſought his Life. As he fled to ſave himſelf, the Night drew on, and proved exceeding dark, overtaking him juſt as he had reached a very uncouth and ſolitary Place, where he felt himſelf grievouſly oppreſſed with Four intolerably heavy Fears and terrible Apprehenſions all at once, which almoſt overwhelmed his Heart with Horror. The Firſt was, His own Fear of the Tyrant's cruel Diſpoſi-

---

of the Water, which being known by the *Jews*, they rejoyced, and their Hearts became eaſy. —— *Lamai*, in his Book called *Lathaif*, writes, That *Pharaoh* often conſulted with the Devil, and was very importunately preſſing, that it might be brought about through his Means, that his Subjects might adore him like a Deity ; but the Anſwer the Devil ſtill made him, was, That it was not yet Time ; but that when it ſhould be ſeaſonable ſo to do, he would not fail of gratifying him in that his Requeſt. —— The *Mahometans* add, That *Pharaoh*'s Magicians being converted at the Sight of *Moſes*'s real Miracles, that tyrannical Prince was ſo incenſed againſt them, that he condemned them to be all put to Death, which Sentence they received and ſuffered with the greateſt Expreſſions of Joy and Satisfaction. The Eaſtern Chriſtians, according to *Ebn Batrick*, give the Name of *Amious* to *Moſes*'s Perſecutor who periſhed in the *Red-Sea*. The Name of *Amious* ſeems to have ſome Reſemblance with *Amiſis* King of *Ægypt*, well known in the *Grecian* Hiſtories. —— There is a Book in the King of *France*'s Library, intitled *Ketab fi Imán Feraun*, treating of the too late Repentance of King *Pharaoh*.

tion

tion if he fell into his Power. The Second was, His
Fear for his Mother, whom he dearly loved, and
highly honoured, ſhe having remained behind him in
the City : This was the moſt grievous to him of all.
The Third was, The Apprehenſions he had for his
People, who were kept by that wicked King in a
cruel Servitude and Oppreſſion. The Fourth and
laſt was, The diſmal Obſcurity of the Night, which
was ſo great, that he could, by no means, dare venture to ſtir out of the Place where he was, either one
Way or the other. Whilſt he was in this terrible Conſternation, he, with very great Devotion, performed
thoſe four Proſtrations, which we *Muſſulmans* are wont
to repeat when we find ourſelves in Fear, or oppreſſed with Terror ; the which we call (a) *The Prayer
of Fear*, in Commemoration of thoſe Four Apprehenſions wherewith the Heart of this Holy Man was at
one Inſtant ſo heavily tormented, but from the which,
by his thus addreſſing himſelf to Him who is only
able to apply a Remedy, he was immediately delivered, and his torturing Aſſaulters put to Flight ; for
he had no ſooner ended his devout Supplication, but
he heard a Voice from Heaven, which called him by
his Name, bidding him *be of good Cheer and fear nothing* ; whereby he took new Courage, and ſhook off
all his Doubts, Fears and Apprehenſions.

(b) *Joſhua* was a moſt magnanimous and valiant
Leader of the *Iſraelites*, to whom God gave this Advantage over the great *Moſes*, that he made an intire
Conqueſt of the numerous Hoſts of his Enemies, and
compleated

(a) This Prayer they call *Salaat el Khouf*, and they uſe it when
they are moſt in Danger. But my Author here calls it by (at leaſt
I think ſo, having never heard it before, to my Knowledge) a new
coined Word, for he has it *A'atema*.

(b) Of *Joſhua* I have little more to add, only what they ſay of
his Gigantick Enemies the *Philiſtines*, with whom he had to do
upon that memorable Day. They call them *Giabbaran*, or *Giababerah*,
and

compleated what he, not being able to accomplish, had left undone. The *Hebrew* Text informs us, That this famous and mighty Warrior, being hotly engaged in an obstinate and bloody Battel, wherein his Party apparently began to have the Better, and observing the Sun to be hastily declining towards the West, and fearing he should not have Day-light enough to prosecute what he had so happily begun, by compleatly destroying the Army of his Adversaries; he, therefore, without alighting from off his Horse, bowed down his Head as low as he could, prostrating himself over the Horse's Mane, and, with extraordinary Humility and Devotion, addressed himself to God, in these few, but memorable Words;

O 3.

" Omni-

---

and say, They were of the Race of the *Amalekites*, and that the lowest in Stature among them, was full Nine Cubits high: But of all those Giants, *Aoug ben Anak*, or *Og*, was the most eminent, both for Valour and Tallness of Stature, and lived 3000 Years. He and his People were of the Posterity of *Ad* (concerning whom I have made Mention already) and are therefore sometimes called *Adian*, or *Adites*. These were then, according to them, the Inhabitants of *Falasthin*, that is, *Palestine*, which the *Arabs*, like us, call the Holy Land, and say, That its Two Capital Cities are *Ilia* and *Areka*, that is, *Jerusalem* and *Jericho*, and that this Province contained 1000 open Towns, with the most curious and delicious Gardens in the whole Universe; that 5 Men could hardly carry a Bunch of their Grapes, and that a Pomegranate Shell in that Country, was sufficiently capacious to contain 5 Men within it, so rich and exuberant was the Soil.——When *Moses*, they say, first arrived near the Confines of this fine Province, he dispatched away 12 Men to make Discoveries: They went; and when they had viewed the Land, and seen all they could, they agreed among themselves, to relate the whole naked Truth to *Moses* and *Aaron*, but to conceal some Particulars from the People, for fear of discouraging them: Yet 10 of them could not keep Counsel, but publickly related all they knew. This raised a great Mutiny and Confusion, and *Joshua* and *Caleb*, who were the Two that kept the Secret, were employed to appease the clamorous Multitude, by letting them know, how much they were in the Wrong to entertain such terrible Ideas and Apprehensions of those Gigantick People, since the Lord had promised infallibly to put them in Possession of that Country. The Land of *Arden*, or *Jordan*, is often mentioned in the

Oriental

" Omnipotent Monarch! Tremendous Lord of all
" Victories! My weak Ability, my infignificant
" Strength, my Want of Power to finifh any Thing
" of my-felf, induce me to implore thy irrefiftable
" Aid, without which I am nothing! " He faid no
more; but as foon as he lifted up his Head again, the
Lord commanded the Sun immediately to ftand ftill,
continuing without moving, 'till *Jofhua* had intirely
routed his Oppofers, and gained a moft compleat
Victory over them.

" This is certainly a very amazing Myftery! A
" moft wonderful Diftinction! A furprizing Conde-
" fcention! The Sun itfelf ftop at the Requeft of a
" Mortal! With what Sincerity, with what a Con-
" fidence of Soul muft that Servant of the Lord have
" uttered thofe fhort Sentences! Thefe Examples are
" all fo many Confirmations, fo many corroborating
" Demonftrations, whereby God gives us to under-
" ftand, That there is nothing but what may be ho-
" ped for, nothing but what is too mean, in Compa-
" rifon to the Excellency of the firft Scheme of our
" Creation, if the Actions of our Lives are but anfwera-
" ble to the glorious Intent for which we were cre-
" ated. "

Oriental Books, as a Part of *Palefline*. A noted Author, called
Abmed el Faffi, writes, That all the Ancient Kings of *Palefline*, bore
the Title of *Gialout*, or *Goliab*, as thofe of *Egypt* did that of *Feraoun*,
or *Pharaob*; though fome Eaftern Authors abfolutely affirm *Goliah*
to have been only King of *Amalek*. ——They likewife fay, That the
Inhabitants of the Holy Land were Twice expelled and drove into
Africa, firft by *Jofhua*, and next by *David*, after having killed
Goliah. The firft Tranfmigration is to be underftood of the *Cana-
anites*, and the fecond of the *Philiflines*. The *Afiaticks* will needs
have the Inhabitants of *Barbary*, along the Coafts of the *Mediter-
ranean*, to be defcended from the *Amalekites*, which agrees with
what fome of our Writers fay of a Pillar or Column found in
Africa, near the *Streights-Mouth*, on which was an Infcription, pro-
ing them to be the People who fled from the Fury of *Jofhua* the
Conqueror of *Palefline*. *Qui fugerunt a facie* Joshuæ *Latronu*.

-*David*

David the Royal Prophet, was in no wife inferior
to, or lefs memorable than the others: Whilft he was
yet a Stripling, without one Hair of Beard upon his
Chin, he vanquifhed and flew the mighty *Golias,* or
Goliah. He left us many very notable Examples of
his Piety and Fear of the Lord ; and inftituted Two
Proftrations at Sun-rifing, and the like at Sun-fetting,
the which he very vigilantly obferved, with the utmoft Affiduity all his Life ; and more than that, he
never omitted paying fome peculiar Devotions to
God the Creator, whenfoever the Moon began to appear, and when fhe abfconded from his Sight ; nor
was he ever weary of inceffantly praifing, glorifying
and calling upon the Name of the Lord both by Day
and by Night, which he did as an Attonement to ex-
piate for the Follies he had fo inconfiderately committed. Thefe, and numberlefs other Aufterities
which he had enjoyned himfelf to obferve, he underwent with moft exemplary Conftancy and Determination ; and fo unfeignedly great was his Penitence
for his Tranfgreffions, that though the Penance he
did was fo far beyond his Strength in thofe his declining Years, yet he would never have defifted from
continuing thofe rigid Severities, without ever refrefh-
ing his exhaufted Spirits with one Moment's Refpite,
had not the Angel *Gabriel* prevailed with him to mitigate them in fome meafure, by putting him in Mind,
That he was in Danger of incurring the Chaftifement
of thofe who run themfelves into the heinous Sin of
El-cafára, or, as we may explain it, of Self-murder.

However, he never afterwards ceafed from ferving
and calling upon the Lord with a moft confummate
Contrition, and an indefatigable Fervency, compofing
and chaunting his excellent *Epigrams* or *Pfalms* to
God's Praife and Glory ; a Book of fo great a Perfectnefs, that it hath been, and ftill *is*, very conducive
towards the World's Happinefs. This Holy Prophet
continually lived in a very aufters Penitence during

the

the Space of Forty Years, excluſive of thoſe (*a*)
Forty Days of his ſo exceſſively rigid Penance, wherein he inceſſantly bewailed his Sin in offending God,
weeping ſcalding hot Tears of Contrition, without
one Minute's Intermiſſion, 'till his Royal Perſon was
reduced to ſuch a lamentable Condition, ſo weak and
debilitated, and his Countenance ſo ſtrangely meta-
morphoſed and disfigured, that he was not to be
known : And from hence it is, we derive the precep-
tary Injunction of mitigating all too rigid Deeds of
Penance, in order to avoid falling into the Error of
over-acting our Parts, and by prejudicing our Health,
become acceſſary to our own Deſtruction ; though certain it is, that nothing is ſo inſtrumental towards the
filling of Paradiſe with Inhabitants, as ſincere and unfeigned Repentance.

" O moſt Pious and Royal Prophet ! How benefi-
" cial has thy Error, and thy voluntary Mortifica-
" tion in Expiation thereof, been to Mankind ! How
" infinite are the Numbers of otherwiſe incurable
" Sores, which have been healed up by the Merit of
" thy Contrition ! How many Spots have thy Tears
" waſhed away ! and how many have turned their
" Backs upon the dreadful Flames of Hell, who would,
" irretrievably, have fallen into the midſt of that
" horrible Furnace, had they not prudently followed
" the Example thou didſt ſet them, by a fervent Re-
" pentance of their Errors. It was not in vain,
" that thy Hours were ſpent in ſuch Auſterities, ſince
" the Lord, through thy meritorious Penance, did
" not only grant thee a full Pardon and Remiſſion

(*a*) The *Mahometans* little differ from our Scripture in their
Accounts of *David*, whom they call *Daoud, ben Iſcha, ben Aouil*, that
is, *Dav d*, the Son of *Jeſſe*, the Son of *Obed*. The Author of the
Taarich Montekheb and ſome others, only add, That the Birds and
the Stones obeyed him ; that Iron grew ſoft in his Hands ; and that,
during the Forty Days he wept for his Sin, the Tears he dropt,
cauſed Herbs and Plants to ſpring up.

" for

" for all thy Offences, thy Adulteries, and thy un-
" godly Murders; but likewife fhowered down up-
" on thee greater Mercies in a more particular Man-
" ner; I mean, That God, of His wonderful Bounty,
" fhould ordain, that the Fruit of thy Incontinency,
" of thy finful and unjuft Adultery, fhould be the
" Great *Solomon.* Hail, O Bleffed King! O lucky
" Miftake! O Illuftrious and Happy Product of In-
" continency! That one fo Holy, fo Wife, fo Honour-
" able, and fo worthy of our higheft Veneration,
" fhould be conceived in Sin and Adultery!

(*a*) *Solomon* the Son of *David*, was the greateft,
the wifeft, the richeft, and the moft magnificent Prince
upon Earth; fince he was fole Lord and Monarch of
all Things between *it* and the Firmament of Heaven.
He had the abfolute Command of the Winds, the
Clouds, all Humane Creatures, the *Genii*, the Birds
of

(*a*) The *Mahometans* call King *Solomon*, *Suliman ben Daoud.* Moft
Eaftern Writers fay, That after his Father's Death, he afcended
his Throne at 12 Years of Age; and, that God fubjected to his
Empire, not only Men, but Good and Evil Spirits, the Birds, the
Beafts and the Winds; and that he fpent 7 Years in building the
Temple of *Jerufalem.* The *Taarick Monthekheb* fays, That he was
Contemporary with *Caicous* Second King of *Perfia*, of the Race of
the *Caianides.* The *Mahometan* Hiftorians tell us a Thoufand Fabulous Stories of *Solomon*'s Ring, which was ftollen from him, whilft
he was in the Bath, by an Evil *Genius*, or *Dæmon*, and by him caft
into the Sea. *Solomon*, having thus loft his Ring, forbore afcending
his Throne for 40 Days, as being deprived of the neceffary Wifdom
for Governing his Kingdom well; but he recovered it, at laft, again,
finding it in the Belly of a Fifh that was ferved up to his Table.
———It would be tedious to repeat all they relate concerning
the Magnificence of his Throne, over which, they fay, the Birds
continually flittered whilft he fat thereon, to fhade him inftead
of a Canopy; and about which were 12000 Seats of Gold on the
Right, for the Patriarchs and Prophets, and 12000 of Silver on
the Left, for the Wife Men and Doctors who attended his Judgments. We fhall add fome few Circumftances concerning his Life
and Reign out of the *Alcoran*, and the Writings of its Expofitors.
The *Alcoran*, in the Chapter intitled *Anam*, has thefe Words;
The

of the Air, and all Beafts of the Field; nothing dared difobey him, but all was at his Difcretion; and he was endowed with Knowledge and Wifdom fufficient to keep them all intirely under his Subjection.

This peculiar Virtue he was poffeffed of, and which none before, or fince him, ever enjoyed, was contained in a Ring he had, upon the Seal whereof was engraven, Triangular-wife, in *Hebrew* Characters thefe Words, tending to the Glory of the Almighty; *Alhamdulillahi,* and again, *Allahu acbar,* that is, *God be praifed!* and *God is Great!* By the myfterious Efficacy of this ineftimable Jewel, this happy Monarch reigned in moft glorious Splendor, Tranquility and Content.

Concerning

They have followed that which the Dœmons and the Magicians their Subftitutes, read and taught in the Days and Reign of Suliman. Houffain Vaez Paraphrafes upon that Text thus; The Malt Genii, or Dœmons, Solomon's Enemies, publifhed Books full of Superftition, intermix'd with fome facred Ceremonies of the Religion and Priefthood of the Jews, and they made the ignorant Vulgar believe, that Solomon made ufe of thofe Books, to gain the Knowledge he had to govern his People Solomon having caufed all thofe Books to be carefully collected, he lockt them up in a Cheft, which he buried under his Throne, that none might be infected thereby Yet after his Death, either the Magicians or the Genii got thofe Books from thence, and fpread them among the Jews, as if they were the genuine Books which were compofed by Solomon, which made many believe that Wife King to have been the Author of them, and had been a great Magician. ———Mouffa ben Abi Ifmael writes That one Day Solomon riding out to take the Air, the Hour of Prayer being come, he would not fuffer that Time to be mifpent in leading his Horfes to Stable, but ordered they fhould be all turned loofe, as if they had no Owners, and that from that Time they fhould be confecrated to God; who, to reward his Zeal, from thence forwards, fupplied him with a Pleafant, but Strong Gale of Wind, which, without having any Occafion for Horfes, conveyed him wherefoever he pleafed to go. All the Eaftern Nations look upon Solomon to have been Univerfal Monarch of the whole Earth, infomuch, that thofe who believe there have been feveral Ages and Revolutions, in which the World has been inhabited and governed by other Creatures befides Men, before the Creation of Adam, do give the Name and Title of Suliman to the Monarchs they fay then governed. Of thefe I fhall give fome Hints below. ———The

Concerning this Great and Universal Monarch *Solomon,* our Beatified Prophet *Mahomet* has Recorded, That his Imperial Power was so great, his Reign so prosperous and undisturbed, his Knowledge and Penetration so exquisitely profound, and, to compleat all, his Treasures so prodigiously immense and inexhaustible, and, in fine, all this so superlatively beyond all Example, Precedent, or Comparison, that these alluring Baits drew him into a Snare, endearing him to the transitory Pleasures and dangerous Calls of the World and the Flesh (those fatal Inciters to, and

---

Asiaticks say, That *Solomon*'s Grand *Vizier,* or Prime Minister, was *Assaf,* of whom the Holy Scripture makes mention, and to whom *David* addresses several of his *Psalms.* The *Persian* Poet *Emadi,* says; That *Solomon*'s Ring, so much talked of, was no other than the Wisdom God had given him, and of which the Ring is the Emblem. However, there are *Rabbies* who affirm, That *Solomon* saw all he desired to know, in the Stone which was set in that Ring; and so the High Priest saw all in the *Urim* and *Thummim* on his Breast-Plate (which also consisted of Precious Stones) whatever he was desirous of knowing from God. ——— The Life of *Solomon* hath been written by several *Turkish, Persian* and *Arabian* Historians, but by all of them very fabulously.——— From the supposed Universal Empire of *Solomon,* the Eastern Romances have taken Occasion to give the Title of *Suliman* to all those they make to have been Lords of the whole World. ——— They affirm, There have been of these *Sulimanes,* or Universal Monarchs, who reigned successively for very many Ages before the Creation of *Adam,* yet some Authors inverse their Numbers to 72. Each of these *Præ-Adamite* Sovereigns ruled over Creatures of his own Kind, whose Forms were different from that of *Adam*'s Posterity, yet Rational, like Mankind. *Argenk,* who reign'd on the imaginary Mountain *Caff,* in the Days of *Tohmurah,* had a Gallery, as their Romances tell us, in which were the Statues of those 72 *Sulimanes,* and Pourtraictures of all the Creatures their Subjects, which were very unlike to Human Kind; for some had several Heads, others many Arms, and some seemed to be composed and made up of several Bodies. Their Heads were also very strange; for some were like that of an Elephant, others resembled that of a Buffalo, or a Wild Boar, others still more hideous and monstrous. These *Sulimanes,* they say, were perpetually at War with the *Dæmons,* the *Dives,* or Evil *Genii* and the Gyants; of which Wars, there are many Fabulous Volumes not worth mentioning. See *D'Herbelot* in *Soliman.*

Sources

Sources of Ambition, Rebellion and all Sin) to such a Degree, that he began wholly to fix his Mind thereupon, and to neglect, and, in a manner, to forget the Mighty Donor. But, as the Lord of all Things never fuffers thofe prefumptuous Incroachments upon His Divinity to pafs unchaftifed, but will have us Mortals acknowledge Him to be the Author of all our Happinefs, and the Fountain-head from whence proceeds the Wealth we enjoy ; His Cœleftial Majefty, therefore, thought fit to deprive him of that Empire, and thofe Riches which he employed only to his own Honour, and not to the Glory of Him who had fo bountifully beftowed them upon him ; and, in lieu of all his fplendid Pomp, to reduce him to a defpicable State of Poverty, Contempt and Mifery.

It was the Cuftom of this King, when he retired into his Clofet to his private Devotions, always to take off his Ring, and to deliver it into the Cuftody of one of his Virgins, to keep it whilft he made his Addreffes to the Lord. Now, as *Solomon* kept all the perverfe and mifchievous *Evil-Genii* under an abfolute and very rigorous Subjection, which they endured not without the greateft Impatience and Reluctance, and were ever contriving, imagining and confpiring by what Means or Invention they might deliver themfelves from fo grievous a Bondage, and fhake off the Yoak to which they had fo mortal an Averfion; it chanced one Day, when the King was gone to his Devotions, as ufual, that One of thofe Enemies of Mankind, whofe Name was *Harico*, affuming the Form of *Solomon*, went to that Damfel who had the Ring in her Keeping, and impofing upon her Credulity, deceived her, and got away that precious Gem, and, with exceffive Joy, went immediately, and caft it into the deepeft Part of the Sea, where, as it was finking, it was caught and fwallowed by a Fifh: And when the King returned, and demanded his Ring of the Virgin he had left it with, fhe, with great Confufion in her Looks, told him, That fhe had returned

it

it to him already; And withal, repeating the same Words he had said to her when he asked for his Ring, as likewise the Answer she made when she gave it him, and which was a certain Form of ceremonious Sentences always used upon that Occasion, she also told him, " That his Majesty had the very " same Robes on when she delivered him the Ring, " that he wore at present.

The good King, upon this disastrous Circumstance, grew sensible, that the Anger of the Lord was kindled against him, and that, without Doubt, this severe Mortification was sent him for a Tryal, and in part of Punishment for his Transgressions and Omissions: So reflecting upon his irreparable Loss, he continued in an inconsolable Condition, overwhelmed with Grief and Anguish, 'till the Evening, and then stripping himself of all his Imperial Ornaments and Princely Robes, he clad himself in very mean Garments; and then taking a Staff in his Hand, he left his Royal Palace, glorifying the Name of the Most High, and uttering many penitential Sighs and Groans for the numerous Sins he had committed, and whereby he had incurred his Lord's Displeasure: And in this poor Condition he wandered about a long while like a Mendicant, passing through many remote Countries, and whereever he went, was always despised, slighted and ill-treated: Nay, he was reduced at last to such an Excess of Poverty and Misery, and his Person was become so very contemptible, that the very Beggars themselves refused to associate themselves with him, nor would they suffer him to go a Begging in their Company; saying, That, for his Sake alone, the People forbore bestowing their Charity upon them; insomuch that he continued Forty Days, and as many Nights, fasting, never tasting the least Sustenance in all that Time, being preserved alive by the Divine Grace alone.

Such was the Wretchedness, and such the Life this Great Prince led, 'till God was pleased in these his miserable Peregrinations, to inrich him with a most
beautiful

beautiful and worthy Lady for a Wife: She was the Daughter of a certain idolatrous King, through whoſe Dominions he paſſed, who having ſeen him, took ſo great a Liking to him, that, without her Father's Conſent, and extremely againſt his Will, ſhe eſpouſed him; which when he came to know, his Indignation was ſo great, that, with many Injuries, and abundance of Ill-treatment and Reproach, he cauſed her to be turned out of his Palace, and, in a manner, quite Naked; And being thus both of them deſtitute of all Comfort, or Relief, they betook themſelves to the Sea-ſide, where they found ſome poor Fiſher-Men caſting out their Nets: The diſconſolate New-married Couple, craving their Charity, they gave them a Couple of Fiſhes, in the Belly of the leaſt of which, King *Solomon* found the precious Jewel he had loſt, and for which he had ſo long languiſhed, and undergone ſo many Miſeries. At the Sight of what he had deſpaired of ever ſeeing again, his Heart rebounded within him, and in an Ecſtaſy of Joy, he kiſſed thoſe dear Characters a Thouſand and a Thouſand Times, with Rapture, giving Praiſe and Glory to God, for having deemed him worthy of again reading thoſe Myſterious Words which ſurrounded the Angles thereof; and for having reſtored his ineſtimable Ring once more to his Finger: And, in effect, the very Moment he had put it on, all Creatures, without Exception, returned again to their Duty, and were as obedient, and as much under his abſolute Subjection, as they had been before he met with that diſaſtrous Loſs: And having cauſed a Cloud to deſcend to the Earth, he and his Beloved Spouſe mounted therein, and were ſpeedily conveyed through the Air to his Capital City, from whence he had been ſo long abſent, and to which he had ſo ardently deſired to return. Soon after this had happened, the Angel of the Lord came down from Heaven, and delivered him a Meſſage, whereby he was ordered to lay the Foundation, in order to erect that great and ſumptuous Temple, which we call *Beit el Moccaddas,*

Moccaddas, or *The Holy-Houſe*, a Fabrick of moſt coſtly and exquiſite Workmanſhip; And the Place where it ſtood, is ſtill held in the higheſt Veneration by all Nations in general.

Daniel was a moſt pious and venerable Prophet: This was he that was preſerved, in ſo miraculous a manner, from the cruel and unjuſt Sentence of the *Aſſyrian* Monarch *Darius* in *Babylon*, whither he had been led into Captivity by *Nebuchadnezzar*. That too credulous King, by the Advice, and at the Inſtigation of his *Satrapa*'s, or Chief Men, cauſed the Holy Prophet to be caſt into a frightful Den, in the Midſt of Seven furious and ravenous Lions, who had been kept Three Days without Meat, on purpoſe that they might ſatiate their hungry Maws upon *Daniel*'s Fleſh: But he, armed with a ſtrong Faith and an intire Confidence, in the Omnipotence of his God, with Sedateneſs in his Looks and an undaunted Courage, intrepidly went down to thoſe fierce Creatures, who, inſtead of devouring, fawned upon him for half a Day and a whole Night that he remained in their Den: And the next Morning, when the King, followed by thoſe Wicked Accuſers of the Holy Man, repaired to the Mouth of that diſmal Cave, expecting to have found ſcarce the Bones of *Daniel* remaining whole; (for the King, in Reality, although he had been ſo inconſiderately weak as to ſuffer himſelf to be over-perſuaded by thoſe vile, malicious Paraſites, was mightily concerned, and had a very particular Love and Eſteem for that virtuous Prophet) and as he approached nearer to the Den, began to call upon him, in a loud and ſorrowful Voice; " O *Daniel!* Hath the " God in whom thou haſt believed, in whom thou " diſt continually put thy Truſt; has He, I ſay, de-" livered thee from the Lyons Jaws?" To which Words *Daniel* replyed; " May thy Life be long and " proſperous, O King! I am alive, ſound, whole and " unhurt. The God in whom I ever have, do, and

" ever

" ever will center my whole Truft and Confidence,
" feeing the Juftice and Innocence of my Caufe, hath
" been gracioufly pleafed to fend down his Angel,
" who, by the Sacred Word and Command of the
" mighty Lord of Heaven, hath interpofed his pro-
" tecting Arm, and hath affuaged the raging Fury
" of thy devouring Lions, and withheld them from
" doing me any Harm ." When the King heard
this, he was exceeding joyful, and immediately
ordered him to be fet at Liberty ; and being highly
incenfed at his malicious and parafitical *Satrapa's,*
he commanded them to be all thrown down headlong among the Lions, who furioufly flew upon them,
and they, being almoft famifhed with Hunger, foon
devoured them, fatiating their ravenous Stomachs
with the mangled Limbs of thofe Wretches.

This memorable Incident was fo exemplary, the
Deliverance fo miraculous, and fo publickly tranfacted, that *Darius* and all his Court immediately
forfook and renounced their Falfe Worfhip, and believed in the God of *Daniel* ; and that King likewife
iffued out his Royal Proclamation, ftrictly enjoyning all his Subjects throughout his whole Dominions,
That under fevere Penalties, they fhould all, without
Diftinction, adore the fame Deity whom the Holy *Daniel* worfhipped and confided in.

Another Time, he was in like Manner, upon his
having incurred the Wrath of King *Cyrus,* by him caft
into a Den, wherein were alfo Seven fierce Lions,
the Mouth whereof was ordered to be clofe ftopped
up ; and he was there confined a whole Week. At
which Time, God commanded *Bacub,* or *Habakkuk,* to
convey the Provifions he was carrying to his Workmen in the Field, to *Daniel* in the Cave ; which he
did in the Twinkling of an *Eye,* though he was many
Leagues diftant from him, becaufe he was born up
through the Air by an Angel : When he came to the
frightful Den, he called out to *Daniel,* who having
opened the Entrance, received the Food from him ;

and

and he returned to his Workmen the ſame Way he came, and all this in the Space of a Moment.

But, at length, when that King, with his Followers and evil Counſellors, came to ſee what the ravenous Creatures had left of *Daniel,* whom they ſuppoſed had, long ſince, been torn Piece-meal, and devoured; the Holy Man, who heard them at the Mouth of the Den, roſe up, and lifted away the vaſt and ponderous Stone which had been laid over it, when they all, with Aſtoniſhment, beheld him feeding thoſe fierce Animals, who fawned upon him, as if he had brought them up. The King, being greatly amazed at this wonderful Prodigy, bad him come out, and embracing him with Joy and Satisfaction, he commanded his Guards to lay hold of thoſe who had been the Perſecutors of this juſt Perſon, and to caſt them all to the Lions, before his Face; which Order being inſtantly executed, they were, in a Moment, pulled all in Pieces; " For it frequently happens, that the " Harms which the Wicked deſign for the Innocent, " light upon the Heads of the Inventors. "

" From the wonderful Preſervation of this beati-" fied Prophet, we are taught, That by a conſtant " firm Faith, and an unſhaken, perſevering Confi-" dence in God's omnipotent Divinity, we ſhall be " delivered out of all Dangers and Afflictions, and " that thereby we may triumphantly go through " the ſevereſt Perſecutions. Let us, therefore, fix " our whole Truſt in God alone : Let none loſe Cou-" rage, or deſpair of his Benevolence, even under the " worſt of Circumſtances ; For where the Danger is " the greateſt, and ſeemingly unavoidable, there, of " a Certainty, his Mercy is more to be hoped for, " and infallibly neareſt at Hand. "

Jonas has taught us the ſame ; ſeeing that his Want of Confidence, and his Unbelief, were ſuffici-

ent

ent to difturb the Tranquility of the very Sea, and to raife a mighty and terrible Tempeft in the, before, peaceable Waves, infomuch, that nothing would appeafe and affuage their Fury, but his cafting himfelf headlong into the midft of them ; where, though he beheld the huge Whale, with its monftrous Jaws widely extended, and waiting for him to fwallow him up, yet there was no Remedy, but he muft fee the Event. When he found himfelf in that enormous Paunch, he began to be fenfible of his heinous Tranfgreffion : He then began to implore Mercy and Forgivenefs : There, with many a bitter Sigh, he reflected upon his paft Offences, and inceffantly invoked the Name of his angry Lord, when he found himfelf involved in that Labyrinth of Woe : There he, with Anguifh of Soul, found himfelf overwhelmed and oppreffed all at one Time, with four difmal and terrifying Obfcurities ; either, or the leaft of which, was more than enough to amaze, fhock, ftupify, and caufe to tremble, both the Body and Soul of the moft determined Mortal ; Thefe were, Firft, The Darknefs of his Sins ; Secondly, The Darknefs of the Waters ; Thirdly, The Darknefs of the Night ; and, Fourthly, The Darknefs and Obfcurity of that monftrous Paunch which was his prefent Abode.

Neverthelefs the tremendous Word of God came down to the mighty *Leviathan*, with a ftrict Command, that *Jonas* fhould be preferved with the fame Care and Regard it would ufe in the Prefervation of its own Bowels : And it was moreover the Lord's Will, that he fhould be difgorged from the Belly of that huge Fifh on the Third Day, and caft up on the dry Land ; which happened to fall out exactly at that Time of the Day when three Parts thereof were diminifhed and paft : And when he found himfelf at Liberty, and fafe upon the Shore, with exceffive Joy at his Delivery from that imminent Danger, he, with unfeigned Devotion, made Four Proftrations to the Lord,

been

in Commemoration of the four Obfcurities he had been oppreffed with, whilft he continued under the Waters, and as a Thankfgiving Offering for His Divine Majefty's having fo gracioufly vouchfafed to preferve him in thofe terrifying Circumftances. This is the fame daily Prayer which is enjoyned us *Muffulmans* to obferve, repeat, and celebrate every Day at the fame Hour, and is what we call *Salaat el Aafar.*

(*a*) *Yabia,* that is *John,* was a moft fanctified Perfon, and whofe great Privileges and Immunities were, as the reverend *Alcoran* tells us, figned with the Lord's own Hand. This was he who, in his early

P 2

Youth,

(*a*) St. *John* the Baptift is, by the *Arabs,* called *Jahia* (or rather, according to our Pronunciation *Yahia*) *ben Zacharia,* and fometimes, after the *Syrians* and other Eaftern Chriftians, *Johanna* and *Mar Johanna.* The Name *Yahia* fignifies the Giver of Life, from *Haiat,* Life; becaufe, they fay, he made the Name of *Zachary* his Father to live, and his Memory immortal; or elfe, becaufe the true Religion, or the Faith in the *Meffiah,* through his Means, received new Life; for, they affirm, That the Doctrine our Bleffed Saviour preached, was *Iflamifm,* but has been fince adulterated and corrupted. The *Alcoran* and *Mahometan* Authors give the fame Account we find in the Holy Gofpel, concerning his being promifed to his Father by the Angel, with only the Addition of fome Circumftances. — The *Taarich Monthekheb* fays, That his Head being cut off by a King of the *Jews,* the Blood that flowed from his Body could never be ftaunched, 'till his Death was revenged upon the *Jews,* by a great Defolation God fent upon them, and that he was the laft Prophet of that Nation. — The *Perfian* Geography fays, His Head was preferved in a Church built by the *Sabians* at *Damafcus* for that Purpofe, and there always honoured both by *Chriftians* and *Mahometans.* Thefe *Sabians* are, with fome Difference, the fame the *Afiaticks* call *Mendai Jahia,* and we, The Chriftians of Saint *John,* many of whom ftill live in and about the City *Baffora.* That Church, now converted into a Mofque, was dedicated to *Zachary* Father to Saint *John,* and was not called Saint *John's* Church, 'till after his Head (found in the City *Hems* in the Reign of the Emperor *Theodofius* the younger) was carried thither and interred. —— The *Mahometans* confound *Zachary* the Father of Saint *John,* with *Zachary* the High-Prieft, whom *Joas* caufed to be

ftoned

Youth, renounced and relinquished the Pleasures of the World, abandoned his indulgent Parents, and embraced an austere, religious Life; wandering, almost naked, through the Mountains, in Company with the wild Beasts of the Fields, his Face and Limbs uncovered, and continually exposed to the Inclemency of the Winds, the Frost, and the scorching Sun-beams, feeding upon raw Herbs and Roots, drinking foul and unsavoury Waters, never Sleeping but in the open Air, without fearing any of its dangerous Consequences. The Birds of the Air became so familiar with him, that they would pitch and sit upon his Head; and the Brute-Beasts followed him up and down where-ever he went, never quitting his Company, all one as if he had been one of their own Species.

---

stoned to Death in the Temple, notwithstanding the mighty Services done him by his Father *Jiada*, and they say, *Gaduz*, that is *Nebuchadnezzar* (whom they all make to be General of the *Persian* Monarch's Armies) came to *Jerusalem* purposely to revenge his Death ——— They also quote many Words, which, in Reality, are our Saviour's, and apply them to Saint *John*, and have formed Dialogues betwixt them. — They give him several Titles besides that of *Nabi* or Prophet, and call him *Assum* and *Massum*, that is, Exempt, Preserved, and Free from all Sin, not only in Regard of his Innocency, and the Austerity of his Life, but also by his Sanctification in his Mother's Womb. —— The Eastern *Christians* keep the Festival of the Nativity of Saint *John* Baptist on the 21st Day of the Month, called in the *Syrian* Calendar, *Haziran*, which answers to our *June*. It is set down in the *Mahometan* Ephemerides *El Mi'ad*, or *Muloud Jahia*. The Festival we call the Decollation of Saint *John*, and they, *Medtal Jahia*, is set down in the same Calendar on the 27th of the Month *Ab*, answerable to our *August*. —— The Disciples of Saint *John* Baptist, who in the primitive Times were called *Hemero Baptistes*, and whose Numbers were considerable amongst the *Jews*, in process of Time, made a particular Religion, by the Name of *Mendai Jahia*: They use a Sort of Baptism very different from ours, which makes our Travellers call them *Christians of Saint John*; but they must not be altogether confounded with the *Sabians*, who are of a different Sect. —— For those Sects, see *D'Herbelot* under the Names *Mendai, Jahia, Suba,* and *Sabi*, and for Saint *John* see *Jobia* and *Johanna.*

He

He once left this Retirement of his, and went to vifit his Mother *Ifabel,* or *Elizabeth,* who was very much afflicted and concerned to behold in her Son fo near a Refemblance to a *Sylvan,* or a Wild Man, his Countenance fo ftrangely disfigured, his Flefh all parched, tanned, and without Covering, his Legs bare and his Feet unfhod, and all over ill-treated by the Thorns, and lamentably chopt with the pinching Frofts. What increafed her Grief was, That, inftead of comforting her for his long Abfence by offering himfelf to ftay at home with her, as fhe, almoft drowned in a tender Shower of Motherly Tears, moft earneftly intreated him to do, he only returned her this Anfwer :

" My Dear and Honoured Mother ! You are not
" ignorant, nor can you have forgot, that I remain-
" ed with you, under your Roof, the whole Time of
" my Infancy and Childhood, and that I was never
" in the leaft undutiful, or difobedient to your Com-
" mands ; but now I am grown up to be a Man, I
" intend to follow my Obligation, and to endeavour
" to anfwer the End of my Creation, by dedicating
" my Time wholly to the Service of my Creator,
" which is what I may, upon no Confideration, pre-
" fume to omit or to neglect. '' From hence it *is,*
that our Holy Book of *El Sunna,* or the Oral Law, ftrictly enjoyns and commands us, That as foon as we are arrived to Years of Maturity, we muft never neglect to be affiduous in the Obfervation of God's Sacred Laws.

Ifa, or *Jefus* was the fame whom we generally call the (*a*) *Meffiah,* becaufe he had the Vertue of Healing any Wound or Sore whatfoever, with only his Touch:

P 3   By

(*a*) My *Moor* has it *Almalit* ; but that I excufe in him, as I am forced to do a thoufand other Words and Names, which he moft
inhu-

By only ftroaking with his Hand the contracted
Limbs of the Lame, he perfectly reftored them to
their proper Ufes and Faculties : He cured the Paralytick, and thofe who were ftruck with the Plague,
or any peftilential Diftemper ; as likewife thofe who
were afflicted with the Gout, and the Falling-Sicknefs :
He reftored the Blind to their Sight, the Dumb to their
Speech, and the Deaf to their Hearing ; nay, the
very Dead he raifed from their Graves. He made
Birds of Clay, and, with one Blaft of his Breath,
caufed them to fly : He expelled Dœmons wherefoever
they were hid. (*a*) All thefe Miracles this Beatified Prophet performed through Divine Grace and
Infpiration, and by the wonderful Efficacy of a
ftrong Faith in God's Omnipotency, but all to little
Effect, and no Benefit, but it all rather proved the
Caufe

---

inhumanely *Spaniolizes*, or rather *Barbarizes*. The *Arabs*, according to *D'Herbelot* and others, call our B'effed Saviour *El Maffih* ; It
is become amongft them the proper Name of many Men ; as is,
likewife, *Ifa*, *Iffa* or *Aifa*, all which are the fame as *Jefus*. They
call him *Ifa ben Mirtam*, or *Jefus* the Son of *Mary*, but never mention him without the moft profound Reverence, and the additional
Title of *Sidinah*, that is, our Lord.

(*a*) I hope the judicious Readers of the following Lines in this
Paragraph, will be fo Candid and Impartial, as to recollect their
Memories, and to confider who was the Author of this Performance,
whereof I am but the Tranflator. Could the tender Confciences of
the *Spanifh Moors*, who were Chriftians in nothing but their Outfides, have digefted the Myfteries of the facred Trinity, they might
peaceably have enjoyed their ample Patrimonies in their Native
Country, which, through the Perfecution of their mercilefs Enemies,
and Fear of the Inquifition, fo many, fo very many Thoufands of
them, were compelled to abandon, and to flee for Sanctuary to
Turkey, and efpecially over to *Barbary*, where they fwarm. ——
This Doctrine is, indeed, very *Anti-chriftian*, but they are the Words
of a *Moor*, and not of a *Chriftian*. He writes the real Sentiments
of his honeft well meaning Heart, which he imbibed with his Mother's Milk, and had been handed down to him by the erroneous
Traditions of his Fore-Fathers, and to them by their fubtle Law-
giver, the Impoftor *Mahomet* ; and I am perfuaded, he delivers
nothing

Caufe of breeding Confufions: For the People, being alarmed and aftonifhed at the Sight of fuch furprizing Myfteries, denyed, and began to forget, *Him*

---

nothing but what, to the utmoft of his Knowledge, are the true Tenets of that Medley of Incoherences, I mean the *Mahometan* Belief, as delivered in the *Alcoran*, and the other Books of *El Sunni*, or their Oral Laws. I would, neverthelefs, fain have omitted this whole Paragraph, or, at leaft, have given it a different Turn; but, upon fecond Thoughts, I confulted fome Gentlemen of Worth and Learning, who all told me, *That if I pretended to give the World a Tranflation, I muft give the real Meaning of my Author, and not my own, except I did it feparately from the Work itfelf.* But for the Reader's further Satisfaction, I give a faithful Tranfcript of the whole Paragraph. *Videlicet.*

Yçe fue el que le llamaron
Almahiz por que fanaba
Tocando qualquiéra herida
Y con fu mano amahaba
Qualquiera cofa contricta
Coxos y mancos curaba
Tullidos y contajiofos
Ya los qui de gota eftaban
Alos ciegos daba vifta
Alos mudos daba habla
Alos fordos el oir
Los muertos Refucitaba
Hazia abes de ba Ro
Y con fu aliento bolaban
Efpelia los Demonios
De donde quiera que eftaban
Y todos eftos milagros
Que con fu dibina gracia
Hizo por fu fe creçida
Y no le approvecho nada
Antes fueron confufiones
Porque la Jente turbada
De tan grandes marabillas
Negaron al que la daba
El fer con que los hazia
Y al menfajero adoraban
Tomando por fenor
Yncitados de la traça

Del maldito luçifer
De do quedo cimentada
La confufa trinidad
Ceguedad Jamas penfada
Y quando yçe entendio
Que per fenor le adoraban
Haziendo le trinidad
Cofa del tan apartada
Fue ala que el fol fe ponia
Quando Efto le denunciaban
Y defendendofe dello
Hizo ad alla tres a Raças
Aquellas que fon de almagrib
Que oi los muzlimes guardan
Negando las dos perfonas
Que a fu fenor le applicaban
Y afirmando la unidad
Sin ponerle feme jança
Alfin alla lo enxalço
Dentre efte Jente engannada
Quedando efcuros fin fe
Sin Salbaçion y fin graçia
En efte fanto anabi
Hizieron parada y Raya
Los profetas y anabies
Los alquitebes y cartas
Que fobre los de yzrael
Fueron del çielo baxadas.

from

from whom he received the Power, by which he did all this ; and fell to adoring the *Meſſenger*, taking *him* for their Lord, and their God, which they did at the ſubtle Inſtigations of the accurſed *Lucifer* : And from hence is derived the Original Source of the *confuſed Trinity* : A *Bl'indneſs* which that Sanctified Prophet never ſo much as dreamt of.

. But when *Iſa* perceived that they had made a Deity of him, and that they adored him as ſuch, by incorporating him into a *Trinity*, which was what was ſo very contrary to his Thoughts and Intentions ; and it being at the Time when the Sun was juſt going to diſappear, when this was denounced to him by his Followers, which he defended himſelf againſt, by an abſolute Refuſal of any ſuch Propoſal ; He performed, before the Preſence of his Creator, thoſe Three Proſtrations (which are the ſame which at this Day we *Muſſulmans* obſerve and repeat at the Hour of *El Magrib*, or Sun-ſet) wherein he abjured the Two Perſons they had incorporated and joyned with his Lord, whoſe Unity he confirmed, denying to acknowledge that God has any Equal or Likeneſs. (*a*) At length God took him up from amongſt thoſe deluded People, and left them groping in the Dark, with-

(*a*) They will, by no Means, allow nor acknowledge that our Saviour *Jeſus Chriſt* was crucified by the *Jews*, but that they fixed a Malefactor upon the Croſs in his ſtead, who much reſembled him : They intended, they ſay, to have done it, but were prevented by his being, the Night before, taken up into the Fourth Heaven, which, according to them, is the *Cœlum Empyreum* ; for they hold the Firſt to be that of the Planets ; the Second the Firmament ; the Third that of the Spirits abſtracted from Bodies, and the Fourth that of the Throne and Glory of God. —— As to his Birth, they ſay, That he was born at *Bethlehem*, near *Jeruſalem*, in the Fifty-ſixth Year of *Auguſtus Cæſar* : That his Mother *Miriam* miraculouſly conceived him in her Womb without having ever known Man ; and, That he was but Three Hours in the Cradle. —— Though they believe him not to be a God (for few can be ignorant of their being *Monothelites* or *Unitarians*) yet they aſſign him a kind

without Faith, without Grace, and in a Word, without Salvation. In this Holy Prophet the Spirit of Prophefy ceafed: This was the Laft of the Prophets or Meffengers, and his Sacred Scripture was the Laft which was fent down from Heaven to the People of *Ifrael.*

---

of Omnipotency, which, they fav, He manifefted upon Earth, by his wonderful Birth, his Doctrine, his Law, his Afcenfion into Heaven, his miraculous Cures, and the like ; and that he is again to confirm all this by returning to the World, and by his Victory over *Daggial* or *Antichrift.* They add, That he exercifes the fame Power in the other World by his Office of a Mediator and Interceffor.

S U P.

SUPPLEMENT

TO

The Ninth CHAPTER.

A S my Author has been filent in fome very Material Heads, I think it neceffary to fupply his Omiffions by what is to be found in other *Mahometan* Books, efpecially concerning the *Jews* in general, and fome of the Patriarchs and Prophets in particular, that have not been treated of by him : And, Firft,

Of the J E W S.

T Hefe People the *Arabs* call *Beni Ifrael,* but more commonly *Lehoud,* in the Singular *Jahoudi,* from *Houd* the Patriarch *Heber:* For, believing, as many of our Hiftorians do, that the Word *Hebrew* comes from *Heber,* by the fame Reafon they conclude,

clude, that of *Jahoudi*, fignifying a *Jew*, muſt infallibly be made of *Houd*, and ſo that *Houd* and *Heber*
were the ſame Name. The *Turks* call them *Tchifout*
or *Tchafut*, Carrion or ſtinking, by way of Contempt. —— All *Mahometans* unanimouſly agree,
That the *Jews* have been condemned to perpetual
Bondage for their ſtubborn Rebellion againſt God,
and for not receiving and acknowledging *Jeſus Chriſt*
for the true *Meſſiah*. This is grounded on the *Alcoran*; all the Expoſitors whereof ſay, That ever ſince
the firſt Rebellion of that hardened Nation, they
have always been liable to be killed, to be made
Slaves, or at leaſt, to be kept under a rigid Yoak,
and to be forcibly compelled to pay Tribute; which
began firſt under *Nebuchadnezzar*, and will continue
'till the World's End. —— In relation to the Diſ-
perſion of the *Jews*, they add, That there is no
Country upon the Earth without ſome of thoſe
People more or leſs. —— *Mahomet* having been obliged to the *Jews* for many Paſſages in his *Alcoran*,
to requite them, in the Chapter *Aaraf*, ſays, *There is
a Race among the People of* Moſes, *which points out and
ſhews the Truth to all the reſt, and is governed with
Juſtice and Equity.* —— The Expoſitors upon this
Paſſage, add, That the *Jews*, after the Death of *Moſes* and *Joſhua*, fell to Idolatry, and embrued their
Hands in the Blood of the Prophets (They ſay, the
whole Number of the Prophets of the Race of *Iſrael*
was 124000) whom God ſent, from Time to Time,
to preach to them, in order to reclaim them. ——
Nevertheleſs, a great Number of them kept the Law,
and implicitly believed in and adored the True God
of their Fore-fathers, inceſſantly praying to God to
deliver them out of the Company of the Wicked.
God heard their Prayers and Supplications, and, by a
ſtrange Miracle, opened for them a very ſpacious
Paſſage, which carried them, with much Eaſe, into
the moſt Eaſtward Parts of the World, far beyond
China, where they ſettled, and where, to this Day,
are

are some Remains of them. —— Other Expofitors add another Fable, no lefs impertinent than this, which is, That *Mahomet*, in the imaginary Pilgrimage he made one Night to Heaven, faw thofe Tribes of *Ifraelites* in his Way; and having read to them Ten Verfes of the *Alcoran*, they were all converted to *Iflamifm*, and that thofe are the *Jews* he fpeaks of in the Chapter *Aaraf*. —— Thefe *Jews* may, perhaps, be the fame whom our Authors will needs have to have been fent into *Tartary*, and the fartheft Eaftern Parts, in the *Affyrian* Captivity. — *Algianabi* and *Abou'l Feda* write, That *Judaifm* was brought into *Arabia* by *Abou Kerb Affaad*, 32d King of *Arabia Fœlix*, 700 Years before *Mahomet*. —— This Prince was of the Family of *Hemiar*, from whom the *Arabs* his Subjects were called *Hemiarites*, and by the *Greeks*, *Homerites*. —— *Dhou Naovas*, 47th King of the fame Race, was fo zealous for *Judaifm*, that he caufed thofe who refufed to profefs it, to be caft into burning Furnaces, which Cruelty of his obliged the *Negaifhi*, or Emperor of *Æthiopia*, who was a Chriftian, to make War upon him, and, in fine, to fubdue his whole Country, which remained under the Subjection of the *Æthiopians* for the Space of 72 Years. —— There were abundance of *Jews* in *Arabia* when *Mahomet* firft ftarted up, and fome were very powerful, and held feveral Caftles and ftrong Holds, wherein they commanded like Sovereign Princes. *Mahomet* had Wars with them, fubdued many, expelled others, and at laft, gave Quarter to the reft, becaufe they had been Witneffes to his Impoftures. —— Formerly the *Jews* in the Eaft wore a Piece of Yellow Cloth upon their Shoulders, or a Yellow, a Red, or Orange-coloured Hat, for a Mark of Diftinction, as they do now in moft Parts of *Italy*, I mean, as to the Hat: At prefent, throughout all the *Mahometan* Dominions, a long Felt Cap, always black, which the *Turks*, in Dirifion, call *Harouz*, which in their Language, fignifies a Clofe-ftool, being fhaped
ped

ped much like it ; and round about it they are suffered to wreath a Turbant of either blue or striped Linnen, but no other: This Privilege they have only in the *Levant*, for in *Barbary* they must only bind a Sort of Handkerchief round it. Their Habits in all *Mahometan* Countries, must be intirely Black. This is of their own Native *Jews*, for those who come from any Part of *Christendom* may wear the Habit of the Place they came from ; but would run a great Hazard of being burnt, if they should presume to wear any thing Green. To conclude, The *Mahometans* assign the *Jews* their Station in Hell one Story or Degree lower than the *Christians* ; which last, I fear, have never had the Civility to return them their Thanks for that Favour.

Of the Patriarchs *S A L E H* and *H E B E R.*

THe *Arabians* call the Patriarch *Saleh* by the Name and Title of *Salah el Nabi,* that is, The Prophet *Salah.* ——He was the Son of *Arphaxad,* and Father to *Heber.* —— They say, He was sent by God to the People of the Tribe of *Themud,* who inhabited *Arabia Petræa,* or the Stony, but found a very bad Reception among those wicked People. The *Themudites* were descended from *Themud* the Son of *Amer,* the Son of *Aram,* and Brother to *Arphaxad.* ———— The *Taarich Montekheb* has it, That *Salah* was the Son of *Asaf,* the Son of *Cassekh,* the Son of *Haver,* the Son of *Khaver* or *Heber,* the Son of *Themud,* the Son of *Aram,* the Son of *Sam,* or *Shem,* the Son of *Noah* ; which Genealogy little agrees with the *Hebrew* Text, which says, That *Saleh* was the Son of *Arphaxad,* and Father to *Heber.* But by the same
Taarich

Taarich Montekheb it appears, that this *Salah* the *Mahometans* fpeak of, is much more modern than the Patriarch *Saleh* mentioned in Scripture. —— The fame Author tells us, That the Prophet *Salah* proved his Miffion by the Miracle he wrought, by caufing a Rock to open, from whence came out a She Camel, which brought forth a young one in the fight of Multitudes of Spectators: But the *Themudites* continuing obftinate in their Unbelief, killed the faid Camel, though fhe, in audible and articulate Words, upbraided them with Incredulity. This drew divine Vengeance upon them; For God fent the Angel *Gabriel* to chaftife them, who ftruck them with a mortal Difeafe, whereby they all perifhed, excepting only fome few, who believed in the Prophet's Words, and with him retired to *Mecca*, where he ended his Days. —— Some will have it, fays the fame Author, that *Salah* went from *Mecca* into *Paleftine*, and is there buried. This very Story is related by *Houffain Vaez*, but much more at large, and with the Addition of feveral Circumftances, though, in the Main, all tending to the fame Effect: But what the *Alcoran* gives us concerning the above-mentioned *Themudites*, ought to have a Place here: It fays; That God having determined thofe People (who were an ancient noble Tribe of *Arabs*, at prefent extinct) for refufing to give Ear to the Prophet *Salah* whom He had fent to convert them, and who at laft told them, That in three Days Time they fhould all infallibly perifh: Upon hearing this, they dug Caves under their Houfes to fhelter them from the impending Storm, in which fubterraneous Vaults they continued hid 'till the Fourth Day after that Prediction, when, imagining all Danger paft, they came out, and, upon finding no Alteration, but every Thing as they had left it, they derided the Prophet more than ever: When the Angel *Gabriel* appeared to them in his own proper Form, which was thus; His Feet ftood upon the Earth, and his Head reach'd up to Heaven: His

Wings

Wings extended from Eaft to Weft; the Colour of his Feet was like the *Aurora,* and his Wings were of a Sea-Green; his Teeth White, Shining and Tranfparent, his Cheeks Flaming, and his Hair as Red as Coral, which covered the whole Horizon. The *Themudites,* terrified at this Sight, retired again to their Houfes, and again hid themfelves in their Caves under Ground, but *Gabriel* cried out with a moft dreadful Voice, *Dye, all ye accurfed Wretches, for the Lord has paffed Sentence of Condemnation upon ye!* This Out-cry of the Angel's was fo exceffive loud and vehement, that it caufed a great Earthquake, which fhook their Towns, *&c.* all down over their Heads, and they remained buried under the Ruins.

This Patriarch, as I have faid before, was the Father of the venerable *Heber,* whom all *Mahometans* call *Houd,* becaufe their Legiflator *Mahomet,* was pleafed to give him that Name in his *Alcoran:* He is held in high Rank and Efteem among them, and they affirm, That he was fent by God, to Preach to the People of *Ad* and *Shedad,* but that his Doctrine had but very little Influence upon them, for few would liften to him at all, but fewer would believe in his Miffion. Their Incredulity, according to the *Alcoran,* fo incenfed the Lord againft them, that He fent a fcorching Wind, which that Book calls *Rih àkim,* whereby thofe Unbelievers were utterly deftroyed.

——*Houd,* according to fome Authors, with a fmall Number of the *Faithful,* retired to *Mecca,* where he fettled his Abode; though others affirm, He went into the Province of *Hadramuth,* and there ended his Days. His Tomb is ftill to be feen in *Arabia Fœlix,* near the Town of *Mirbath,* and there is a fmall Town built about it called *Cabar,* or *Cubr Houd,* that is, The Sepulchre of *Houd.*——The *Taarich Montekheb* fays, That this Patriarch lived in the Days of *Giamfhid* King of *Perfia.* The aforefaid Chronicle gives this fhort Account of *Houd,* but *Khondemir* and *Houffain Vaez* deliver it much more at large.—— They

fay,

say, He was born in *Arabia* among the *Adites*, who descended from *Ad* the Son of *Avus*, or *Hus* the Son of *Aram*, the Son of *Shem*, the Son of *Noah*. Their Tradition of him is, That God sent *Houd* the Prophet to Preach to the *Adites*, and to convert them from their false Worship they made to Idols. ——— Those Idols were *Sakiub*, whom they invoked when they wanted Rain. *Hesedhak*, that they called upon to be protected in Travelling. *Razekah*, to supply them with Necessaries for Life. And *Salemah* for Health in Sickness. This potent Tribe of *Arabs*, as I have said, had for their Founder *Ad*, who was the Father of *Shodad* and *Shedid*, who became so Powerful and Wealthy in *Arabia*, that they perfectly finished the mighty and stupendous Structures their Father had began. They are mentioned in the *Alcoran* with Detestation, whose Expositors tell Wonders of that fabulous City and Garden called *Iram*, those Princes, who, it seems were huge and monstrous Giants, had built and planted, and where they deposited all the immense Riches they had amassed in their Conquests of the *Arabias* and other Countries. This City, which was called *Gennet*, or *Paradise*, having built it in Imitation thereof, especially the Garden, is only now and then visible, they pretending it appears to some particular Persons, with abundance of such Chimæras. ——— But to return. The *Adites* inhabited *Arabia Fælix*, in a Country called *Akcaf*, in *Arabick* signifying Craggy Hills, all that Space of Land between *Hadramuth* and *Oman* upon the *Persian* Gulph, being full of such Hills of Sand. ——— *Houd* Preached to these People for several Years without any Success, 'till God became so angry with them, that He resolved to allow them no longer Time. ——— The first Token God sent them of His Indignation, was a Famine of Three Years Continuance, which, accompanied with other Plagues and infectious Distempers, carried off vast Numbers of those People, who were at that Time the wealthiest, most formidable and most numerous Tribe in all

Arabia.

Arabia. The *Adites* in this Extremity finding no Relief from their falfe Gods, refolved to go in Pilgrimage to the Province of *Hegiaz*, to that Place where now the *Muffulmans* refort to perform their Pilgrimage, being the fame where ftands the Temple which is at *Mecca.*——— There was then near that Place a Hill of Red Sand, about which there was continually a great Concourfe of People from all Parts; and all thefe, as well the *Infidels* as the *Faithful*, firmly and implicitly believed, That by devoutly applying themfelves to God in that Place, they fhould infallibly obtain from Him whatfoever they demanded for the fupplying their Wants, as to what was requifite for the Support of Life.———Having then refolved upon this Religious Journey, they made Choice of 70 Men, and at their Head they placed *Mortadh* and *Kil*, the Two richeft and moft refpected Chiefs among all their Tribes, who fet out, in the Name of all the People, upon this fanctified Pilgrimage to demand Rain, without which they muft inevitably perifh. This Cavalcade was very kindly received by *Moavia*, who who at that Time reigned in the Province of *Hegiaz*.
————As for *Mortadh*, who was the wifeft Man of the whole Company, he often pofitively told them, That it would be in vain for them to go in Pilgrimage to that Holy Place, except they gave Ear to the Doctrine of the Prophet *Houd*, and did Penance for their Incredulity: But *Kil*, who was an obftinate Unbeliever, and had an extreme Averfion to that Prophet, defired King *Moavia* to keep his Colleague *Mortadh* under Confinement in Prifon, 'till he and his Companions went to perform their Devotions at the aforefaid Hill. *Moavia* complied with his Requeft, and kept *Mortadh* Prifoner, and difmiffed the reft to go and fulfil their Vow.————*Kil* being now the only Chief of thofe mifled People, when he arrived at the Place, prayed thus; *O Lord! give the People of* Ad *fuch Rain as thou fhalt think proper for them.* When he had fo faid, Three Clouds appeared, the one White,

Q

the other Black, and the third Red; and at the same Time a Voice was heard, which said; *Chuse which of the Three you will have.* After some little Pausing, *Kil* chose the Black one, as imagining it contained the greatest Quantity of Rain, and departed full of Joy, thinking his Supplication had been heard, according to his Desire. In his Way home, so soon as he came to the Valley of *Mogaith*, in the Country of the *Adites*, he acquainted them with his imagined Success, and these senseless, misguided People ran out to meet the Cloud, which was full of nothing but divine Vengeance, and instead of the desired and expected Showers of Rain, produced a most violent Wind, excessive cold and piercing, which continually blowing for Seven Days, destroyed all the Infidels in the Country, and none were left alive but only *Houd*, and such as had embraced the Faith.

Of the Patriarch L O T.

NOtwithstanding I could say much upon this Head, as well as upon several others, yet I rather chuse to translate the Words of Monsieur *D'Herbelot*, a grave and learned Author, who was perfectly versed in the Oriental Tongues, and who had, for many Years, made it his whole Business to peruse their Books, and to study their Maxims, &c. whereby it will appear, that their detestable Practice of the Sins of *Sodom*, is not looked upon to be no Crime, as many believe. —— He has it *Verbatim* thus ——*Loth* or *Louth*; According to the *Taarich Montekheb*, he was the Son of *Haran*, the Son of *Tareh*, and consequently, Nephew to *Abraham* the Patriarch. He is one of those the *Mahometans* acknowledge as Prophets,

phets, and was particularly sent from God, to preach the Faith, and the Worship of the true Deity, to the People of *Sodom*, and to dissuade them from the detestable Sin whereof they were the first Inventors. These Wretches having had no Regard to *Lot's* Preaching, *Gabriel* was sent by the Lord, who overturned Five of their Cities and destroyed all the Inhabitants. From that Time, the Word *Louth*, or *Laouth*, signifies, in the *Arabick*, the Sin of those People, and they generally call those who are guilty of it, *Caoum Louth*, or *Lot's* People, as also *Lothi* or *Louthi*. A noted Author named *Saadi*, writes, That *Lot*, being debauch'd by conversing with the *Sodomites*, was the Cause that the Spirit of Prophecy ceased in *Lot's* Family. The Expositors of the *Alcoran* agree with the *Hebrew* Text touching *Lot's* Genealogy. The five Cities which were destroyed, the *Arabs* call, *Sedouma*, *Amoura*, *Daoura*, *Saboura* and *Saouda*. The *Alcoran* says, That *Lot* spent Twenty Years in Preaching to them the Doctrine of the true God, and exhorting them to forsake that abominable Sin, which had never been committed by any but by them. All his Preaching being of no Effect, God took *Lot* out of *Sodom*, but his Wife being corrupted, would not go, and when he was out, it rained, some say, Stones and Flints, but according to others, Brimstone and Fire, whereby they were all destroyed. This same *Sodom* is, by the *Mahometans*, likewise called *Lonathat*, from *Lot*, because the Inhabitants of those Five Cities, are, in the *Alcoran*, called *Lot's* People. The Story of *Abraham* and the Angels, and what happened to them, with *Lot*, at *Sodom*, is delivered by the *Mahometans* much after the same Manner as we have it, only they enlarge and add many particular Circumstances; and for the over-turning the Cities, they say, That *Gabriel*, the most powerful of those Angels, lifted them altogether off their Foundations, so high, that the Inhabitants of the hithermost or lowest Heaven could hear the Crowing of

Q 2

the

the Cocks, and the Barking of the Dogs, and then letting them drop, they were utterly annihilated. After the Subverfion of thofe Cities, God rained down upon them burning Stones, baked in the Furnace of Hell, on every one of which, was written the Name of one of thofe Criminals; fo that even thofe who chanced to be abfent from the Towns, were ftruck down and deftroyed. They add, That one of thofe Wretches, who was then within the Inclofure of the Temple at *Mecca,* built by *Abraham,* efcaped for the Space of 40 Days he continued there; but as foon as he fet his Foot out of it, he was ftruck and killed by one of thofe Stones, which had remained hanging in the Air. Thefe Fables, added to the Truth of the Hiftory, were invented to give the *Mahometans* a Horror of that deteftable Sin, and the *Alcoran* threatens thofe that fhall be found guilty thereof with the fame Punifhment. *D'Herbelot* in *Loth.* Which fee.

Of the Patriarch *J O B.*

HIS Genealogy they deliver thus; *Aiub ben Razbac, ben Ais, ben Is-hak,* whereby they make him of the Race of *Efau,* whom the *Arabs* call *Ais.* He is reckoned among the *Anbia,* the Plural of *Nabi,* or Prophets. The *Taarick Montheckheb,* which is a General Chronicle, and held in great Efteem, fays; He laboured under great Sicknefs and Afflictions 3 Years (though others have it 7) after which he recovered perfect Health at 80 Years of Age, and then begot a Son called *Bafch ben Aiub.* Some Hiftorians fay, He had 5 Sons, and that with them he made War upon a Nation of *Arabs,* who in their hinder Parts, had fome Refemblance to the

hinder

hinder Parts of a Horfe, and utterly deftroyed them, becaufe they would not hear his Doctrine.——*Khondemir*, another celebrated Hiftorian, often quoted by *Pocock*, *Prideaux*, *Ockley* and others, relates the whole Story of *Job* as our Scriptures have it; but adds the following Fable. He fays, *Job* by his Father defcended from *Efau*, and by his Mother, from *Lot*; (of whom I have been treating, by reafon my *Moor* has left him out of his Catalogue, as he has feveral others) That he Preached to the People of *Thaniah*, inhabiting betwixt *Ramlah* and *Damafcus*, Cities of *Syria*; but that only 3 Perfons were converted: Yet his Zeal was rewarded by God with large Poffeffions and many Children: This his Profperity raifed the Devil's Envy, who told God, That *Job* ferved Him becaufe of his Wealth; but if He withdrew it by reducing him to Poverty and Affliction, he was certain, that he would rebel, and not pray once a Day. Thus far he fticks pretty clofe to our Scripture; but adds, That when the Devil had Power given him over *Job*'s Body, he blew fuch a Peftilential Heat up his Noftrils, that the Infernal Blaft corrupted the whole Mafs of his Blood, and caufed him to break out all over in Ulcers. He became fo miferable an Object, that he was forfaken by all but his Wife *Rafima*, who carried him what-ever he wanted; but the malicious Fiend ftole it all away, 'till fhe had no more to give him. The Devil then appeared to her in the Likenefs of an Old Woman, and told her, That if fhe would give her the Two Treffes of her Hair that hung on her Neck, fhe would every Day provide her wherewithal to maintain her wretched Hufband: To which Propofal *Rafima* immediately confented. The Devil, upon this, went away to *Job*, and told him, That his Wife, having been found committing Adultery, had her Treffes cut off: And he feeing her, when fhe came next, without her Hair, believed it to be true; and this put him into a raging Paffion, infomuch that he fwore, if ever he recovered,

he

he would make an Example of her. The Devil, pleafed with the Succefs of his Fraud, took the Form of an Angel of Light, and appearing to the People, told them, That he was fent by God to acquaint them, that *Job*, whom they had thought a Prophet, had incenfed God againft him, and incurred his higheft Indignation, and therefore they ought in no-wife to regard his Words. *Job*, under this new Affliction, had Recourfe to God, and his Supplication being heard, his Sufferings ceafed; for the Angel *Gabriel* defcended and raifed him up; and then, ftriking with his Foot upon the Ground, a Spring gufhed out, whereof *Job* drinking and wafhing himfelf in it, he was reftored to perfect Health. After this, his Wealth was fo multiplied, that the Rain and Snow which fell where he was, became precious Stones; and fome Authors affirm, that it rained *Tibr*, or Gold-Duft. See *D'Herbelot* in *Aiub*.

Of the Prophet S A M U E L, and of King S A U L.

THIS great Prophet the *Mahometans* call *Shamouil*, or *Afhamouil.* The Account they give of him is this; In the Time of *Ali*, or *Hali el Imam*, that is, *Heli*, the High Prieft of the *Jews*, the *Philiftines* having defeated the Children of *Ifrael* in a great Battle, they took from them the Ark of the Covenant, which in *Arabick* they call *Tabout Sekinah*, and put to Death moft of the Sons of the Prophets. ——This Ark, fome fay, had been made in Paradife, and delivered down from Hand to Hand 'till it fell into *Mofes*'s Poffeffion; though the Generality affirm it to have been made by *Mofes* himfelf, and was compofed

poſed of ſeveral different Sorts of Metals. In it he
ſhut up ſeveral ſacred Relicts; as the Tables of the
Law he had received from God's own Hand, a Baſon
wherein the Angels waſhed, cleanſed, and purified the
Hearts of the Prophets, as alſo the *Tiara*, or Mitre,
and all the reſt of *Haroun's* or *Aaron's*, Pontifical
Robes. The *Iſraelites* uſed to uncover the Ark, and
to expoſe it to Publick View, whenever any Calamity
threatned them, and God always delivered them from
it, by Virtue of thoſe ſacred Things contained therein. ——— As for the *Sekinah* [ſee below] which was
at the Top of it, and from whence the Ark took its
Name, the *Mahometans* affirm, That it was the Figure of a Beaſt like a Leopard, which, always when
the Ark was carried out againſt their Enemies, was
wont to ſtand up, and to make ſo dreadful a Noiſe,
that they, being utterly aſtoniſhed and diſmayed,
would fall down with their Faces flat upon the Ground.
———This is their fabulous and ridiculous Expoſition of the Force and Uſe of the Cherubims; For the
Word *Sekinah* is *Hebrew*, and ſignifies, The Majeſty
and Glory of God, which appeared on the Ark between the Two Cherubims. However, this extravagant Notion they have taken from the Ancient *Rabbins*,
who have aſcribed ſeveral Shapes and Motions to
thoſe Cherubims.——But to return. The *Iſraelites*
aſtoniſhed and confounded at the Loſs of the Ark,
prayed to God to ſend them a Prophet; whereupon
Samuel was ſent, whom they obeyed and held in high
Eſteem for ſome Time; but then, with that Levity
ſo conformable to the Unſettledneſs of their Natural
Diſpoſition, they again began to murmur, and to
call aloud upon him to chuſe them a King.——The
King they elected was *Thalout ben Kiſſui*, as *Mahomet* calls him in the *Alcoran*, and after him, all of
that Perſuaſion do the like. This was *Saul* the Son
of *Kiſh*, firſt King of *Iſrael*, of whoſe Advancement
to the Throne of *Iſrael*, the *Mahometans* in moſt of
their Chronicles give the following Account. (The

Spanifh-Moors fometimes call him *Shaoul*, as do like-wife fome others, but it may be fuppofed to be only in Imitation of the *Jews* and the *Chriftians*.) The Word *Thalout* is derived from the Verb *Thal*, which, amongft other Things, fignifies, To be greater than another; becaufe *Saul* was taller than all the reft of the *Ifraelites*, and for that particular Reafon, was chofen their King.———For, according to the *Maho-metan* Traditions, when the *Jews* defired a King to guide and protect them againft the *Philiftines* their Enemies, God gave to *Samuel* a Veffel of Oyl and a Rod or Wand, and, at the fame Time giving him to underftand, That he, in whofe Prefence the Oyl boiled up, and whofe Stature fhould be exactly the Length of that Wand, fhould be chofen King. This being made known to the *Ifraelites*, all the Great Men among them flocked to *Samuel*, but the Oyl neither boiled up, nor were any of them of the Height of the Rod or Staff.——— *Saul*, who, as fome fay, was but a Currier by Trade, (and others affirm him to have been a Water-Carrier, and that the Name of *Thalout* was given him for his Talnefs of Stature) coming to the Prophet's Houfe after the reft, but up-on fome different Occafion, the facred Oyl began to boil up amain, and he being meafured, his Height was found exactly to anfwer the Length of the Staff; where-upon the Holy Prophet declared, that *Saul* was the Perfon appointed by God to rule over *Ifrael*.———The *Grandees* all muttered, and expreffed great Difcontent, that a Man of fo mean an Extraction and fo bafe an Occupation, fhould be propofed to them for their King; but *Samuel* told them, It was the Will of God, the Difpofer of Crowns and Kingdoms, and that they muft fubmit.——— *Saul* being thus declared and an-ointed King of *Ifrael*, the People demanded of *Sa-muel* a Sign or Miracle to demonftrate that it was the Will of God, that *Saul* fhould reign over them. *Sa-muel* told them, the Sign fhould be, That the Ark which had been taken away by the *Philiftines*, fhould

be

be brought back again by Angels; which accordingly happened, the Ark inftantly appearing upon their
Borders. The Manner of its being recovered out of
the Hands of the *Philiftines,* is thus related by *Abou
Giafar* : At the Time when the Ark was carryed
away, *Giolout* or *Goliath* was King of the *Philiftines,*
and out of the Hatred he bore the *Jewifh* Nation,
caufed it to be caft into a very filthy, indecent Place ;
but all the Inhabitants of that City, being fmitten
with a foul Difeafe in their private Parts, they were
forced to remove it ; and where-ever it was carryed,
the fame loathfome Difeafe followed the Inhabitants.
This Punifhment made the *Philiftines* convey it to the
Country of the *Ifraelites,* where it was taken up by
Angels, and carryed to the Tabernacle where *Saul*
had been anointed King but juft before : This fettled
his Reputation among the *Jews.* ———— The *Taa-
rik Montekheb* fays, That *Samuel* lived in the Reign of
Caikobah, firft King of *Perfia,* of the Second Race.
———— The Expofitors of the *Alcoran* write, That
round about the Ark were the Effigies of all the Patriarchs and Prophets which had or fhould appear, over
which was placed the *Sakinah,* which the *Hebrews* call
Shekina, and fignifies, as I have faid, in that Language,
God's Glory and Majefty. Yet the *Mahometans* fay, That
Sakinah implies *Taskin Khathir,* That which fets the
Mind at Reft, as it happened to the *Ifraelites,* whenever they, unfeignedly, thought that God dwelt among
them. They add, That the *Sakinah* was more particularly a Cherubim, whofe Eyes, like two Lamps,
were fo bright, that none were able to endure their
Splendor. They have alfo a Tradition taken from
the *Rabbins,* That the Head of this Cherubim was
like that of a Man ; that he had two Wings, and that
in War-Time, he came out of the Ark like a violent
Guft of Wind, which bore down before it all the Enemies of the then Believing *Ifraelites,* and for this Reafon, they always caufed the Ark to march at the
Head of their Army. ———— In the Ark were kept
the

the Rod of *Moſes*, the Mitre and other *Pontificalibus* of *Aaron*, a Veſſel full of *Manna* gathered in the Deſart, and a Piece of the Wood called *Alouab*, which made the bitter Waters of *Mara* ſweet.

Of the Fairies, Genii, &c.

BEcauſe, what has been ſaid concerning *Solomon's* having the abſolute Dominion over all thoſe Species of *Beings*, by the Virtue of his Ring, has, perhaps, rais'd the Curioſity of the Reader to be, in ſome Meaſure, acquainted with the Ideas the *Orientals* have of thoſe (as ſome think) imaginary Creatures; I preſent him with the few following Hints. To pretend to ſet down at large the Tythe of all the fabulous Stories I have heard, concerning Fairies, &c. would be both an endleſs and ridiculous Taſk: Their Romances abound with them; and, 'tis to be preſum'd, That moſt of what we find in ours, upon that Subject, owes its Original to the pregnant Brains of the Eaſtern Writers, who were in all Ages very fruitful in Inventions of that Kind. ―――― The *Arabians* call them *El Jinnoon*, which is the Plural of *Jinn* or *Gen*; the *Turks* likewiſe call them *Jinler*, in the Plural; and the *Perſians* call them by the Names of *Dives* and *Peri*, which laſt ſeems to be ſomething like *Fairy*; and from the firſt, certainly came the *Latin* Word *Divus*, and the *Greek* Διⓢ; for, in ſhort, the *Divi* of the *Gentiles* were no other than *Genii*, *Dæmons*, and ſuch like Creatures of a different Species from Men, as *D'Herbelot* affirms. See the Word *Div*. ―――― The *Mahometans* hold them to be neither Angels, Men, nor Devils, but *Genii* and *Dæmons*, as the *Greeks* had it, and a Sort of *Giants*, not of Humane

mane Race, but compos'd of a more refin'd Matter.—
Among these *Dives* or *Jinnoon*, there are some which
are distinguished (particularly by the *Persian* Authors)
by the Name of *Ner* or *Nere*, and are looked upon
as the most dangerous and dreadful of all the others;
These are held to be the Males, and are always at
War with the *Peri*, who pass for Females, and are
not thought to be so wicked and mischievous as the former, but mild and harmless : Nor are they, say the
Mahometans, begot by the *Neri*, or Male *Dives*, but
are of a quite different Species. ——— They have
a *Fairy-Land* as well as we, which they call by the
Name of *Jiniftan*. ——— Their *Mythologists* all agree,
That these *Peri* are kind, good and benevolent, and
do no Manner of Harm, unless provoked by very ill
Usage. They figure them to be of an exquisite lovely
and beautiful Form; and an exceeding beautiful Woman is by the *Persians* (especially the Poets) called
Peri-zadeh, or, Born of a *Peri* or *Fairy*; from which
the *Greeks*, by Corruption, have made the Name *Pa-
risatis* the Daughter of *Darius*, as they have that of
Statira from *Sitarah*, and *Roxana* from *Roushen*, which
signify a *Star*, and *Light*. ——— They hold, that
they were created, and governed the World, long before *Adam*; and in the Number of these *Fairies*, are included, as I have said, all the Good and Evil *Genii*,
and the Giants who waged War with Men in the first
Ages. ——— *Abou Giafar* in his Chronicle, says,
That the *Dives* rul'd the Universe Seven thousand
Years; after which, they, for their Wickedness, had
the Monarchy taken from them by God, and were
succeeded by the *Peri*, who held the Government for
Two thousand Years longer, under the Command of
Gian ben Gian their sole and sovereign Monarch : But
these likewise having offended God, He sent *Eblis* or
Satan to have the absolute Command upon Earth,
who then being an Angel composed out of the Element of Fire, and, consequently, of a nobler Nature
than they, had his Abode in Heaven. When he had

receiv-

received these Orders from his Lord, he descended into this World, and made War upon the *Dives* and the *Peri*, who had now confederated together for their mutual Defence. In these Wars some of the *Dives* siding with *Eblis*, had leave to remain in this World, whilst the rest, and by far the greatest Part, being vanquish'd, were expelled and confined in *Jinnistan* or *Fairy-Land*: Here they continued 'till the Days of *Adam*, and after that, down to the Time of *Solomon*, who had them all under his Subjection. But to return to *Eblis*, who being grown more formidable by the Assistance of those New-comers, attack'd, and intirely defeated the Monarch *Gian ben Gian*, (of whose Exploits and mysterious Shield, many Fables are told) and soon became absolute Master of all the lower World, which had, at that Time, no other Inhabitants but those two Sorts of Creatures. *Eblis*, though he was of the Order of the chief Angels, when he saw himself Victorious, and so very powerful, shew'd he had no more Sense than the other Creatures, so far forgetting himself, as to say, *Who is like unto me? I go up to Heaven whenever I please, and the Earth is absolutely subject to my Will!* God, offended at this his Pride and Insolence, resolved to humble him, by creating Man, *&c.* as is before related in the Chapter of the Creation. Which see. —————— All paralytick Persons, as likewise those who are afflicted with Convulsions and the Falling-Sickness, are by the *Arabians*, &c. called *Mejinnoon*, and *Miskoon* in the Singular, which Words, by adding *een* become Plural; and is as much as to say, Possessed or Inhabited by *Genii* or *Dæmons*, which, as I have already hinted, are not to be understood as *Devils*, but rather what we call *Fairies*. ——— Among all the *Mahometans*, there are Abundance of *Talibs* or Students, who are publick Professors of *Magick*, and who pretend by Exorcisms, Talismans, Casting of Figures, Writings in odd unintelligible Characters, and such like, to expel these *Genii* from the Bodies and Limbs of such Creatures who are troubled

with

with them, whether Rational or Brutes. The Methods practifed by thefe Operators, are various and different: In moft Cafes where we *Europeans* have Recourfe to an able Phyfician, the *Afiaticks* and *Africans* fend for a *Talib Hakim*, or a fkilful *Talib*, meaning one of thofe Students in the *Black-Art* who has acquired the Reputation of having the *Genii* (at leaft fome of them) under his Subjection. Nothing is more common than to fee People with a Scrip of Paper, written all over, and folded up in a fmall Compafs, hang dangling down their Foreheads for fore Eyes, or the Head-ach, Pain in the Ears, Tooth-ach, *&c.*: Nay, for all Sorts of Fevers, and, in a Word, for all Diftempers, thefe Impoftors are generally fent for, and never put Pen to Paper without a Fee, and are treated with great Refpect, the Patients and their Friends kiffing their Hands and Veftments. They burn feveral Sorts of Drugs and Perfumes in their Operations, and though, generally fpeaking, their fallacious Charms are writ upon white Paper, others upon red, blew, yellow, black, *&c.* yet fome of them, on divers Occafions, write upon Parchment and the dry'd Skins of feveral Beafts, as Goats, Sheep, Camels, Oxen, *&c,* and fometimes upon the Leaves of Trees, and a hundred fuch fantaftical Abfurdities. Some of this Trafh they burn under the Nofe of the fick or ailing Perfons, with a Sheet or Blanket drawn over their Heads, to prevent the Smoak of thofe precious Remedies from evaporating in vain: Others they faften about their Arms, Necks, *&c.*: For they are fo ftupidly bigotted to this Superftition, that they believe, with an implicite Credulity, That thofe Scrauls have an efficacious Power to affuage any Pain, and to cure any Ailing whatfoever; imputing fcarce any Diftemper to natural Caufes, but imagine that moft proceed from the *Genii.* Thefe Writings, which they call *Harrouz*, are ufed by Way of Anticipation and Prevention; and here are few of either Sex, but what have fome of hem upon their Arms, Heads, *&c.* and many topping
ping

ping Men will have a dozen or more, neatly ftitch'd up in fine Leather, (either embroider'd or without) and hung under their Arms in a Silk String. The Caps of their Children are feldom without fome of the fame, few'd in Bits of Silk, *&c.* to preferve them from Sicknefs, but, more efpecially, from Evil Eyes, and Witchcraft. The fame Method they take with their Cattle, and one can very rarely meet with a Horfe, Mare or Mule of any Value, without one about its Neck. They fancy the *Genii* frequent the Stables, *&c.* very much, and therefore, can't endure any Body fhould make Water upon the Dung of Horfes, or the like. It is taken as a very grofs Affront, and fcarcely pardonable to mention thefe *Præternatural Beings* where Children are, efpecially when they are very young; nor is it mannerly to commend a Child, Horfe, *&c.* for its Beauty, without adding *Allah-baric*, God blefs it; for they have terrible Apprehenfions of *Fafcination* by *evil* or *envious* Eyes. —— The Ancient *Romans* were no Strangers to this Notion; for *Virgil* fays,

Nefcio quis teneros oculus mihi fafcinat agnos.

To enumerate one half of the Stories I could tell upon this Subject, would be to fwell this Volume to an enormous Bulk, and to tire the Reader's Patience; but, perhaps, he might take it unkindly fhould I drop it without giving him a Tafte: I'll therefore, as fuccinctly as poffible, relate a notable Inftance, which I affure him to be Matter of Fact; and, tho' fomewhat long, I hope will be found entertaining.

In the City of *Coftantina*, the Capital of *New Numidia*, now belonging to the *Algerines*, about the Mid-way between that *Neft of Sea-Rovers* and *Tunis*, lives a very famous *Talib*, whofe Name is *Sidi Meffoud ben Bou-Saadia*, held in high Efteem and Veneration by the Inhabitants of that City and Province. He is reforted to like an Oracle, and is reported to have effected innumerable Cures. 'Tis fome Years

since

ſince he firſt gave out, That he was effectually join'd in Marriage to a Daughter of the King of the *Red Genii* (for they diſtinguiſh the *Fairies* under different Tribes and Colours; theſe are to be underſtood of the *Peri*, or harmleſs and benevolent Species) and that every *Thurſday* Night, this beautiful Fairy-Lady came, inviſible to all Eyes but his, and was Sharer with him in his Bed. At which Times he never fail'd of being ready to receive her, after he had purified himſelf at the Bagnio, and put on clean and perfumed Garments. Her Appartment was always kept extremely neat, and ſmelt like a Perfumer's Shop, with the great Quantity of the choiceſt Incenſe continually burnt therein; nor would he ever ſacrilegiouſly ſuffer either of his other Wives (for he had Two of *Mortal Extraction*) to pollute that Chamber with their groſſer Perſpirations, but held it inviolably ſacred for the Scene of more refined Embraces in the Arms of their *Immortal* Rival; ſo that thoſe good Ladies could never hope for any Family-Benevolence upon a *Thurſday* Night. All this, like dutiful and ſubmiſſive Wives, they bore without Murmuring. But, to make ſhort, this till then happy Man, had diſoblig'd ſome of the principal *Turks* (of whom there are many Hundreds in the Town, and are far from being ſo credulous, or having ſo mighty a Veneration for thoſe ſanctified Folks, as the Native *Moors*) who reſolving to be reveng'd, went to the *Bey*, or *Vice-Roy* of the Province, and maliciouſly inſinuated, That they had heard him ſpeak very diſreſpectfully of his Excellency, who thereupon, inſtantly, ſent to have him apprehended and caſt into Priſon; for thoſe greedy Governors are ſeldom deaf to ſuch Propoſals, eſpecially when any thing is to be got by it; and, in Effect, our *Talib* was threatned with a ſevere *Baſtinado*, in Caſe he would not buy it off at the Price of Four Thouſand Dollars. The Priſoner, who imagin'd the great Credit and Reputation he had always lived in, as well with the Country

try

try People, as the former *Beys,* would have been a fufficient Protection for him, fancy'd the *Bey* was in Jeft, or, at leaft, that his Friends and Admirers would not fail to make Interceffion for his Releafe, upon much eafier Terms, as in Reality they did, in Swarms, but to very little Purpofe ; for the avaritious *Turk* was inexorable ; and having, in more menacing Terms, fent to him again for a conclufive Anfwer, the poor Devil was obliged to fet his Hand to the fatal Inftrument, wherein he acknowledged himfelf indebted the full Sum of Four Thoufand Crowns to the *Beylick* or Government. But as Four Thoufand Crowns is, in thofe Parts, a great Sum of Money, and can hardly be made up out of the Purfes of feveral Families, who yet live tolerably well, and have ten times the Value in Cattle, Corn, and other Effects, he was at a lamentable Lofs how to raife them; and the *Bey,* at the Inftigation of the *Taleb's* Adverfaries, pofitively declared, That he would accept of nothing in Payment, but Dollars *in Specie.* He alledged, That *Sidi Meffoud* was a rich Man, and added, with a right *Turkifh* Sneer, " That, certainly, one who had the Honour of " having a *Fairy-King's* Daughter lie by his Side once a " Week, could never want fo paltry trifling a Sum as " that which he demanded ": Telling withal thofe grave *Dons* who came to intercede for their great Phyfician, " That nothing but his Regard to them had prevail'd " with him, to lay upon that Offender fo moderate a Fine " as Four Thoufand Dollars, inftead of Forty Thoufand, " as he at firft intended. " This artful Procedure of the *Bey* effectually ftopp'd their Mouths ; for they well knew, That thofe unmanageable Petty-Tyrants are dangerous Edg'd-Tools to meddle with. —— In a Word, our Criminal was forced to procure the Security of Twelve of the moft refponfible Houfe-keepers in the Town, for the fpeedy Payment of the demanded Sum ; upon which Terms, he had the Liberty of returning Home, that his Royal Bride might not be difappointed. As his Difpofition was naturally generous, and
him-

himself something inclining to *Epicurism*, he had lived too high to be Master of much ready Cash; so that he found he was obliged to strip himself and his Wives of all their most valuable Moveables, as Things for which he could get a speedy Sale, and, with some Difficulty, made up Two thousand Five hundred *Pieces of Eight*: But the *Bey*, by his reiterated Messages, giving him to understand, that if the remaining Fifteen hundred were not ready, and punctually paid at the appointed Day, he should infallibly receive Fifteen hundred Bastinadoes, which should be no Inducement to his abating him one single *Asper*; and his Corn, Cattle, and the like, being, at that Time, mere Drugs; he was quite at his Wits End, and could not avoid parting with his fine House, having nothing else he could dispose of for ready Money, in so short a Time. This the politick *Bey* had foreseen, and was therefore the more urgent with him for his Debt, the Justice whereof no-body dared call in Question, though the Town's-people whisper'd, that he could never prosper; that the *Fairies* would certainly break his Neck, and look'd upon his whole Proceeding to be not a whit better than Sacrilege. He was sure none of the *Moors* would buy the House, nor even live in it, if they might have it for nothing; and the *Turks*, tho' not so superstitious, could not, in Manners, propose the Purchasing it without asking their Governor's Leave. Poor *Sidi Messoud*, in this woful Plight, being perpetually in Fear of the insupportable Torture he was hourly threatned with, and not being ignorant of the Absoluteness of the Tyrant he had to deal withal, from whose Sentence there was no Appeal, sent him Word, in very melancholy pathetick Terms, That he had nothing he could rake Money of against the Time, but the House he dwelt in, except he would be pleased to have Patience a Month longer: To which the *Bey* coldly answered; That he had present Occasion for Money to pay his Troops; but that, to do him a Kindness, and to rid him of the

R

Trouble he lay under, he himſelf would take the
Houſe for the Remainder of the Debt, though he
knew little what to do with it when he had it ; withal ordering the *Chiaus* who carried this Meſſage, to
intimate, that if he continued to trifle with his Excellency, as he had done hitherto, he might be ſure of
what he had promis'd him. Theſe hard Lines our unfortunate *Talib* was forc'd to comply with, and, as an
Additional Mortification, two or three Days after was
informed, That the *Bey* had ſold it for Two thouſand,
to one of his moſt inveterate Accuſers, who, mightily
pleas'd with his good Bargain, went with his Family
to inhabit it; chuſing for himſelf that very Appartment which had been conſecrated for the Reſidence of
the *Fairy* Princeſs : Nor did I ever hear, that *that* injured Lady ever ſhew'd the leaſt Reſentment for her
having been ſo uncivilly turn'd out of her Lodging;
though for a while it was the univerſal Subject of
Diſcourſe throughout the whole Province, eſpecially
that of the Women, who waited with Impatience to
hear what Diſaſter had befel the Family, few making
any Doubt, but that the ſacrilegious Purchaſer, at
leaſt, would aſſuredly one Night or other, have his
Neck wrung round. —— Some Time after, *Sidi
Meſſoud*, having had Leiſure to diſpoſe of ſome Effects,
and to pick up his Crumbs again, made ſhift to pur-
chaſe another Dwelling though much inferior to the
former, and followed his Vocation as before, though
with ſomewhat leſs Reputation of Infallibility. He
made his Peace with the Princeſs, who had abandon'd him under his Misfortunes, and would never
honour him with her Company while he was but a
Lodger ; but now he was once more become a Houſe-
keeper, and had provided her a tolerable good and
very neat Appartment, ſhe condeſcended to bleſs him
with her enchanting Embraces. This was what he
himſelf gave out, nor had any-body any other Authority for this Part of the Story, but his; and he would
conſtantly declare, That of all his Loſſes and Misfortunes,

tunes, he regretted nothing but the ill Treatment ſhe had met withal. ———— When all this happen'd to him, he was about the Age of Forty, and a Man of a goodly Stature, graceful Mien and comely Aſpect, and the Report went, That he had been married to the *Fairy* Lady upwards of Fifteen Years. His Method of exerting his Faculty was ſingular, and peculiar to himſelf; for, as I obſerv'd above, every Pretender to that Science, practiſes after a different Manner : *Sidi Meſſoud's* was thus; When he was ſent for to inſpect into the Cauſe of any Diſeaſe, or to ſolve any difficult Queſtion, he order'd a Pan of Charcoal to be kindled and ſet before him, wherein he caſt ſeveral *Aromatick* Gums and Perfumes, and gave the Paper in which thoſe Drugs were, to one of the Company, to keep throwing the Powder into the Fire by little and little, that thoſe efficacious Fumigations (in which he ſaid, the inviſible Gueſts whom he was about to invoke, exceedingly delighted) might meet with no Interruption during the whole Ceremony of his Exorciſms, which if they ſhould, the Operation would prove not only abortive, but dangerous. Next he would enquire into the Nature of the Patient's Diſtemper, or whatever elſe he was ſent for about, neither more nor leſs than our reputed Conjurers do. Some of the moſt Unwary would tell him more than he aſk'd, and theſe were certainly his beſt Cuſtomers : But many, of a more retentive Faculty, would be ſparing of their Loquacity, and deliver themſelves in ambiguous Terms, or only ſay; *Alas, Sir, You ask nothing of us, but what you will ſoon be better inform'd of than we are able to tell you, by the ſubterraneous Gentry, who, through your Means, are to honour our poor Habitation with their Preſence. It is the Confidence we put in your great Art that has made us give you the Trouble of coming hither. It is We who are to enquire of You, and not You of Us.* Sidi Meſſoud, if the Truth was known, had no great Veneration for ſuch puzzling Chaps as theſe, and would, without

Dispute, have willingly dispensed with their Compliments, and mighty Opinion of his deep Learning and unerring Skill, could he but have prevailed with them to have told him more of their Case : However, he always put a good Face of Assurance upon the Matter, and proceeded with his wonted Regularity. His next Step was to demand Silence, and then to draw out a Figure with Ink in the Palm of his Left-hand, holding it extended over the Smoak of the Incense, muttering, for near half an Hour, some strange unintelligible Words, raising, falling and altering his Voice, and, at last, distorting his Face in a very odd frightful Manner, and cramping up the Fingers of that Hand wherein he had made the magical Characters, as if the whole Hand was lame and out of Joint. He still mutter'd on, and as a Signal that the expected Guests were arrived, he began to speak very loud, and in different Tones, as if several People were talking together (as *Moliere* makes *Scapin* do, while he thrashes the old Gentleman he has upon his Shoulder in a Sack) in divers Languages. This is what he is so highly valued for by the Women and ignorant Vulgar, who have no Knowledge of any Tongue but their maternal *Arabick* ; for this Arch-Impostor religiously confines himself never to utter a single Syllable of any Language but that, and positively denies his having the least Notion of any other : *For, say they, supposing every Word of what* Sidi Messoud's *Enemies alledge against him to be true, and that many Incidents happen quite contrary to his Predictions, yet how is it possible, that he, who never learnt a Word of any Tongue but his own, should, at those Times, speak all the Languages of the World so fluently?* This, indeed, is a material Question, and very worthy our Consideration ; but, as I told you, It is only started by those who know none but the Tongue their Mothers taught them. I myself, who have a Smattering in several besides my own, have had the Curiosity to be present at his Conjurations Four Times, and can therefore,

both

both as an Eye and Ear-Witnefs, affure the Reader,
that what he gabbles is nothing in Nature, but an unintelligible Gibberifh, a Medley of confufed Non-
fenfe, undiftinguifhable, in any Refpect, from the
Language of a *Gander*, but in here and there a Sentence of broken *Turkifh*, and worfe *Italian*, without
the leaft Connexion or Coherence; fo that after having
feen the Repute this Man had got among his Compatriots, I no longer admired at the amazing Progrefs
the erroneous Doctrine of their infamous Law-giver,
the grand Impofter *Mahomet* has made throughout
fo great a Part of the Univerfe; fince, as near as
leffer Things may hold a Comparifon with greater,
the Impoftures of them both, feem to have been
grounded upon the fame Foundation, and to have
fome Affinity, and has confirm'd me in my Opinion,
*That nothing is infuperable to one armed with a deter-
mined Refolution, and a large Stock of Impudence.* ——
But to beg Pardon for this Digreffion, and to return
to our Magician. After he had frighten'd the moft
timorous of his Auditors with his ugly Geftures and
uncouth Jargon, he told them, That fo many Kings,
with their prime Minifters, Courtiers and Attendants
had made their Entry, he, all the while, ufhering them
in with loud Acclamations, bidding them *Welcome !
Welcome !* Then, in a weak faint Voice, he went on
with his Farce, telling his Story in *Arabick*, fuch as
the *Turks* and other Foreigners fpeak, which, notwithftanding its harfh and barbarous Sound, yet they
are, without much Difficulty, underftood: This, to give
him his Due, he mimicks to Admiration; and I can
compare it to nothing it more exactly refembles, than
the *Englifh* fome of our *Frenchmen* talk, who, though
they underftand our Language very well, yet their
Accent and Pronunciation is extremely different from
that of the Natives. He generally tells the Patients,
That their Ailing proceeds from their having-ftruck,
wounded, trod, or pifs'd upon fome of the *Fairy* Children, who were playing in fuch and fuch a Place, as,

R 3

perhaps, near a Fountain, or the like, and that the Child's Parents, Relations or Friends are reſolv'd upon Revenge, unleſs the Party makes ſufficient Atonement, by ſacrificing ſome Beaſt, or Fowl, of ſuch or ſuch Colour or Marks ; not forgetting to put them in Mind, That it is the Pleaſure of his Majeſty, his moſt honoured Father-in-Law, (who never fails to be preſent in thoſe Royal Aſſemblies) that the Offender muſt have Recourſe to his truſty Secretary, (you may be ſure he means himſelf) who, by writing for him ſome never-failing *Herrouz,* has in his Power, and only his, to appeaſe the Wrath of the injured *Fairy,* and to mitigate the Sufferings of the Patient. This, when the Show is all over, and he is intreated to write the ſaid Charms, he ſeems to make ſtrange of, and to know nothing of the Matter; but, as ſure as Death, either ſends or brings them the next Day, and receives a Reward for his Trouble and Condeſcention, according to the Circumſtances or Generoſity of the Party who requeſted that mighty Favour at his Hands ; for his Fee for coming is never more nor leſs than half a Dollar, which, he ſays, his Royal Bride allows him to demand of his Patients, Poor or Rich, and no more.

———— Theſe are the Means this Impoſtor has to get his Living by, and which coſts him nothing but what he lays out in Drugs, *&c.* and by thus defrauding the blind deluded People, has maintained, for ſeveral Years, himſelf, three Wives (including the *Fairy* Princeſs) and all his other Domeſticks, with a couple of fine Saddle Mares, ſeveral good Mules, *&c.* ———— But the Cream of the Jeſt is ſtill behind. When he has play'd over all his Monkey Tricks, he feigns to come to himſelf, which he has not been all this while. The *Fairies* take their Leave and depart, and the Operator ſeems to rouze out of a Dream or Lethargy ; he yawns, he gapes, he ſtretches, looks heavy-Ey'd, his diſtorted Viſage and his disjointed Fingers aſſume their priſtine natural Forms; he complains of Pains in all his Limbs, ſpeaks faintly in a languid

Tone,

Tone, and tells his admiring Audience, That his Charity and Readiness to assist the Afflicted, visibly impairs his Health, and will, in the End, bring him to his Grave : He now begs Leave to depart, while the Master of the House earnestly presses him to stay and take a small Repast, which he seldom or never accepts of. Then some one in the Company asks him, If he will not try, whether or no his Lady will give him any thing ? He shakes his Head, and answers sorrowfully, *Tis in Vain! tis in Vain*! This Farce is really very pleasant, humoursome and diverting ; for, with much Intreaty, he at last prepares to gratify their longing Desire, and standing up, with much seeming Weakness, he extends out over his Arms the Lappet of his large *Bornoos* or Cloak, muttering something between his Teeth, which, it seems, are pathetick Invocations to his *Fairy-Lady* ; when, with a sudden Jerk, he closes his Arms together, having, clumsily enough in all Conscience, conveyed something from under him, which we hear jingle in his Lap. This is look'd upon, as the profoundest Piece of *Magick* any Mortal ever attain'd to, and an authentick and infallible Instance of *Sidi Messoud*'s uncommon Knowledge in the *Black Art*. —— Upon this, his Countenance begins to clear up, for now he smiles and looks pleasant, yet seems agitated between Hope and Doubt ; however, he very gingerly opens his Lap, that himself and the By-standers may see what has been sent him, and never misses finding Five full-weight *Spanish* Dollars, and a great Lump of the finest Sort of *Benjuy*, or *Benjamin*, near as big as one's Fist. The Present is beheld by all the Spectators, with the greatest Admiration imaginable, though the good *Sidi Messoud* assures them, That his capricious invisible Spouse has tantaliz'd him after this Manner a Million of Times, but always takes back her Bounty as soon as ever he is got out of the House, leaving him nothing but the *Half-Dollar*, which she calls his *undeniable Right :* Nevertheless, he desires

the

the Perſon who ſent for him, or ſome other of the Company, to take hold of it as it is wrapp'd up in a Corner of his long, looſe Garment, and ſo to lead him out a Pace or two from the Door, to try if it be once poſſible to prevent the ſaid Preſent being re-taken from him. This the requeſted Party never re-fuſes to comply with, and *Sidi Meſſoud* takes his Leave of the Company, and marches off with his Conducter, ſhewing great Signs of being weak and out of Order; and when they are paſt the Threſhold, I don't know how he contrives it, but with a vigo-rous Puſh, he forces the Man to let go his Hold, and with a much neater Slight of Hand than he convey'd them thither, he cauſes the Dollars, *&c.* to vaniſh, ſhewing the Lookers on the empty Place, where there remains nothing but the Half-Dollar he had receiv'd for his Fee. —— Though this, by ſuch poor credu-lous Mortals as the *Moors* of *Barbary*, may be thought a clever Trick, a clean Conveyance, or downright *Magick*; yet, upon ſeeing ſuch a clumſy Bungler paſs among them for an infallible Conjurer, I am fully perſuaded, That one of our neat *European* Artiſts at *Legerdemain*, Poſture-Maſters, or Fire-Eaters, might very well paſs there for the Devil *in propriâ Per-ſonâ.*

But I fear I have tir'd the Reader's Patience too much, by amuſing his Thoughts with ſo ridiculous a Scene. I could inſtance many of his bungling Tricks enough to make any but the blind bigotted *Afri-cans* eaſily perceive themſelves to be groſsly impo-ſed upon; but, to have done with this ſilly Subject, ſhall ſet down only one, whereat I was preſent, and which has been far more prejudicial to his Reputati-on, than all the Incidents of his paſt Life. It runs thus;

A Smart Rakiſh Young Fellow, an Officer in the *Bey's* Troops, with whom I was intimately acquainted, rode to a *Douar*, or Village of Tents, about Fifteen Miles out of Town, on purpoſe to beſpeak a Saddle-
tree

tree of a very noted Workman, who had positively assured him, he should have it in a Week at furtheft; but that Week and another pass'd, and not the least News of his Saddle-tree, which he impatiently expected, his own being broken and useless.———Whoever has travelled to those Parts of the World, know, that the *African Turks* are not to be treated in that Manner, especially by the Native *Moors*, who are their Vassals, and little better than Slaves, in Competition with the imperious Tyrants their Conquerors, who hold them in a more abject Subjection than the *Lord-Danes* did our vanquished Ancestors. At this unpardonable Disappointment, the blustering young Hector stormed, fumed, and, as may be supposed, breathed nothing less than an unmerciful Drubbing to the audacious Varlet who had dared to play him such a Trick; and not being able to endure his Insolence one single Moment longer, sent to a Friend to borrow his Saddle, and mounting his Horse, ordered his Servant to take a Cudgel in his Hand, and to follow him upon his Baggage-Mule.———The Wife and Daughter of the Poor Fellow, when they saw him come towards their Tent, his Eyes glowing with Wrath, and his Horse all on a Foam, fled, and abandoned all to the Mercy of the furious Invader of their Quiet. He instantly threw himself out of the Saddle, and entering the Tenement of the offending Vassal, he found an Object rather of Compassion than of Anger: The poor *Moor* lay extended upon a Mat, his Mouth drawn to his Ear, his Hands and Arms turned quite backwards, and his Fingers stretched out and spreading in a most lamentable Manner. In the first Heat of his Fury, he accosted him in these thundering Words; *Presumptuous Villain! Dog! Slave! How dare you use me thus? Do you think me a proper Person to be so imposed upon? This Evasion shall not serve your Turn!* and at the same Time discharged Three or Four hearty Blows upon his Hips, as he lay immoveable, before the Neighbours (who, by this began to flock about him)

him) could possibly prevent it; for he fancied this to be an Artifice invented purely to amuse him, and to divert his just Resentment at his having been so basely disappointed: But the Womens Outcries having assembled the Inhabitants of the Village, they, with much Intreaty, brought him to hearken to Reason, and to examine further into the Matter. They told him, That the poor Man had been in that helpless Condition, ever since he had washed himself at a certain Fountain, which they named, and that this Disaster happened to him Ten Days ago, he being then as well as ever he had been in his Life; and all this was likewise affirmed by the Patient himself and his Wife, with Tears in their Eyes.————The deplorable Object, and the moving Manner in which the Story was told him, wrought very much upon the Gentleman, who was now grown cool, and was in Reality, neither ill-natured nor uncharitable; but had abundance of Compassion and Humanity. He expressed a great Regret for what he had said and done in his Passion, asking the Man, What he could do to serve him? promising to use his utmost Endeavours. He returned him many Thanks and Compliments for his kind Offer; but told him (which was likewise unanimously confirmed by all the rest there present) "That God alone, and under Him, "Sidi Messoud ben Bou-Saadia, could restore him to "his Health, and the Use of his Limbs; but as he "was a poor Wretch, he could never hope, that "so eminent a Person would condescend to come "to him; and being an intire Stranger in the "Town, he had no Friend's House to resort to, and "must, for those Reasons, lie and perish in that mi-"serable Condition, destitute of all Assistance." To which the generous Gentleman replied, "That shall "be no manner of Hindrance to your Recovery: If "you are well enough to sit upon my Mule, my Man "shall ride behind, and hold you up. You shall be "very welcome at our House, you and your Family,

"as

" as long as you stay; nor have you any Occasion
" for Money, since I'll freely defray all your Expen-
" ces, and whatever lies in my Power, you may ab-
" folutely depend upon. But the only Objection I
" make is, That I not being one of those who pin
" their Faith upon *Sidi Messoud*, or upon any of his
" Class, can no-wise conceive, that he has it in his
" Power to do you any good: Yet, if you imagine
" he can help you, 'tis your Fault if you don't ac-
" cept my Offer." In effect, he conveyed him, his
Wife and Daughter, to his House, where he ordered,
that every thing should be provided for their Accommodation with most exemplary Humanity and Generosity; and, to humour those his superstitious Guests,
who looked upon *Sidi Messoud* as their only Refuge,
the next Morning he sent for that Mountebank (for
he deserves no other Title) who accordingly came.
The Person imployed to fetch him being our charitable Gentleman's Valet, who attended him in this
Adventure, the cunning Impostor, in the Way as they
came, exerting his laudable Faculty of Pumping,
wheedled out of him all the whole Story, not omitting
one Circumstance (as we were informed afterwards)
and every thing being placed in Order, he Apishly
ran over the whole Pageantry, exactly as I have described it above. When the *Invisible Gentry* had
made the ceremonial Entrance, and all their Formali-
ties were explained to us by their Interpreter, he, in
his Jargon, began to tell his wondering Audience all
the Particulars of this poor Man's disastrous Bathing
at the Fountain, and added, by way of Interrogation,
" If he did not remember, he had taken up a rough
" Stone of a blueish Colour, to rub his Heels, and
" the Bottom of his Feet withal?" Though this is a
Thing of Course, and all he told beside was nothing
but what he heard from the Fellow, and (his Memory being good) had repeated again *verbatim*, yet the
poor Wretch, in great Astonishment, could not contain himself from uttering several Times these Exclamations,

mations, Wonderful Man! Prodigy of Nature! Unfathomable Myſteries! Incomprehenſible Science! and
many ſuch like; proteſting, That he had not uttered
one Syllable but what was inconteſtable Truth: Nor
was the Admiration of his Wife, and of ſome others
in Preſence, a Jot leſs than his. The Magician went
on in his Interrogatories when all was again ſilent,
and firſt aſked him once more the ſame Queſtion, to
which he replied in the Affirmative thus; *Yes, my dear
Lord! I do remember! I well remember I did ſo! Did
you not,* ſaid the *Taleb, after you had made Uſe of it
in the Manner I told you, caſt it from you over your
Right Shoulder? I am not abſolutely poſitive over which
Shoulder I threw it, but that I caſt it from me, when I
had done with it, I am very certain.*——" Ay! ſaid the
" Conjurer, I am likewiſe very certain you did ſo:
" That Stone was the moſt unlucky Stone you ever
" handled in your Life; for with that very Stone
" you ſorely wounded in the Forehead the Green
" King's beloved Nephew, his only Siſter's Son, who
" was dancing Hand in Hand with his beautiful Twin-
" Siſter, who was to have been married on the Mor-
" row to the Yellow King's Grandſon; but that un-
" fortunate Blow of yours has obſtructed the Wed-
" ding, and has put both the Courts into deep Mourn-
" ing: The young Princeſs is inconſolable for her
" Brother's Diſaſter, and will hear nothing of Mar-
" riage 'till his Recovery, which the Phyſicians almoſt
" deſpair of. It was the wounded Prince's Governeſs
" that did you the Damage you labour under; for ſhe
" being frightned to ſee him bleed ſo faſt, ran and
" ſtruck you acroſs the Face, and turned your Arms
" round, leaving you in this Condition.——Did you
" feel nothing?——I felt a ſuddain Pain, anſwered the
" wretched Cripple, but know not how to deſcribe it:
" But is there no Remedy, my Lord? Has your Art
" nothing in Store for a poor penitent Wretch? *Ad-
" viſe with my Secretary; adviſe with my Secretary,*
" ſays the other. Who is your Lordſhip's Secretary?
" What's

" What's his Name, I beseech you?" says the Patient.
This being a Question *Sidi Messoud* had never been used
to have put to him, all his Customers knowing *that*
of Course, it utterly confounded him, as appeared
visible in his Countenance; and being at a Loss what
to answer, said, *His Name! His Name! I'll inquire.*
O, says a by-standing Neighbour, *I'll tell you that; you
must not ask him!* This set him a little to rights again,
and he proceeded with his Comedy. But, to make
short, after he had done all his Tricks as he was ac-
customed, he desired Leave of our Gentleman to be
gone, who, being of the Disposition I have described,
and loving Mirth, told me, I should see something
very diverting before he parted with the Conjurer,
who, he was resolved, should not put him and his
House to all that Trouble with his Impertinence for
nothing.   I, who had full as an indifferent an Opinion
of him and his Performances as my Friend could
possibly have, said, I should not be sorry to see
that Impostor detected in his Knavery, and would
very willingly laugh a little at his Expence. ———
" *Sidi Messoud*, said he, This *Fairy-Lady* of yours is
" very unkind; I hear she always takes away your
" Money from you : I'll try if I can procure you
" better Success upon this Occasion, than you have
" hitherto met with. "   *Alas!* reply'd he, *'twill be
all to no Purpose : It is but striving against the Stream.
I can but do my Endeavour,* said the Wag; *If this Money is ty'd fast in your Garment, I am almost persuaded
she can't come at it to deprive you of it. Come! who
knows but I may be lucky to you? Besides, I'll hold it
as fast as possibly I can.* ————Accordingly, he ty'd
it up very fast with a strong Packthread, and went
holding it Cheek-by-Joll with him, to the Street-Door,
and then, whipping it off with a sharp Pen-knife I lent
him, he suddenly fell down (having cleanly convey'd his Prize into his Sash about his Middle) feign-
ing to have been forcibly beaten from his Hold by
an unseen Hand, leaving the amazed *Sidi Messoud* in
the

the Street with Crouds of People gathered about him, all wondering at the Unaccountablenefs of the Accident. As for the poor Devil himfelf, he look'd very blank at his Difgrace, and to fee himfelf fo dextroufly bit, and deprived of his *Five remarkable Pieces of Eight*, about half a Pound of coftly Incenfe, his own *juft Fee* he had received for his Trouble, and which the Lady never offered to take from him before, and, to complete all, a great Hole in his beft *Burnoos*, wide enough to thruft his Head through. —————— While the People were bufy in condoling with *Sidi Meffoud* for this Misfortune, our Spark, having otherwife difpofed of the Fruits of his Artifice, went out amongft them, and whether or no they miftrufted his having any Hand in that Affair, I am not able to determine, but this I am fure of, That if they did, none dared tax him with it. He faid, *He was never fo terrify'd in all his Days* ; *That doubtlefs the* Fairy *took it ill that any Body fhould pretend to contradict her in her Proceedings* ; He mightily condemn'd himfelf of Imprudence in acting fo rafh and inconfiderate a Part ; begg'd *Sidi Meffoud's* Pardon, faying, *He had nothing in View, but to do him a Piece of Service*, &c. However, this Matter foon became the univerfal Town-talk, and few, befides the moft credulous Zealots, and the very ignorant Part of the Town, had ever a good Opinion of his Exorcifms after this. His *Burnoos* being too good to be thrown away, he got it repair'd with a fuitable Patch ; and that very Evening, we, and three or four more Friends, made merry at the poor *Talib's* Coft.

As to the Patient, whofe Diftemper was no other than very ftrong and violent Convulfions, he dy'd in Six Weeks Time, though the hofpitable Gentleman omitted nothing to fave him, if poffible. The Widow he retain'd as a Domeftick in his Houfe, and not long after married the Daughter (who was a modeft, pretty Girl about Fifteen Years of Age) by her own Confent, and that of her Mother, to his above-mentioned

tioned Serv ant, having firſt made him his *Wakkaff*, or Manager of his Farm.

This Relation I have been the more particular in, both to paint the Nature of this Sort of Impoſture in its true Colours, and to diſabuſe thoſe who imagine that a generous Action is ſeldom or never met with among the *Barbarians.* ———— I hope, that, as it may be depended upon for Truth, and the Sub-ject in itſelf is not uncurious, the Reader will favour-ably accept it, and think thoſe Reaſons ſufficient Amends for its Length.

Of JETHRO.

I Shall conclude this Supplement with what I find in *D'Herbelot* concerning *Jethro*, whom the *Ori-entals* call *Shoaib.* See that Name. ———— It is true, it might more properly have been plac'd in the next Chapter, which treats of the Line of *Iſhmael,* from whom they hold him to be deſcended. ————

That learned Traveller has it thus ; *Shoaib* is the ſame the Holy Scripture calls *Jethro* and *Raguel.* The *Mahometans* reckon him among the Prophets, and ſay, He was ſent by God to the People of *Mi-dian,* his Compatriots, to convert and reclaim them from Idolatry, and to preach to them God's Unity. ——— The *Taarich Montekheb* makes him the Son of *Mikil* or *Michael,* who was the Son of *Taskhir,* the Son of *Midian,* from whom thoſe Tribes of *Arabs* call'd *Midianites,* took their Name. ——— The *Alco-ran* ſays, This Prophet wrought Miracles to authorize his Miſſion, but mentions none of them. But the Author of the Book called *Aıbat Baberat,* The viſi-ble Miracles, tells us, That when this Prophet would

go

go up to a high Mountain to pray, the ſaid Mountain ſtoop'd, to render the Aſcent leſs troubleſome and difficult. —— *Houſſain Vaez*, in his Paraphraſe on the *Alcoran*, ſays, This Prophet did not only labour to eſtabliſh the true Faith among the *Midianites*, with ſome Succeſs, but that he alſo endeavour'd to root out the reigning Vices of thoſe People. They were moſt notorious Cheats in buying and ſelling, plundered Paſſengers upon the Road, and threatned to expel the Prophet and all his Adherers out of their Country, if they did not return to the Religion, or rather the Impiety of their Fore-fathers. This their Inſolence provoked the Lord to ſend the Angel *Gabriel*, who, with one hideous Out-cry, cauſed ſo tremendous an Earthquake, that they all periſhed, except *Shoaib*, and thoſe of his Followers who profeſſed the true Faith. —— It was after this Puniſhment and Deſtruction of the *Midianites*, that *Shoaib* left the Country, and went to his Son-in-Law *Moſes*, as we read in *Geneſis*, where no Mention is made of that Incident.

CHAP.

The GENEALOGY

Taken from the

1. Ifhmael. 2. Kedar. 3. Selam
Beauty. 10. Moad, *a great Com*
Day. 12. Modar. 13. Elias.
the Prophets. 19. Phahir. 20

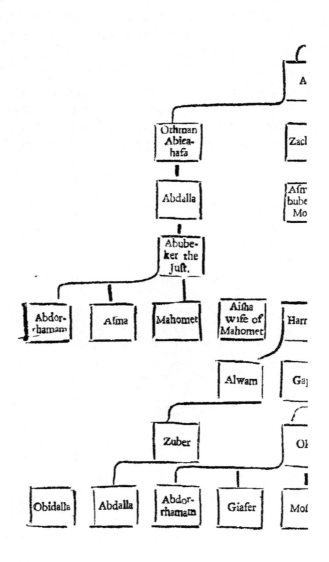

. 4. Jesjab. 5. Hemaifa. 6. Jafe. 7. Ader. 8. Ad. 9. Ed
nander, and Enemy of the Jews. 11. Nifar, *whofe Standard the* Turk
14. Madrac. 15. Chazaima. 16. Canaan. 17. Nodar. 18
. Galib. 21. Loway. 22. Kaab.

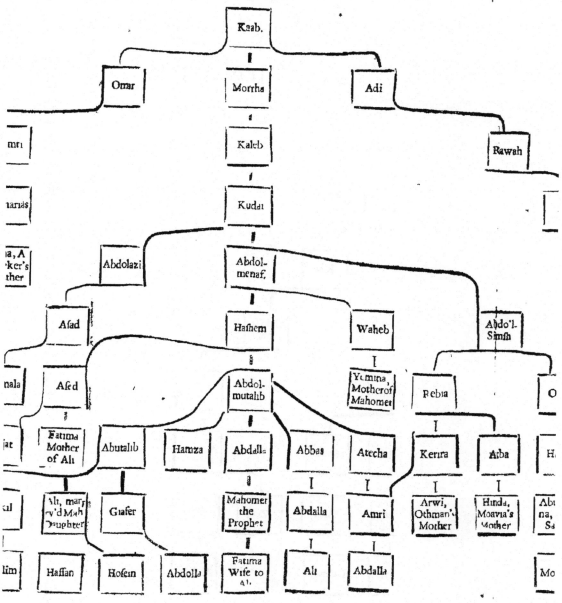

TIONS.

nah, *a Person of singular*
s *are said to possess at this*
3. Malic, *celebrated among*

[Page 257.]

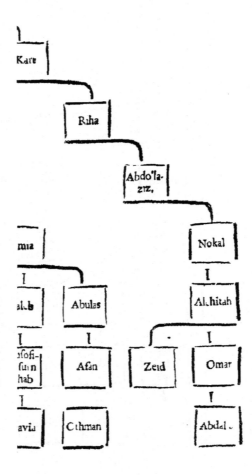

RADITIONS.

9. Ednah, *a Person of singular*
e Turks *are said to possess at this*
ar.   18. Malic, *celebrated among*

[*Page* 257.]

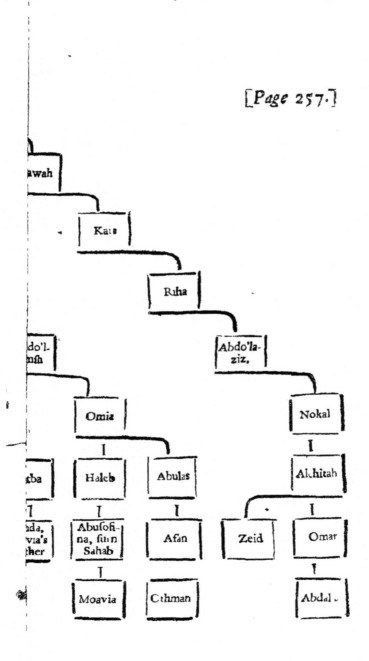

C H A P. X.

The LINE of ISHMAEL.

Ishmael's great Character. He marries in Arabia
Fœlix. *Has Twelve Sons. His Wealth, exemplary
Charity, Hospitality, &c. Has all* Arabia *assigned to
him and his Posterity for their Inheritance. He is
look'd upon to be the Founder of the* Arabs, *as* Isaac
is of the Hebrews, *whose Patrimony was the River*
Jordan, *and its circumjacent Lands ;* Abraham *being the common Father of both those mighty Nations.*
Cebid *the Son of* Ishmael *elected by the Lord to
inherit the imaginary Light, and has the City of* Mecca *appointed him for his Seat. The Succession of that
Light carried down from Father to Son.* Khedhir's
*great Devotion, and wonderful Visions for Three suc-
cessive Nights. His Prayer. Is visited by the Angel*
Gabriel. *His Character. For his uncommon Piety,
is certified in another Dream that he shall be admitted
among the Choirs of Heavenly Chanters, which is
likewise confirmed to him by the Angel* Gabriel. *The
Succession of the* Light *continued down to* Abdulmenaf *the Father of* Hashem, *Great Grandfather to
the Prophet* Mahomet. *

Ishmael, the First-born Son of the Patriarch *Abraham*, Grandson of the mighty
Monarch King *Agar*, who was to have
been offered up as a Victim to the Lord,
and was elected for the Propagation
of the *Light*, was a most memorable,
prudent and upright Person. He was very strong

S and

---

* The Title the *Mahometan* Author gives this his 10th Chapter,

and robuft of Body, daring, couragious and enter-
prizing in War, exceedingly fkilful in military Affairs, and dextrous in all the martial Exercifes of the
Field.

He married a noble Virgin of fingular Vertue and
Merit, high Birth and Condition, and Heirefs to a
vaft Inheritance in *Teman*, or *Arabia Fœlix* : And he
himfelf was likewife abundantly bleft with the Goods
of Fortune, being very wealthy ; his Droves of Camels, Herds of Cattle, and Flocks of Sheep, large
and numerous. He was a ftrenuous Obferver of all
the Precepts of his Lord, and more particularly imi-
tated him in being Bountiful, Munificent and Compaffionate ; for he was exceedingly free and hofpitable, courteoufly entertaining Travellers, charitably
and generoufly fuccouring the Indigent, pioufly vifiting the Sick, and comforting the Afflicted. It was
his conftant Cuftom to have Part of his Flocks near
fuch Roads as were moft frequented, and he himfelf
would ufually carry out Provifions, and wait in the
Highways for the Shepherds, and there diftribute to
all Comers and Goers, Cakes and Milk, with a confummate Benevolence, and a moft exemplary Charity ; Thefe and fuch like laudable Occupations were
his chief Delight, and in which he took the greateft
Pleafure and Satisfaction : Nay, whenever his Affairs
obliged him to be abfent from Home, he never failed
to leave the ftricteft Orders with his Domefticks, and
all who belonged to him, that the fame Regard

---

is as follows ; *Yftoria quarta del difcurfo de la Luz de Muhammad
çalam. Acabaffe de declarar el afiento ae los dos pueblos de Yfrael y
de Arabia.* ———— *La Revelatiun de Al-Hadir. Pafa a la Baronia
de la Luz hafta / exim Bifiguelo de nueftro anabi Muhammad çalam.*
Which, in Englifh, runs thus ; The fourth Hiftory of the Difcourfe
of the Light of the Bleffed *Mahomet.* The Settlement of the two
Nations, viz The People of *Ifrael* and the People of *Arabia*
(or the *Arab*) is concluded. ———— The Revelation of *Khedbir.*
The Male-Line of the *Light* paffes down to *Hafhem* the Great
Grandfather of our bleffed Prophet *Mahomet.*

fhould

should be shewed to all Paffengers and Strangers, without Diftinction, as when he was himfelf prefent.

He was the Father of Twelve Sons, all Princes of the higheft Fame and Renown ; from amongft which, the juft *Cebid*, a moft pious and accomplifhed Chieftain, was the *Elected* to be the Inheritor of the mighty Kingdom, and the Standard-Bearer of the myfterious *Light*.

When he was grown up to Man's Eftate, and had entered into Matrimonial Bonds, his Father *Ifhmael* affigned to him, and to his Pofterity, the City of *Mecca*, with all its Territories, for a Patrimony and Inheritance, as, likewife, for their ordinary Seat and Refidence ; by Reafon, That his illuftrious Lineage was chofen from among all the Nations of the Earth, to be the Poffeffors of that *ever-celebrated* Station, which, from the Beginning of Time, had been appointed for, and promifed to the Great *Mohammed*, of bleffed Memory : And thefe were they who followed *his* Banner, and thofe who feparated from the other Tribes, according as they were delineated and ftamped upon the (*a*) Parchment or Cloth which *Adam* delivered and recommended to the Care of his Son *Seth*, as he had been commanded by the Lord of Heaven to do.

Ifaac, as I have already faid, laid the Foundation of the *Hebrew* Nation, and of all its Defcendants ; to whom his Father had left the Charge, that he and his Offspring fhould people that fpacious Tract of Land which is watered by the River *Jordan*, which they continued to do for many fucceeding Ages.

(*a*) See Page 60.

Iſhmael, for the Reaſons we have ſpecified, remained in *Arabia*, and was, as we are endeavouring to make appear, the chief Founder of that moſt exalted Generation, which was carried on, in the Male Line, from Father to Son :   " For God never fails bounti-
" fully to reward the Merits of thoſe, who piouſly
" dedicate their whole Lives to his divine Service,
" and manifeſt their Zeal and ardent Love to Him
" in all their Actions ſince, notwithſtanding *Abraham* ;
" that bleſſed and elected Servant of the Moſt High,
" underwent ſo many *expiating* Tryals, ſuch grievous
" Troubles, Perſecutions and Afflictions, as hath been
" largely related, yet, for his uncommon Piety and
" Humility, he was deemed worthy to be the Pa-
" tron and Father of Two ſo honourable Nations,
" and ſo illuſtrious Lineages, the beſt and the moſt
" noble that were ever created !

For the Honour of *Iſaac*, a Multitude of thoſe of his Race dedicated themſelves to the Lord, and walked uprightly before Him ; all whoſe notable Deeds are gradually to be found in the *Hebrew* Scriptures · And to eternize the Memory of *Iſhmael*, the *True Faith*, with all its *Spiritual Rules* and *Documents*, had its Riſe in his Line (which hath ſince been expanded with an amazing Velocity and Succeſs in its Propagation) the original Source and ſucceeding Emanation whereof, with all the other Particulars, and the Deeds of the *Elected*, we learn from our honoured *Alcoran.*

To avoid Prolixity (and yet not wholly to omit making Mention of Perſons ſo worthy to be remembered) I ſhall only juſt rehearſe the Names of thoſe *choſen Males* who carried the *Blazon* of that *Hereditary Light*, 'till I bring it down as far as *Abdulmenaf* ; and notwithſtanding it may be very well ſuppoſed, that an Infinity of Tranſactions, worthy immortal Praiſe, and equally meritorious with any we have hitherto treated of, might be related concerning
ing

ing thofe Heroes, yet I fhall only enlarge upon thofe who are more immediately the Subjects of our prefent Purpofe, and juft mention the others in fucceffive Order one by one.

I have already faid, that *Cebid* inherited that precious and ineftimable *Gift* from his Father, the good and pious *Ifhmael*, being the *Elected* from among thofe Twelve Brethren, his Sons. By *Cebid* it was recommended to *Kebil*; from whom it was tranfmitted to *Zelib*; who was fucceeded by *Muhebid*; and he begat *Emin*; from whom it paffed to *Laguan*; who left it to *Azaret*; after whom followed *Munir*; and after him *Hamir*; who transferred it to *Zileb*; whofe Succeffor was *Yulad*, after whom came *Admen*; and he was followed by *Galib Mador*; the next to him was *Mador*, whofe Son and Succeffor was *Amador*; and this was the Father of the Sanctified (a) *Khedhir*: And though the Courfe of this our Genealogy

S 3   logy

(a) This Name, although my Author calls it *Al Hadir*, is no other than that highly refpected Prophet of theirs, whom the *Arabians* call *Sidi Khedhir*, and the *Turks* and *Perfians* pronounce *Khizir* and *Hizir*. —— They all in general confound the Prophets *Elijah*, *Elifha*, and *Elias* with this *Khedhir* of theirs, whom they fometimes call likewife *Ilia* or *Elia*. —— They write, (but more particularly a certain *Perfian* Poet) That *Khedhir* found the Fountain *Abou Hiat*, or, of Life, of which having drank plentifully, he obtained Immortal Life, which is the Nature of that Water, though they add, That his Abode is fometimes in Heaven, but oftner upon Earth, upon which Account of his Immortality, he got the Name of *Khedhir*, which fignifies *Green* and *Flourifhing*. —— The *Tarich Montekheb* makes this Prophet to have been born in *Abraham*'s Days, and to be the Nephew of that Patriarch, as likewife, to have been *Mofes*'s Guide through the *Red Sea*, and the Defait. —— The *Eaftern* Chriftians call the Prophet *Eliah* by a Name compounded of the Two, *viz. Khedirlas*, quafi *Khedoir Elias*, and fo the *Turks* call St *George*. —— According to the Oriental Traditions, This *Khedhir* was a Companion, Counfellor and General to *Efcander Dhoulcarnin*, who is not *Alexander* the Great, as fome imagine, and who is likewife fo called, but a Monarch of the whole Univerfe, antienter than he, and who had that Name before the

other

logy will be hereby obftructed for fome little Space, yet it is very neceffary that we call to Mind, in this Place, what we are indebted to, and what we inherit from this Holy Prophet.   This

---

other more modern *Alexander*.   This mighty Monarch fought for the Fountain of Life a long Time in vain, but could never find it; but his more fortunate Friend *Khedhir* obtain'd that Bleffing, and Drinking thereof, became Immortal. —— So fay they. ——
This Notion of the Immortality of this Prophet, is prefumed to be borrowed from *Elijah*'s being taken up into Heaven. —— As to their affirming him to have been Contemporary with *Abraham* and *Mofes*, they have it from fome Jewifh *Rabbins*, who were of Opinion, that *Elijah* was the fame as *Phineas* the Son of *Eleazer*, and Grandfon to *Aaron*, becaufe of the Fervency of both in their Zeal to ferve and glorify God; But after all, how they can bring that about to bear, I muft needs own, paffes my Comprehenfion: Yet this grofs Error, grounded, I fuppofe, upon the Tranfmigration of Souls, is embraced by moft of the *Mahometans*, and even by many *Afiatick Chriftians*. ——The *Mahometans* further believe, That *Elia* (and by Confequence *Khedhir*, being the fame) was fent by God to preach the Unity of the Deity to the Inhabitants of *Baalbeck*, by many thought to be the ancient *Palmyra*, and to perfuade them to forfake the Worfhip of *Baal*, from which Idol their City took its Name. —— The *Magi* of *Perfia* pretend, That their great Prophet *Zoroaftres* was one of the Difciples of *Elijah*, or, at leaft, what their Anceftors were inftructed by fome of the Difciples of *Elijah*, or *Ehfha*; which Fable proceeds from *Elijah*'s caufing Fire to fall from Heaven, and his being taken up in a fiery Chariot, which Element the *Zoroaftrians* make the chief Object of their Worfhip and Adoration.——The *Mahometans* firmly believe, that *Elijah*, *Elia*, or *Khedhir* will appear again publickly upon Earth before the End of the World. —— I fhall conclude this Subject with a notable, though romantick Story, which the Author of *Nighiariftan* gives us concerning this Prophet, under the Name of *Zerib ben Bar Elia*, and is to be found in *D'Herbelot* upon that Name.
After the *Arabs* had taken the City *Holvan*, in the Year 620. Three hundred Horfe, returning from that Expedition, under the Command of *Fadhilah*, came towards Evening to encamp betwixt two certain Mountains in *Syria*.   The Time of Prayer being come, *Fadhilah* going to perform his Devotion, faid, as ufual, with an audible Voice, *Allah Acbar!* God is Great! a Voice repeated the fame Words after him, and fo continued to do till the Prayers were ended, repeating every Syllable he faid, in a very loud Voice. *Fadhilah*, who might have imagined that the Eccho had retorted his firft Words, was extremely furprized to hear the Voice pronounce
                                                            nounce

This venerable Patriarch dedicated to the Lord a very laudable Inſtitution ; for every Night conſtantly, before he went to Reſt, he performed Ten Proſtrations, &c. of Devotion, with a Hundred *Tazbibes* (a) ; this he never failed to do, without omitting the leaſt Tittle of what he obliged himſelf, by a ſolemn Vow, to obſerve. But one Night, finding

---

nounce all he utter'd, ſo diſtinctly plain, and cry'd out ; " O " thou who anſwereſt me ! If thou art of the Rank of Angels, " the Virtue of the Lord be with thee ; and if thou art of any of " the Species of the *Genii,* or other Spirits, fare thee well ; but " if thou art a Man like me, appear viſibly before my Eyes, that " I may enjoy thy Sight and Converſation ! " No ſooner had he ſpoke theſe Words, but an old Man with a bald Head, looking like a *Derviſh,* with a Staff in his Hand, appeared before him. ———— When they had courteouſly ſaluted one another, *Fadhilab* asked the ancient Stranger, Who he was ? Who replyed ; " I am " here by the Command of *Sidi Iſa,* (or my Lord *Jeſus*) who has " left me to live here in this World, 'till he returns to the Earth " a ſecond Time. I abide here in Expectation of the Coming of " that Bleſſed Lord, and my Reſidence, by his Appointment, is behind that Mountain. " Upon this, *Fadhilab* inquired of the old Man, When the Lord *Iſa* was to appear ? To which he anſwered ; " His coming will be at the End of the World, and at the laſt " Judgment. " But the Curioſity of *Fadhilab* increaſing, he aſked him ; " What were to be the Tokens of the Approach of that Cataſtrophe of Time ? " To that over-curious Queſtion, *Zerib ben Bar Elia* or *Kheahir* (for he it was) return'd him this prophetick Anſwer ; " When Males and Females ſhall promiſcuouſly mingle to- " gether, without Diſtinction of Sex ; When Plenty of all Things ' ſhall be no Inducement to the Owners to fall the Prices of Pro- " viſions ; When the Blood of the Innocent ſhall be ſpilt ; When " Charity is grown ſo cold, that the poor Mendicants ſhall not be " able to ſubſiſt by begging of Alms ; When the Word of God in " the Holy Scriptures ſhall be turned into Songs, and the Temples " which were dedicated to the Lord, ſhall be filed with Statues " and Idols ; Know, That then the Day of Judgment is very near. " And having ſaid this, he immediately vaniſhed, and was ſeen no more.

(*a*) This Word here, means the Repetition of God's Attributes ſo many Times, which the *Mahometans* very frequently do, counting them upon their Fingers or Beads : A Set of Beads in *Arabick* is called by this Name.

himſelf

himfelf tired and indifpofed, he chanced to go to Bed without recollecting that he had not been at his accuftomary Devotions ; and as he was in his foundeft Sleep, he beheld a Vifion in the Air, of two Trees, exactly of the fame Form and Bignefs, oppofite to one another, and from the uppermoft Parts of each of thofe marvellous Trees, proceeded three Branches of *Light*, exceeding bright and refplendent. This ftrange Vifion made him pafs the whole Night in great Agony and Terror ; and the next Day his Thoughts were very much difturbed and reftlefs, occafioned by his Reflections upon the Fault he had been guilty of, in neglecting his obligatory Duty.

When Night came, having with great Diligence and Circumfpection, for fear of another fuch an Omiffion, purified his Body with the neceffary Ablution, and performed his Prayers, *&c.* he foon after betook himfelf to Reft, and clofing his Eyes, fell afleep. No fooner was he in a fweet Slumber, but the fame Vifion of the two Trees appeared to him again the fecond Time, but with this Difference, That they were now more verdant and flourifhing than before, with the Boughs ftuck full of blueifh-white Flowers, which, to all Appearance, gave evident Signs of being ready to produce Fruit ; and fo bright a Splendor proceeded from thofe Branches of *Light*, that the whole Earth was illuminated therewith : He thought, that, ftretching out his Hand, he gathered fome of thofe odoriferous Bloffoms, and that their Scent exceeded that of Mufk : But awaking at Day-break, he found himfelf deprived of fo exquifite a Regale.

On the Third Night, after having made the ufual Preparations of Wafhing, *&c.* and compleatly performed his Devotions, he went to Bed very penfive and melancholy, as he had been ever fince his firft beholding that myfterious Vifion : As he flept, the fame Trees were once more reprefented to his View, but now loaded with moft beautiful ripe Fruit

of

of an incomparable fine yellow Colour, looking like burniſhed Gold as they hung in Cluſters upon the Trees, and all round about them he ſaw innumerable Creatures flying like Birds, and ſhewing Signs of Worſhipping and Proſtrating, as it were, before thoſe Viſions, as they flew, which he was given to underſtand, was their continual Exerciſe Day and Night.

Beſides all this, he beheld Two (*a*) *Alohes* of glorious Fabrick, each of which had a (*b*) Pen belonging to it, the which were employed in Writing thereon, without being touched by any viſible Hand.

In the Morning *Khedhir* aroſe very thoughtful, and in a terrible Fright and Conſternation at what had happened to him for thoſe three ſucceeding Nights; being no wiſe capable how to account for thoſe wonderful Viſions he had ſeen, or what Conſtruction to make thereof; at all which, being under the deepeſt Concern, he prepared himſelf, and addreſſed his Almighty Creator in theſe few, but memorable, Sentences.

KHEDHIR's *PRAYER.*

TO *Thee I proſtrate, myſelf, O moſt powerful Monarch! O King of the Cœleſtial Luminaries! O impartial Judge of all our Actions! O Puniſher of our Sins and Errors! Munificent Donor of everlaſting Life! All thou doſt is without* Why, How, *or* When*! O*

(*a*) This Word ſignifies any Plank or Board; but here it means a thin Board, cut in long Square like the Leaf of a Book. Theſe are made of a very cloſe light Sort of Wood, of all Sizes, for Children to learn to read and write upon: They are very ſmooth, and being rubbed with a certain white Earth called *Ack*, may be written upon, when dry, like Paper, and then waſh'd off again.

(*b*) The Word here is *Al Calim*, which is a Pen made of a Cane; for they uſe no others.

Sove-

Sovereign Protector of thy Servants, and Distributer of their Rewards! ——O Lord! since it is Thou who givest us Life and Breath by thy divine Influence, and hast endowed us with Reason, which is the essential Cause of all our Deeds: Yet since, Lord! thou art not pleased with our weak Endeavours, our mistaken and erroneous Performances (thy own mighty Actions being wholly sublime, and altogether inimitable) it seems, if we follow the Earthly Way of Reasoning, that we are not by thee bound under any effectual Obligation to serve thee as we ought, but are rather intirely free from any such Bond, seeing all proceeds from Thee, and it never appears, that thy Divinity ties the Hands of any Mortal, to prevent him from doing amiss. —— Lord! I am not forgetful of thy Holy Precepts and Decrees, neither am I refractory or unwilling to be obedient to thy Commands; but without thy Assistance I have no Strength, nor any Knowledge, but what I have received from thee. —— If I am indebted to thee for any additional Devotion, besides what I use to pay, or if I must perform any Act of Contrition, or Atonement for my Negligence and Omissions, I humbly intreat thee to make it clearly manifest to me, that I may rightly comprehend the Nature of my Offence, and thereby be enabled to comply with my Duty and Obligation, which I sincerely engage myself to accomplish with the utmost Diligence and Punctuality.

At the Conclusion of this expostulatory Harangue, *Gabriel* descended, being sent by the Almighty to comfort him with a joyful Message: *For God is never unmindful of those who fervently call upon His Holy Name!* The Angel said unto him; " Righteous " *Khedhir!* Do not meditate any Innovations, nor " entertain the least Scruple concerning your Proceed- " ings, but persevere as you have done hitherto: " To which, *Khedhir* replyed; " My Lord and Friend! " For these three last successive Nights, to my great " Amazement, I have visibly seen astonishing Visi- " ons in my Dreams, wherein Trees, bearing Flow-
"   ers,

" ers, and Autumnal Fruits, were expofed to my
" View ; and I am exceedingly terrified and con-
" founded to conjecture what can be the Signification
" of thefe Prodigies ! " The Angel made Anfwer in
thefe Words ; " O *Khedhir !* The Lord of Heaven
" hath manifefted unto thee, in thefe Vifions thou
" fpeakeft of, that He hath prepared and allotted for
" thee an exalted, glorious Station, far fuperior to
" thy Hopes, or Expectations : Rejoice and live in
" Confidence, and perfevere in thy Praife-worthy Be-
" ginnings, as I have already counfelled thee to
" do. "

Our Sage *Aalims* and learned Expofitors tell us,
That this Vifion of *Khedhir* had fo great an Influence
over him, and made fo deep an Impreffion in his
Heart, that 'till the Hour of his Death, he would
never have ceafed from making his moft earneft and
importunate Supplications to God, to let him know
what was the Reward he fhould obtain for his fedu-
lous Application to His Divine Service; and that at
laft in a Dream, he faw himfelf placed and inclofed
round about with Hofts of the Cœleftial Chanters,
all employed in their accuftomary Occupations of
finging Divine Hymns. To this they add, That
the Seraphick *Gabriel* again came to him, and, with
a fmiling Countenance, told him, " That his Lord
" had vouchfafed to make him a Partaker of the
" greateft and moft confummate Glory that ever was
" granted to any Mortal upon (Earth, that of being
" admitted a Companion of the Heavenly Chanters)
" nor even the moft fanctified of all the Prophets were
" ever favoured in fo high a Degree.

As there are none of the Rites and Ceremonies
which are celebrated and obferved amongft us at this
Day, but what moft certainly derive their Original
from the remoteft Antiquity, or, as it were, *ab initio,*
fo the divine Majefty was pleafed to ordain, That
thofe Prayers, *&c.* we inherit from this Holy Prophet,

phet, fhould be peculiarly adapted to be ufed in the Months of *Rejeb* and *Shaaban,* and are exceedingly meritorious.

After what we have related concerning this venerable Saint, he underwent many heavy Troubles and Afflictions. This was the fame who accompanied the mighty Monarch *Alexander* in his Progrefs, and was held in high Efteem by him, participating many dangerous and hazardous Enterprizes with that ever-famous Champion.

But to return to our Courfe of the Emanation of the *Light,* from which we have made this Digreffion; I fay, That from this righteous *Khedhir,* it defcended to *Madrac;* whofe Succeffor was *Jucaibet;* and after him it paffed down to *Madir;* who tranfmitted it to *Malic,* who recommended it to *Galib;* from whence it went to *Aluai;* and after him it was inherited by the great *Caebu;* who left it to his Son *Murad;* and from him it defcended down to *Kelem;* and thence to *Kufai;* whofe Son and Inheritor was the moft valiant *Koreifh,* from whom proceeded the ever-renowned Name acquired by thefe couragious Warriors, the (a) *Koreifhites* fo famous in Hiftory, and fo much feared, honoured and revered in all Parts, and who were the Glory of *Arabia* and all its neighbouring Countries.

From this great Man and noble Tribe, defcended *Abdulmenaf,* Father of the moft illuftrious *Hafhem,* who was Great Grandfather to our bleffed Prophet; whofe Hiftory and memorable Exploits, require Time and more Leifure.

(a) Thefe *Koreifhites* are often mentioned by Dr. *Prideaux* and many other Writers. Though *Mahomet* was of this Tribe, they were ever his moft implacable Enemies.

C H A P.

CHAP. XI.

The Hiſtory *of* Haſhem *the Son of* Abdulmenaf.

The Method of tranſmitting the Hereditary Light *downwards.* Haſhem's *Diſcontent at his having, as yet, no* Elected *Son to inherit it. He hears a* Voice *in his Sleep, commanding him to go to* Yathrib *to marry* Salma, *who was to bear him ſuch a Son. The* Zeal *of his Brother* Almutalib *on this Occaſion, who makes a fine Elogy upon that Lady.* Haſhem, *accompanied by forty gallant Cavaliers, prepares and ſets out, in a very ſplendid Manner, for* Yathrib. *Arrives there. The Aſtoniſhment of the Inhabitants of that City in beholding the Splendor of his Countenance. They are courteouſly received, and nobly entertained by* Omar *Father to* Salma. *The great Malice of the* Jews, *and their Apprehenſions upon this Account.* Haſhem's *extraordinary Beauty and Merit.* Salma *falls in Love with him at firſt Sight. She endeavours to diſguiſe it. Her Character. The Devil, hoping to obſtruct ftruct the Match, goes to* Salma *thrice, and tells her a very infamous Story of* Hafhem. *She, highly incenfed, yet diffident of the Truth of fo vile a Character, refolves an Interview with him, and goes to him in a Difguife. She is con-vinced of the Falfity of the Accufation, and con-fents to marry him. The Devil affembles the* Jews, *and engages them in a Confpiracy to deftroy* Hafhem *and his Companions.* Hafhem *is advertifed of it in a Dream, and exhorts his Cavaliers to be upon their Guard.*

E have already taken Notice in another Place, That the miraculous *Light,* pre-deftined to be centered in our Prophet *Mahomet,* was always tranfmitted from the Foreheads of thofe who carried that *Blazon,* to thofe of their Wives, from the Moment they had conceived with Child of *him* who was *Elected* and deemed worthy to inherit the fame ; the beautiful Countenances of whofe Mothers were, all the while, 'till their Delivery, brighter than the Moon in her Glory ; and that then it departed, and was fixed upon the Illuftrious New-born *Elected.*

According to what we are informed by *El Haffan,* it appears, That all the Time *Hafhem* co-habited with the Wives whom he had married out of his own Tribe, and by whom he had Seven Children, including the Females, the *Light* ftill continued fixed upon his own Forehead, the Hour appointed for its Removal being not yet come. This was a fore Mortification to him, and made him fo reftlefs and uneafy, that he was every Day walking very penfively round the (a) *Ca-*

(a) The little fquare Chapel in the Temple of *Mecca.* See Pages 120, to 130, in the Notes.

aba,

aba, and there devoutly praying and making fervent Intercession to God, that he would be pleased to send him a Son worthy of that *Banner*, to whom the Hereditary *Light* might be transferred, in order to *its* descending in the same regular Method *it* hitherto had done.

Whilst he continued under this daily Affliction and Perplexity, he heard a Voice one Night in his Sleep, which said thus to him; " Go to *Yathrib* (now *Me-*" *dina*) where thou shalt find a Woman of high Me-" rit and Condition, rich, chaste, unblemished, ver-" tuous, of noble Parentage, and who has a nume-" rous Band of most illustrious Relations: This Wo-" man waits thy coming; with her thou shalt marry," and to her this *Light*, concerning which thou " art so anxious, shall pass from thee; for she is in-" tirely worthy of that Honour: She shall bear thee " a Son of the illustrious Line of the *Elected*:" Her Name is *Salma*, and she is the Daughter of " *Omar*.

Hashem awoke in a very great Surprize, and getting up, sent for his Friends and Companions, to whom he gave an Account of all that had happened, concealing from them nothing of what the Lord had revealed unto him. They were all in general exceedingly pleased at their hearing these Tydings; but he who shewed more Zeal in this Affair, of so great Importance, than any of the rest, was his Brother *Almutalib*, who made this Reply to what *Hashem* had told them;

" You may remember, my beloved Brother, that " you have had several Daughters of mighty Princes, " and other Persons of the highest Rank, propos'd to " you in Marriage, which Overtures, as being out of " our Tribe, were always rejected on our Part, and " never met with the least Encouragement from any of " us; for this illustrious Stock of ours is much more " to be esteemed for the Purity of our Blood, than the " Alliance of Kings: But I now agree, that what

" has

" has been refused to so many, should be granted to
" the Lady in Question, because I deem her well de-
" serving the Honour of being allyed to our Family.
" I am very well acquainted with *Salma*, her Father,
" and all who belong to her : She is a most beautiful,
" graceful and accomplished young Lady ; nor has
" any a better Character for vertuous Inclinations,
" and all other amiable Qualities : She is endowed
" with a most compleat Portion of Sense and Know-
" ledge. She is engaging and affable in her Deport-
" ment, and, in a Word, her whole Behaviour is
" exceeding courteous and endearing : She is univer-
" sally known, beloved, respected and esteemed by
" the whole City of *Yathrib*, and all the Country
" round it ; so great is her Fame in those Parts.
" Consider now with yourself, after what Manner
" you will have this Negotiation carried on : If you
" think proper that I go thither to demand her for
" you in Marriage, I'll most willingly undertake the
" Journey immediately, without the least Delay ;
" for to lose Time in prolonging an Affair of this
" Nature, is the highest Imprudence, and may prove
" very prejudicial. "

Hashem returned these Words in Answer ; " If
" you think it convenient, I my-self will be the
" Messenger in this joyful Journey, and, indeed, I
" am commanded by the Lord of Heaven so to do ;
" I'll bear you Company in this Expedition to
" which I am called ; and will go my own self an
" Eye-witness of the Perfections of this Woman, to
" whom you give such superlative Commendations. "
To this the whole Company replyed ; " Do in this
" Case what you please, for we are all at your De-
" votion, and are, with all sincere Love and Affecti-
" on, willing to follow you

With this Resolution and Agreement, they all departed to make Preparation ; and the next Morning,
having got every Thing in a Readiness, *Hashem*, accompanied by Forty gallant Cavaliers, most of them
his

his near Relations, of the House of *Abdulmenaf*, began to set out, very joyful and in great Order. Abundance of Camels were laden with their Arms and Provisions, and thus, in a very splendid Equipage, *Hashem* took his Leave, and marched on his Way, followed by his Forty Cavaliers, who were all Nobles of the greatest Account, and in whose Countenances were evident Signs of Satisfaction and Content. *Hashem* himself was decently arrayed in new Garments brought him out of *Arabia Fœlix*, with a Sash round his Head of a rich and curious Texture: The ancient Standard of *Egypt* was displayed and carried before him, which Royal Banner is the venerable and original Ensign of this Noble and Illustrious Tribe.

It was Night when they arrived at *Yathrib*, and as they entred into the City, the *Light*, which shone on the Forehead of *Hashem*, cast so great a Splendor, that it passed into the Windows of the Houses, insomuch, that the People opened their Doors, and came out in great Surprize, wondering from whence could proceed so resplendent and unusual a *Light*; for it pierced into their very innermost Appartments, thro' the Windows, Chinks and Crannies of the Doors, shining like the Rays of the Sun; or, at least, far brighter than the Full-Moon: But when they beheld so noble and beautiful a Cavalcade passing along the Streets, they began, with loud Voices, to call upon others to come out and see this splendid Entry of so many Gallant Persons, who made so noble an Appearance: Every one was inquisitive in examining, (being extremely desirous to know them) *Who they were? and upon what Business they were come thither?* Asking them thus; " We beseech you to tell us, What People " are you, whose Miens and Garbs appear so noble and " uncommon? We never beheld such goodly Perso- " nages as you in our Country; but especially we " intreat you to let us know, Who is he, from whose " Countenance proceed those *Beams of Light*, which " descend from Heaven, and settle thereon?

T

To

To theſe Interrogations *Almutalıb* anſwered; " We
" are Natives and Inhabitants of *The Holy Houſe,* or,
" *The Houſe of God,* where his Divine Majeſty hath
" fixed his Throne upon Earth : By Race and Pedigree
" we are *Koreiſhites,* of the Noble and Illuſtrious
" Houſe of *Caebu* the Son of *Aluai* ; Our Reſidence, I
" ſay, is in *Mecca,* the City choſen by God Himſelf
" for His Seat : This Perſon concerning whom you
" inquire, is our Brother *Haſhem,* and who is diſtin-
" guiſhed by a peculiar Portion of Cœleſtial Influence :
" His coming hither is to do you Honour ; *May his*
" *own be augmented,* Amen.   To explain my ſelf, His
" Intention is, That this glorious *Light* remain fixed
" amongſt you, thro' the Means of *Salma,* the only
" Daughter of *Omar* : And this is the Occaſion that
" made us leave our own Habitations, as you ſee,
" and come into your Territories. "

Omar, who happened to be there among the reſt of
the wondering Spectators, and had heard all that *Almutalıb* had ſaid, was exceeding joyful, and made this
Reply ;

" Moſt Illuſtrious and Praiſe-worthy Lords ! High
" and Potent Prince of the Supreme Throne ! May
" your Arrival into our Country be propitious ! You,
" who are the Quinteſſence of Hoſpitality and Gene-
" roſity ; whoſe liberal Hands are always open to en-
" tertain the *Haggies* who, with a pious Devotion,
" reſort in Pilgrimage to viſit *God's Houſe* ; never refu-
" ſing to laviſh your Stores to accommodate thoſe who
" ſtand in Need of your Aſſiſtance ; I bid you a
" hearty Welcome : All you require at my Hands,
" and even more, ſhall moſt willingly be complied
" with.   The Damſel you have been pleaſed to men-
" tion, is my own Dearly-beloved Daughter ; tho'
" ſhe has the intire Management and Diſpoſal of her
" Perſon, Houſe and Affairs.   She went hence Yeſ-
" terday, accompanied by a great Number of her
" Servants and Dependants, to the famous *Fair* of *Cai-*
" *canea,* about ſome Negotiations of Importance.   If,
" in

" in the mean while, you will be pleafed to remain
" my Guefts, I fhall think my Houfe highly honour-
" ed with your worthy Prefence, and engage myfelf
" to ferve you to the very utmoft of my Power, as I
" think myfelf in Duty bound to do. "

In fine, without more Arguments, they were all conducted, and took up their Lodging at *Omar's* Houfe, Father to the intended Bride, where they were entertained with all the Courtefy and Magnificence imaginable, and the Tables were covered with vaft Plenty of exquifite Dainties, abundance of Prefents and Regales being brought by the principal Gentry of the Town; and fo they paffed the greateft Part of that Night in Mirth and Rejoicing, and then betook themfelves to Reft.

The next Morning early, *Omar's* Houfe was throng'd with Ladies; no one Matron, or Virgin, of any confiderable Fafhion or Condition in that City, being able to deny her felf the Satisfaction of repairing thither, to behold the extraordinary Beauty and Graceful Mien of *Hafhem*, each tender Breaft burning with refiftlefs Love, and, with Emulation, coveting to enjoy the Poffeffor of that refulgent *Light*.

But the Joy and unfeigned Satisfaction thefe good People fhewed upon this Occafion, was a very fevere Mortification and Eye-fore to the perfidious misbelieving *Jews*, whofe Malice and Hatred towards *Hafhem*, was fo infuperably implacable, that, upon feeing the great Deference and Veneration the Citizens of *Yathrib* expreffed in his Regard, they were ready to burft with Rage and Defpair: For they had found it foretold in their Scriptures, That the laft Poffeffor of that *Light* which appeared upon his Forehead and Countenance, fhould infallibly prove the Sword to deftroy and bring them to Confufion; a Judgment they had merited for their Perfidy, and the bafe Degeneracy into which they had precipitated themfelves.

A great Number of that falfe and accurfed Generation of Men affembled together to treat of this important Affair; when the Elders and Diviners, their

Eyes all flowing with Tears, chofe the moft ancient of their Fraternity to fpeak for the reft: The Name of this Man was *Armon* the Son of *Caiton*, and he had the Reputation of being the wifeft Perfon in the whole City, among thofe of his own Perfuafion: He made his Auditors the following Harangue; —— " You, " and only You, O Sons of *Ifrael!* have Caufe " to grieve, weep, and forely lament: To You, in " particular, Sorrow and Anguifh are left as an In- " heritance: Weep and lament then, fince you have " fuch mighty Caufe; for the Hour is already come, " wherein the *Lord of Time* approacheth, according " to the Decrees of Fate, foretold in Prophecy.

Prepofterous Blindnefs! unheard-of Stupidity! Stubborn Barbarian! Stiff-necked Obftinacy of a partial Enemy! Unbelief confpicuoufly vifible! Errors undeniably confirmed! Was any other Generation but this ever heard of, to harbour Malice and Prejudice fo inconfiftent with Reafon? What! abominate and perfecute that, which, at the fame Inftant, they cannot avoid praifing! Strange Incoherency! To utter, with the very fame Breath, Encomiums and Execrations upon the fame Subject!

Armon continuing his Speech, goes on thus; " O " pernicious and fatal Accident! O moft deplorable, " mortal, and inevitable Stroke! This Wound, in- " ftead of healing, becomes wider and more danger- " ous, and will foon bring us to the Earth, and bury " our very Name in the Duft! This unhappy Stroke " will be the utter Deft: iction of all your fruitful " Lands and ftately Edifices! This will throw down " your ftrong Walls and your Fences; it will dif- " comfit your Warriors, blunt your Weapons, and " deftroy your Caftles! It will make your Habita- " tions defolate, pollute your Wives and Sifters, and " deflower your Daughters! It will fpill the Blood of " your Veins, and will lay open all your fecret Im- " purities! All this, and much more, will be brought " to pafs by Him, whofe Guardians and perpetual
" Pro-

" Protectors will be the Angels of God ; Him, I say,
" of whom it is prophefied in Sacred Writ, *That such*
" *a One shall come* ; And this new arrived Gueft carries
" that very fame *Light* in his Forehead, which our
" Scriptures inform us, fhall be the *Blazon* of that
" our fo dreaded Enemy. "

At the pathetick Arguments their highly-revered
Orator had vomited with fo much Spleen and Rancour, that invidious and tumultuous Rabble, thofe
abandoned murmuring Wretches, wept bitterly, and
began, all with one Voice, to cry out, " Advife us, thou
" unerring Oracle! Let us know what thou thinkeft
" proper to command us to do in this Exigence,
" that we may be delivered from this impending Ruin
" and Defolation, which thou haft denounced unto us!"
To which *Armon*, in Defpair, with a mournful Voice,
replied ; " Alas! Alas! Woe, Woe unto ye ! All will
" be in vain ! Your Efforts will prove Abortive,
" and of no Effect! Your Swords and Spears will
" nothing avail you ! Alas! we find it written in
" our Holy Scriptures, That this *promifed* Prophet
" *Mahomet*, fhall be fo compleatly endowed with all
" Perfections, that he fhall gain Admittance to fit
" *Hand in Hand* with God Himfelf, and to com-
" municate with his Divine Majefty *Face to Face!* —
" Since then it is fo, faid they, and feeing that this
" New-comer bears the Refemblance of him who is
" to follow, and from whom we are threatned with
" fuch unavoidable Deftruction ; to prevent and anti-
" cipate thofe prophetick Evils, we will extinguifh
" that fatal and deftructive *Light* before *it* produceth
" any more Branches ; Let us cut it off, that he
" who is to be the true Owner thereof, may never be
" born to our Ruin ! "

This they faid, and it was unanimoufly approved
of by the whole Congregation, who were now all bufily
employed in fetting their Inventions upon the Rack,
and forming Schemes how they might deftroy *Hafhem*
and his Affociates : And from hence, the Hatred and

Rancour they have ſince manifeſted, on innumerable Occaſions, againſt the *Light* of *Mahomet*, had its Original Riſe.

But I will leave thoſe malicious Wretches and their impious Intentions for awhile; *for they who are among wicked Perſons, cannot be long before they hear ſome of their infamous Exploits:* They will ſoon be introduced again upon the Stage in a proper Place, when what I have hinted above will be fully confirmed. Let us now return to our Worthies, and put ourſelves on their Side; for, as the Proverb ſays, *The Society of the Vertuous is a main Step towards Grace.*

They were all making Preparations to go to the *Fair*, where, as I ſaid before, *Salma* was already gone with a numerous Train of Followers. Their Horſes, Arms and fine Veſtments, were all got in a Readineſs betimes in the Morning; Upon that Occaſion, they ſet themſelves off to the beſt Advantage, their Habits and Equipage being all extreamly pompous and magnificent; Their Heads were adorned with Laurel-Diadems, and the Banner of *Egypt*, diſplayed and waving in the Air, led the Van. *Haſhem* rode in the Middle of all thoſe, with *Omar* at his Side, who, followed by all his Relations and the beſt part of the Nobility of *Yatbrib*, would needs bear them Company: And, as this Splendid and Gallant Troop, which conſiſted of the Flower of *Arabia*, was thus marching towards the *Fair*, it was conſiderably augmented by the Gentry from all the adjacent Parts, who joyned them in the Way thither.

When they were arrived at the *Fair*, the *Light* which ſhone upon the Forehead of *Haſhem*, had aſſembled all the Inhabitants of thoſe Parts, as well as the Strangers who happened to be there, in that great *Piazza* of *Caicanea*: Every Soul left their Houſes, Shops and Tents, their Merchandize, their Wealth, and their moſt urgent Negotiations, abandoning all, to run, with a promiſcuous Confuſion, to glut their Eyes with gazing, in Amazement and Surprize, upon ſo very extraordinary

ordinary a Cavalcade: But the Spectators in general, were more particularly intent, and, as it were, inchanted, when they beheld the resplendent Brightness of *Hashem*'s Countenance, whose Rays of *Light* still increased more and more by the Peoples Admiration and Gazing: *For the Almighty always brings Things about by unexpected Means, when He designs the Accomplishment of His unsearchable Decrees.*

Salma, in the mean while, was so placed, that she had a fair Prospect of the whole Cavalcade, of the glorious *Light*, and of *Hashem* himself, without being seen by any; and whilst she was, in the most agreeable manner, amusing herself with contemplating upon the uncommon Gracefulness, the refulgent Splendor, and the intoxicating Beauty of *Hashem*, she uttered this Soliloquy with Rapture and Ecstasy; " O how " inexpressibly happy must that Woman be, who shall " have the good Fortune to be blest in thy conjugal " Embraces! O thou Wonder of Men, how transcen- " dantly bright is thy Countenance, and how exqui- " sitely desirable is thy most amiable Person! "

Whilst her Breast was glowing with these pleasing Thoughts, and her lovely Eyes were feasting upon that dear Object, which gave her such Emotions and Agitations, that her very Flesh trembled with ecstatick Desire, her Father came, and, very eager to unload his Bosom, without giving her Time to speak a Word, he said thus; " My dearest Child! I have exceeding " good News to tell thee of an Embassy which fills " my Heart with Joy, and ennobles thee far beyond " Expression. " " Let me alone, I beseech you, my " Dear Father, replied she: Leave me at present, I " humbly intreat you, to my soothing Thoughts; Go " not about to obstruct my Sight from the present " Object of my wondering Eyes: Say nothing to me, " I beg you; for the greatest Tydings in the World, " the highest Honours upon Earth, the most pompous " Grandeur, Popularity, Adulation. Wealth, nay, " the utmost Summit of Human Felicity, or, in a

T 4 " Word,

" Word, all that is contained, comprehended, and
" created in the Univerſal Globe, is nothing in Com-
" pariſon to what my raviſhed Eyes now behold
" upon the Forehead of that Man, whoſe Counte-
" nance caſts forth ſo glorious a Brightneſs!" "Why,
" that is what I meant, my beloved Daughter, ſaid
" the overjoyed *Omar*; thoſe are the joyful Tydings
" I came to impart to you: That moſt mighty Per-
" ſonage is the greateſt Champion of our Times,
" and of the higheſt Fame and Renown in all the
" Land: He is the celebrated *Haſhem*, the Son of
" *Abdulmenaf*, whoſe noble Stock and Family hath no
" Equal for Honour and Purity of Blood: They
" are the Chieftains of the Tribe of *Koreiſh*,
" and Sovereign Lords of the Holy City *Mecca*: The
" true and only Cauſe of his coming hither, is to
" demand you, my Dear, with the Intent of making
" you his Wife!"

When *Salma* heard this unexpected Explanation of
the Cauſe of *Haſhem*'s Journey, ſhe was quite confounded and out of Countenance; her Cheeks
glowing with Modeſty and Shame, for having ſo
plainly expreſſed the tender Sentiments of her
Love-ſick Heart, in her Father's Preſence; and
after many contradictory and evaſive Speeches to
extenuate her inconſiderate Error in owning what
ſhe now endeavoured to conceal, ſhe ſaid to him;
" I deſire you, Sir, to make no manner of Scruple in
" believing, That, notwithſtanding this noble and
" illuſtrious Family you have been mentioning, is
" the very Center of Honour itſelf, and hath the Ad-
" vantage over all the Tribes and Nations in the
" Univerſe; yet, if they are come, in Reality, to
" treat of a Marriage with me, and are ſatisfied with
" my Perſon, Character, &c. and agree, that the
" Propoſal ſhall be made to me concerning that Mat-
" ter, or have any Hopes, that I ſhould give my Con-
" ſent; they may reſt aſſured, That it ſhall never
" be, but upon Condition, that they give me a
" Dowry,

" Dowry, with all other Preſents, Feſtival Ceremonies,
" &c. ſuitable to my Birth, Honour and Condition ; of
" all which, if the leaſt Tittle is omitted or neglected, I
" am poſitively reſolved never to yield to their Deſires,
" and their having come ſo far will be to no purpoſe.

This *Salma* ſaid to retrieve what ſhe had been too
precipitate in diſcovering, and as a Blind, that her
Father might not too clearly dive into her Inclinations
and ardent Affection. —— This Lady was moſt tran-
ſcendantly replete with Prudence, Good-Conduct and
Diſcretion : The Features of her Face were admirable,
and of a moſt exquiſite Symmetry, and her Air and Mien
both charming and majeſtick. Her Stature was complete, and her Shape and Make perfectly fine and exact,
nothing inclining to either Extreme, but from Head to
Foot ſhe was all Perfection. Her Speech was graceful, and the Accent of her Voice ſweet and melodious :
She had a happy Volubility of Tongue, and her Re-
plies were always ſolid and pertinent to the Subject,
and ſometimes ſharp and witty. Her nice Education
and profound Learning had much improved her own
admirable Genius. She was wonderfully courteous,
affable and pleaſant to all ; benevolent, charitable,
compaſſionate, and intirely free from the leaſt Speck
of Sordidneſs or Ill-nature ; and, in fine, ſhe was a
complete Compound of all Graces and Perfections :
And, with all theſe amiable Qualifications, *Haſhem*
equalled, or rather exceeded her in every one ; for
his extraordinary Merits made him both envied
and admired by all who ſaw him, and none ever heard
him ſpeak but was charmed with the Eloquence of
his Expreſſions.

Omar, ſcarce able to contain himſelf for Joy, returned to the Place where he had left the Company :
He very impatiently burnt with the Deſire of ſeeing
the happy Hour arrive when his Daughter ſhould be
joyned in Wedlock with *Haſhem.*

But what ſhall I ſay of the infernal Malice, Rage
and Fury of the accurſed *Lucifer* ? His fiery Entrails

were

were fcorched with Envy, feeking what Diabolical Schemes he might invent to obftruct and difannul this conjugal Union: And, to accomplifh and bring about this his prefidious Defign, this his bafe, implacable and mortal Hatred and Rancour, he affumed the Appearance of an ancient Man, with long grey Locks and fnowy white Garments; and fo, with a venerable Afpect, a fluent Tongue, and a plaufible Pretence, he went, and, in a mighty courteous refpectful Manner, prefented himfelf before *Salma*, and after having, like a complete Courtier, given her the ufual *Salam*, or Salutation, he drew her away from her Company into a private Appartment, and then addreffed himfelf to her in thefe Words;

" Be pleafed, moft noble Lady, to underftand,
" That I am one of the Retinue of *Hafhem*, and that I
" left my own Houfe purely upon his Account: I am
" now fent hither from him, to acquaint you with the
" Caufe of his having undertaken this Journey. Now,
" Madam, it is a very prepofterous unfeemly Office
" for Men of my Age and Gravity to prevaricate,
" or to tell Lyes to fuch a worthy Lady as you are,
" whereby the Honour and Refpect due to my grey
" Hairs would be intirely forfeited, and I fhould
" become infamous wherefoever I go: And notwith-
" ftanding I am of the Number of thofe who came
" to make up this Match, and am bound by Obli-
" gation to comply with *Hafhem's* Injunction of pay-
" ing you this Vifit on his Part, yet I will difabufe
" you fo far, as to let you know his Ill-Qualities,
" his Defects, and the Unworthinefs of his true Chara-
" cter; that you may never have Caufe, in future
" Times, to caft any Reflexion upon me, and to pre-
" vent my becoming liable to the Affronts or Re-
" proaches of your Family. "

Salma, in a great Surprize, replied; " I intreat
" you, obliging, venerable Old-Man, that you will
" conceal nothing from me, but relate the naked
" Truth in all its Particulars; *for a Lye in the Mouth*
" *of*

" *of a Man is ever the Destroyer of his good Name,*
" *and nothing can possibly be baser than that Man who*
" *maliciously endeavours to deceive another.*

The invidious *Fire-brand* returned this Answer;
" *Hashem,* as your Eyes have been Witnesses, Madam,
" is a very graceful, beautiful and agreeable Gentle-
" man, as to his external Form; but his insupport-
" able Temper, and his base vicious Inclinations, blot
" out all the Perfections of his Person, and debase them
" into Deformities. His Behaviour towards his Wives
" is very brutish, and unlike a Man of Honour, never
" shewing them the least Tenderness or Respect: (a)
" Nor can any of them, be they ever so chast, good,
" modest or vertuous, continue long with him; some
" have been turned off, and sent home to their Friends
" in Ten Days, others in a Month, which was thought
" a great while; nay, the most prudent, cautious
" and discreet Woman that ever was born, if she
" was a Miracle of Nature, and the best Oeconomist
" under Heaven, could not possibly stay out her Year.
" Besides all this, he is of a vile, mean, groveling
" Spirit, without the least Sense of Honour or Ge-
" nerosity: A Guest was never seen to be entertained
" within his Gates; He is, besides all this, a base
" timorous Coward, and always runs away in an
" Engagement, or hides himself to avoid being pre-
" sent upon such Occasions: His Vices and bad Quali-
" ties being already so well known to every body
" in our City, and the Country round about us, that
" he was forced to have Recourse hither, as to a San-
" ctuary; where, for the Remoteness, he fancies his
" Exploits have never been heard of; and there is not
" one Woman in our Territories, but what hath had
" such a Character of him, from those poor unhappy

(a) The Reader must recollect here, that the *Mahometans* are allowed four lawful Wives, at the same Time, besides Female Slaves,
&c. and that they may part from them when they please.

Wives

" Wives of his, who have had ſo woful Experience of
" his Baſeneſs, inſomuch, that with one Voice, they
" all abſolutely refuſe to have any Dealings with him,
" and keep themſelves upon their Guard.   Now,
" Madam, I leave it to your own Judgment to deter-
" mine how what I have told you will agree with your
" good Liking, or anſwer your Expectation; aſſuring
" you, I have not uttered one Syllable but what is
" the very Truth.

" What Liking do you think I ſhould have, replied
" *Salma*, to a Man in whom are to be found ſuch a
" Maſs of infamous Qualities, as you have been re-
" citing? Since the leaſt of them all, would have
" been more than ſufficient to make his Errand inef-
" fectual, and to frighten away all Thoughts I might
" ever have entertained of conſenting to be his Wife:
" How much greater, then, muſt my Averſion be to
" ſuch a Propoſal, after having heard him to be
" tainted with Three ſo deteſtable and abhorred Pro-
" perties, ſo extremely odious to all thoſe who have
" any Spark or Notion of Honour in them? I mean,
" Cowardice in Battle, Poorneſs of Spirit, and Levity
" and Brutality, in abuſing and caſting off the Wo-
" men he has Married.   I therefore ſolemnly vow to
" Almighty God, that I never will yield to his De-
" mand, except I am compelled ſo to do by the utmoſt
" Rigour, and by main Force and Compulſion. So I
" deſire you, Father, to leave me to myſelf, without
" ſaying one Word more to me, upon this Subject."

Upon this, *Satan*, that Enemy to God and Mankind, took his Leave and departed, the Lady remaining
with her Blood all in a Ferment, and exceedingly ſorrowful at her Diſappointment, very angry with herſelf, and heartily repenting her having ſo deeply ſettled her whole Affections upon a Man ſo unworthy the
leaſt of them.   But *Satan*, not ſatisfied with what he
had already done, returned to her again, the ſame
Day, Three Times, always in a different Garb and
Appearance, telling her ſtill the like malicious Falſi-
ties,

ties, with some Variations, and several Aggravations, insomuch that at last he reduced her to such a State of Rage and Indignation, that she was quite out of her Senses, being no longer Mistress of her Reason, or able to contain herself within Bounds.

In the Height of this her Disquiet and Perturbation of Mind, her Father came in; who finding her in a Disorder so apparently great, and so very different from that State of Satisfaction and Sedateness, into which his imparting those welcome Tydings had put her, was much concerned, and inquired the Cause of that strange Alteration. She made him this Reply; " How " can you expect or desire, my dear Father, that I " should marry a Man, of whose own Retinue I " have had here with me Three or Four Persons, " who have told me a Thousand and a Thousand of " his Enormities, Villainies and Blemishes?" And at the same Time, gave him an Account of all that the Devil had told her.

This surprized *Omar* in the highest Degree; and notwithstanding he used all possible Arguments to endeavour to drive away those Thoughts from her Breast, which were so prejudicial to her Repose, yet all he could say was of little Effect, so well had *Satan* succeeded in his malicious Scheme, and had raised so fierce a Combustion in her before pacifick Mind, that her Father was, at last, obliged to leave her to her melancholy Reflections; telling her, as he went out, " That " she was at Liberty to do just what she pleased in " that Affair, for it was not his Intent to intermeddle, " or to force her Inclinations. "

She remained in so much Uneasiness, such Resentment, and so very much confounded to find, as she imagined, herself deceived and imposed upon, that she scarce knew where she was; for, *As it is true, that Hearts are composed of frail Flesh, as well as the rest of the Body, so it is likewise certain, that He who formed them out of nothing, formed them in an unconfined Liberty, and not to be compelled either to Love or to its Contrary.*

How-

However, thro' the Divine Goodneſs of the Almighty, all the Snares and Subtleties of *Satan* were baffled and brought to nought; for the Heart of *Salma* being inſpired with a pure and indelible Love, ſhe could take no Reſt, the Flame increaſing to ſuch a Pitch, that it had now taken Poſſeſſion of her very Soul. She could not yet be ſatisfied as to the ſeveral various Accounts given her that Day; which, though they all tended towards the rendring the Object of her Deſires infamous and odious to her Imaginations, yet ſhe was reſolved to be better convinced of the Reality of thoſe vile Aſperſions: Therefore, ſo ſoon as it was dark, ſhe laid aſide her own Garments, and putting on a Diſguiſe, reſolved to go out and ſearch for the lovely Man who was the Cauſer of that ſo violent and unextinguiſhable a Flame; a Fire, that preyed upon her Vitals, and conſumed her whole Fabrick.

Her Diſguiſe being ſuch that ſhe could not eaſily be diſcovered, ſhe, armed with Reſolution and ardent Love, left her Habitation, and went roaming about the City, inquiring of all ſhe met, If they had ſeen *Haſhem*? and this ſhe did, till ſhe ſaw the Heavenly *Light*, deſcending from the Firmament and centering upon the Forehead of him ſhe had been ſeeking with ſo much Eagerneſs and Concern: And he, at the ſame Time, hearing himſelf inquired for, anſwered; "I am *Haſhem*; Who is it wants him?" And as he turned his Face towards her, the *Light* ſtruck ſo full in her Eyes, that, not being able to endure its great Splendor, in great Aſtoniſhment, ſhe turned her Head on one ſide, which when *Haſhem* obſerved, he covered his Forehead.

To make ſhort, *Haſhem*, with a Lover's Eye, ſoon diſcovered the Fair *Salma*, and, at this Interview, thoſe Two Lovers, by interchanging a few amorous Glances, inſtantly came to a perfect Underſtanding. Their Flames were reciprocal, and burnt with an equal Ardour; neither of the Two, having the leaſt Advantage over the other. They, at firſt, only
amuſed

amufed themfelves with gazing at, and in Compli-
menting one another, with Expreffions of Joy and
Refpect; and then they began to explain to each
other their refpective Pretenfions; by which means
Salma became intirely difabufed and convinced of the
Falfities and vile Malice of *Satan*, in all the Afper-
fions he had caft upon the Character of *Hafbem*; and
fo, to conclude all, fhe faid to him thus; " In An-
" fwer to what you have been faying to me, O *Hafbem*,
" I affure you, and give you my Word, that I am
" contented with your honourable Propofal, and am
" very willing to become your Spoufe, as you de-
" fire: But I give you Notice of one Particular, That,
" concerning the Dowry and Prefents you are to
" make me, if my Relations fhould happen to re-
" quire any thing extraordinary, or unreafonable,
" you make no Hefitation in complying with their
" Demands. And obferve, that there are many Per-
" fons of the higheft Rank who would do all they
" poffibly could to obftruct this Marriage, and among
" whom my Name is held in great Efteem and
" Veneration: Yet, notwithftanding all Obftacles, I
" make you whole and fole Lord of my Perfon, For-
" tune, Affections and Defires; folemnly protefting
" to you, by the Almighty and all his Cœleftial
" Glories, That there fhall be no manner of Change
" or Prevarication in this Promife which I have made
" you, but it fhall be as fixed and immoveable as the
" Center.

Hafbem returned her a very grateful and courteous
Acknowledgment for her fo kind and generous a
Compliance, and faid; " You fhall affuredly be
" treated in every Refpect conformable to your high
" Merit and Condition; and I engage my felf to
" agree to whatfoever is demanded or required of me
" upon your Account, even to the leaft Tittle.

" There is one Circumftance upon which I fhall in-
" fift, faid *Salma*, if you pleafe to grant it; which is,
" That I being, as you well know, a Woman fo
" much

" much valued and looked upon in this my native
" City, and that every one makes ſo great Account of
" my Word, and is willing to obey me in whatſoever
" I deſire, you never offer to remove me from hence,
" or propoſe my leaving *Yathrib* to go to *Mecca.* "
" I conſent, Madam, ſaid *Haſhem*; I grant your
" Requeſt: Have you any thing more to demand?
" Yes, ſaid ſhe, If I ſhould chance to bear you Iſſue,
" I require, that my Children may never be ſeparated
" from me, but be always left to my Care. I conſent
" to that likewiſe, anſwered *Haſhem*, and happy ſhall
" I think myſelf, nor no leſs happy ſhall you be, if
" you bring me a Son, that I may ſhew my Willing-
" neſs to pleaſure you in this your Deſire. Have
" you any other Requeſt? Only replied ſhe, that, if
" you neglect me, and leave my Company to aſ-
" ſociate yourſelf with other Women, I may then
" in ſuch a Caſe, be free from all Obligations, and at
" my own Liberty to ſue a Divorce, nor be compelled
" to cohabit any longer with you upon any Account
" whatſoever. All you have, or can ask, anſwered
" *Haſhem*, I moſt willingly comply with; but this
" your laſt Propoſal, I neither can, nor will agree
" to: Think if there is nothing elſe I can ſerve
" or oblige you in. I am throughly ſatisfied, ſaid
" *Salma*; I have asked enough; and ſhall think my-
" ſelf both fully requited with what you have already
" condeſcended to, and bound in Duty to conform to
" your Pleaſure in all Things. In the Morning
" you may ſummon my Friends to conclude the
" Marriage: You have my free Conſent to proceed
" therein without Delay. " After this, they took
their Leaves of each other and departed to their
own Abodes.

But *Satan*, when he ſaw himſelf repulſed and derided, and that all his perfidious Projects had proved
ineffectual, made it now his whole Buſineſs to aſſemble
together and exaſperate the Malice of the *Jews*, who
were come from divers Parts to negotiate their Affairs

at

at this noted *Mart.* All this his Diligence and indefatigable Affiduity, proceeded from the inveterate
and implacable Hatred that Infernal Fiend bears to
our Holy Prophet *Mahomet,* and to prevent, if poffibly he could, *his* Appearance upon Earth; becaufe
fo many Evils were denounced to him from the Birth
of that *Beatified Saint,* who was predeftined to be the
Overthrower and *Deftroyer* of Herefies and Falfe-
Worfhips, the which are the very Effence, the Life
and Soul of that *Traytor.*

The *Fair* was, that Day, very full of *Jews* ; as
well thofe who were Inhabitants of the City and its
Neighbourhood, as of others who came in great Numbers from more diftant Towns and Caftles of the
Country ; for there was fcarce one *Jew* in the whole
Land, who failed to be prefent at that famous and
celebrated *Fair,* efpecially upon this remarkable Occafion.

In the midft of fuch a numerous Congregation of
People, who were all fworn Enemies to that *Elected*
Company, the invidious and pernicious Fiend prefented himfelf; being prepared for the Part he was to
act, by affuming the Form of an ancient grave Man,
with a long grey Beard, and very decent Apparel,
his Garments touching his Feet: By his Prefence and
Afpect, he appeared to be a Perfon of great Sanctity,
and profound Knowledge.

When that blood-thirfty deteftable Generation beheld him, they received him with great Reverence
and Honour ; kiffing his Hands, his Garments, and
the very Ground where he had fet his Feet; incom-
paffing him about with extraordinary Tokens of Veneration and Refpect, and calling him their Tutelar-
Angel, their Protector and Redeemer; faying unto
him ; ' How came it to pafs, Great Lord! that you
' did not give us Notice of your Approach? Had we
' but the leaft Intelligence thereof, we would never
' have been guilty of fo unpardonable a Fault, as to
' have neglected coming out to meet and receive your

U
' Lord

' Lord∫hip: We be∫eech you pardon the Omi∫∫ion,
' which was wholly cau∫ed by our Ignorance.

The Fiend replied; ' My coming hither was by
' Night, and Oh that I had never come! Would I had
' never ∫et my Feet within your City, nor had been
' a Witne∫s of what is going forward! Do not you
' ∫ee what I ∫ee? Are you not ∫en∫ible of the impen-
' ding Evil as well as I? Are you blind? Have you
' not beheld and con∫idered this Company, the∫e new
' Gue∫ts who came from *Mecca?* " To all this they
an∫wered in the Affirmative. ' Well then, ∫aid *Satan,*
' Have you not, in that Cavalcade, ob∫erved among
' the re∫t, one, in particular, of a mo∫t comely, beau-
' tiful and ∫tately Per∫onage, who hath a ∫hining *Light*
' on his Forehead, and who∫e Name is *Ha∫hem*; and
' who, as it is reported, comes to be married to *Sal-*
' *ma?* ' To this they likewi∫e replied, *Yes.* ' Then,
' ∫aid he, You may depend upon it, as an unavoid-
' able Certainty, That if that Man ever ∫hould take
' a Wife who is a Native of your Country, he will
' *Fi∫h in your very Bowels*; for he will infallibly de-
' prive you of your Patrimony, and de∫troy your
' Inheritance; and your future Tranquility is in the
' mo∫t imminent Danger: He will devour up your
' whole Sub∫tance; your Children will become his
' Slaves and Va∫∫als; and your Po∫terity, both far and
' near, will bear his in∫upportable Yoke. This is
' he, concerning whom the Sacred Scriptures make
' mention, and call *The Spiller of Torrents of Blood,*
' and of whom the Learned Sages progno∫ticate ∫uch
' dreadful Prodigies! Con∫ider, therefore, with your
' ∫elves the∫e dire Pre∫ages, and the terrible Confu∫ion
' and De∫olation wherewithal you are threatned;
' and think upon ∫ome Remedy how to avert and
' extingui∫h this de∫tructive Flame, which will admit
' of no Delay, but requires the utmo∫t Re∫olution, and
' a ∫peedy Determination.

Armon replied; ' I have already told them, That
' this is he who is called, The *Subverter* and *Rooter-*

out

' *out* of all Laws which are not conformable to *his*
' *own*; and that he is actually conſpiring and ripen-
' ing moſt Treaſonable Practices, all tending to our
' utter Ruin. Then, ſaid *Satan*, if you are deter-
' mined to apply a certain Remedy, *Cut down the*
' *Tree, and that will ſurely prevent the Branches from*
' *growing :* In ſo doing, you will attain your Ends, and
' will deliver your Country from this *Monſter with-*
' *out a Second:* And, to bring this about, that the
' Event may ſucceed anſwerable to your Wiſhes, it
' muſt be ſo contrived, in the Morning, when the
' intended Bridegroom goes, attended by his Follow-
' ers, to demand his Bride of her Relations, in a
' publick Manner, that then, in the middle of his
' Harangue, you all, in one unanimous Voice, diſ-
' turb the whole Treaty, by exclaiming and proteſt-
' ing againſt the Match, ſaying; That *You neither*
' *can, nor will, ever conſent, that ſhe ſhall marry a*
' *Foreigner* : And then, at the firſt Reply they make
' you, attack them ſuddenly with Vigour and Re-
' ſolution, employing your Weapons to the beſt Ad-
' vantage you can, ſo that they may every one die by
' your Hands with the Edge of your Swords ; for
' this muſt, of neceſſity, be the Conſequence ; they
' being but a ſmall, deſpicable Company of Wretches,
' and wholly unprovided to receive your Hoſtilities,
' as not in the leaſt dreaming of ſuch an Aſſault.
' And ſince you are ſo numerous a Band, I would
' have you ſelect a choice Squadron of Four hundred
' of your beſt *Men, armed at all Points, that there
' may be Ten of you, to every one of them ; and this
' do for your own better Security, and that you
' may be ſure of not miſſing your Aim. I, in the
' mean while, will not fail of being preſent amongſt
' you, and will moſt zealouſly act all whatſoever
' Damage lies in my Power to do, againſt the con-
' trary Party. " —— This was the Speech made them
by the accurſed Fiend, and the Counſel he had given
them was unanimouſly affirmed, by the whole Aſ-

ſembly, to be good and wholſome: And accordingly, they ſpent that Night in making themſelves ready to put it in Execution the next Morning.

The ſame Night, as *Haſhem* was ſleeping in his Bed, he dreamt, that he was ſurrounded by a great Number of Dogs, which, with ravenous Looks, and their Tails erected and briſtled up, in a furious manner, barking, ſnarling, yelling and howling, made ſhew of being juſt ready to ſeize upon him; and that, when their Rage was at higheſt, he drew out his Sabre, ſtriking at, and wounding the Faces of thoſe who ſeemed the moſt courageous, and moſt eager to faſten upon him, to whom he ſtill gave the greateſt and deepeſt Wounds; his Weapon never miſſing to reach them.

This Dream diſturbed his Mind exceedingly, and awaking in a terrible Conſternation, he ſent for all his Friends and Companions; and when they came, he communicated to them the whole Purport of that Viſion, not omitting one Circumſtance; At the Rehearſal whereof, they were all filled with Wonder and Aſtoniſhment, asking him, If he could conjecture the Signification of ſo ſtrange and frightful a Dream, and what Interpretation might be made thereof? To which he replied;

' You are to underſtand, That by thoſe Snarling
' Dogs, is meant, a malicious, perverſe and wicked
' Generation of People, who are contriving all ſorts
' of Villainy and Perfidiouſneſs. The Almighty be
' ·with us, to guide, protect and defend us from the
' Snares and Treacheries of thoſe who lie in wait to
' deſtroy us! I adviſe you, my beloved Friends and
' Kinſmen, that, as I am not unacquainted with your
' great Prudence and Conduct, your hearty Friend-
' ſhip and Fidelity to me, your Heroick Valour and
' Reſolution, you be likewiſe, all of you alert and
' fully prepared for what may happen: Go provided
' with your Arms, all in good Order, and caſt your
' Eyes attentively round about you on every Side:
' Be careful and vigilant; and be in no wiſe negligent
' or

' or over-secure: Keep your Hands continually upon
' the Hilts of your *Sabres*, that if any Attempt be
' made against our Lives, we may be in a Readiness
' to exercise our Weapons in our Defence; for, assure
' your selves, That the Success of our Undertaking,
' and even our future Welfare, is wholly depending
' upon God's Protection, and the Force of your
' Arms. '

They all promised to be mindful of his Admonitions,
and began to prepare themselves for the great Affair
in Agitation.

U 3   C H A P.

C H A P. XII.

Hashem *and his Followers prepare to go to demand the Bride. The Cavalcade defcrib'd, and Salma's particular Care for their Accommodation. Hashem's gallant Appearance, and with what Ornaments and facred Relicks he was array'd. The Reception he and his Company had from the Bride and her Relations, &c. The Harangue made them by* Almutalib, *Brother to the Bridegroom, concerning the Nobility of the moft Illuftrious Family, the Poffeffors of the Hereditary Light. Anfwered by* Omar, *the Bride's Father. Offers made by* Almutalib, *in the Behalf of his Brother* Hashem. *Rejected, at the Inftigation and inveterate Malice of* Satan, *who is there prefent, under the Likenefs of a grave, religious Perfon, accompanied by great Numbers of* Jews, *all mortal Enemies to the Caufe.* Satan's *shamelefs Infolence; at which* Omar *is at laft quite fcandalized, and rebukes him. His Perfeverance in his malicious Impudence, and the unreafonable Propofal he makes to the Princes of* Mecca. *The Refentment of* Almutalib *at the Impoffibilities demanded, and the fcandalous Impofition of of the* Fiend; *who thereupon gives the appointed Signal to the* Jews, *who attack the Bridegroom and his Companions, but are intirely routed by them, with very great Slaughter; and, among the reſt,* Armon *their Chief, falls by the Hand of* Almutalib. *The exceeding Valour of the Princes of* Mecca. *The Fiend endeavouring to get away, is overtaken by* Haſhem. *Their Encounter, and the Devil's Words to* Haſhem, &c. *The Bride's Fear and Concern for her Lover. The Marriage concluded,* &c.

T the Time when the beautiful *Aurora* began to ſhew her chearful Countenance, and, with her Brightneſs, to diſſipate the intenſe Obſcurity of the Night; when the Clearneſs of the *Eaſt* gave Notice of the Morn's Approach to the other *Quarters,* and that the Ruddy *Phœbus* would not be long before he made his glorious Appearance, to gild the Hills and verdant Plains: When the nocturnal Birds began to retire to their Places of Reſt, and the other Species of thoſe winged Choriſters, that delight in the Sun's Preſence, began to pierce the thin and paſſive Air with their ſhrill and melodious Notes: When human Creatures began to ſhake of their ſweet Slumbers, and to rouze themſelves from their ſoft Repoſe, in order to pay the Debt they owe to their Creator.

In a Word, the wiſh'd-for Day appeared, and the Son of *Abdulmenaf,* with his whole Company, aroſe from their Beds, in order to prepare themſelves for the great Matrimonial Solemnity, having, in the firſt Place, with ſingular Piety and Devotion, performed the uſual Ablutions and Prayers.

U 4   Their

Their coftly magnificent Garments were richly perfumed with Mufk, Amber, and many other precious odoriferous Drugs and Gums ; and, mounting their beautiful Steeds (which were all moft pompoufly adorned with Princely Furniture) attended by their Pages and Followers, they marched, in a very gallant and fightly Manner, towards the great Market-Place, where the *Fair* was kept.

Salma, being told that this noble Cavalcade was coming, defired her Father and the reft of her Relations to get all Things in a Readinefs to receive thofe Princes of *Mecca,* infifting, with fome Earneftnefs, that they fhould prepare for their Accommodation with the utmoft Magnificence imaginable ; and that they fhould be entertained according to their high Dignity and Merit. She caufed a very fine Tent to be fet up in the moft confpicuous Part of the Plain, wherein fhe intended to receive her Company : The Ground was fpread with exceeding rich Carpets and Tapiftry, and covered with many Tables, abundantly furnifhed with great Variety of moft exquifite Viands, and delicious Refrefhments. Every Thing being in due Order, the Banner appearing waving in the Air, gave Notice of the Approach of thofe Forty Princes, with *Hafhem* at their Head : A moft gallant Troop of Princely Heroes it certainly was ; and who had not their Equals in the World ! Their Horfes, which were the fineft and the fwifteft in the whole Country, came prancing on, all covered with very fine and impenetrable Coats of Mail, under their richly imbroider'd Caparifons. Their Riders, nobly arrayed in long graceful Garments, and very fine Scarves, forgot not to put on their beft and ftrongeft Armour under thofe Garments, that they might be ready againft all that fhould happen.

Hafhem himfelf made a moft gallant Appearance, fuitable to his high Rank and Condition. He was clad after the Mode of the remoteft Antiquity ; and

not-

notwithstanding many of the Ornaments, &c. he had on, were of a most ancient Fabrick, yet they were all exceeding fresh, and seemed to be perfectly new; nor had Time done them the least Damage: (*a*) *For Time can never wear out those Things which were created before Time itself; but, on the contrary, they still continue in the same Condition:* All which were delivered to him by his Father *Abdulmenaf*, and were gloriously inriched with Embroidery, Gold and Jewels. His beautiful Forehead was adorned with the Crown of *Cusai*, from whose illustrious Loins he was descended; and he had the Scarf of *Koreish*, who was a most famous Sovereign Prince, and his Progenitor as well as the other. He had upon his Feet the Shoes of the venerable *Seth*, as all the Princes of that most *sanctified Stock* were wont to have, upon such solemn Occasions; and it is very remarkable, that those sacred Relicks always fit the Feet of all who are worthy to wear them, as exactly as if they were made on Purpose for them. He carried the Staff of *Abraham*, and the Bow of the mighty *Ishmael*; and for his Device, had the venerable Banner of *Ægypt* displayed and bore before him; in this triumphant Manner, riding in the midst of all his Company, he approached the Market-Place; and, as the Sun from the East, at his first Appearance in the Morning, expanding his glorious Rays all around, gilds the Surface of the Earth, and brings a joyful Chearfulness along with him, even so did *Hashem*, at his first Entrance into that vast Square, enliven the Spirits of all the expecting Assembly; the glorious Rays of his Countenance spreading intirely over the Place, and striking the admiring Eyes of his Beholders

---

(*a*) Here the Author alludes to the fabulous Traditions of the *Mahometans*, concerning many Things they hold to have been actually sent down from Heaven, ready made. See Page 62. about *Adam*'s Shoes, &c. he left to his *Elected* Son *Seth*.

with

with an awful Dread, mixt with Deference and Veneration.

When the Relations of *Salma*, and the rest of the Nobility, saw their Arrival, with Signs of universal Joy and Respect, they advanced towards them, with great State and Gravity ; yet so, that Satisfaction, Peace and a hearty Welcome, were evidently visible in every Feature of their Faces ; and, assisting them to alight from their Horses, they were conducted to, and seated in the Stations prepared for their Reception, according to the laudable Customs and Hospitality of those People ; and the Place where these noble Guests had dismounted, was instantly surrounded with infinite Numbers of Spectators ; amongst whom the accursed *Satan*, followed by many Hundreds of Blood-thirsty, misbelieving *Jews*, from *Yathrib*, and several other Parts of the Country, failed not to be present at this ever-memorable Marriage-Treaty.

Silence having been commanded, and so strictly observed, that not the least Whisper was to be heard among all that great Concourse of People ; it was first broken by *Almutalib*, Brother to *Hashem*, who was the greatest Orator, and the most eloquent of Speech of all his Tribe, and whose Prudence was held in high Esteem by all. This illustrious Spokesman standing up, looking all round the Assembly, and saluting them all with a graceful and courteous Gesture, and a pleasant smiling Countenance, he made them the following Harangue ;

" To God alone, who is the most Mighty King of
" all Kings, be the Praise! To Him who hath seated
" us in his own City, and hath appointed us to be
" the Princes and Rulers thereof ; who hath endow-
" ed us with His divine Grace, and hath poured
" down upon us so large a Share of his Bounties,
" Blessings and Mercies : To Him alone be all Glory!
" We are God's own peculiar Guests, inhabiting His
" sanctified Mansion, in which we are distinguished
" by the Honourable Titles of *The Lord's own Ser-*
" *vants,*

" *vants*, both we and all our Pofterity.   We are the
" *efpecially Elected* from among all the Nations of
" the Earth; the *Chofen of* the Almighty; particula-
" rized by the Blazon of a glorious and refplendent
" *Light*, whereby we are guided; and which defcendeth
" down to us from the fupreme Throne, its native
" Center, that beatified Abode of all Purity, where
" no Uncleannefs can exift : And this fame ineftima-
" ble and peculiar Mark of Diftinction hath been
" tranfmitted to us, as an Inheritance, even from our
" firft Original Father; paffing through the Loins
" of the moft eminent Worthies, and the Wombs of
" the chaftest and moft reclufe Matrons, from Fa-
" ther to Son fucceffively, in a direct, uninterrupted
" Line, down to *Luai*, *Caebu*, and *Kufai*, 'till at laft
" *it* came to be inherited by our Father and Ante-
" ceffor *Abdulmenaf*, who held *it*, 'till having run
" the regular Courfe, *it* was by him, transferred to
" this our Brother *Hafhem*, who, among all Men, is
" the Lamp and Luminary of the prefent Age, and
" the Protector and Defender of our Laws.   We
" are free from all Manner of Fornication or Impu-
" rity, and all the vile Confequences thereof; which
" unclean Practices, as the Almighty Creator hath
" ftrictly forbidden us to ufe, but, on the contrary,
" commanding us to join in lawful Matrimony,
" in order to avoid that Sin ; fo our Brother *Hafhem*,
" guided by God, and having His Fear before his
" Eyes, is come hither, as you fee, accompanied by
" his Brethren and Kinfmen, to afk of you, with all
" due Honour and Refpect, That you confent to give
" him for his lawful Spoufe the matchlefs *Salma*, only
" Daughter to *Omar* ; which illuftrious Lady is here
" in the Prefence of all this honourable Company.
" Confider now among yourfelves what Anfwer you
" think proper to return to this our Propofal ; and
" affure yourfelves, that we will readily agree to
" all your Demands, without the leaft Hefitation
" or Omiffion of any one fingle Particular: Nor will
" we

" we offer any Thing, but what shall intirely tend
" to your Honour and Advantage. And now, since
" we have acquainted you with our Intentions, I de-
" sire you will be pleased to let us know your Re-
" solutions in this Affair.

Here *Almutalib* concluded his Speech, and waited in
Expectation of an Answer; when *Omar*, whom it most
of all concerned to speak, began thus; " Peace and
" Eternal Bliss, the highest Honour and Veneration,
" all Reverence and Regard is due to you alone, O
" most select and illustrious Heroes! Noblest among
" all the Tribes! Chief of the Inhabitants of the
" sacred and venerable Temple! In Answer to your
" Affair, I say, in the Name of us all here present,
" That we are wholly content to gratify your graci-
" ous and honourable Request, and joyfully agree,
" that the Marriage may be concluded; since it is
" highly our own Interest, and so much for our own
" Honour, to consent to a Proposal, which so con-
" spicuously tends to the ennobling our Country, and
" our Family. I say, therefore, O *Hashem*, That
" both I and my Daughter, are intirely at your
" Service and Devotion; and we shall esteem your Ac-
" ceptance as the greatest Honour could happen to us.
" But as my Daughter's high Rank, her great Wealth,
" Interest and Estate, the high Esteem and Veneration
" the whole Country hath for her, and her own Vir-
" tue and unblemished Character, are all sufficiently
" notorious to recommend her, I make it my Re-
" quest, that you will assign her a competent and
" equivalent Dowry, Presents, *&c.* which may be to
" the Liking, Satisfaction and Approbation of all this
" Assembly.

" We will give you, said *Almutalib*, One hundred
" She-Camels, all of them young, strong and sound,
" without any Blemish: See what you desire more. "

—— The *Infernal Serpent*, upon this Occasion, failed
not to place himself, just at *Omar's* Elbow, and gave
him private Advice, to say, That the Offer was too
little,

little, and that he could not agree to it. — *Omar* then replied; *What you promife us, Young-Man, is no wife conformable to my Daughter's Condition and Rank; You muft bid higher, if you intend to have her.* " We will, befides " the Camels, faid *Almutalib*, give you a Thoufand " Golden-Ducats. " — The accurfed *Satan* faid to *Omar*; " Tell him, that it is too little; that you " will not take it; and that it is not at all anfwerable " to your Daughter's Fortune and Merit. " *Omar* anfwered; " Your Offers, Sir, are good; but you " muft ftill advance higher; I cannot agree to this. " " Well, replied *Almutalib*; Becaufe you fhall be in- " tirely fatisfied, and have no Caufe of Complaint, " we will prefent her wherewithal to adorn her Perfon, " Thirty Changes of Rayment, of the choiceft Silks, " wrought with Gold, of the Fabrick and Texture of (a) " *Ægypt* and *Alireque* or *Iraquia*; Will all this content " you? "

(a) *Ægypt* is by the *Arabs* call'd *Mefr*, and by the *Turks* and *Perfians, Miffir*. When the Country is meant, the *Arabians* fay *Berr Mefr*, that is, The Land of *Ægypt*; but the Word is more particularly adapted to the Capital City, which the *Europeans* call *Grand Cairo*, formerly *Memphu*, corruptly fo called by the *Greeks*, from its more ancient Name *Monf*. —— The proper Signification of *Mefr*, is, A very populous Province, or a great City; in the Plural *Amfar*. —— The *Hebrews* call *Ægypt*, in the Dual Number, *Mifhraim*, alluding to the Upper and Lower *Ægypt*, or the Northern and Southern, or the Eaftern and Weftern, as it is divided by the *Nile*. — It muft be obferved, That the old *Monf*, or *Memphu*, was feated on the Weft-fide of the *Nile*, and all that has been fince built by the *Arabs*, from Time to Time, is on the Eaft-fide, oppofite to it. —— My *Spanifh Moor* always writes it *Mifera*. By *Alireque* he furely muft mean that Province our Hiftorians call *Iraquia*, and the *Mahometans Erac* or *Irac*. This is, indeed, the proper Name of two Countries, diftinguifhed by the Titles of *Erac el Agemi*, the *Perfian Erac*, and *Erac Arabi*, and fometimes *Erac Babeli*, that is, the *Arabian* and the *Babylonian Erac*. —— The ancient Geographers and Hiftorians called this *Erac*, and the other *Giabal*, or the Mountains, which is likewife often called *Kouheftan*. —— *Iraquia* is a Province of *Afia*, which, on the Weft, Borders upon the Defart of *Arabia* and *Gezirah*, otherwife *Diarbiker* or *Mefopotamia*; its Border on the South, is another Defart adjoining to the former, and the Gulph of *Perfia*, with Part of *Khozıftan*

" you? " The Fiend ftill made Signs to *Omar*, that he
fhould return a negative Anfwer; who, almoft out of
Countenance, replied to *Almutalib*; " Your Offers, Sir,
" are, in Reality very great; for the which you have
" my thankful Acknowledgements; but if you pleafe
" to make fome fmall Addition to what you have al-
" ready promifed us, it will be taken as an Obliga-
" tion. " " To oblige you, faid *Almutalib*, I will
" add One hundred (a) *Aludas* of Amber-greafe, and
" the fame Quantity of Musk, with Ten large Chefts
" of Camphire: See if you can be fatisfied with what
" we have condefcended to grant. " But as nothing
is fufficient, to abafh the fhamelefs *Satan*, fo he manifefted his notorious Impudence upon this Occafion,
faying out aloud; " All they have hitherto propofed
" to give for your Daughter, is by far too little. "
Omar, quite out of Patience, turned towards the
Fiend, and faid; " Have you neither Fear nor Shame
" in you, you malicious, unmannerly old Dotard,
" to affront me after this manner, to exact from them,
" a larger Dowry, *&c.* than what, in Reafon, they

Khouziftan or *Sufiana*; on the Eaft is borders on *Giabal*, the Mountain *Erac*, which is the *Parthia* of the Ancients. The laft Town of
Iraquia, on that fide is *Hulvan*, from whence it ftretches towards the
North as far as *Mefopotamia*. —— This Province runs along both fides
of the *Tigris*, as *Ægypt* includes both fides of the *Nile*. The Length
of it from *Takrit* to *Abadan*, where the *Tigris* falls into the Gulph
of *Perfia*, which is North Eaft and South-Weft, is Twenty Days
Journey, according to the *Perfian* Geographers. —— This is the
Province the *Greeks* and *Romans* called *Chaldea* and *Babylon*; and it is
not unlikely, that the Name of *Erac*, given it by the *Arabs*, comes
from the Hebrew *Irek*, a Town in the Province of *Cafhdim* or *Chaldea*.
——*Babel* or *Babylon*, was its Metropolis under the *Affyrians*; under
the *Cofroes* it was *Madani*, and under the *Saracens* or *Arabs* it was
and ftill is, the City *Bagdat*.

(a) Here I can but guefs at my Author's meaning, this Word
Aludas being very obfcure, nor do I know any thing like it but thofe
little Shells we vulgarly call Blackmoor's Teeth, and the Negro
Women in *Barbary* are very fond of, and call *El Oudah*. It is probable
the Word here means fome fort of Weights.

" ought

" ought to give ? How long muſt I endure your
" ſhameleſs Inſolence ? I, for my Part, am altogether
" confounded and out of Countenance, to ſee their
" great Patience at ſuch prodigious and extravagant
" Demands, and at what they have already had the
" Goodneſs to agree to! If you imagine their Conde-
" ſcentions great, replied the Infernal Fiend, we look
" upon them with a different Eye ; and, in our
" Opinions, all their Preſents are very inſignificant :
" You ought to ask of them more than they are able
" to comply with ; for we will anſwer all your De-
" mands, far more to your Daughter's Intereſt and
" Advantage, than they can ever pretend to do ; and
" amongſt us, we will lay down upon the Spot,
" both Camels, Apparel, Slaves, &c. for the Secu-
" rity of the Performance of all we agree to, till you
" are intirely ſatisfied : And therefore, ſince theſe
" Strangers ought to have no further Pretenſions of
" marrying *Salma*, it is your Buſineſs to demand
" of them more than they are worth, or able to ac-
" compliſh.

To this *Almutalib* replied in theſe Words ; " Speak
" your Mind, Old-Man ; Let us hear your Propoſals ;
" and if your Words carry any thing that is reaſon-
" able along with them, we will ſtill condeſcend, tho'
" it ſhould at our further Expence. Well, ſaid the
" Devil, obſerve then, what I have to ſay : The
" Dowry you are to make this Lady, ſuitable to her
" Fortune, Character and Condition, is this ; You
" muſt build for her an *Alcaſſer*, or Palace, which
" ſhall be ſuſtained in the Air, in ſuch wiſe, that it
" may be the Admiration of all that behold it : It
" muſt be in Length a whole Day's Journey, the
" ſame in Breadth, and as much in Height; inſomuch,
" that no Fabrick that ever was, or ever will be in
" the World, can hold the leaſt Competition with it ;
" and from the Turrets whereof the Proſpect may be ſo
" ſituated, that the Sight may reach ſo far, as plainly
" and clearly to diſcern the Ships in the Sea, as they are
" ſailing

" failing towards the Weft, and every thing that in-
" tervenes between the faid Palace, and the Diftance of
" a Month's Journey from it : And likewife, that you
" caufe a River, divided into Three Branches, to enter
" into the *Alcaffer* ; each of which Branches, fhall be
" very deep, large and rapid Currents, capable for
" Ships to fail therein ; and upon the Banks of all thefe
" Torrents, you fhall plant Date-Trees, at an exact
" Diftance from each other, meafured by Compafs,
" and fo ordered, that the Boughs of one may touch
" that which is next it ; and that thefe Trees may
" produce ripe and delicious Fruits of all Sorts, at
" all Seafons ; And, laftly, that thefe Rivers, planted
" after the manner I have defcribed, may take their
" Courfe from the Sea of *Uzmen,* 'till they evacuate
" themfelves into *Iraquia.*

Almutalib, who by this Time, had intirely loft all
Patience, made the pernicious Serpent in Difguife
this Anfwer ; " Hold your Tongue, you malicious,
" lying, prevaricating old Villain ! Your impotent Envy
" is vifibly evident in all you fay : Nor need you add
" any more, to convince us of your incoherent Folly,
" or rather Madnefs ; as likewife of the Bafenefs of
" your Principles. —— I will accomplifh, faid the
" Devil, all this, and much more, if it is required at
" my Hands, provided they will marry me to *Salma,*
" and will but drive away all thefe *New-Comers* from
" hence ; and I am certain, that it is very convenient,
" and the intire Intereft and Defire of all her Family,
" that fhe fhould rather be married here amongft our-
" felves, than to a *Foreigner.*

Salma, upon hearing this, cryed out from within,
with an audible Voice, that fhe might be heard by the
whole Affembly, faying ; That they fhould, by no means,
give heed or agree to any Thing that was propofed
to them, by that falfe, lying, impertinent *Old Ruf-
fian.* To which, *Armon,* that rebellious, blood-
thirfty Tyrant, made Anfwer ; " I am very forry to
" hear you talk fo, and to give fuch pernicious Counfel:
" This

"This Holy Man is the wifeft and moft learned
"among the Learned and the Wife; his great Fame,
"for Piety, Sanctity and Wifdom, is fpread all over
"*Arabia* and *Iraquia:* The Caufe which he defends is
"juft and equitable; it being but reafonable, that you
"marry and remain among ourfelves, and not be carried
"away from hence; and we will fully agree to, and
"comply with all, whatfoever they have offered you,
"without omitting the leaft Particular; nay, we will
"give more if required.

Salma replied; "You have, certainly, no Senfe
"of Shame in thofe *brazen, deformed* Faces of yours!
"How can you, elfe, be fo importunately trouble-
"fome to one who abhorreth and detefteth you fo
"much as I do? I never will accept of any of your
"Goods or Prefents, no more than I will receive thofe
"of that infamous Old Infidel, who maketh fuch ma-
"licious and inconfiftent Propofals; and who, in all he
"hath uttered here, hath not faid one Syllable of
"Truth: Affure yourfelves, that I will never have
"any thing to do, either with you or with him;
"and, that though the whole Fabrick of the World
"fhould be reverfed, I can never be content with any
"Man but *Hafhem*; fo let me be no more importuned
"or molefted by any of you.

Then faid the Traytor *Armon*; "You fhall never
"then have your Will, you may depend upon it; and
"here you are like to continue in fpite of all Oppo-
"fers whatfoever:" And, immediately, rifing up,
he beckoned to the *Jews* and called upon them, (in a
Tone which gave evident Signs of his villainous
Intents) who were all ready waiting, and approached
in a tumultuous Manner, with their naked Weapons
in their Hands, which, till then, they had kept concealed under their Garments.

When our Heroes, the Sons, *&c.* of *Abdulmenaf*,
beheld this, inftantly recollecting the Dream of
their Brother *Hafhem*, they took it for granted, that
what he had prognofticated to them, concerning that

X   Dream,

Dream, was now fulfilled; and, with a Greatnefs of Soul peculiar to themfelves, thofe Forty Champions drew out their Sabres, and, like fearlefs undaunted Lions, intrepidly fell upon that fierce, accurfed and numerous Band of mifbelieving Infidels; and, notwith-ftanding the vaft Difproportion of Numbers, our Wor-thies began the Affault, fpurred on by their innate Valour and Magnanimity, and by the illuftrious generous Blood that boiled within their noble Breafts, nothing regarding the great Advantage thofe cowardly Traytors had over them, but made a glorious Attack upon thofe their unworthy Adverfaries; wounding, hacking, difmembring, fplitting, cutting in two at the Wafte, killing and deftroying them, running here and there on every Side, driving them out of Order, and, where-ever they appear'd, filling thefe bafe Scoun-drels with Terror and Confufion; breaking all their Ranks in fo effectual a Manner, that having, intirely routed them, they finally ran away in a Fright, cur-fing and blafpheming. The whole Market-Place was covered with Blood, which ran like a Torrent from the numerous Wounds our Heroes diftributed, and the Carcaffes of thofe who fell by their Hands, lay in Heaps all about, nor could any Refiftance avail them againft thofe Thunder-bolts of Death, who fought like Lions. —— *Almutalib* fingled out the execrable Traytor *Armon*; and notwithftanding the Mifcreant made fome Efforts in his own Defence, he was laid extended on the Ground, divided into two Pieces, without its being in the Power of any of his Followers to prevent his Fate.

When *He* who is the Author of all Confufion, faw this great Deftruction and Ruin, which had been all of his own kindling, he endeavoured to make off from the Field of Battle, and to put himfelf in Security, to avoid further Shame, according to his ufual Cuftom; And as he was about to withdraw, *Hafhem* chanced to fee him, and flew upon the bafe Wretch before he could hide himfelf, and laid him on fo home,

giving

giving him such stupifying Strokes on the Head, that he fell down at his Feet, groveling with his Mouth in the Dust, *Hashem* himself falling likewise at the same Time; and when the *Light* which *Hashem* bore on his Forehead, shined upon the Fiend and covered him, he lay *yelling* and *hissing* like a Serpent.

Salma, hearing the extraordinary Shouts which were made upon that Occasion, ran out of her Tent, stumbling and treading upon her Garments as she ran; and when she beheld them in that manner wallowing on the Ground, she cryed out and said; " O Lord of " Power! Help *Hashem,* I beseech thee, and grant " that he may obtain the Victory over his treacher- " ous and blood-thirsty Adversary! " And the Devil, when he found himself in such an Extremity, felled to the Earth after that manner, and that all his Falsities, Disguise and Snares were insufficient to conceal him, he said; " *Hashem,* desist! Let me alone! " Proceed no farther! How far in your fruitless At- " tempts do you pretend to go? For know, that your " Efforts are all very much in vain, if you imagine " to take away my Life; your Strength, at present, " you may rest assured, can in no wise compass any " such Intent; nor does the Almighty permit you so " to do; for know, That (*a*) I am of the Number of " those who are Doomed to *complain* until the Day " of Judgment.

Hashem then replied; " Avaunt, *Satan,* thou base " Miscreant! Mayst thou be confounded and all thy " Devices! Thou who hast been the Cause of so many " Mischiefs among the Servants of the Almighty " Creator! " And having said this, he left him, and went to see what was become of his Companions, and what they had done with their faithless Enemies. He found them all, not one being lost or missing; neither

---

(*a*) Alluding to that Notion of theirs, That on the Last-Day, when *Israfil* sounds his Trumpet, all Living Creatures Angels, Men and Devils shall die, and last of all *Azarael* the Angel of Death.

was

was there much Danger, conſidering the worthleſs Wretches they had to deal withal. He called them together, deſiring them to put an End to the Slaughter, telling them, That he had Reaſon to be ſure, That all the Blood that had been ſpilt was through the means of *Satan*. In this manner ended the Battle, at the Expence of ſo many Lives, which were taken away by thoſe our invincible Heroes, the impenetrable Bulwark of the *Light*; the *Jews* remaining ſo highly incenſed, that their implacable Hatred and Malice, againſt our Holy Prophet *Mahomet*, hath continued ever ſince, to this Day.

Omar ben Azadin, the Bride's Father, pacified all, and made Peace for the preſent; and the Marriage Rites were concluded without any Interruption or Inconveniency; And, inſtead of a Collation or Feaſt, as was uſual, to entertain the Company and all who came upon ſuch Occaſions, *Salma* ordered many rich and conſiderable Preſents to be given out, and diſtributed large Sums of Money among all the People, who happened to be there; and, after having, with her own Hands, perfumed the Robes of *Haſhem*, and his Friends, with moſt precious and coſtly Gums, they all joyfully took their Way towards *Yathrib*.

C H A P.

C H A P. XIII.

Almutalib goes with a rich Prefent to Salma, which fhe requites with one much greater. Her Relation of her firft Marriage to Uchaichate. His vaft Wealth. The number of his Wives. Salma's Contract with him. His fordid Temper, and groundlefs Jealoufy. He treats her very unworthily, and confines her in a Caftle, where he perpetually watches and perfecutes her. She endeavours to efcape, but cannot. Is delivered of a Son. Her politick Contrivance and Efcape. Gets fafe to her Father. Her Proteftation and firm Refolution, never to return to her unworthy Husband. Her Requeft to Almutalib. The Confummation of the Nuptials. The Bride conceiveth with a Male-Child the firft Night, which was known by the Light's *being tranfmitted from* Hafhem's *Forehead to hers.* Hafhem's *great Joy thereat.*

THE fame Evening, after the Celebration of the Nuptials, *Hafhem* fent his Brother *Almutalib* to pay a Vifit to *Salma*, and to convey to her a great Quantity of very rich and coftly Jewels from him, which he fent as a Pledge or Confirmation of her being his Spoufe. She received the Prefent, and in Re-

quital

quital for the fame, returned a Prefent much greater than an Equivalent. The Difcourfe that fhe held with *Almutalib* was as follows.

The HISTORY *of* SALMA.

I Intreat you, my worthy Brother *Almutalib*, give Ear to my Words, and hear me out patiently, without Interruption, while I relate to you my whole Hiftory at large.——— You are to underftand, That I was married once before, and have been under the Subjection of another Hufband, befides this to whom I am now wedded.

The Name of that my firft Spoufe was *Uchaichate*: He was the moft wealthy Man of h's Time, both in Lands and Effects, and in Nobility and Defcent he was inferior to none, nor had he fcarce any Equals. He was poffeffed of innumerable Droves and Herds of all Sorts of Cattle, Camels, Cows and Sheep; and was the Owner of a great Number of Slaves and Servants, prodigious Groves of Date-Trees, and Grounds of vaft Extent.

Befides her, who is now in your Prefence, he had Ninety-nine Wives, all which he had taken when they were young and beautiful Virgins. When he married me, I made fuch an Agreement with him, that had he afterwards ftood firm to his Word and Promife, my Happinefs had been complete: In my Capitulation I engaged him, That if, at any Time, either in Earneft or in Jeft, he fhould act any thing contrary to my Inclination, or fhould make me uneafy by the leaft Ill-treatment, which I fhould not have deferved through bad Conduct, nor had given him any other Provocation to ufe me fo, that then,

in

in such Case, it should be lawful for me to leave him, without being obliged to give him any Reason for my so doing; nor should it be in his Power to prevent my being divorced from him, and to remain intirely free from his Yoke.

But as the Accounts which are cast up by the Vassals, seldom agree with those of the Lord; so my Reckoning proved quite wrong, as is said to happen always to them, who *reckon without their Host*. My Destiny would have it so, that after I became his Wife, his natural Temper was quite altered : For first he conceived an Antipathy to my Father, and a perfect Abhorrence to my whole Family, and I, insensibly, found myself miserably oppressed and misused, and, in a Word, treated as if I had actually been his Servant or Slave.

When I perceived that all my Hopes were nipped in the Bud, and that my Spring was changed into a most rigid Winter; that my Health was impaired, and began to droop and decay, through the intolerable Captivity in which I passed my Life, I thought of having Recourse to the Remedy I had pitched upon when I was a Virgin; but where-ever I went, I always found the Gates and Doors secured with a Thousand Locks. Seeing myself in so wretched a State, I sought all Means and Methods how I might deliver myself from such a miserable Bondage, passing my Days very disconsolately, racking my Invention perpetually to little purpose, and my Nights were always spent without Sleeping, revolving a Thousand *Chimera's* in my Brain, which all proved abortive; for my Husband had entertained so strong a Suspicion of me, and mistrusted me so much, that he was generally upon the Watch; and to such a Pitch was his Diffidence and Jealousy arrived, that he wholly neglected all his Negotiations and Affairs, letting his most important Concerns run at Random, to apply himself intirely to inspect, with a vigilant Eye, into my Actions, which were now become his sole Care.

He

He conveyed me out of my Native City, **at a great** Diftance from all my Friends and Relations, **to a** Caftle which he had purchafed and fitted on purpofe to make me unhappy : Here he held me under a clofe Confinement, which, in thofe my tender Years, was fo grievous to me, that my Life perfectly confumed away in Mifery.

While I laboured under thefe Streights and Afflictions, it pleafed the Divine Goodnefs, that, amidft fo many Torments and fo much Anguifh, I fhould conceive and bring forth a Son, as fome Affuagement of my Sorrow ; not by Reafon his Father altered my wretched Condition, or made my Life one Jot the eafier, as Fathers, who rejoice at the Birth of their Children, or who take Delight in them, are wont to do ; for, on the contrary, his infupportable Humours rather ftill increafed every Moment, as I found to my Coft. He was perpetually at my Side, and would never be a Minute out of my Sight : And as it is a certain Truth, that *the Part which is the moft ftrained, and pulled at moft in Earneft, never fails to break in Time* ; fo I, unable to endure it any longer, plucked up a Refolution, and firmly determined to fet my-felf at Liberty, even if I loft my Life in the Attempt, and give one Pufh, to try if Fortune, who had turned her Wheel fo much to my Damage, would affift me at the laft Pinch.

One Night, after I had lain down in my Bed, with my Hufband and my little Son, my Thoughts wholly taken up with the Indignities I underwent, my Heart ready to burft with Anger and Refentment, and, in fhort, in a very ill Humour, and in great Sufpence, I took a ftrong twifted Silk-Thread, which I bound as hard as poffibly I could, about the tender Leg of my beloved Child : The poor innocent Infant, whom I made fuffer for the Crimes of another, cryed out moft bitterly ; as it is faid, That *the Son fhall fometimes be punifhed for the Sins of his Parents who begot him.* His Father, who knew nothing of my Contri-

vance,

vance, was in great Trouble and Concern, and lay awake much longer than ordinary, the poor Child still crying; till, when the Night was about half spent, I softly loosened and took off the String from the harmless Babe's Leg, upon which he instantly was quiet, and both he and his Father closed their Eyes, and fell into a profound Sleep; but for my Part, I never once closed mine.

Resolving to be sure, I called my Husband Twice, to try whether he was asleep or awake; but finding he made me no Answer, I began to harbour some Hopes that my evil Destiny was weary of persecuting me, and intended to afford me some Respite. So that, when I perceived all was safe, I leaped out of the Bed, as if it had been all on a Flame, and just ready to be reduced to Ashes; when taking a Cord I had prepared, I tyed it round my Body, and, fastening the other End between Two of the Parapets on the Top of the Tower in the Castle, I let my self down from thence, by Degrees, and with a great deal of Silence and Caution, till I had fixed my Feet upon the Ground; which I had scarce touched, when immediately I loosened myself and took the Way towards my Father's House with incredible Swiftness. After the same Manner as doth a Bird, which hath escaped out of a Net or Snare, who hath no sooner got loose, but away he flies with much greater Velocity than at other Times, just so did I; and soon reached our House; where, when I arrived, I was very joyfully received, and set up an inviolable Resolution never again to return to *Uchiachate*'s intolerable and detested Yoke: Nor will I ever return to him again, tho' the whole Earth and all its Powers should conspire and combine together to compel me to it.

" Now, dear *Almutalib*, I desire you to repeat all
" you have heard from my Mouth to your Brother,
" that he may be fully apprized of all my Misfortunes;
" and that, as he is going to have the Remnant of
" my once so unhappy Days within his Power, he
" may

" may take Care to make Amends for what I
" have already suffered; and that he may ever have
" the Cataſtrophe of that wretched Union freſh in
" his Memory, and may be better both in his Be-
" haviour, Treatment and Conditions, than that my
" firſt Huſband; and may ſo order it, that when
" he hath me in his Power, the continual Jarrings
" and Uneaſineſs I then underwent, may be changed
" into Concord and Unity, as I flatter myſelf with
" the Confidence of finding with him. "

Here *Salma* concluded her Diſcourſe, and *Almutalib*
took his Leave, and returned to his Brother, to whom
he related all he had heard, at the which he was
highly ſurprized. That very Night the Nuptials were
conſummated with exceeding great Joy, to the mutual
Satisfaction of thoſe Two illuſtrious Lovers: And the
more exquiſite was *Haſhem*'s Joy, becauſe, on that
ſame Night, the *Light* paſſed away from him to *Salma* (through the Permiſſion and immenſe Goodneſs
of God) which was the Thing he moſt of all deſired
and languiſhed for: So that in the Morning, the Bride
was known to have conceived with a Male Branch of
the pure and immaculate *Light*, which was the Banner
or Blazon of the Heir-Male of that *Choſen Lineage*.

C H A P.

˙ C H A P. XIV.

*Hashem's excessive Joy at his Bride's Conception.
Prepares to take a Journey. His Discourse
with her before his Departure. His Speech to his
Brethren, &c. at his taking his Leave ; with his
Charge to them. Appoints his Brother Almutalib to Officiate in his Absence. He sets out.
Arrives at Axem, where he buys abundance of
rich Things for Salma. Being ready to return, he
falls dangerously ill. His Speech to his Friends
and Followers. His Letter to his Brothers and
Sisters at Mecca. His Death and Burial. The
Cavalcade of Mourners return to Yathrib. Their
sorrowful Procession. Are met by Salma and
great Numbers of People, with inexpressible Grief
and Lamentation. Salma's sad Complaints.
The universal Mourning that was made for Hashem's Death, especially at Mecca, upon the
reading his Letter. Abdolmutalib is born.*

IN the Morning, when *Hashem* found that
the *Light* of the Sacred Homage was
gone from him, and had passed away to
his Bride, he conceived the greatest Joy
and Satisfaction he ever had in the
Course of his whole Life before ; seeing
he had now begot an Heir and Successor of the Number
of

of the *Elected?* And that he might acquit himself of the Promifes he had made, and the Obligation he was under to his dear and deferving Spoufe, he made Preparations to go and take a Journey, in order to purchafe for her the Pearls, Jewels and Apparel which of Right belonged to her. Before his Departure, he called her afide into a private Appartment, and, in a moft affectionate and tender Manner, fpake to her in thefe Words;

"My deareft and moft beloved Spoufe! Give Ear
" to what I am about to fay unto you, which I fpeak
" with all Honour and Deference due to your great
" Merit. The Child you have conceived in your
" Womb, is a moft Holy and Beatified Male-Child;
" and whom I recommend to your Care, in the fame
" Manner as *Adam* recommended his Off-fpring, and
" as his After-Pofterity have ever fince continued to
" do, from Father to Son, with the utmoft Caution
" and Regard. If it fhall fo happen, that you are de-
" livered of him in my Abfence, I charge you, that
" you have the fame Care for him, as you have
" for the *Light of your Eyes.* Be mindful, my Dear,
" he hath many Enemies: Depend upon it, thofe
" perfidious Traytors the *Jews,* bear him a mortal
" Hatred; *for the Enemies of the Father, will, affured-*
" *ly, be fo to the Son likewife.* When he is grown up
" paft his Childhood, fend him, under the Protection
" of his Uncles, to the ancient and noble City of
" *Mecca,* the Seat of his Anceftors, the Abode of all
" his Friends and Kindred, and the Source from
" whence he deriveth his Honour, and which is his
" Patrimony and rightful Inheritance. I conjure you,
" *Salma,* That you never deviate, in one fingle Tittle,
" from this my Injunction; in the punctual Obfer-
" vance whereof, you will infallibly do what is plea-
" fing in the Sight of the Almighty Lord, and give
" me the higheft Satisfaction.

Salma replyed; " I fhall moft willingly obey you
" in all you have enjoyned me, exactly according to
" your

" your Defire, and I folemnly promife you it fhall
" be punctually performed; and although, with your
" Words and Proceedings, you have ftrangely furpri-
" zed and difturbed my Thoughts, yet I truft in God
" you will return again in Safety.

Prefently after this, *Hafhem* called together his Brothers and Kinfmen, and began to admonifh them
with Expreffions of the moft fincere Love and Friendfhip; and, in fuch a Manner, as if he had abfolutely
forefeen, that it would be the laft Advice he fhould
ever give them: *And it is a Token of the greateft Prudence in any one who hath the Fore-knowledge of his approaching End, to fettle Affairs for the Time to come
as if his laft Hour was actually arrived.*

" O Sons of *Abdulmenaf*, faid he, my Brothers, my
" Kinfmen, and my deareft Friends! upon whofe
" Shoulders refteth the great Charge of cultivating
" and propagating the Sacred Worfhip of the True
" Divinity: You are very fenfible, that Death is the
" common and univerfal Road by which all Crea-
" tures that have once breathed the Breath of Life,
" muft indubitably pafs: The Old, the Young, and
" the Infant, muft, of neceffity, tafte the Bitternefs
" thereof; Emperors and Kings, Peafants and Beg-
" gars, It is a Lot whereof every one muft partake,
" without any Exception of Perfons; for, when the
" Hour is come, All are indifpenfibly obliged to fub-
" mit to the fatal Stroke.——— I am now going to
" leave you, and am uncertain whether or no His
" Divine Majefty, in this my intended Journey,
" will think fit to ordain, that I fhall be removed from
" this Life to the next; wherefore, I recommend unto
" you Peace, Concord and Brotherly Love. Be hof-
" pitable and liberal in your Houfes, and charitably
" affift and comfort the Poor and the Diftreffed. Let
" there be no Divifions nor Animofities among you,
" but be unanimous in your Councils; for, if you
" cherifh an inviolable Union among yourfelves, you
" will be refpected and revered above Kings and
" Monarchs.

" Monarchs. It is my Will and Defire, that my
" dearly beloved Brother *Almutalib*, be inftituted to
" officiate in my Name and Station, during my Ab-
" fence ; he being qualified and highly worthy of that
" Dignity : And, if I happen to die, I charge you
" to inftall him, and to put into his Poffeffion
" my whole Eftate and Dominions ; Refpect and
" Honour him in my Name, and deliver up to him
" the Keys of *Mecca*, of the Temple, and of the Holy
" Relicks ; give him the Keys of the Council-Chamber,
" and of all the Archives ; give into his Poffeffion the
" Banner of *Ægypt*, the ancient Shoes, and the Bow of
" *Ifhmael* ; and, in fine, the whole Patrimony which
" I inherited from my Father. Do, in all Refpects, as
" I have enjoyned you ; And, as I intirely confide in
" you, I charge you, above all Things, That you
" have particular Care and Regard of the Infant
" *Salma* fhall bring forth, who will prove a very
" eminent and famous Man ; and that when he ar-
" riveth to Years of Maturity, you deliver up into
" his Poffeffion every individual Article, in the fame
" Manner as I now deliver the fame, and recommend
" all to your Management ; it being his undoubted
" Right, and, in Juftice, belonging unto him. "——
This they all unanimoufly promifed to fee punctually
performed, tho' they were very much troubled at his
Difcourfe ; *for it generally happeneth, That the Hearts
of Men are apt to be touched and difturbed at fuch
Prophetick and Ominous Arguments, as if they portended
fome approaching Evil.*

After thefe Difcourfes had paffed between them,
Hafhem, with Joy and Serenenefs in his Countenance,
took his Leave, and departed from *Yathrib* : He was
accompanied in this Journey by feveral noble Per-
fonages of his own chufing, befides a numerous Train
of Menial Servants and Followers, who conftantly
attended upon him where-ever he went.

With this Retinue he arrived at *Axem*, where he
bought all Things neceffary : He purchafed a great
Quantity

Quantity of very rich and coftly Garments, and all
the fineft Curiofities he could find ; and when all was
in a Readinefs, and depofited in perfumed Chefts, and
every Thing in proper Order for his Departure and
Return Home (which he intended to do early the next
Morning) it pleafed the Divine Majefty, that his Intents fhould be fruftrated, and that he fhould there
end his Days ; for fo it was Written ; That was his
Deftiny, and his Hour was come : And as he was gone
to Bed in order to take his Reft, he was wounded with
that fatal and conclufive Stroke, whereof every Living-
Creature muft indifpenfibly partake.

When he found himfelf oppreffed with an exceffive
and mortal Pain, he caufed all thofe of his Retinue
who had accompanied him thither, to be affembled together about him ; to whom he faid ; " I charge you
" all to depart from hence, and let nothing detain
" you here any longer ; for moft certain it is, that I
" am a dead Man, and my Time of Life is compleat-
" ed : You fhall be the Meffengers of my Death ; for
" the Divine Decrees of the Almighty muft be accom-
" plifhed, when and where He pleafeth, nor is His
" Sacred Will to be contradicted. O how true is
" that Prophetick Saying of Old, That *One Friend*
" *fhall be parted from another !* Happy is he who
" breathes his Laft among his deareft Friends and
" Relations, in his own Houfe, where he is cherifhed
" and affifted by All!

His Friends and Companions omitted nothing they
could fay to comfort him, though they were all exceedingly overwhelmed with Sorrow to behold him in
that Condition, he being extremely beloved and refpected by all in general ; and, notwithftanding the many
preffing Arguments he ufed, he could never prevail
with any one of them all to leave him, they being
fully determined to ftay till they had feen the definitive Gafp of their beloved Prince. —— He paffed the
whole Night in a perfect Agony, and, at Break of Day,
he, with a very weak and faint Voice, called for

Pen

Pen, Ink and Paper, and as he lay upon the Bed, so much spent that he could scarce support himself, he, with a trembling Hand, wrote the following short Letter.

HASHEM's LETTER to his Brothers, &c.

TO You, my Brethren of the Elected Tribe, in these Lines I now write, I send my Wishes for your Health and Salvation. I give you hereby to understand, That as I was ready to take my Journey, in order to return to you, the Command of the Most High Lord was sent me, whose Holy Pleasure it is, That I go and appear before the Tribunal of His most strict Justice; That I bid Farewell to this World, and to all its Vanities, Snares and bewitching Allurements: And seeing that Life and Death are at the Disposal of the Almighty Creator, and that every Mortal must, indispensibly, appear before His Judgment Seat, His Holy Decree must be obeyed, both here and in every other Place whatsoever.

I herewith send you my Worldly Goods to be divided amongst you; and I remit to your honourable, just and impartial Direction, all my other Affairs in general. My Daughters I recommend to your Care, confiding, that you will rank them in the Number of your own Children: And, when they are Marriageable, fail not to procure suitable Matches for them, with no less Candour than if they were your own. Deliver from me my tenderest Remembrance and Salutation to her, who, in this Life, was the Lamp and the Light of mine Eyes, the Joy of my Heart, and my greatest Regale: I beg of you, for the Love of God, if I ever deserved any Favour at your Hands, That you visit and comfort her, oftner, or with more Affection, than if I had been Living: Call to mind, That she beareth in her Womb my Son and your Nephew;

and

*and who is endowed with that Light which is the honour-
able Blazon of your illustrious Name, and whom I recommend to your Love and Protection; and since he hath
the Misfortune to become an Orphan before he is born,
and to be deprived of the Knowledge of his Father, let
him find a Father in the Love and Protection of his
Uncles; and when he is past his Childhood, remove him
from Yathrib, and take him under your own Care.*

When he had concluded this Epistle, with the tenderest and most moving Expressions, he, with a profound Sigh, folded it up, and sealed it with his usual
Signet: He then desired his Friends to assist him to
lie down, being unable to help himself. His Spirits
were quite spent and exhausted, his Strength gone,
a cold Sweat followed, and the last Agonies of Death
were upon him; whereupon, with the utmost Hū-
mility, Contrition and Resignation, lifting up his
Eyes towards Heaven, he said; " Have Mercy, O
" Lord, upon this thy helpless Servant, if it be thy
" Holy Will, for the Merit of that Sacred *Light* of
" thy *Elected Messenger* (the most Excellent of all
" who ever drew, do draw, or ever shall, the Breath
" of Life) which I have borne so long upon my Fore-
" head! " And when he had uttered these Words,
he was seized with his last Convulsion, and *Azarael*,
the Angel of Death, took Possession of that holy and
immaculate Spirit.

His Body was taken Care of, had all due Rites performed to it, and afterwards Interred, by his Friends
who accompanied him in that Journey, in the best
and most decent Manner that they were able; and
when his Funeral Obsequies were over, they packed
up all the Baggage, mounted the Slaves which had
been bought, and directed their Way towards *Yathrib*
with the greatest Expedition, and most visible Signs of
Sorrow appearing on every Countenance.

When

When *Salma* was apprized of their Coming, she, not knowing of *Hashem*'s Death, caused all Things to be ready prepared, and went out a great Way, with a numerous Train of Followers, to meet and receive *Hashem* and his Company: But as the Two Cavalcades came within Sight of one another upon the Plain, the Band of Mourners began to manifest their Grief, and what Cause they had for it. They rent their Garments, tore their Faces with their Nails, and approached with a general Weeping and Lamentation; the neighbouring Mountains resounded, in sorrowful Ecchoes, with their loud and repeated Outcries of unfeigned Sorrow. The very Horses, Mules and Camels seemed to sympathize, and to be affected with the same universal Mourning; their Fore-tops, Manes and Tails being all cut off, and, as an additional Token of the great Reason they had to weep and lament, as likewise to render the mournful Procession the more solemn and melancholy, each loaded Beast had one of *Hashem*'s Garments exposed to view, and spread over the Burden he carried. All this, with the dolorous Cries and Complaints of the whole Cavalcade, who, at every Step they made, repeated and called upon the Name of their deceased Prince, made a most dismal and moving Scene.

But who is able, in a succinct Manner, to form a true and intelligible Idea of the racking Sentiments, the anxious Doubts and Fears of *Salma* and her Followers, who were waiting with Impatience, to know the real Meaning of that dismal Scene of Horror and Despair, that was coming towards them? Or, what Words can be used to express the Perturbation of Thought, the excessive Uneasiness of Mind, the Agitation of Soul, which must rend the impatient Breast of that tender Lady, from Moment to Moment, at such an Object? How cruel must her boding Fears be! She, who had made such mighty Preparations for Mirth and Rejoicing! She, who had caused so plentiful a Store of the

rarest

rareft Dainties to be provided! Who had already fpread fo many Tables with moft exquifite Viands, and had invited fo great a Number of noble and honourable Friends and Relations, as Guefts, to be Partakers of a joyful Feaft, and to honour the fafe Return of her Hufband! And now, to think that all her Joy muft be changed into Sorrow, Mourning and Funeral Obfequies! *Though it is meet, that one who was the Center of Honour whilft Living, fhould be likewife honoured at his Death.*

When the fatal Tydings were (alas! but too foon) brought to the Ears of the fufpenfeful *Salma,* the Extremity of her Grief is not to be expreffed, without infpiring the Soul with the moft feeling Sentiments of Horror and Compaffion: Sitting upon the cold Earth, fhe cruelly abufeth and disfigureth her beautiful Face with mercilefs Blows, tearing her Flefh with her Nails, a Sight moft lamentable to behold! inflicting upon her lovely Perfon, a moft deplorable Martyrdom, exalting her Voice in forrowful Outcries, faying; "Alas, *Hafhem!* Alas! my deareft Lord and "Friend! The only Light of her who adored Thee! "My fole Delight! Where art Thou? Where haft "thou abfented thyfelf from me? From her who had "centered her very Soul, her whole Being in Thee! "In the extinguifhing thy Name, the Light of all "the Plains is extinguifhed! I am now deprived of "all my Comfort, my Joy and my Sanctuary! "Who will now be the other Half, the Companion "and the Safeguard of thy beloved Wife? Who muft "now be the tender Father, the faithful Protector of "thy unhappy wretched Son? Alas! Alas! Woe, "Woe is me!

Her Sorrow and Defpair were fo exceffive, and fhe took on, wept and lamented to fuch a Degree of Extremity, that the beft Method can be taken, upon this Subject, is to break off the Thread of the Defcription;

X 2

for

for the Tongue is never capable of expressing the true Sentiments of an unfeigning and sincere Heart.

But what shall we say of *Mecca*, when the doleful News was carried to his Brothers and Sisters, his Kinsmen and his Friends ? How shall we delineate the Impatience of his Daughters? Or how shall we express the sorrowful Lamentations they incessantly uttered ? How can we paint the terrible Confusion, the Emotions, the Swoonings and Agitations of Soul which were felt, the Heart racking Groans, the Sighs and Sobs which were heard at every Syllable, while the Letter, which contained his last Words and Testament, was reading? A Scene truly moving, and not to be described.

When the Excess of Weeping and Grief was somewhat abated, they put *Almutalib* into the Possession of the Government, according as *Hashem* had appointed. A Hero well worthy of such a Charge. Amidst all this Sorrow and Mourning, it pleased the Almighty to send his Divine Comfort and Assistance ; *for Misfortunes never come without some Alleviation.* For in those Days of Mourning *Salma* was delivered of a young Prince, endowed with the Mysterious *Light*, who was observed to come into the World laughing, giving certain Tokens of Rejoicings and great Benefits which would accrue to Mankind from the Birth of one of the most eminent amongst the Lord's *Elected.* He was born with the Hair of his Head quite grey, from whence he had the Surname of (*a*) *Jaibacanas* given

---

(*a*) This Surname, I presume, is compounded of Two Words, one *Arabick* and the other *Spanish*, and is peculiar to the *Spanish Moors.* —— *Sh-yeb* in *Arabick*, is the same as *Canas* in *Spanish*, both signifying Gray-Hairs: And as the *Spanish* Alphabet has no Letter or Letters equivalent to the *Arabick Shin*, or our *Sh*, they some-

given him. He proved a moſt notable and worthy Champion ; and it is, by no means, proper, that the famous Deeds and Atchievements of ſo illuſtrious a Perſonage ſhould remain in Oblivion: Wherefore, I deſire, that, whilſt I rehearſe them, I may be heard with Attention.

ſometimes uſe the *X*, and ſometimes the *Ƒ,* to ſupply that De-feƈt, though very imperfeƈtly. ———— The Perſon here meant, is *Abdolmutzlib*, or, as many call him, *Abdolmotbleb*, Father to *Ab-dillah*, and Grand-Father to the Falſe Prophet. He is mentioned by Dr. *Prideaux* and many others.

CHAP. XV.

The HISTORY *of* Abdolmutalib.

Abdolmutalib's Education at Yathrib. *He is hated by the* Jews. *His promising Infancy. His Uncle* Almutalib *persuades him to escape from* Yathrib. *They are pursued and overtaken by the* Jews, *who came with Intent to murder them. Almutalib's Concern and Apprehension. The Child's Prayer, and wonderful Courage and Resolution. Miraculous Instances of the* Light. *The hypocritical Speech of the Captain of the* Jews. *They are disheartned by the Child's Valour, who kills Four of their stoutest Men. Almutalib challenges the Enemy to single Combat,* &c. Salma, *with her Father,* &c. *arrive, and destroy all the* Jews.

Bdolmutalib was brought up in the ancient and noble City of *Yathrib,* under the Tuition of his Mother, who was exceedingly careful of his Education, causing him to be instructed, by learned Masters, in good and pious Doctrine. As it was no-wise practicable, or indeed proper, to conceal

ceal one of his high and illuftrious Defcent, he was foon known; and became an intolerable Eye-fore to the malicious and perfidious *Jews*, who all bore him a mortal and implacable Hatred; according to that well known Rule, That *Averfion generally becomes Hereditary; whereas Friendfhip is oftner feen to increafe than to diminifh.*

He was fcarce arrived to his Seventh Year, when the bare Mention of his Name ufed to make them tremble; and the leaft of his Infant Actions would ftrike them with Terror; fo great was his Fame; and fo dreadful was the *Light* of his Countenance to them, that the very Thoughts of *it* confumed their Vitals. Whereever he went, he would ftill be faying out aloud, *I am the Son of* Hafhem; *I am the Heir of the* Elected Tribe! This, this was their greateft Abomination; This was what they abhorred; and infomuch, that they always fought to take away his Life, whenever they heard him utter thofe Words.

It chanced one Day, that a certain Inhabitant of *Mecca*, paffing by where he was at play, and taking particular Notice of his extraordinary Beauty, and of fome Expreffions he ufed, came up to him, and calling him afide, faid; " I intreat you to tell me, Child, who " you are, and from whom you are defcended? " *Ab-dolmutalib*, with great Courtefy, readily returned him a fatisfactory Anfwer, and told him his own Name, and that of his Father, with fome Account of the Houfes to which he owed his Birth: And being given to underftand, that the Perfon who was fo curious in his Concerns, was a Native and Inhabitant of *Mecca*, he went on thus; " Since, Sir, your Occafions or " Chance, have brought you this Way, I beg you " deliver this Meffage to my illuftrious Uncles: Afk " them, as from me, How it hath come to pafs, that " in fo fhort a Time, the Memory of their Brother

" *Hafhem* is forgotten? For what Reafon are all thofe
" Things he recommended to their Care, fo foon
" banifhed from their Thoughts? Why have they fo
" foon abandoned and forgot me? Why have they left
" me here, fo folitary, in the midft of this wicked
" Generation of People, my mortal and inveterate
" Enemies? Why am I kept fo far from my own
" rightful Country, an unhappy folitary Orphan,
" without knowing my Relations and Friends, or
" ever feeing the Place of their Abode? And fo may
" the Lord affift and comfort you under all your
" Troubles, as you will oblige and comfort me in de-
" livering this my Meffage, without fail, as foon as
" you reach *Mecca*; Forget not, I befeech you, but
" rather commiferate my lonefome and forlorn Con-
" dition.

The Man failed not to carry the Meffage faithfully,
as he had been defired; and the very next Day *Almutalib*
prepared himfelf to depart for *Yathrib*, mounted upon
an exceeding fwift Horfe, his good Sabre girt at his
Side, which Weapon he fo well knew how to manage,
whenever he had Occafion to make ufe of it: His
Buckler he carried upon his left Arm, and at the
Pummel of his Saddle hung the Bow of the ftrong and
mighty *Ifhmael*, which belonged now to him, as left
him by his deceafed Brother *Hafhem*. [This *Almutalib*
was the fame who for his Heroick Actions had gained
fuch high Renown in all Parts, that where-ever his
Name reached, his Sword was revered and trembled
at.] He concealed part of his Face, by wreathing one
Turn of his Turbant acrofs it, to prevent his being
known, if he fhould chance to meet any who had feen
him before; and becaufe he was firmly refolved to
carry off his Nephew, either by Stealth or by Force,
either peaceably or otherwife, as he could bring it
about; but he was fully determined not to return
without him.

He

He ſoon arrived at his Journey's End, and was going into the City ; but ſeeing a Company of young Lads playing without the Gate, he went aſide to look upon them. They were exerciſing themſelves at ſeveral different Games, and making Tryals of their Strength and Activity, and among them was his Nephew *Abdolmutalib*, who, among other Proofs of his Strength he had been ſhewing with his Companions, was now very intent in throwing a heavy Quoit, to ſee who could caſt it fartheſt.

As *Almutalib* came near him, he ſoon perceived and knew the Hereditary Blazon of the *Light* upon the Countenance of his Nephew, at the Sight of which he rejoiced exceedingly ; but more when he heard him, every Time he caſt the Quoit from him, ſay ; *Now, Son of* Haſhem, *Lord of the Holy City!*

Almutalib beckoned him aſide, and with tender Words and Careſſes made himſelf known to him, and told him the Cauſe of his Coming. " Conſider, ſaid " *Almutalib*, whether or no you are willing to go along " with me to the Place of your Anceſtors Abode, and " to live among your own Kindred, in your own Seat " and Principality, which, for ſo many Ages, was " poſſeſſed by your illuſtrious Predeceſſors ; and which " the Almighty hath ordained for the Throne of their " Male-Poſterity : Think now, my beloved Kinſman, " what you intend to reſolve upon ; for I am come " from *Mecca* upon no other Account but this.

Like unto an Arrow out of a Bow, or a Falcon that waits for the Signal to fly at his Game, ſo this vigorous and generous Youth, hearing the ſo long wiſhed-for Signal from his Uncle's Mouth, without anſwering one Syllable, leaped up behind him with an incredible Agility, ſaying ; " Slack your Reins, " Uncle, and ſpur away ! Let us get from among " theſe People, before my Mother hath Notice of my " Departure, who may, otherwiſe, prevent it !" And ſo they fled away upon the Horſe, with all imaginable Speed.

Al-

Almutalib was overjoyed to find that his Expedition had fucceeded fo profperoufly, and that he had been able fo eafily to bring off his Nephew, who was dearer to him than his own felf. They arrived, about Sunfet, at a Place called *Delhuilefata*, where they refted themfelves, and took a little Refrefhment, being very much fatigued ; and when it was dark they advanced up into the Mountain, intending to take that Way, to avoid meeting any who might obftruct their Journey. But as they were proceeding on very cautioufly, and thought themfelves the moft fecure and freeft from Danger, they heard a very great Noife of Voices, as of many Men talking and hallowing loudly to one another : This made them ftop to fee if they could difcover what it was ; and they were foon convinced that the Voices approached nearer and nearer, and that they were purfued clofe at the Heels.

Almutalib was in a great Concern, and faid ; " My " dear Nephew, what fhall we do in this Cafe ? Where " fhall we hide ourfelves ? This *Light* which Heaven " hath influenced upon your Forehead, will infallibly " difcover us ! My much honoured Uncle, faid *Abdolmutalib*, if you would have my *Light* concealed, " cover my Face with my Turbant, and that will " hide it. " *Almutalib* did fo ; but the more he endeavoured to conceal it, the more it appeared, and the Rays fhone out but fo much the brighter, and difplayed their Splendor more than ever.

When *Almutalib* beheld this wonderful Myftery, he was greatly furprized, and faid ; " This is certain" ly very prodigious, Nephew ! I fee no Method how " to hide this cœleftial *Light*, the Lord hath been " pleafed to endow thee with ! But He who hath ho" noured thee therewith, will be our Guide, our Pro" tector, and our Redeemer ; to Him alone I recom" mend thee ; He will affuredly blefs and deliver " thee.

Al-

Almutalib had no fooner faid this, but they difcovered, at a Diftance, a confiderable Troop of Horfe-
men, armed at all Points. They all along concluded
that thofe who had purfued them were the Troops of
the Nobility and Cavaliers who belonged to the illuftrious Family of *Salma*, who had conftantly a great
Number of their Relations, befides many others, who
having their whole Dependance upon them, were
always ready upon any Occafion that offered; and
that they were now come on Purpofe to carry back
Abdolmutalib to his Mother: But that illuftrious Youth,
who knew them all perfectly well, foon perceived how
greatly they had been miftaken in their Conjectures;
and turning towards his Uncle, faid; " Thefe are
" very bad Signs! There is fome Treachery going
" forwards. It is quite different from what we ima-
" gined, and even much worfe, if well confidered.
" We have been all this while in the Dark; for, if my
" Eyes deceive me not, thefe we fee making towards
" us, are my Enemies, who are come to feek me
" out: This is not the firft Time they have fought
" my Life, having made many Attempts to get rid
" of me.

The good *Almutalib* was very much terrified at
thefe Words of his Nephew, fcarce knowing what
Courfe to take. His Concern for his own Life was
nothing in Comparifon to his Apprehenfions for that
of the beloved Child. He could not refrain from weeping bitterly, when he beheld his tender promifing Youth,
and that refplendent beautiful Countenance, the *Light*
whereof caft its Rays up to the Skies; and feeing
him, almoft, in the Midft of fo many of his moft mortal Enemies, from whom there was no Probability of
efcaping, he quite loft his Courage, and utterly de-
fpaired of being able to prevent their Fate. He, in this
Agony, turned to him, putting his Arm round his
Neck, and kiffing him *between the Eyes*, faid; " My
" dearoft Child! Had I had the leaft Notice or Sufpi-
" cion

" cion of thy being ſo purſued and perſecuted by thoſe
" baſe Wretches, who bear thee ſuch an inveterate
" Hatred, I would never have brought thee from
" *Yathrib :* But, I proteſt to thee, in the Preſence of
" the Eternal God, That thou ſhalt behold my Body
" extended here upon the Earth, all diſmembred and
" hacked in Pieces, before I will ſuffer one ſingle Drop
" of thy Blood to be ſpilt." "Take Courage my
" generous Uncle, replied the Youth, be not diſmayed
" nor afflicted: With God's Aſſiſtance I intend to ſur-
" prize you, with letting you ſee, yet before Morning,
" what your Brother's Son can do." And then they
were ſilent for a while, and continued looking upon
each other, till at length the Enemies were come up
very cloſe to them.

El Haſſan tells us, That the Occaſion of their coming out upon this Expedition, was the Report given
by thoſe Boys who were contending with *Abdolmutalib,*
about throwing the Quoit or Bar; and who having
heard the Words had paſt between the Uncle and the
Nephew, and had ſeen them ride away ſo faſt, had
carried the News to their Fathers, and this being
ſpread about among the malicious *Jews,* they had,
that ſame Night, mounted Seventy armed Men of
their Tribe, and had ſent them out in queſt of them,
with the Blood-thirſty View of accompliſhing what
they had been ſo long hatching with ſuch treacherous
Eagerneſs; I mean to find *Abdolmutalib* in a convenient Place, where, by taking away his Life, they
might revenge themſelves and ſatiate the implacable
Hatred and Rage they had againſt the *Prophetick
Light.*

They imagined now they were arrived at their
ſo much deſired Point; ſo they made their Approach,
all mounted upon light Horſes, with large Lances advanced in their Right Hands, with Targets on their
Left Arms, and, in fine, armed at all Points: And, to
cn-

encounter all these Arms, so much Hatred and so much Fury, a Child, a naked and unarmed Child sallies out; an Infant, who hath scarcely seen his Tenth Year; a true Emblem of the Great *David* when he went forth to encounter with the Haughty *Goliah*! He slipt away from his Uncle, whom he left weeping, and went a considerable Way towards those vile Traytors to meet them, with surprizing Courage and Intrepidity: But before they came up to him, he lifted up his Eyes towards Heaven, and, with great Humility, thus addressed himself to God to deliver them.

The Child's PRAYER.

O LORD, *by whose radiant Rays the most intense Obscurities are illuminated! Thou, who dost influence Thy Light into all who worship and adore Thee, with a contrite Spirit! All-wise Monarch, who penetratest into the profoundest Recesses of every Heart, and discoverest the most hidden Secrets; for to Thee nothing can be a Secret! Thou, who hearest all who call upon Thee in their greatest Afflictions! Thou, who art the only Succourer in Time of Need; the Accepter and Receiver of our Endeavours; the Regulater and Distributer of all the Blessings and Mercies Thy Creatures enjoy; Since nothing can advance or recoil one Tittle, but according to Thy Divine Decree! If, in Thy unsearchable Judgment, Thou hast any peculiar Regard to (a) this distinguish-*

(a) Alluding to the *Prophetick Light,* pretended to be Hereditary in that Family.

ing

ing Mercy which Thy Elected ever have, and still do enjoy; I supplicate Thy most immense Bounty, That, at this Juncture, Thou wilt not permit that Branch of it, which I possess, to be extinguished; my own Strength being so inconsiderable, and so little capable of defending it: But, I intreat Thee rather, that my Force may be augmented with a double Portion of that Grace, wherewith Thou hast already illustrated and adorned me; and, that Thy Light, in me, may be exalted higher than ever it hath been hitherto. Lord! for the Sake of this precious Blazon of Thy Sacred Light, wherewith Thou hast Sealed my Forehead, and with which inestimable Ornament Thou hast ennobled me, I beseech Thee to protect and defend me from these faithless, cowardly Traytors, whose Design is to extinguish this Light, because they are ignorant of its high Value. But since I know that every wrathfully armed Hand must yield before Thine, and that the most formidable Powers must fall prostrate at the Mention of Thy Name, Why should I be afraid of those who have presumptuously dared to lift up their impious Arms, with infernal Fury, to offend Thy Majesty? If in me, therefore, Lord, Thou hast deposited any secret Mystery that is of Importance, or beneficial to Mankind, and hast distinguished me from others, as this Blazon seemeth to signify, I, once more, intreat Thee, for its Sake, that Thou wilt strengthen and assist me in this Extremity; and so, that those who attempt to destroy it, may be made sensible of Thy Power; and that the direful Scourge of the Infernal Caverns may fall upon them: For it is Thou who throwest down the Proud into the Deep Abysses, and exaltest the Meek and Humble; whom Thou rewardest with Diadems!

Great

Great God! cried out *Almutalib*, who, at that very Moment, beheld those base Cowards dart a whole Volley of Lances at his beloved Nephew. But, as a Ball, when forcibly struck against the Ground, reboundeth towards him who cast it; or if thrown against a Stone-Wall, flies off again; even so, and no otherwise, did those Lances recoil backwards towards their Perfidious Owners, piercing their Breasts, as if they had been returned by the Strength of vigorous Arms. They, astonished and quite confounded at this Prodigy, spurred on their Horses amain, thinking to take *Abdolmutalib* alive; but they only wounded the poor Horses to no purpose; for those Creatures, with their Necks drawn in, and their Manes and Fore-tops standing upright, snorting, trembling, wincing and raising themselves up an end, refused to stir a step forwards.

The magnanimous Youth, who had faced them all without the least Fear or Terror, beholding them so astonished and out of Countenance, called to them, in a loud Voice, saying: " Base, treacherous Infidels! Ac-
" curfed vile Miscreants! whose Dispositions more
" resemble Brutes, than Human Creatures! You in-
" famous abandoned Generation! What think you of
" the Mystery, wherewith God is pleased to forewarn
" you? This Mystery which serveth to exalt our *Light*,
" and to punish your most detestable Attempt? What!
" would you extinguish a *Light*, whose Center is fixed
" in Heaven, and which the Lord of all Power, out
" of His great Wisdom, hath ordained to be a Guide
" to His Servants, to abolish Idolatry and all false
" Worship, and is pleased Himself to protect with
" His All-powerful Hand? Would you destroy this?
" Dare you attempt it? Your Number is already
" considerably diminished by the Destruction of so
" many of you; Return, therefore, while you are well,
" and desist from these fruitless Chimæra's; other-
" wise I will supplicate my Creator to confound you
" all. "

To this, their Captain, whoſe Name was *Letia*, re-turned Anſwer: " O Son of the Mighty *Haſhem*; " deſiſt from this thy Obſtinacy ; for we are no wife " ſcrupulous to acknowledge the great Worth of the " Illuſtrious Houſe of *Abdulmenaf*, to which all the " Tribes and Nations pay ſuch Reſpect and Venera-" tion: But you are aſſuredly in the wrong to ima-" gine, as your Words ſeem to intimate, that our " coming from *Yatbrib* hither, was with the Intent of " deſtroying you. No, we came, ſent by thy Mother, " and at her earneſt Requeſt, to conduct thee in Safe-" ty back to her, that her Eyes may be rejoiced with " thy Preſence ; for ſhe is very ſorrowful and diſ-" conſolate at thy leaving her. Beſides, thou canſt " not be ignorant of the great Love and Friendſhip " we bear thee, and well knoweſt how courteous and " obliging we have all of us been to thee ; ſo that " thou haſt no manner of Reaſon to harbour any " ſuch Thought ; for we always looked upon thee as " our chiefeſt Joy, Comfort and Content: Thou art " the Light of our Eyes, my Dear, and the greateſt " Pleaſure of our Lives!" " It is well known, replied " the fearleſs Youth, That you are all my mortal " Enemies, and this your baſe treacherous Attempt " hath fully confirmed it: You always hated me, " and have ever looked upon me with an evil, de-" ceitful and hypocritical Eye, and you utter no-" thing but what is founded upon Lyes and Treachery, " ſeeing your perfidious Scheme hath proved abortive, " and not anſwerable to your Hopes and Expectations, " becauſe the Sacred Promiſes of the Almighty are " inviolable, and muſt be accompliſhed." Then, with a noble Diſdain, without the leaſt Sign of Fear or Concern, he turned away from them, and went to his Uncle, who was all the while an admiring Spe-ctator.

When the baſe *Jews* ſaw he had left them, they ſpeedily alighted from their Horſes, and with infer-nal Fury they drew out their mighty Sabres, run-ning

ning towards him, like hungry Wolves, to attack him. *Almutalib,* when he faw them coming, made ready for the Encounter, and was going to meet them, but was hindred by his Nephew, who held him by the Arm, faying: " Stay, Sir; Now you fhall be Eye-
" witnefs to a fecond Miracle; I befeech you to be
" quiet, and for the prefent only ftand ftill and look
" on: Give me your Bow and Quiver, and I'll affure
" you of the Victory." " You are far from being able,
" anfwered *Almutalib,* with your tender Arms and
" little Strength, to bend this Bow; for there is not
" one Man in all *Mecca,* or its Territories, who
" hath the Prefumption to attempt fhooting with it,
" except thofe of our Family, to whom it belongeth
" by Divine Ordinance: This is *Ifhmael's* Bow; your
" Father had it in his Life-time, and at his Death
" bequeathed it to me: With it, in droughty Seafons,
" we intercede for Rain, and many other Bleffings,
" in Cafes of Neceffity and Diftrefs, and which the
" Almighty, of His immenfe Bounty, never faileth to
" grant us." " Let me have it, then, faid *Abdol-*
" *mutalib,* for I being, likewife, a Branch of that
" noble Stock, have fome Right to that precious
" Relick; notwithftanding my want of Years, may
" feem to deny me that Privilege:" And taking it in his Hands, he bent it with fuch Force, that he made the Two Ends almoft meet together, and then ftrung it with as much Eafe, as the ftrongeft full-grown Man could have done, or as if the Bow had been made only of a green, pliable Switch.

The *Jews* were now approached very near them, when the dexterous Youth, fixing an Arrow in the Bow, took his Aim, and fent it into the Heart of him, who, among all the reft, feemed to be the proudeft and moft infolent, who immediately fell groveling on the Earth, yelling like a Salvage Beaft, and vomited out his impious Soul. And, without lofing Time, he took another, and after that another, and then a Fourth; all which he let fly with fuch admirable Dexterity

Z   and

and ſo ſure an Aim, that with each of thoſe Four Shafts he pierced one of their perfidious Breaſts, who lay yelling out their Vitals upon the Ground; and every Time he ſtretched the Bow and diſmiſſed the Arrow, he ſaid; *I am the Son of* Haſhem: *My Name is* Abdolmutalib.

When the Traytor *Letia* ſaw this, he ſaid; " This " verifieth the Proverb, " *The Serpent can produce nothing but venomous Vipers!* Then turning towards his Companions, " Degenerate, faint-hearted Wret- " ches! ſaid he; are you not aſhamed to let a Child " baffle your Strength and effeminate your Courage? " Let us pour in upon them all at once, and with " vigorous Impetuoſity, let us attack them in ſo " effectual a Manner, that they may not ſurvive " our Strokes; and if Ten of us ſhould happen to " fall by their Hands, with the Proviſo they fall " too, thoſe who are ſo fortunate among us as to " eſcape, will enjoy a glorious and honourable Life, " after the Death of our greateſt Enemy.

Thus ſpake that perfidious Enemy to God's Cauſe; And now they all form themſelves into a Body, in order to make the Onſet; but as they were advancing, their Courage began to ſlacken, being fearful of the Arrows, and not forgetting with what Force and Dexterity they had been before ſent amongſt them; They, therefore, upon ſecond Thoughts, determined rather, to try what they could do by way of Parley and Capitulation; when *Letia*, calling out to the un- daunted Youth, ſaid;

" Hear, O *Abdolmutalib*, what we have to ſay: As " you are truly valiant, generous, and magnanimous, " we intreat that you will, out of your innate Cour- " teſie, withold your Arm from ſhooting any more " of thoſe fatal Shafts, which you ſo, without Rea- " ſon, or Provocation, let fly amongſt us; and let " us conſult deliberately of the beſt and moſt whole- " ſome Means, that you may return Home with us. " Conſider, Deareſt Child, that it is an unſpeakable
" Grief

" Grief to us all, that you ſhould leave our Country;
" nor do we think ourſelves a little affronted and
" injured by your ſo doing. Remember, that you was
" born, and drew your firſt Breath amongſt us; and
" forget not, that all our Wives have been Nurſes to
" you; you have ſucked Milk out of their Breaſts,
" and have been bred up in their Laps: And is this
" the Return you make us, for all our Love and un-
" feigned Tenderneſs? Is this the Recompence where-
" with you reward us, for all the Pangs and Agonies
" we ſuffer upon your Account, and for your Sake?
" You have ſlain Four of our Company; Men of the
" greateſt Note and Conſideration of our whole
" Tribe; and yet we are all contented to ſit down
" with their Loſs, and to forget all that's paſt; as
" we would do had you killed as many more. Be
" ſatisfied, that we value you more, and have a
" greater Regard for your Intereſt and Content, than
" for all the Comforts, Pleaſures and Advantages of
" this Life. Take your Leave of your Uncle *Almuta-
" lib,* and let him depart on his Way in Peace, and
" wiſh him, as we ſincerely do, a good and proſ-
" perous Journey; and do you return back again with
" us to your own native Place, your ſafeſt Sanctuary,
" where you will paſs your Days in the higheſt Ho-
" nour and Eſteem, and the greateſt Satisfaction and
" Tranquility; and where it is but reaſonable you
" ſhould abide, were it only to avoid having the Sin
" to anſwer, of grieving the Souls of your tender Mo-
" ther, and indulgent Grand-father; and to baniſh
" the Sorrow, and tormenting Affliction of thoſe dear
" Parents, who are inconſolable at your cruel Abſence;
" but moſt of all, for your departing abruptly, with-
" out taking leave of them, without their Privacy or
" Conſent, or the Knowledge of any of your Relations.
" Did you but ſee, O unthinking, inconſiderate
" Youth! Could you but once behold the Torrents of
" Tears they pour out! How they rend and disfigure
" their Faces; or hear their pitiful Groans and

Z 2   " doleful

" doleful Lamentations! and how inceſſantly they
" call upon thy Name! It muſt needs move you to
" pity them. Come, therefore, my deareſt Child;
" pluck up your uſual and innate Courage, and de-
" termine (without farther Heſitation, but with a
" deliberate Conſideration of my Words) to do what
" is ſo very reaſonable for you to comply with; a
" Reſolution of Duty and Generoſity, ſo very worthy
" of finding a Place in a Breaſt ſo truly noble and
" generous as yours.

Theſe were the Words, and ſuch the Arguments,
and Propoſals that treacherous Hypocrite made uſe of;
and, had they been ſincere, were ſo pathetick and
moving, that *Almutalib* began to be under a Concern
leſt his Nephew ſhould waver, and, in reality, was
in pain, and doubtful of his Conſtancy; and, with
Tears in his Eyes, ſpoke to him thus;

" You well know, Child, That I undertook this
" Journey, from *Mecca*, hither, purely for your
" Sake, to induce you to go and take your Abode in
" your own rightful Seat and Patrimony, and enjoy
" it, as your Fore-Fathers have done, in a direct
" Line down to you: But hearing the plauſible Ar-
" guments theſe People uſe to make you alter your
" firſt Intent, the affectionate Expreſſions of Love
" and Sincerity they make you; the great Honour
" and Deference they give you; the mighty Eſteem
" in which you are held among them; and the Re-
" ſpect they ſeem to have for you, through the Know-
" ledge they have of your high Birth, Deſcent, Eſtate
" and Condition, I am at a Loſs to know what I
" ought to ſay! Yet if you are willing to return home
" again with them, go in God's Name, and under
" His Protection; and when you are arrived to Years
" of Maturity, you may then repair to *Mecca*, the
" ancient Seat of your Anceſtors; and whither, as it
" is the Abode of your whole Paternal Family, you
" are called by all the Ties of Conſanguinity." " How
" wrong are your Conjectures! ſaid *Abdolmuta-*
" *lib;*

" *lib*: How readily have you given Credit to the de-
" luding Words of thofe vile Wretches! Do not you
" know that they are *Jews*? a Generation of Infa-
" mous, bafe, fcandalous, accurfed, perfidious, degene-
" rate People, full of Falfity, Fraud and Deceit?
" Suffer not their fair Speeches to gain upon your
" Credulity, or to have any Effect upon your Imagi-
" nation; for there is not the leaft Truth in all they
" fay: They are the Servants and Companions of
" *Lucifer*, who are perpetually walking in his Paths.
" Let them begone from hence, therefore, and may
" the Curfe of God go along with them!

Almutalib, hearing his Nephew exprefs himfelf with
fuch Refolution, rejoiced exceedingly, and immediately made ready to give the Onfet; and covering
himfelf with his Shield, with his good Sabre drawn in
his right Hand, he advanced towards the Traytor
Letia: *So treads the Lion, when he finds himfelf in
Danger*: And fo, nor with lefs Intrepidity, did the
generous Worthy advance to meet the Hoftile Band;
when, exalting his Voice, calling out to *Letia*, he
faid;

" O Thou Hypocrite! who haft wafted and caft
" into the Air fo many fpecious Arguments, wrapt
" up in Perfidy and Diffimulation, Lies and Deceit!
" Defift from fpending any Time and Breath in Fal-
" fities, and Prevarications; and fee, if among you
" all, You have any that dare venture himfelf in
" fingle Combat with me, in order to bring thefe our
" mutual Pretenfions to a Conclufion: If any fuch
" there be, let him come out, for I am here in Ex-
" pectation; it being, in my Opinion, but reafon-
" able, That *what the Tongue is fo liberal in blazoning*,
" *fhould be made good by Actions*.

Letia then faid to his Followers; " You hear how
" we are challenged, and fet at Defiance by him,
" who is the moft famous and renowned Champion of
" his whole Tribe; by him, who is the chief Leader
" of the redoubted *Koreifhites*, who are the Flower of

" all

" all the *Arabian* Nobility; by him, who is held in
" ∫uch high E∫teem throughout the Three *Arabias,*
" and in all the Cities and Provinces around them;
" who hath no Equal, nor was yet any Man found
" able to with∫tand the Force of his invincible Arm.
" If we can but de∫troy him, his Nephew will then
" be in our Power, and that de∫tructive *Light* he is pof-
" ∫e∫∫ed of, may be extingui∫hed without Danger
" or Difficulty. Come on, renowned Warriors;
" Courage! I promi∫e to him who ∫hall deprive this
" dangerous Enemy of his Life, a Reward of One
" hundred young, flouri∫hing, * *Female* Date-Trees,
" as an Encouragement for his Bravery.

To this, one of the Company, who∫e Name was
Chemio, made An∫wer; " If I undertake this Combat
" again∫t our Enemy, and have the good Fortune to
" obtain the Victory, I ∫hall require no other Reward
" from you, but that you give me an Acquittance for
" the Debt I owe you. " " I am very well contented,
" replied the Traytor *Letia.* I will forgive you
" that Debt, and give you as much more. " Upon
this he went forth to encounter *Almutalib,* who ∫eeing
him coming, advanced to meet him; by who∫e
valiant Arm, the Infidel ∫oon lo∫t his mi∫believing
Life, being ∫plit down to his Brea∫t at one Stroke.

When *Letia* beheld this, he ∫aid; " *Chemio* is
" dead! Let another of our mo∫t valiant Warriors go
" out and try his Fortune. " Another did, and another; and by the ∫ame Means, ∫everal of their be∫t

---

* *Le mando cien Datileras, nuevas, tiernas, femininas.* —— The
Palm or *Date* Trees are Male or Female; as are likewi∫e the *Fig-
Trees.* The Female *Date-Trees* only bear the Fruit; for that which
the Male produces is not eatable. They commonly plant ∫ome Male
Trees among the Females, which makes them bear the better; and,
as an Eye-witne∫s, I can affirm, that the Female Trees always grow
∫omewhat crooked, if any Male ones are near them, ∫till bending
and inclining towards them: But upon tho∫e where none of the Male
ones are, the Owners hang ∫ome of the Fruit they bear; as they like-
wi∫e do to their Fig-Trees.

Men

Men loft their Lives. But one of them at laft, faid;
" *Letia*, this all carries a very ominous Appear-
" ance! Would you have us all Sacrificed, one by one,
" whilft you ftand by an idle, ufelefs Spectator? Go
" out yourfelf and encounter this Challenger, whom
" none but you amongft us all, is able to engage
" with; as we are, likewife, fenfible, that when he
" once feeleth the Force of your Arm, his Pride will
" be laid in the Duft, and our Strife will be at an
" End.

To this the treacherous *Letia* replied; " I would
" before this have undertook the Combat, without
" ftaying 'till I was told of it, had it not been for the
" Refpect I had for *Salma*, the Stripling's Mother;
" and that neither fhe, nor any of that Family,
" fhould have it to fay, that I had a Hand in killing
" her Son: But fince I perceive 'tis your Defire I
" fhould do it, and you think it neceffary, fuppofing
" the Victory dependeth upon me, I freely engage my-
" felf to go out and encounter this Boafter.

The Traytor then ftripped off his upper Garment,
and fhewed great Signs of an undaunted Refolution,
mixed with a difdainful, daring Haughtinefs. He
was a Man of the largeft Size and Stature, and his
ftrong-knit Limbs were inclofed in the fineft burnifhed
Steel; His left Arm bore a mighty Target, and his
right Hand carried a keen Sabre; the Belt whereof
was girded round his potent Loins, and the Scabbard
hung at his left Side. He feemed, in Agility, to exceed a wild Stag, and his very Afpect had fomething
which infpired Awe and Terror. As he approached,
he called out to *Almutalib*, faying; " Call your
" Nephew to come to your Affiftance, and that our
" Combat may be the fooner over; for I am refolved,
" you fhall both fall with the Edge of my Sword. "
" Call, rather, replied *Almutalib*, to your own
" cowardly Squadron of Scoundrels, to come and help
" to deliver you out of my Hands; for before the
Z 4 " Day

" Day appeareth, you shall every one of you be laid
" wallowing in your Blood upon the Ground."

Now the Two Combatants advanced one against
the other, and, at their Meeting, the Shock was so
violent, as if two Rocks had met together, so well
were they matched, and so equal their Strength. The
Blows they mutually dealt, were nothing inferior to
those of Smiths beating with their heavy Hammers upon
an Anvil, and with such equal Fury and Resolution,
that no Words are sufficient to describe this memorable
Encounter. The *Jews* encouraged one another, and,
with continual Shouts and Huzzaes, they animated
their valiant Leader; greatly wondering, that *Almu-*
talib was able to defend himself so long against him:
Whilst the magnanimous *Abdolmutalib* stood fuming
with Rage and Madness, to behold his noble Uncle,
a Man so renowned for Feats of Arms, so hardly put
to it; and to think, that any single Man should be
able to withstand him so long, and to make so notable
a Resistance, which several, with their united Forces
had never before been capable of doing; and not being
enough Master of himself to bridle his Passion a Moment longer, he fixed an Arrow in the Bow, bending
it with all his Might, and aiming at the perfidious
Letia, he let fly the Shaft with so great a Force, that
entering between his Shoulders, it passed down to his
Bowels.

When the *Jews* beheld him, who had so manfully
defended them, and upon whose Valour they wholly
relyed; When they saw him, I say, fall to the Ground
and expire, they were exceedingly enraged, and ga-
thering themselves all together in a Body, were coming
furiously to fall upon *Abdolmutalib*, and to dispatch
him; but were diverted and prevented by a sudden
Noise they heard behind them, of very loud Shouts
and Outcries; when, facing about towards the Quarter
from whence the Noise came, they beheld a great
Dust, and, a Moment, after plainly perceived the
Glittering of bright Armour, naked Sabres and Lances,

Helmets,

Helmets, Shields, and all such Warlike Accoutrements; and, in a Word, a numerous Troop of most gallant Cavalry, who, tho' all covered with Sweat and Dust, yet appeared very Noble and Magnificent. They galloped on a great Pace, and were now all come up, proving to be Four hundred Cavaliers from *Yathrib*, among whom were *Salma*, her Father, and many of their Relations; who having had Notice of the Designs of the treacherous *Jews*, were come, in all speed to prevent it; and as soon as ever they came up, without suffering them to speak one Word for themselves, they cut in Pieces every one of those vile execrable Villains, not one escaping to carry the Tydings of their disastrous Overthrow.

C H A P,

C H A P. XVI.

*Almutalib resolves to lose his Life rather than
suffer his Nephew to be taken from him.* Salma's
*angry Speech to him before she knew him. His re-
solute Answer. Discovers himself. She mildly
reproaches him and her Son. Leaves the Child to
his own Choice, either to go with his Uncle, or to
return home with her; who chuses to proceed to*
Mecca. *Almutalib enjoins his Nephew to conceal his Name, and to pass for his Servant. They
arrive at* Mecca. *The Child's Beauty, and his
enlightned Countenance so much admired, and
venerated by the People of* Mecca, *that they ask
their Necessities of God in his Name. The secret
Malice the* Jews *bear to him. His excellent
Qualifications. The Government of* Mecca *vested
in him. The Deposed Governor highly resents it,
and makes him a very reproachful Speech, upbraid-
ing his Want of Children.* Abdolmutalib's *Answer, with his Vow, if ever he was the Father of
Ten Sons, to offer up One of them to God as a
Sacrifice. His Prayer upon that Subject. His
Petition is heard; he having Ten Sons born of Six
Wives, of which Number* Abdallah, *the Youngest,
inherits the* Prophetick Light.

T HE perfidious *Jews* being all destroyed,
in the Manner I have related, and the
great and terrible Noise of clashing
Armour, and redoubled Strokes, being
now at an End; the Ground all about
appeared to be covered with Streams of
Blood, and Breathless Carcasses; and those who had
been

been concerned in that difmal Encounter, and bloody
Carnage, were fufficiently tired with diftributing fo
many Wounds, and with hewing off fuch a Number
of Limbs, as they had done. But the Valiant and
Invincible *Almutalib*, who had, for a great Part of the
Night, fuftained a Combat fo furious and obftinate,
had now remounted his Steed, and was retired with
the Child, at a fmall Diftance from the Company,
where he ftood ftill panting for Breath; as, indeed,
well he might; having undergone a Fatigue fufficient
to weary him out, *had he been made of Brafs.* He
now, having refted himfelf during that whole Action,
had fomewhat recovered his wafted Spirits, and began afrefh to prepare his nervous Arm, and mortife-
rous Weapons, for a more unequal Encounter; being
fully determined to employ them, and that never-
failing Courage with which his great Heart was animated, againft the whole Band of noble Warriors,
who had come to their Affiftance, and that fo very
feafonably; as not looking upon that, to be worthy
the Name of Succour, or friendly Affiftance, which
cometh with any View of Self-Intereft, as he well
imagined theirs was. He refolved, if they infifted
upon taking his Nephew from him, that he would
fooner dye in defending his Pretenfions, without putting himfelf to the Trouble of giving them any Reafons, or ufing any Arguments or Capitulations in the
Matter. So taking his Bow in his Hand, and with
the Child behind him, he intrepidly advanced towards
that whole Friendly Troop of Four hundred Warriors,
who were ranked in moft feemly Order, and prefented the Point of his Arrow, with a fteady Aim
amongft them.

As he approached, *Salma*, who was in the Front,
called out to him in a loud Voice, that fhe might be
eafily heard by them both, faying; "Who is the
" Audacious Man, that hath been fo daringly pre-
" fumptuous, as, with fo little Ceremony or Refpect,
" to take away my Son from my Houfe and Pro-
" tection,

" tection, without acquainting me, therewith, or
" giving the leaft Notice to any of my Family of this
" his bold Attempt?" " I am he, anfwered *Almuta-*
" *lib*, who conducted him hither to this Place, and
" who likewife pretend to accomplifh my juft Refolu-
" tion of conveying him from hence to his honourable
" Patrimony, in order to inftall him Prince of that
" noble City and Territories, which have been the
" Seat of all his Anceftors, from Times immemorial;
" and which is the nobleft and moft famous Inheri-
" tance in the whole Univerfe. If my prefent Dif-
" guife preventeth your knowing who I am; or if
" you only pretend not to know me, and to have for-
" got the Friendfhip and Acquaintance there former-
" ly was between us; know, that I am a *Koreifhite*,
" and my Name is *Almutalib*; that I defcend from
" the illuftrious and valiant *Koreifh*, whofe Grand-
" fon I am, and the Son of *Abdulmenaf*: The gallant
" and matchlefs *Hafhem*, your Hufband, was my Bro-
" ther, and whofe infeparable Companion I was du-
" ring his whole Life. I am he who managed the
" Affair, and who made up the Match between you
" and him; and if your Memory faileth you not, you
" may call to Mind how much Blood, both of our
" own and others, was fpilt, in your Behalf, upon
" that Occafion. In fine, I am your Son's own
" Uncle, and, in all my Actions, I am a Father to
" him; and who am tenderer of his Life and Wel-
" fare, and more defirous of his Profperity, than you
" your own felf can poffibly be.

Salma, when fhe heard this, was highly fatisfied,
and joyfully came up to the worthy *Almultaib*, and
beholding him with a pleafant fmiling Countenance,
fhe fpeak to him in thefe Terms; " How came you,
" my deareft Brother, to be guilty of fo great an Over-
" fight, and to ufe fo little Ceremony, or have fo
" fmall Confideration for her who brought into the
" World this your Nephew, for whom you exprefs fo
" much Tendernefs and Regard, or for *my* Father
" and

" and Relations, as to convey him away from his
" Friends, and the Place of his Nativity, and run
" him into so great a Danger, that, had it not been
" for these worthy Gentlemen, you had, both of you,
" infallibly lost your Lives? And you, my dear
" Darling! Have you so soon forgot these your in-
" dulgent Mother's Breasts which gave you Suck,
" that you treat me as if I was a Stranger? I protest,
" by the living Creator, (you may believe what I
" affirm) That had it not been, that we had Notice
" given us, of the vile Designs of those blood-thirsty
" Traytors, and that they had followed you on Pur-
" pose to take away your Life, I should never have
" been against your going with your Uncle; for I
" should rather have looked upon it as the greatest Ho-
" nour you can have on this Side Paradise: But since
" Things have so happened, and you are come so far,
" as likewise I am come hither, with all this Train
" after me, and your Uncle is here present, I leave it
" intirely at your own Discretion, to chuse the Com-
" pany you like best: If your Inclinations lead you
" most to go along with him, I shall not contradict,
" or endeavour to compel you to the contrary; and if
" you have a Mind to return back with me, you are
" sensible of my Love and Affection, and how wel-
" come you are to me.

Abdolmutalib, with his Eyes fixed on the Ground, remained some Moments in a silent Suspence, and his
Cheeks, all covered with Blushes, evidently demon-
strated the Nonplus he was at for a suitable Answer.
He looked first upon his dear Mother, who had given
him his first Nourishment, and who had carried him
Nine Months in her Womb, whose tender Breasts had
given him Milk, and who was so extremely fond of
him: Then lifting up his Eyes again, his worthy Uncle
presented himself to his View; and, upon recollecting
the strong Ties of Consanguinity, the high Obligations
he had to him, for the great Love he bore him, as, likewise, the last Injunction of so noble a Father, whose
Desire

Deſire and Commands he thought himſelf in Duty
bound to accompliſh ; ſo that after having continued
ſilent for ſome Time, he at laſt, with a moſt reſpectful
Geſture and Accent, (and moſt juſtly did her extraordinary Merit claim the higheſt Reſpect) returned his
Mother this Anſwer;

" If going to *Mecca* with my Uncle will not be
" counted an Act of Diſobedience to You, my Incli-
" nation is to proceed in my Journey thither : But,
" in offending you, I fear I ſhall likewiſe offend my
" Creator ; I therefore am determined to act nothing
" contrary to your Pleaſure and Commands, but will
" either proceed or return as you ſhall pleaſe to ap-
" point.

Salma being now ſatisfied which Way her Son's Deſires chiefly led him, would no longer detain him;
but, on the contrary, with the greateſt Tokens of Tenderneſs, Conſent, and even Willingneſs, ſhe kiſſed,
embraced, and gave him her Bleſſing ; after which,
with the ſincereſt Expreſſions of mutual Friendſhip,
Love, Acknowledgment and Reſpect, with great Offers and Proteſtations on either ſide, they took their
Leaves of each other ; *Salma,* with her Company
taking the Road back to *Yathrib,* whilſt the noble Uncle with the Child purſued their Journey to *Mecca.*

As they were proceeding on their Way, very joyfully, *Almutalib* ſaid to his beloved Nephew thus;
" Liſten, my dear Child, to what I am about to ſay :
" My Counſel is, that if you are asked who you are,
" be ſure you conceal your Name, and let no body
" know that you are, any wiſe related to me; but,
" to all who inquire, tell them, you are my Servant :
" For, if at *Yathrib* you have had Snares laid for
" your Life, and have been perſecuted by thoſe Tray-
" tors; in the City we are now going to, we have
" likewiſe many of that perfidious, blood-thirſty
" Generation; wherefore, ſeeing you are not imme-
" diately to take the Government of *Mecca* into
" your own Hands, it is not at all convenient, that
" in

" in the *Interim,* they fhould know any thing of your
" Birth, or Defcent, or even have the leaft Sufpicion
" of it.

Having given him this neceffary Precaution, and
being now arrived at the City Gate, they began to
make their Entry; the refplendent Rays of the *Prophetick Light* ftill going before them; which from the
Forehead of *Abdolmutalib* caft no lefs bright Refle-
ction, than doth a Cryftal Mirror reverberating the
Beams of the Mid-day Sun.

All who beheld that moft beautiful Countenance,
were very inquifitive in afking the Uncle, *Who that
lovely Child was, and from whence he brought him? Almutalib* very readily told all who inquired, *That he
was a Youth he had brought from a diftant Country, where
he had lately been, and whom he intended to breed up in
his Family as a Domeftick.* And, in Effect, from thence-
forwards, he was ever after called by the Name of
(*a*) *Abdolmutalib,* inftead of *Jaibacanas,* [rather *Shéryb*]
being thought by every body to be really *Almutalib's*
Favourite-Page or Servant, upon which account they
gave him that Name. He was extremely beloved
and refpected by the whole City; every one who beheld that glorious *Light,* which was fo confpicuous
upon his lovely Countenance, being inclined to have
a more than ordinary Affection for him, and were in-
fenfibly infpired to beftow their Benedictions upon
him. Nay, the People, in all their Neceffities, and
Misfortunes, and upon all Occafions, as want of Rain
in a droughty Year, or any fuch like Vifitations,
and Tokens of God's Wrath, which frequently occur
to Mankind, they would intercede, and implore the
Mercy and Affiftance of the Lord of all Things, in
his Name; which Interceffions His Divine Majefty,
out of his immenfe Bounty, would never fail to give
Ear to, when made in the Name of that Poffeffor of
the

(*a*) *Abd,* in *Arabick,* fignifies Servant, or Creature.

the Myſterious *Light*, and of his future Succeſſor, the beatified Prophet *Mahomet*.

The Fame of his exceeding Beauty, uncommon Qualifications, and great Actions extended itſelf, not only throughout *Mecca*, but over all its Territories, both far and near: And as it always happeneth, that thoſe who are the moſt eminently conſpicuous for their extraordinary Merits and Perfections, are ever the moſt liable to the Envy and Malice of Rivals, and ſecret Enemies, (who are none but Men of baſe Principles; nor do they ever perſecute any but the Good and the Righteous) and by how much the more they excel in Virtue, and Piety, by ſo much the ſurer they are to be expoſed to the Hatred and dangerous Treacheries of the Wicked and Invidious. An undeniable Proof of all this we have in this worthy Perſon; for, from the very Moment of his Birth, till the Hour of his Death, his wicked Enemies were continually racking their Inventions to find out Means to deſtroy him.

In thoſe Days, there lived in *Mecca* a certain near Relation of this *Abdolmutalib*'s, being his Couſin Germain, and Grandſon to the great *Abdulmenaf*, who was a Man of good Parts, and Qualifications, but of an ambitious, haughty Mind; yet was honoured and reſpected by all, for his high Deſcent, and immenſe Riches. He was Grand Preſident of the Council, a very able Stateſman, and had, in a manner, the whole Management of the Affairs of the City *Mecca*; being the chief Miniſter at the Helm of the Government, and ſo highly revered, and even feared by all the Inhabitants, that none dared to diſobey or contradict him; as knowing the dangerous Conſequences of having ſo great a Politician for their Enemy: *For, as Skill and Penetration in State Politicks are the principal Steps to high Stations and Dignities, ſo an able Politician is a dangerous Enemy.*

Now *Abdolmutalib* being grown up to Man's Eſtate, and was married and had got a Child (though he ſtill retained the *Prophetick Light*, that Son being not the
Elected

Elected Inheritor thereof) the People began to ſlacken in their Reſpect and Eſteem they were wont to have for his above-mentioned Kinſman, and, in fine, they took no more notice of him, and he was as much forgotten, as if he had been in the other World; none applying to him in publick Matters, nor indeed upon any other Account; nor was the leaſt Regard ſhewed to any of his Commands; but, on the contrary, they committed all their Affairs to *Abdolmutalib*'s Management, delivering into his Cuſtody the Keys of the City, and of the Council-Chamber, giving into his Poſſeſſion all the Archives and publick Writings, with the ſole Government of the Holy Temple; making him their Leader and General in the Field: And all the Inhabitants, in general, moſt willingly and readily ſubmitted themſelves to his Obedience; nor did they ever repent their putting the Power into his Hands.

The depoſed Governor, enraged at theſe Proceedings, his jealous Breaſt boiling with Indignation, Envy, Ambition and Reſentment, ſought all Occaſions to ſhew the Sentiments of his incenſed Mind in ſome Diſcourſe with his newly advanced Kinſman: When one Day he chanced to find him in the Company of ſeveral People; at what time, quite blinded with Rage, and ready to burſt with Malice, he accoſted him in theſe extravagant and reproachful Terms;

" Whither, vain Boy, do your ambitious, haugh-
" ty Thoughts intend to hurry you? Tell me, thou
" worthleſs, fantaſtical Trifler, how high would thy
" Vanity make thee aſpire at laſt, that thou thus
" fooliſhly expoſeſt thy wretched Ignorance to the
" open Air, without the leaſt Solidity, or Founda-
" tion? Or tell me, if, perhaps, thou imagineſt us to
" be ignorant who thou art. We know thee perfectly
" well. It was but Yeſterday, as it were, that thou
" wert brought almoſt naked hither to this City from
" *Tatbrib*, where thou hadſt led thy Life among the
" *Jews* of that Place, a poor, deſpicable, forlorn
" Wretch, a Servant-Boy; and here amongſt us thou

A a " wert

" wert always known, and looked upon as one of our
" Lackeys, a poor Boy to run of an Errant: And
" now, all on a ſudden, we behold thee reſpected,
" honoured, and revered; advanced to the higheſt
" Employs, and Poſts of the greateſt Dignity! We
" ſee thee puffed up with Pride and Ambition, forget-
" ful of thy mean, deſpicable Original, and thy poor
" Capacity to go through what thou haſt undertaken.
" Thou haſt no Children, nor art thou Man ſufficient
" to beget them: From whence, therefore, comes it,
" that thou carrieſt thyſelf with ſo much Haughtineſs
" towards us; ſince thou muſt needs know, that God
" would have bleſſed thee with Children, had he found
" thee worthy of ſuch a Bleſſing; and that the only
" Cauſe he denieth to grant thee that Bleſſing, is thy
" own Unworthineſs to enjoy them.

Abdolmutalib, quite ſcandalized, and out of Countenance at a Diſcourſe ſo diſdainful and haughty, could
not avoid ſhewing his juſt Reſentment; and with that
undaunted Reſolution, which was ſo natural to him,
he made him this Return, with an Accent and Geſture
ſomewhat diſcovering the Diſturbance of his Mind,
and how much he was touched to the Quick:

" Were it not, ſaid he, for the Nearneſs of Blood
" which God hath thought fit to infuſe into our Veins,
" and which with holds my Arm, and to which, and
" nothing elſe, I have ſome Regard, I would moſt
" certainly diſfigure that Face of yours, and ſet my
" Mark upon that your ſhameleſs Front, for your
" ſcurrilous, diſreſpectful Language, and would, in-
" fallibly, make you unſay every Syllable you have
" ſo ſcandalouſly and unadviſedly uttered. It is un-
" pardonably baſe in you to upbraid me with my
" Want of Children, when it is far from being un-
" likely, or improbable, that I may be the Father of
" many: Muſt you endeavour to caſt a Blemiſh up-
" on my Honour, becauſe, as yet I have but one? I
" ſolemnly proteſt to the Almighty, and dedicate
" this inviolable Vow before the Preſence of his Sa-
" cred

" cred Divinity, That, if He fhall ever vouchfafe
" to make me the Father of Ten Sons, I will offer up
" One of them to His Holy Name, as a *Corban*,
" or Sacrifice." And, as a farther Confirmation of
this Vow, he immediately repaired to the Holy Temple; and approaching the venerable *Caaba*, embracing
and clinging clofe to thofe fanctified Rails, he affirmed the Sincerity of his Intent in the following devout
Addrefs to his Creator.

ABDOLMUTALIB's *Vow* in the TEMPLE.

OMnipotent Lord of the exalted Throne of Eternal Glory, who from Thy immenfe Altitudes
art continually beholding all the Tranfactions of both
the One and the Other World! Thou, whofe Incom-
prehenfibility is in every Place, and yet cannot be
properly faid to be in any Place! But, notwithftanding, thou art to be found in every Place by thofe who
implore Thy Affiftance in their Diftrefs! Thou, to
whom alone all devout Prayers and Supplications are
due, as being the univerfal and only Lord, who art
the Infpector, the Mover, the Tolerator, the great
Judge and Arbiter of all Th ngs! Thou, who alone
knoweft the Number of Thy Creatures; and who a-
lone delivereft them out of the Wombs wherein they
have been borne and formed after the Manner and
Figure which Thou alone haft feen fit to appoint!
Thou, whofe Divine Effence and Influence infpireth
the Soul, and filleth it with joyful Tydings; and
who gracioufly turneft from us the Evils, which,
without Thy Protection, would continually befal us,
and doft change them into their Contraries! Thou,
who well knoweft, that I am reproached for what I
am in no wife blameable; fince nothing can ever be
effected without Thy Permiffion, and all thou pleafeft

to ordain, muſt ever be accompliſhed! If, therefore, Lord, my Enemies upbraid and revile me, by imputing to me the Want of a Bleſſing Thou haſt not been pleaſed to grant me, I humbly preſume, moſt bountiful Lord, that it is but juſt and equitable, that Thy Divine Grace and Goodneſs ſhould ſupply thoſe my Defects. O Lord! if Thou ſhalt think fit to make me the Father of Ten Sons, who ſhall be Followers and Obſervers of Thy Holy Laws, and ſhall aſſociate themſelves with Thy true and faithful Servants, in an intire Obedience to Thee, and to none but Thee alone; I here again repeat my late voluntary Vow, with the utmoſt Sincerity and Reſignation, of devoting One of that Number to Thy Divine Service, by offering him up as a Sacrifice to Thy Holy Name; which ſolemn Vow I promiſe to keep ſacred and inviolable, without the leaſt Scruple or Prevarication.

This ſolemn Addreſs he made with ſo unfeigned a Contrition of Heart, and ſuch a Sincerity and Fervency of Mind in his Expreſſions, that the Divine Goodneſs heard, and granted his Supplication: For, in Proceſs of Time, he became the Father of (a) Ten Male Children, which were brought him by Six ſeveral Wives he married; all of them worthy Ladies of great Merit, and noble Extraction, ſelected out of the moſt Illuſtrious Tribes. Of theſe Sons, the Youngeſt of all was the *Elected* Inheritor of the reſplendent *Light.*
They

(a) See ſomething of this, Pag. 123, 124, in the Note, mention'd by *D'Herbelot,* under the Name *Abdelmothleb.* —— Dean *Prideaux* in his Life of *Mahomet,* ſays, That " *Abdolmutalib* (whom he " calls *Abdol-Mutallab*) had Thirteen Sons; and that *Abdallah,* the " Impoſter's Father, was the *Eldeſt,*" and not the *Youngeſt,* as my Author affirms; though the ſame is likewiſe affirmed by *D'Herbelot,* under the Name *Mohammed Aboul Kaſſem, Ben Abdallah,* in theſe very Words, viz. *Abdelmothleb,* the Son of *Haſhem,* and Grandfather to *Mahomet,* had Ten Sons; *Hareth, Gaidac, Aboulchebel, Abdel Caabah, Dheran, Abbas, Hamzah, Zobeir, Abou Talib,* and *Abdallah.*
This

They gave him the Name of *Abdallah* [i. e. God's Servant.]   He was a Child of incomparable, Beauty, Shape, Mien, and Qualifications; upon whom Heaven poured down its Bleffings, and whofe Birth was the Subject of infinite Joy to the whole Earth.

This *Abdallah*, the Tenth and Laft, was Father to *Mahomet*, and the other Nine were his Uncles, among whom *Aboulckefel* was his greateft and moft implacable Enemy.

Aa 3   C H A P.

CHAP. XVII.

*The Caution which ought to be ufed in making fo-
lemn Vows; with the Neceffity of keeping them
when made.   Abdolmutalib's Rafhnefs.   He
propofeth the Sacrifice to his Sons.   Their Obedience, but more efpecially Abdallah's, with his dutiful Anfwer.   His great Refolution.   They caft
Lots.   Abdallah is chofen.   His Mother's Grief
and Complaints.   They make ready for the Sacrifice in the Temple.   The great Joy of the Jews.
Abdallah's Refignation.   Abutalib offers himfelf in his ftead.   Abdolmutalib's Prayer.   The
People prevent the Sacrifice, &c.   They go to con-
fult a wife Woman.*

VOWS or Offerings ought to be kept, only according to the Advantage or Benefit which may accrue from the keeping
them, if well and properly chofen; or
difpenfed with, omitted, and neglected,
if, on the contrary, the Performance can
produce nothing but evil Effects: For, by how much
the more acceptable the Obfervance thereof fhall appear in the Sight of the Almighty Creator, by fo much
the

the more the Dedicator offendeth the Supreme Majeſty of God, and accumulateth his Sins, in failing of accompliſhing what he hath dedicated. Vows and Promiſes are (or at leaſt always ſhould be) free, ſpontaneous and voluntary, not forced and conſtra.ned; and more eſpecially when made to God, and Himſelf is called upon to be the Witneſs; for then they become an Obligatory Precept; and to derogate from that, is a Perjury of an unpardonable Nature: For, let us extenuate the Sin ever ſo much, by alledging, that it was a Vow better to be broken than kept; yet ſtill, he who is guilty of ſuch a Perjury, certainly loſeth the Nan e of a faithful Servant, and forfeiteth his Word, and blaſteth his Character, and his Reputation, thereby rendering himſelf for ever infamous Wherefore every one, who deſigneth to make any ſolemn Promiſe, ought ſeriouſly and very deliberately to conſider what he is about, and to compute and calculate the Nature of the Promiſe he is going to make, and of Him to whom he is going to dedicate it, maturely weighing it againſt his own Sufficiency and Ability, before he proceed too far, by raſhly, inconſiderately, and irretrievably offending his great Maker. But when once his Reſolution is firmly fixed, then, indeed, let him confirm it with ſuch ſacred and inviolable Ties, that he may look upon the punctual Performance thereof, as the higheſt of all Obligations; becauſe, in thoſe Things, wherein Heaven and its mighty Lord are concerned, there muſt never be the leaſt Equivocation or Prevarication, but the naked Truth in all its Purity; ſince, even in worldly Affairs, they are highly diſpleaſing to God.

It is the moſt undoubted Sign of an unfeigned Virtue in that Perſon, who, while in the Vigour of his Youth, and bleſſed with the Enjoyment of a perfect State of Health, ſhutteth his Eyes againſt the alluring Pleaſures and Vanities of the World, purely to look upwards towards Heaven, and Divine Things; and who, with that only View, voluntarily depriveth himſelf of his

Liberty,

Liberty, by retiring into fome lonefome Solitude, re-pulfing all his Inclinations, and bridling and fubduing all his Appetites. This is the Virtue which our *Aâ-lims,* or Teachers, fo highly extol, applaud and approve of; affirming, that it is moft grateful and acceptable in the Sight of God: But, above all other good Works, thofe which they moft of all approve of, as more fuperlatively meritorious than all others whatfoever, are Vows and Offerings made to Heaven; the which, they fay, *caufe both God and His Angels to re-joice:* And, in Effect, a folemn Vow, dedicated and addreffed to God, is fuperlatively meritorious, and to which nothing is any ways comparable; provided that what the Tongue hath uttered, is firmly grounded in the Heart; and when, to confirm it, the Dedicator maketh ufe of a ftrenuous Vehemency, and an irradicable Refolution; when all his Senfes and Faculties are agreed, and ftrongly bent upon the Performance: Then it is, that the Action becometh meritoriofly weighty; then it is, the Maker of that Vow dif-ingageth himfelf from the Snares of the World and the Flefh, and meritoriofly chargeth himfelf with that Obligation. It is, indeed, very true, that it would be far better, if our Lives and Deportment were fuch, that there might be no Neceffity for thefe Tryals; but fince we are, through the Frailty of our Natural Difpofitions, fo very *brittle,* and, by Confequence, liable to the fame Aptnefs to *break,* as all other *brittle* Bodies are, we frequently *fall afunder;* and therefore, it is very requifite we fhould be *fouldred* and *made whole* by fuch *Amendments.* Yet let us do our beft to avoid all Occafions, of making rafh and inconfiderate Refolutions; fuch always make our Vows and Oblations lefs weighty and meritorious; they being extorted, as it were, by Force. Seeing, therefore, that we have Leifure and Opportunity offered us to prevent thofe evil Confequences, let us not be the Authors of our own Misfortunes: But if

we

we make juft and reafonable Vows, it is very juft and reafonable we fhould perform them.

It cannot be difputed, but that *Abdolmutalib*, in the before mentioned Controverfy, had fome fort of a reafonable Provocation to act as he did. Who doubts, but that the Affront and Indignity offered him, was very grofs? Certainly he thought it fo; and *that* even in the higheft Degree; or elfe he could never have been prevailed with to make fuch a Vow, as the Offering to the Lord as a Victim, the Life of one of his own Children; a Life which muft of Neceffity be fo dear to him, and which muft coft him fo much; and that only through the Refentment thofe grofs Expreffions gave him! In thofe Days, at *Mecca*, and throughout all thofe Parts of the World, a Man who had no Children, was looked upon with a very defpicable Eye, as one worthy of little, or no Regard: And for certain, had his Antagonift known, or been able to have thought upon any Thing that would have been taken as a greater Affront, and have touched him more to the Quick, he would, infallibly, have faid it; for, upon fuch Occafions, when Men are blinded with Choler, their Anger will generally provoke them to utter the worft of Words; nay, tho' what they fay, is rather an Affront to him who fpeaketh, than to the Perfon to whom they are directed, as it happened in the Cafe before us: For, to treat a Man who was held in fuch high Efteem as was *Abdolmutalib*, in fo vile a Manner, and to give him fo grofs Language, only for accepting of what was his lawful Right, his own Patrimony of Inheritance, which had, in fo direct a Line, been tranfmitted down to him from his Anceftors, was moft apparently the greateft and moft unpardonable Piece of Brutality ever heard of! Yet let that be as it will, or his Provocation ever fo grievous, to induce him to come to fo cruel a Refolution and to oblige himfelf to take fuch a violent Satisfaction, it was ftill exerting his Refentment by much too far; a ftrange Derogation from his great natural Prudence

and

and Sagacity. Nothing could well be a greater Inſtance of Temerity, than to make a Vow of Sacrificing a Life which was none of his to offer, and which was alſo a Thing ſo very uncertain, as to the Performance. And in caſe he ſhould be able to accompliſh his Promiſe, he left an Example of his Cruelty and Inhumaniy to his whole Poſterity. An Example which ought ſo carefully to be avoided by all, but more particularly by thoſe whom God hath placed upon Earth to be Precedents or Patterns for others; whoſe Office it rather is, to ſet Examples, whereby their Inferiors may edify; as being thoſe, upon whoſe Actions the Eyes of the Vulgar are perpetually fixed, and to whom they are to appeal upon all Occaſions.

Abdolmutalib was now become the Father of Ten proper Sons, moſt of which, being full grown Men, were married, and very happily ſettled in their own Families and Eſtates, and ſome had ſeveral Children. And at the Time, when he took the greateſt Satisfaction in ſeeing them all together; when the beholding them before his Eyes, afforded him the higheſt Joy and Content; at the very Time, which, that his paſt Promiſe was more out of his Thoughts, than ever it had been ſince he made it; then it was, that, according to the natural Inſtability of Worldly Affairs, with one Turn of Time's variable and inconſtant Wheel, (though God is never unmindful of the Actions of his *Friends,* and, indeed, put it into his Mind, leſt the Glory of ſuch a Reſignation ſhould be loſt) that ſolemn Vow he had dedicated to the Supreme Majeſty, returned afreſh in his Memory; I mean, that of Sacrificing one of his Sons to the Lord, if he ever had the compleat Number of Ten.

Upon this Recollection of his Vow, though it gave him an exceſſive Grief and Anguiſh of Soul, yet, without loſing a Moment's Time, he immediately ſet about it; *for Delays are never good;* but, *in Matters of ſuch a Nature as this, it is always beſt to take them in Hand,*
with

with all poffible Expedition. To this Intent, he fent for his beloved Sons, and when all the Ten were come into his Prefence, he made them an open Declaration of the Offering he had vowed to the Lord.

When they heard this, they were all in a ftrange Confternation, remaining motionlefs and in deep Sufpence; hanging down their Heads, with their Eyes fixed on the Ground, without moving their Tongues, for a confiderable while; and then looking upon one another, with great Signs of inward Emotions, and Perturbations of Mind; For the Image of Death, which feemed to be in the Midft of them, had intirely ftagnated and congealed their Blood, and difpirited them to fuch a Degree, that not one of them returned the leaft Syllable in Anfwer to what their Father had faid; nor is it any Wonder they fhould be fo furprized, fince every one of them, muft needs lie under the Apprehenfion of the fatal Lot's falling to his own Share, and that he muft be the Victim.

But after they had continued fo long mute, *Abdallah*, the Youngeft of them all, at length broke Silence, and with a chearful, fedate, and fmiling Countenance, ftood forth, and made his Father the following Reply; " Moft certain it is, my beloved
" Parent! that you have engaged your felf in an
" Undertaking, that none but you was ever heard to
" have thought upon, in any Age whatfoever: But
" fince you have done it, and your Vow is paft re-
" calling, there remaineth nothing now but that you
" immediately go about it, and fhew your Obedience
" by accomplifhing what you have fo folemnly pro-
" mifed to His Divinity, without any farther Delay:
" And may the Supreme Lord never permit, that,
" in any of us, there fhould be the leaft Sign of any
" Thing, but what may tend towards the Serving and
" Obeying you, in all whatfoever you fhall pleafe to
" command or defire. We are, all Ten of us, your
" Sons; and we all refign to pay an intire Obedience
" to the Lord who created us, and to the Father who
" be-

" begat us: We are every one of us ſatisfied and
" contented, and offer our Lives with an humble
" and dutiful Reſignation; and I am the firſt, who,
" for all the reſt, offer my own Throat to the
" Knife. "

His Father, upon this, turned towards the others,
to ſee whether or no they approved of what had been
ſaid; and they all, with one Voice, anſwered in the
like Terms, ſaying; " Not only *One* of us; but,
" if it be your Pleaſure to command us *All* to die,
" we will moſt freely, moſt ſincerely, and moſt wil-
" lingly reſign our Lives. "

The pious Father, was ſo highly pleaſed and comforted at the great Dutifulneſs and Humility of this
Reply, as likewiſe, at the noble Generoſity and Reſolution they expreſſed, in ſo frankly offering their
Lives, without ſhewing the leaſt Weakneſs or Fear,
that, with his Eyes all drowned in Tears of Tenderneſs and Affection, he poured out a Thouſand and a
Thouſand Benedictions upon them, and ſaid; " My
" dear Children; Since your Submiſſion and Reſigna-
" tion is ſo exemplary and ſpontaneous, and you give
" me ſuch Encouragement to proceed in my Deſign,
" my Deſire is, That to morrow, early in the Mor-
" ning, you purify your Bodies with the neceſſary
" Waſhings, cloath yourſelves in new Garments,
" and recommend yourſelves to God, as if you were
" going to leave the World: Take your Leaves of
" your Mothers, and let thoſe among you who are
" the Fathers of Children, take Leave of them like-
" wiſe, and then repair to the Holy Temple; where,
" that neither of you may think himſelf injured, or
" partially dealt withal, you ſhall caſt Lots; and he
" upon whom it is God's Pleaſure the Lot ſhall fall,
" Him it ſhall be, from among the reſt, who ſhall be
" the choſen Victim for the Sacrifice; " Which they all
willingly agreed to, and very punctually obſerved.

At Break of Day *Abdolmutalib* aroſe, and began to
prepare for what he had reſolved upon. He firſt of all
washed

wafhed his Body, put on his beft Apparel, adorned himfelf with many precious Relicks of the Ancient Patriarchs and Prophets, performed his Devotions, re-
commending himfelf to his Creator; and then, being
provided with a keen Weapon, of *Indian* Temper and
Fabrick, he went forth in order to put his Undertaking
in Execution, calling upon his Sons to follow him, who all
immediately came out at the firft Call, and prefented
themfelves before their Father, except *Abdallah*, who
ftayed behind; Not that he was in the leaft backward or
unwilling to come, but was detained by the forrowful
afflicted *Fatima* his Mother, who could by no Means be
prevailed upon to part with him. At length he endeavoured to force himfelf out, fhe ftill hanging upon,
and embracing him; and he, that he might get loofe
and dif-ingage himfelf from her, unkindly denied and
refufed thofe tender Demonftrations of Maternal
Love and Affection, though fo excessively moving,
that they were enough to mollify the very Rocks.
" Let me go, faid he to her, to my Father, who is
" yonder waiting for me, left he fhould accufe me
" of Negligence, or deem me to be a Pufilanimous,
" faint-hearted Coward; For I have far more Regard
" to my Reputation, my Duty and my Obligation,
" than to all your Tears. Let me go, therefore, I
" fay; for if the Lord fhall decree that I lofe my
" Life, I fhall then have been found worthy of that
" Palm of Glory, whereof my Soul is fo defirous; and
" fhall thereby deliver my Brethren, and acquit my
" Father of this obligatory Debt: But if God feeth
" proper that I efcape, I fhall return to you again. "
He had no fooner faid thefe Words, but his Father
came in great Hafte, to call him; and *Fatima*, her
Eyes flowing with Showers of Tears, turned towards
him, and thus befpake him; " In what Part of the
" World have you ever feen, or heard; in what
" Book have you read, an Example or Precedent
" of a Father's imbruing his Hands in the Blood of
" his own begotten Son, and that, without the leaft
" Provocation, or forcible Compulfion! Is there any
" Cruelty

" Cruelty in the whole Univerſe to be compared to ſo
" inhuman a Deed? When it ſhall be known in the
" World, that you cut your Son's Throat, nay, ſup-
" poſing it done in Paſſion, or for ſome great Crime,
" what will be ſaid of you? But ſtill ſuppoſing, that
" this Undertaking of yours cannot poſſibly be diſ-
" penſed with, or prevented, take one of the other
" Nine, and let this your youngeſt Child alone; Have
" Pity upon his tender Years; conſider his uncommon
" Beauty; have Regard to that radiant Light upon
" his Forehead, whoſe reſplendent Beams reach to the
" very Skies, and remember, that this my own wretch-
" ed Life dependeth upon his; for, aſſuredly, I ſhall
" never ſurvive my Child one Moment.

To this *Abdolmutalib* made Anſwer in theſe Words;
" You may aſſure yourſelf, that I have the greateſt
" Reluctancy imaginable, to hurt even one Hair of
" the Head, much more to take away the Life, of him
" who is the very Light of my Eyes; but it is not
" reaſonable that the Lord's due Sacrifice ſhould be
" neglected or refuſed, upon the Account of your Son's
" Beauty, or your Grief, or indeed, upon any other
" Worldly Conſideration whatſoever. I feel more
" Compaſſion for him, and love him with a more
" tender and unfeigned Affection, than all thoſe who
" make Profeſſion of their Love and Concern, be
" the outward Signs of their Grief ever ſo great, or
" their Lamentations ever ſo many. I'll conduct him
" with the reſt to the Temple, where, Oh! may it
" be the Divine Will of the Almighty, of His infinite
" and boundleſs Mercy, that he may be ſentenced to
" live, and not to die! But if the fatal Lot falleth
" upon him, it is our Duty to obey; *For there is no*
" *contradicting, or contending with the Pleaſure or De-*
" *crees of Him whoſe Creatures we are, and who com-*
" *mandeth and forbiddeth what He Himſelf pleaſeth.*

When *Abdolmutalib* had ſaid this, the Youth immediately got himſelf ready, and turned towards his
ſorrowful Mother to take his Leave of her; who kiſ-

ſing;

fing, embracing, and blessing him, with Expressions
and Gestures which would have softned the hardest
Stones, fell into these passionate Exclamations; "My
" dearest darling Child! Thou, whom the Lord hath
" pleased to ordain, that thy Father shall cut thy
" Throat before my Face! That these my Eyes shall
" behold thy beautiful Countenance all besmeared
" with the Blood of thy precious Veins! O my Child!
" Thou who wert wont, with only looking upon thee,
" to alleviate all my Pains, all my Sorrow and my
" Discontent, and now thy Sight affordeth me no-
" thing but mortal Affliction, Grief and Despair!
" This unhappy Day putteth an End to all my Com-
" fort and Joy, and is the Beginning of my Anguish,
" my Bitterness, and my Woe; since, from this
" wretched fatal Minute, my Breast can never more
" be capable of hoping for the least Glimpse of Rest
" or Consolation! This Day *Mecca* will be deprived of
" its *Luminary!* This Day it will be involved in Dark-
" ness! For when it no longer enjoyeth thy *Light*, it
" must, of necessity, be covered with Clouds of Ob-
" scurity! Let those who are in her Walls accompany
" me, this cruel Day, in my Tears and Lamenta-
" tions; and let the Inhabitants of Places far and near
" repair hither, to be Witnesses of my unutterable
" Grief! O my Child! for whose Ransom I would
" freely sacrifice my own Life, were it valuable
" enough to redeem thine, or would it do thee any
" Service! But alas! I do but, by vainly forming
" effectless Chimæras, wish I could apply a Re-
" medy; for I see, by no human Means, how, or
" which Way I can deliver thee! My Eyes shall
" flow with watry Floods of Brine, as long
" as those Membranes which cover them shall
" endure, and when they are rent and torn out,
" the Torrent shall then be converted into Blood!
" From this Day I bid *Adieu* to all Comfort, and re-
" nounce every Spark of Joy; since all that I have

" hitherto

" hitherto enjoyed, from hence-forwards, will be the
" Subject of my eternal Anguish! "

Thus spake the disconsolate *Fatima,* weeping all the
while, without Intermission, as if in Reality her Son
had been massacred in her very Sight. *Abdolmutalib,*
likewise, was so dissolved, as we may say, in Torrents of bitter Tears, that he *melted away like Wax
in the Heat:* Nor is it to be wondered at, that Tears
vented with so much *Ardency,* should reduce him to
such a *Softness.* But at last he resolved upon departing, without farther Delay, or suffering himself
to be detained any longer, by giving Ear to Weeping
and Complaints; and so, ordering his Son to come
after him, they went into the Street, followed by the
sorrowful *Fatima,* close behind them. Like an Ewe from
whom her tender Lamb hath been snatched away,
and is shewed to her at a Distance, just so did this
afflicted Mother run after them, overwhelmed with
Floods of Tears, and so confounded, that she scarce
knew what she did; her very Garments being a
Trouble to her, she trampling upon them as she went
along.

The News of this great Incident was soon dispersed
throughout *Mecca,* and all the circumjacent Country,
and all who heard it repaired thither; insomuch, that
such prodigious Numbers of People flocked to be Spectators of that Tragical Scene, that the City was much
too small to contain them. Nor did the Sages and
Diviners of that perverse Generation of People, the
Jews, with Multitudes of their Followers, fail to be
there; That accursed Race! who were continually inventing treacherous Snares and Practices against the
Lord's *Elected,* Possessors of the *Light;* and that because those impious Traytors were ever apprehensive,
and had sure Grounds of their Suspicion, that the true
Lord and Possessor of that Sacred *Light,* would overthrow and abolish their false Sect. And the more,
because amongst their ancient Relicks, those wicked
Magicians had preserved a Shirt which had been dip-
ped

ped in the Blood of the Righteous (a) *Yahia,* concerning which their Writings made mention, That whenever the Blood, which, for so many Ages, had been upon that Garment, should be perceived to liquify, and to drop apace from it, that then, of a Certainty, *the destroying Sword of Wrath* approached.

These Tokens were manifestly shewn them at the Time of *Abdallah's* Birth; for the Blood was seen to drop very fast from that holy Relick; and by this they were fully convinced, that their Ruin and Perdition was at Hand. For this Reason they had assembled together all their stoutest Warriors from all the Cities and Towns in the Country, and, upon Consultation, had firmly resolved, and given express Orders to destroy the *Light,* by killing *Abdallah,* when and where-ever they could find a favourable Occasion: And with that perfidious bloody Design, after which they so much thirsted, they were now come to *Mecca,* upon hearing the News of this Sacrifice, to see whether or no it would fall to his Lot to become the Victim; and to further which, they had privately offered vast Sums of Money, and prodigious rich Presents of Jewels and other valuable Things.

Abdolmutalib was now come to the Temple, preceded by his Ten Sons, and gave Orders, that the Lots, according to the Custom of those Times, should be brought him, which he delivered into the Hands of the Person appointed for that Office, and then gave him the Charge of his Children. This Person took them, and, followed by all the Ten Brothers, went into the Temple, the good Father staying without, with his drawn Weapon ready in his Hand; tho' scarce able to contain himself, but stood trembling, and felt all the Convulsions to which the Frailty of Human Flesh is subject; and before the Lots were cast, he went up to the Rails, and laying hold of them, he devoutly be-

---

(a) St. *John* the Baptist.

fought

fought God to accept of this his Sacrifice, with the fame Pleafure as he offered it, and that it might be as grateful in His Sight, as he defired it fhould. He likewife implored the Almighty, that his Son *Abd-allah* might be exempted from the fatal Lot, and that it might rather fall upon any other of the Nine. And indeed, this was what gave him the greateft Difquiet, becaufe he bore him a tenderer Affection, than he fhould have done to Fifty Sons, had he had fo many.

Having ended his Prayer, he departed from the holy Rails (which all the while he had been embracing) and calling out aloud to the Perfon who had the Lots, he bad him do his Office, without Delay. The Cafe of this pious and venerable Perfonage, was at that Juncture, certainly very extraordinary, and, as we may term it, as if he had been put to publick Sale; fo intirely were the Thoughts and Eyes of the whole Multitude taken up with his Concerns: For that vaft Concourfe of People were all crouding around the fpacious Portico of the Temple, impatiently waiting the Refult of this great Affair, and the coming out of him whom Chance fhould have condemned to be the fuffering Victim. That numerous Congregation was compofed of his Relations, Friends and Well-wifhers, as alfo of abundance of his invidious Enemies and Perfecutors, who bore him a mortal Hatred. Thofe were extremely moved with Commiferation and Fellow-feeling, at his prefent unhappy Circumftances, and inexpreflible Agitation of Mind, as every well-intentioned difinterefted Perfon muft undoubtedly conceive his to be; whilft thefe others would indifputably have been, in their Souls, far better pleafed to have feen him ftill deeper involved in Grief, Anguifh and Mifery; *for the Wick-ed have always abundantly more Malice concealed in their Hearts, than what they openly make Profeffion of.* Some are weeping and lamenting for the unfortunate Father, whilft others, who hate him, inwardly rejoice at his Afflictions. Whilft fome pity the rigid Fate of the unhappy Youth, whofe Lot it fhall be to fwallow the

bitter

bitter Draught, others have, by way of Anticipation, already paſſed Sentence upon him.

Thus, as is uſual in all mixed Aſſemblies, were the Thoughts of the whole Multitude variouſly employed; the unconſtant Rabble, who are profeſſed Enemies to the Good, and to all Piety, having their Minds moſt at Eaſe, according to their Cuſtom upon all ſuch Occaſions. The ſorrowful Mothers of thoſe illuſtrious Youths were all preſent, overwhelmed with anxious Doubts and Apprehenſions, each being filled with Fear and Horror, leſt the fatal Lot ſhould fall upon her own Son. Theſe racking Thoughts gave them unutterable Diſquiets and Perturbations of Soul: This inſupportable Uncertainty made them wring their delicate, lilly Hands, and cauſed them to tremble with Anguiſh and Deſpair, and to vent innumerable bitter Sighs, at the ſhocking Thoughts of what might happen.

When that numberleſs Congreſs of People had a conſiderable while continued with their Eyes always fixed upon the Gate of the ſanctified Temple, without once moving them off from that Object, ſome clambering up one upon another to ſee the better, others ſtanding on tip-toe, ſtretching their Necks as much as poſſible, and all in general looking that way, with the utmoſt Attention; the Temple Door at laſt was ſeen to open, and the Lot-Caſter came forth, leading after him the noble Youth *Abdallab* (by a Saſh which he had faſtened to his beautiful Neck, by giving it one Turn round it) his Viſage pale, wan and diſcoloured, and not the leaſt Glimpſe of his wonted glorious *Light* appearing on his Countenance; after whom followed his Nine Brothers, all weeping and making lamentable Outcries for him, and uttering the ſame Expreſſions of exceſſive Concern, as if the Caſe had been their own; all which, when the good *Abdolmutalib* beheld, he had certainly fainted away, and fallen to the Ground, had not the noble, undaunted Spirit of his magnanimous Anceſtors, and his own innate Great-

heſs

nefs of Soul, infpired him with Courage to bear up a-
gainft fo killing a Sight.

No fooner was this moving Scene opened, but a fudden Noife of Sighs, Groans and compaffionate Murmuring was heard among the Spectators, at an Object
fo extremely fhocking. To behold the lovelieft, fpright-
lieft Youth that Nature had ever formed, juft ready
to have the fatal Steel applied to his delicate Throat,
and that in his tendereft and moft promifing Bloom!
But, what fhall we fay of his Mother, when fhe is
at laft clearly convinced that all thofe racking Fears
and Doubts, which till then were but uncertain Sufpi-
cions, are now but too heart-breaking Truths; who
is now fo plainly confirmed in what before fhe only
dreaded, and feeth the whole Myftery unravelled before her Eyes? This let the Mothers confider, who
upon every (even the leaft) Hurt that happeneth to
their Children, feel mortal Pains, afflict themfelves to
the higheft Degree, not being able to bear it with any
Patience: What then muft fhe do who beholdeth her
Darling, like an Ox tied down in a Ditch to be flaugh-
tered?

This diftreffed Lady had another Son, a Youth of
very great Merits, who was Brother, both by Father
and Mother, to him who was now appointed to be
offered up as a Sacrifice: His Name was (a) *Abutalib.*
This magnanimous young Hero, ftirred up and infpired by that tranfcendent Generofity and Greatnefs of
Soul, which he had inherited, in a direct Line, from
his illuftrious Anceftors, came and caft himfelf, with
great Piety and Humility, at his Father's Feet, and,
with a ferene, fmiling Countenance, intreated him,
That he would be pleafed to accept of the voluntary

(a) This *Abutalib* was *Mahomet's* Uncle, who, after the Death of
his Grandfather *Abdolmutalib,* took him under his Care and Protection. He was the Father of the famous *Aly,* who married the Impoft-
or's Daughter *Fatima.* He is often mentioned by Dean *Prideaux,*
and others.

Offering he was defirous of making to the Lord in Defence of his Brother's Life, proffering freely to lay
down his own in Exchange.

" I dare act nothing contrary to the Lord's Plea-
" fure, faid his Father, neither will His Divinity confent
" to have His holy Decrees contradicted or difobeyed."
Why then, replied *Abutalib,* to avoid committing any
Error, or proving difobedient to God, let the Lots be caft
once more, to try if it may light upon me, and I
will go and intercede with His Sacred Majefty, whofe
Ears are always open to thofe who feek Him, that,
out of His immenfe Bounty, He will vouchfafe to accept this my free Offering: And having faid thefe
Words, he went into the Temple, where, taking hold
of the Rails, he moft devoutly made his Addrefs to
his Creator in the following Terms.

Abutalib's PRAYER.

O *Sovereign of all the Nations, which, out of Thy incomprehenfible Wifdom, Thou haft created! O Diftri-
buter of all Mercies! O Maker and Erecter of Thrones!
Thou haft been pleafed to pafs what Judgment upon us
Thou faweft moft meet and agreeable to Thy Holy Will,
wherewith all of us, both our Father and our felves, are
fully fatisfied, and to obey which, we are perfectly refigned. The Vow our Father made, was, in reality, fomewhat
inconfiderate, and of an uncommon Nature, fince he promifed our Lives before we were born, or had an Exiftence.
Thou wert pleafed to comply with his ardent Requeft, in
granting him what he fought for at Thy Hands; and he is
now come to accomplifh his Vow, and to offer up to Thee
that which he had confecrated to Thy Holy Name. We
all of us caft Lots, that neither of us might think himfelf
injurioufly treated, and the Lot hath fallen upon him,*

who,

who, as Lord, Thou well knoweſt, is the moſt eſteemed, and the worthieſt of us all.   He is our Light, *and our* Content; *He is our chief* Conſolation *in our Adverſities; He is the* very Light *of our Eyes, and the* Ornament *of his whole Tribe.   If therefore, Lord, it ſhall be Thy Pleaſure to content Thy ſelf with me for Thy Victim, and to exempt my dear Brother, and ſuffer him to be ſet at Liberty, I here affirm, in Thy Preſence, that I am freely ſatisfied to reſign my own Life to redeem his, if Thou wilt vouchſafe to accept me in his ſtead.   This I willingly, and of my free Choice offer, out of the ardent and unfeigned Affection I bear him; and, I beſeech Thee, I may be permitted to lay down my Life for his, and prevent his Blood from being ſpilt by ſacrificing my own.   O Lord, I intreat Thee, deliver my Brother, have Compaſſion upon his afflicted Mother, and accept of this my Petition; for Thou throughly knoweſt the Intent with which I make it.*

When he had ſaid this, he departed from the Rails, and returning to his Father, he intreated him to accompliſh his Vow upon him, by paſſing his Weapon upon his Throat.   The good Father, to put them out of Suſpence, caſt Lots a ſecond time, and it fell again upon *Abdallah,* as it had done before.   This having put an End to all farther Diſputes, the Thing being now ſo fairly confirmed, there remained nothing more to do, but to obey the Sentence, as God had thought fit to ordain; and, in order to put it in Execution, he inſtantly laid hold of that his choſen Son, and conducted him into that Sacred Manſion, worthy of ſo noble a Sacrifice.

The Youth, whoſe ſo beautiful Countenance was now quite deprived of every Ray of its wonted Light, very reſolutely encouraged his pious Father, ſaying; " Be not afraid, Sir, but, without Delay or Heſitation, " tie my Hands and my Feet very faſt, that you " may meet with no Impediment to obſtruct your " Deſign: And if you apprehend, that, when the cru- " el Steel ſhall have penetrated my Veins, the Sight " thereof

"thereof will move you to Compaſſion; I beſeech
"you, ſhut your Eyes, and then paſs it over my
"Throat as faſt as you can; ſhaking off all Thoughts
"of Pity or Tenderneſs, and arming yourſelf with
"Patience, and a firm Reſolution; for, in obeying the
"Lord's Decrees, you will receive a ſufficient Conſo-
"lation for my Loſs. For my own Part, I am
"intirely content, and exceeding joyful, that the Al-
"mighty is pleaſed to accept of me, in this my im-
"mature Age, for an expiatory Offering, and think
"myſelf highly honoured, in being deemed a Victim
"worthy enough to acquit you from this your Obli-
"gation, for which you are ſo extremely concerned. But
"I adviſe you to order it ſo, that your Garments may
"not be ſtained with any Drops of my Blood, as well
"to avoid giving you the Occaſion of making melan-
"choly Reflections at ſuch an Object, as likewiſe, to
"prevent my Mother from falling in a Paſſion with you,
"when ſhe ſhall behold it, which muſt certainly bring
"the Remembrance afreſh into her Mind, and lay all
"the Blame upon you: And I intreat you, my beloved
"Father, that if ſhe ſheweth any Reſentment, or maketh
"any Complaints (which ſhe will have, in Juſtice,
"ſome Reaſon to do) be not offended at her for ſo doing,
"but rather comfort her in her Mourning and Sorrow,
"and endeavour to dry up thoſe Tears ſhe may pro-
"bably ſhed for her Loſs of me: For, in fine, ſhe is a
"Woman, and an indulgent tender Mother, and, upon
"that Account, ought to be conſidered. May God be
"pleaſed to comfort you both under your Afflictions;
"and I beg you, at preſent, to ſpare your Grief,
"and to think upon nothing but fulfilling the Al-
"mighty Decree, and offering up to His Sacred Name
"the intended Sacrifice. "

The tender Youth had no ſooner inclined his lovely
Neck to receive the cruel Wound, but immediately
from his beautiful Forehead proceeded ſuch a glorious
Splendor, that the radiant Beams of that refulgent
Light, mounting aloft, pierced the Clouds, through

which

which having paffed, they entered into the Spheres of the Cœleftial Courts, till they arrived up to the Seventh Heaven ; where the (a) Favourite Angels, who are employed in bearing the Throne of Glory, cryed out, and humbling themfelves before the Lord of all Bounty and Clemency, they faid ; " Moft Merciful Lord ! " have Compaffion, we befeech Thee, upon thefe pious " Worfhippers of Thy Divinity, fince Thou fully " knoweft their Sincerity, and the Integrity of their " Hearts ! " God replied ; " I fee all ; They do " nothing but what I perfectly well behold : Although " I am tardy, and do not immediately haften to their " Affiftance, it is only to make a full Tryal of their " Conftancy and Perfeverance ; and I will furely de- " liver all thofe who remember me, and who call " upon me. "

But when *Fatima* beheld the *Light of her Eyes,* her Darling Child, juft ready to undergo the cruel Stroke of the keen Weapon, and that her Mifery was now paft Remedy, her Hufband being bufily employed in faft binding his delicate Limbs with hard Cords, and, in Earneft, preparing to begin the fatal Sacrifice ; fhe, no longer able to contain herfelf, or to endure that inhuman Sight with any Patience, forced her Way out from amidft the Croud, like an inraged Lionefs, when deprived of her Young, or a Wild Cow, whofe Calf hath been taken from her, and ran about like one diftracted, weeping, fobbing, raving, lamenting, complaining, and tearing her Face with her Nails, roaming up and down through every Street, knocking and calling aloud at every Houfe fhe came by, for the People to commiferate her Sufferings, and to come to her Affiftance, begging and imploring them to refcue her dear Son, either by Force of Arms, or otherwife, as beft they could : And fo numerous were her Complaints, and fo loud the Out-cries fhe made, that *every Corner of Mecca,* its publick Places, and

(a) See p 12, 13, 25, 53. in the Notes.

its Suburbs rang with them ; and so moving was her
Grief, that all the Men, I mean all those of her own Tribe
and Family, as likewise all others, who upon such
Occasions, value themselves upon their Honour and
Generosity, were stirred up to succour her in her
Distress ; insomuch, that with a resistless Impetuosity,
they broke through the Multitude, bearing down, and
trampling under their Feet all who stood in their
Way, and, with their naked Sabres in their Hands,
came up to *Abdolmutalib*, at the very Moment when he
had applied the murdering Steel to his Son's Throat, in
order to accomplish the cruel Sacrifice ; and, with a
generous ·Zeal, they resolutely laid hold of his Arm,
and wrested the Weapon out of his Hand, not omitting
to give him some severe Reprimands for his unnatural
Intent ; saying, " For Shame! For Shame ! Desist
" from this Impiety! Forbear to think of injuring
" this Woman in so violent a Manner, by murdering
" her Child, without the least Provocation or Grounds
" for committing this cruel Piece of Barbarity ; for,
" assure yourself, that before you shall ever see this
" your Knife stained with that innocent Blood, every
" one you see here are resolved to die in his Defence ;
" nor will we ever suffer you to perpetrate so foul and
" inhuman a Deed. " To whom *Abdolmutalib* made
this Reply ; " For what Reason would you compel
" me to disobey my Creator, and act contrary to His
" Holy Decrees? Judge, O Lord, the Equity of this
" Cause between me and these People, who violently
" and forcibly prevent me from performing the Obli-
" gation I owe to Thy Divinity ! "
While they were thus contending, they heard a certain Man calling out to them very loud at a Distance,
and saw him forcing his Way towards them as fast as
he could, making Signs as he came, that they should
proceed no farther, for, that he would put them in a
Method to set all Things right, and to end their Con-
troversy ; and as soon as the said Person came where
they were, he, addressing himself to *Abdolmutalib*, spake
thus ;

thus; " You are the Prince and chief Ruler of
" *Mecca* and all its Territories, and the whole Govern-
" ment thereof is wholly lodged in your Breaſt; and
" if you ſhould thus murder your Son, it is very pro-
" bable that hereafter you may be liable to the
" Peoples Reproaches, who may, perhaps, blame, up-
" braid and caſt Reflections upon you for this Deed,
" as having ſet an Example to your Succeſſors, which,
" it is to be feared, they might be too apt to follow,
" and ſo, upon every Occaſion, make a Practice of
" Sacrificing their Children, ſince you have left them
" ſuch a Precedent; and ſuch Actions as theſe are
" very ill becoming Princes and Sovereigns. Now
" ſhould your Poſterity do amiſs, by imitating the
" Example you ſhall have ſet them, all the Crimes
" they are guilty of will be laid to your Charge,
" and you muſt aſſuredly anſwer for the ſame: Nor
" doubt in the leaſt, *Abdolmutalib*, but that, for a
" Perſon of your uncommon Parts and Qualifications,
" to ſet evil Examples to others, is an unpardonable
" Overſight, and what ſoundeth extremely ill. "
   Abdolmutalib to this made Anſwer; " Is it then
" meet, or would it any wiſe be excuſable, that the
" Vow which I have ſo ſolemnly made to my Great
" Creator, ſhould be neglected for any Earthly Con-
" ſideration whatſoever? " To which the good *Yqrama*
" (for ſo was this Perſon called) replied; " I'll give
" you wholeſome Advice, and will ſet you in a right
" Method, if you will but follow my Counſel. Here
" in this Province of *Hegiaze*, not very far from hence,
" liveth a moſt Wiſe and Learned Woman, who, in
" Caſes and Diſputes of this Nature, applyeth many
" ſucceſsful Remedies, and thereby very frequently
" preventeth the worſt of Diſaſters: Thither, if you
" ſo pleaſe, we will repair, with all Diligence; where,
" I am fully perſuaded, we ſhall find a ſatisfactory
" Medium for what now ſo deeply troubleth your
" Mind. "

This

This Advice given them by *Ygrama*, was well approved of by all; and fo, putting a Stop to the Sacrifice, *Abdolmutalib* determined to make a Tryal if any Expedient could be found to fave the Youth, and to accomplifh his Vow without deviating, in any Point, from his Obligation; and fo they refolved upon taking a Journey to the Place of this Sage Woman's Abode: *For they who are in Darkness, are ftill in Hopes of getting out of it, and of arriving where they may once again behold the Light of the Sun.*

CHAP.

C H A P. XVIII.

The direful Effects of Envy. Abdolmutalib fets out to go to the Wife Woman. She receives great Prefents from him and his Followers. Her Counfel to him. Abdallah's pious Refignation. His Mother's great Offers for his Ranfom. They all repair to the Temple. The Lots being feveral Times caft, always fall upon Abdallah. His Reproof to his Father. Afflictions beneficial to the Righteous. The Lot falls upon the Camels. A Prophetick Voice heard in the Temple. The general Rejoicing for Abdallah's Deliverance. The hundred Camels facrificed, &c.

Envy, thou corrupted incurable Wound! Thou bitter, deadly, infernal Poifon! Thou corroding Cancer! Thou dangerous Homicide, againft whofe fatal Stroke no Human Arts or Means can avail! Thou who haft deftroyed and laid in the Duft fo many good and righteous Men! How many illuftrious and noble Worthies haft thou reduced to the loweft and moft abject Condition, and how many bafe, mean Wretches haft thou exalted! To fetch Examples from a remote Diftance; What became of the Righteous (*a*) *Abel* ?

(*a*) See p. 57. in the Notes.

What

What was it that induced that ungracious (a) Son to dethrone his Father from his mighty Monarchy? What was it that cauſed *Jacob* to undergo ſo much Sorrow and Affliction? What was the Cauſe of his Son *Joſeph*'s being caſt into the Well, and of being afterwards ſold as a Slave? What made *Daniel* be put into a Den, and *David* to be ſent into Baniſhment, inſtead of crowning him with Laurels, according to his Merits? And what was it that ſhortned the Days of that invincible Monarch *Alexander*, and cut him off in his moſt flouriſhing Prime? And, to come nearer to our preſent Purpoſe, What brought the noble Youth *Abdallah* to ſuch a deplorable Criſis, as to be bound Hand and Foot, and a Knife at his Throat ready to ſpill his innocent Blood? And finally, What ſent the good *Abdolmutalib* a wandring in Pilgrimage, his Heart burſting with Grief, reſtleſs, comfortleſs, and in Deſpair, ſeeking ſome Remedy and Conſolation under his Afflictions? What was it that cauſed his Family, all his Friends, Well-wiſhers and Dependants to be ſo diſquieted and ſo involved in Anguiſh? What divided the whole City *Mecca* into Parties and Controverſies; ſome excuſing his Procedure, and extenuating his Offence, whilſt others ſeverely blamed the Raſhneſs of his Vow, and highly condemned his unnatural Attempt? *O what cruel Afflictions doth many a Righteous Perſon undergo, and how great are the Evils which a Wicked Man is often the Cauſe of!*

On the Third Day after the intended Sacrifice, above treated of, the worthy *Abdolmutalib* (whoſe Mind was now ſomewhat more at Eaſe from thoſe inſupportable Convulſions, wherewith that Tragical Circumſtance had racked his Soul) ſet forwards towards the Place he had been adviſed to repair to by the prudent *Tqrama*, who was a very notable, ſage and

---

(a) Here we can but gueſs who he means.

learned

learned Perfon. He was accompanied in that Journey by Eighty gallant Cavaliers, all of them Men of extraordinary Worth and high Extraction, being his own near Relations; and were, every one of them, under a deep Concern for the Troubles and Misfortunes of their Chieftain; but what moft of all moved them, was, The imminent Danger his Son's Life lay under, whom they left at *Mecca,* not being willing to take him along with them.

When they were at their Journey's End, and had arrived at the Habitation of the faid Wife Woman, they were introduced into her Prefence; where, after many Compliments and Civilities had pafs'd on both Sides, they liberally prefented her with feveral Jewels and Things of Value, with abundance of Promifes of a much more confiderable Gratification, which each of the Guefts feparately offered, and engaged to fee performed, if, by any Method, fhe could put them in a Way of obtaining what they fought for; acquainting her, at the fame Time, with the whole Affair. She gave them a very courteous Reception, calling them her Brothers, and, with great Sincerity, returned them this Anfwer; *That they fhould take Courage; that they fhould have no Caufe to repent their Trouble in coming thither; for that, with the Affiftance of the Almighty, fhe would fet them intirely at Eafe, and expound every Point concerning which they made Inquiry, the very next Morning.*

They having taken their Leaves, departed, and paffed that Night in great Expectation of the Refult of that her Promife; and no fooner the Day appeared, but they went to her again; who, after mutual Salutations, faid to them; *Moft noble and felect Company! Lords of the higheft Degree! Inhabitants of the* Manfion *of certain Pardon! Return in Peace: Rejoyce and be glad; ever trufting in God's Bounty and Clemency, who, from His munificent Hand, will grant you a happy Deliveryout of all your Troubles.*

As to this obligatory Sacrifice in which you are engaged, my Anfwer is, That, in order to its being compleatly ac-

ком-

complished, and may remain deficient in no one Respect, you must provide a great Number of Camels, and convey them to the Place appointed for the Sacrifice, together with the Youth in Question: Then separating Ten of those Camels from the rest, cast Lots between the Youth and them, and if the Lot again falleth upon the Child, set them aside, and take Ten more, and so more, still continuing to cast the Lot, 'till it shall fall upon the Camels; when, taking all those Camels which shall have been so set apart, cut their Throats, and offer them up for Victims to the Lord, who, with the Blood of those Creatures, will assuredly be satisfied and appeased.

Upon this they took took their Leaves of this good Woman, and very joyfully departed in order to return to *Mecca*. Some of the Company hastened on before the rest to comfort *Fatima* with the good News they brought, and to put her in Hopes of saving her Son. As *Abdolmutalib* and the rest approached, *Abdallah*, with his Nine Brothers went out to meet them; and *Abdallah*, addressing himself to his Father, said; It grieveth me to the very Soul, Sir, to see all this Trouble you put yourself to; I for, my Part, shall be very well satisfied if you proceed as you at first intended, and comply with the Divine Decree. But let me know, I beseech you, whether or no you have found any Remedy for your disturbed Mind, or any Expedient which may be capable of setting your Heart at Ease, which is the Thing I most of all desire. To which his Father, taking him in his Arms, and kissing him *between the Eyes*, made Answer; My darling Child! Thou Joy of my Life! I have found an Expedient of fulfilling my promised Sacrifice at a less Expence than that of thy dear Life; which, tho' it will cost me part of my Substance, yet I should think thy Redemption bought at a very cheap Rate, though I should be obliged to purchase it with all I have in the World. The Experiment I intend to make, with the Permission of the Most High God, to Morrow Morning, in thy Presence and before a full Assembly of the

People.

People. *Do what ever you please, Sir, replied the virtuous Youth, I shall always be resigned, and, in every Respect, obedient to your Commands.*

As he spake this, his Mother, who had never ceased from weeping all that Interval, came to them, her Face all miserably torn and disfigured, and her Eyes almost swoln out of her Head with incessant Weeping, saying to her Husband; *Take no Thought for any Loss or Expence; for my Mother and I, between us, have a Thousand Camels ready prepared for my Son's Ransom, all which you are at Liberty to make Victims of : And if the Almighty still requireth more, we will supply the Defect with Oxen, Cows, Sheep, &c. And if yet more is required, I'll willingly undertake plentifully to entertain all the Pilgrims who resort to the Holy Temple, at my own Costs and Charges : And if still this is not enough, we will freely bestow all our Treasure, our Jewels, our Ornaments, our Gold and our Silver, both wrought and unwrought : And still, if all this is not sufficient, my Relations have ordered me to acquaint you, that they are ready to deposite, towards my Child's Redemption, Camels, Gold, &c. But if, after all, we are still deficient, I my-self will go a Begging for the rest into Foreign Countries : I'll wander through all Arabia and Syria : I'll implore the Aid of the Roman Prelates ; nay, I'll go from one End of the Universe to the other, rather than fail. But if all this is too little, and His Divine Majesty will be appeased with nothing but my Son's Life, why then, Praised be His Name, and let His Sacred Will be fulfilled! To whose Judgment I submit my-self, and make my Appeal.*

Abdolmutalib returned her this Answer ; *You oblige me exceedingly, and give me a very great Consolation with these liberal Offers you so generously make me : But I trust in the Lord, that my own Stock will be sufficient, without my having any Occasion to meddle with any Part of yours.* And he forthwith sent away Orders to his Servants, who had the Care of his Droves of Camels,

Cows,

Cows, &c. and to his Shepherds who looked to the Flocks of Sheep and Goats he had at Pasture, both in the Mountains, and on the Plains, that they should drive them home, to be ready at Hand at the appointed Time.

When the Morning came, and every Thing, (as Cords, &c.) being in a Readiness, he took his Weapon in his Hand, and, with his Son *Abdallah* marching before him, he went to the spacious Square before the Temple, which was the Place appointed to perform that Oblation to the Lord; where he found a vast Concourse of the People waiting, with an innumerable Multitude of Camels and other Cattle, standing ready. The first Thing he did, he took hold of his pious Child, and, laying him down upon the Ground, with a determined Courage and Resolution, he fast bound his Hands and his Feet; after which, he caused Ten Camels to be tied likewise, and to be placed behind his Son: And then going into the Temple, he went up to the holy *Rails*, and laying his two Hands upon them, he, in an audible Voice, called upon his Creator in these Words; *Lord! what I am about to offer up unto thee, is thy just Due, and an indispensible Obligation · Thy Judgment and Sentence is right and equitable, and must, of Necessity, be fulfilled and complied withal; for there is no contradicting thy incomprehensible Decrees. Lord! the Servant is thy Servant, the Wealth is thy Wealth, and the Cattle are thy Creatures! If thou requirest the Servant, he is here, with all Humility and Resignation, ready prepared: If thou wilt be satisfied with these other Victims, I only wait to observe thy Will, and to obey thy Command.*

When he had said this, he instantly ordered the Lots to be cast, as before, and it fell again upon *Abdallah*; upon which, Ten Camels more were brought and made fast with the first Ten: Then the Lots were cast the second Time, which fell again upon *Abdallah*; upon which, Ten other Camels were added to the Twenty, which made the Number Thirty: And the casting the

C c

Lots

Lots still going on, and the fatal Lot always falling upon *Abdallah*, Ten more were added, and after them Ten others, which made Fifty : And they still continuing as they had begun, and the cruel Lot, at every Cast, running its usual Way, the Number was now increased to Ninety.

The zealous Youth, notwithstanding he lay bound Hand and Foot, upon the Ground, could not avoid being somewhat moved, and called out aloud, in these Terms ; *How long do you vainly pretend to spend your Time to no Purpose? Cast away those trifling Lots into the Air ; for I am quite scandalized and ashamed to see, that, so contrary to all Right or Reason, you persist in contradicting the Almighty's Ordinances ! I see the Merit of my voluntary Resignation diminished, and my Obedience vilified ! You make my Services unacceptable, and, in the End, you will render them despicable ! It becometh not the Servant to be remiss in his Duty, nor to be over-assured ; nor, if his Lord requireth one Thing, to persist obstinately and contumaciously in acting the quite contrary ! Since, therefore, you are so plainly convinced how much you are in the wrong, come hither (unless you intend to persevere in your Disobedience) and put an End to what you have undertaken ; in doing which, you will acquit your self of the Debt the Lord requireth at your Hands.*

At these Words there was heard a very great Murmuring, with a confused Noise of Outcries, Weeping, and Complaints, from every Part of that spacious Place : And the good *Abdolmutalib*, still firmly fixed in his pious Intent, replied, *He who continueth incessantly knocking at the same Door, may rationally hope to be heard, and pitied at last.* And having once more cast the Lot, and the Camels being now increased to the equal Number of One hundred ; he, lifting up his Countenance towards Heaven, spake thus ; *O most Soveraign Monarch ! O King of the supreme Throne ! Arbiter of all Things, and Distributer of all Mercies ! Receive, I implore thee, this Expiation I offer thee ! I*

intreat

intreat thee, for the Sake of this radiant Light, *where-with thou haſt been pleaſed to illuſtrate and to ennoble us ; which* Light *was created* * *long before thou didſt create Humane Species, deſcending, in an uninterrupted Line, upon the pureſt, moſt honourable, and moſt venerable Worthies, 'till, out of thy immenſe and unſearchable Knowledge, thou didſt recommend it to us, and delivered it into our Poſſeſſion ; for the precious Sake and Merits whereof, I now implore thy Divine Aſſiſtance and Protection.*

Having ſaid thus, he, with Shews of a deep Concern, (ſtill invoking the Almighty's Name) ordered the Lots to be caſt again ; and, at the ſame Time, the whole Aſſembly, I mean thoſe whoſe Breaſts were filled with Righteouſneſs and Integrity, interceded, and ſincerely beſought the munificent Creator, that he would graciouſly be appeaſed, and contented with the offered Victims.

The Incomprehenſible and All-powerful Monarch, who, out of His impenetrable Wiſdom, frequently reduceth thoſe His Servants whom He beſt loveth, to the greateſt Streights, nay, even 'till they are at the very laſt Extremity, and all for their Good, and future Felicity ; by which He giveth the Mortals, who inhabit this World, to underſtand, that His merciful Hand hath created them out of a Compoſition ſo very pure and refined, that (provided they will but uſe their utmoſt Endeavours) they may eaſily get the better of all Sorts of Temptations, and bring them under their Yoke : And when the Lord hath made a ſufficient Tryal of their Integrity, and is ſenſible that their Hearts are Proof againſt ever being induced to commit any Crimes to render them worthy of His Diſpleaſure ; it is then that His Divinity beſtoweth upon the Sons of *Adam*, the moſt glorious Rewards for all their Sufferings ; but ſtill conſidering, that thoſe whom He

---

* See in the Chapter of the Creation, p. 14, &c.

C c 2

is pleafed to afflict, are Men, and consequently unable to endure all He could inflict upon them ; *for the compaffionate Creator never inflicteth more upon any of His Creatures, than what is anfwerable to the Strength He hath given them where-withal to fupport it.*

So it happened with' thofe righteous Perfons we are treating of, who, being firmly determined to accomplish their Sacrifice, had Relief fent them from the powerful Hand of the Almighty, when they leaft of all expected it : For the Lots being now caft, it fell upon the Camels; which happy Turn made many Hearts rejoyce ; and, at the fame Time, a Voice was heard to refound within the Holy Temple, (the moft joyful Sound that ever was heard upon Earth) faying, It *is received. The Expiation and Redemption, inftead of my due Victim, is accepted ; and the Time is now near at Hand in which the fo-long-wifhed-for* Mahomet *is to come forth to rejoice the World!* Which Words the Voice had no fooner pronounced, but the Rays of the refplendent *Light* fhone fo tranfcendently bright from the Forehead of *Abdallah,* that both the Heavens and the Earth were illuminated therewith.

Who can exprefs the Extremity of Joy, and the numberlefs Praifes and Glorifications given to the Lord's moft facred Name, by all the People (I mean the Good) when they beheld that happy Turn of Chance, which was ardently hoped for by fo many ; and when they heard the Voice pronounce fuch bleffed Tydings, fome ran with the utmoft Speed and Diligence to untie the Child's Bands ; and others, in the greateft and moft precipitate Vehemence, hafted away, in order to flaughter the Camels, which had been fet apart for that Purpofe, meeting, joftling, throwing down, and ftumbling over one another in a joyful and diverting Confufion.

Have a little Patience, cry'd out *Abdolmutalib* to them ; *be quiet a few Moments longer : Who knoweth but that there may be fome Miftake in the Lots ? For, feeing it hath fallen already Ten fucceffive Times upon*

my

my Son, it is not just that One single Caft should be thought sufficient to counterpoize what hath been confirmed by Ten, one after another. Let us caft the Lots again, nay, if it is an hundred Times ; for we should be inexcufable, if we should offer to proceed but upon a very fure Foundation.

The People being fenfible that what he fpoke was found and reafonable, immediately defifted, and the Lots were caft again, and again, Four Times in all, and every Time it fell upon the Camels ; fo that being now fully confirmed that the Lord was intirely appeafed, and that the Offering was become acceptable in his Sight, they prevented *Abdolmutalib* from making any farther Trials, as he would fain have done, and went and lifted up that Pattern of Patience and Humility, the illuftrious *Abdallah*, whilft his Nine Brothers ran and unty'd the Cords wherewith he was bound. His tender Mother ran to him, and, taking him in her Arms, almoft fmothered him with affectionate Kiffes and Embraces, giving to the Almighty an Infinity of Praifes and Thankfgivings, for having fo gracioufly delivered him ; nor was there, among all that Multitude, fcarce one Man or Woman but what gave him a joyful Embrace, and would have conveyed him home away from that Place, which had like to have been fo fatal to him : But his Father would not permit it, faying, *Let him alone ; for I think it convenient, that he should be prefent at this Expiation Offering.* And fo, in his Prefence, the Throats of the Hundred Camels were immediately cut, and, being divided into equal Portions, *Abdolmutalib* gave Orders, that the Pieces should be diftributed among all the Affembly, to every one a like Portion ; to Relations, Friends and Strangers, to Rich and Poor, Pilgrims, Paffengers, Sick and Afflicted, to all an equal Share ; cafting many Pieces to the Birds of Prey, and to four-footed Beafts who eat Flefh, that all alike might partake of that Sacrifice. After which *Abdolmutalib*, and his Family, returned to their

Habi-

Habitation, giving Glory to their Creator, who had ſo happily delivered them from that great Affliction.

The END *of the Firſt* VOLUME.

N. B. The Seaſon of the Year being ſo far advanced, I had not Time to finiſh the whole Tranſlation of this Work; but if what I here offer to the Publick, be thought Worthy of their Acceptance, the Second Volume ſhall follow with all convenient ſpeed. Which will contain, I. Some Remarks upon the Lives of *Haſhem* and *Abdolmatalib,* with the Continuation of the Life of *Abdallah, Mahomet*'s Father. II. The Birth, Qualities, Excellencies, Life, Death and Burial of *Mahomet,* with a notable Account of his Journey to Heaven; of the *Alcoran,* and many other Things worth Notice. III. Their Rites, *&c.* And a large and very remarkable Deſcription of the Laſt Day. IV. Of their Lunar Year, with the particular Feſtivals, Faſts, Holydays, Devotions, Ceremonies, *&c.* the *Mahometans* uſe throughout the whole Year; with ſeveral other Curioſities, treated of by no *European* Writers. V. Notable Maxims, Sayings, Obſervations, *&c.* collected out of the beſt Oriental Authors, never before in *Engliſh.*

J. M.